"America's leading source of self-help legal information." ★★★★

—YAHOO!

DATE DUE

SUBJECT TO OVERDUE FINES
CALL 465-2330 TO RENEW

AUG 09 2010

MAR 13 2010

ORMATION
ANYTIME
s a day
lo.com

AT THE NOLO.COM SELF

- **Nolo's comprehensiv**   nglish
  information on a variety
- **Nolo's Law Dictionary**
- **Auntie Nolo—if you'**
- **The Law Store—over**
  Downloadable Softw
- **Legal and product upda**
- **Frequently Asked Ques**
- **NoloBriefs, our free monthly email newsletter**
- **Legal Research Center, for access to state and federal statutes**
- **Our ever-popular lawyer jokes**

Quality LAW BOOKS & SOFTWARE FOR EVERYONE

Nolo's user-friendly products are consistently first-rate. Here's why:

- A dozen in-house legal editors, working with highly skilled authors, ensure that our products are accurate, up-to-date and easy to use

- We continually update every book and software program to keep up with changes in the law

- Our commitment to a more democratic legal system informs all of our work

- We appreciate & listen to your feedback. Please fill out and return the card at the back of this book.

OUR "NO-HASSLE" GUARANTEE

Return anything you buy directly from Nolo for any reason and we'll cheerfully refund your purchase price. No ifs, ands or buts.

Read This First

The information in this book is as up to date and accurate as we can make it. But it's important to realize that the law changes frequently, as do fees, forms and procedures. If you handle your own legal matters, it's up to you to be sure that all information you use—including the information in this book—is accurate. Here are some suggestions to help you:

First, make sure you've got the most recent edition of this book. To learn whether a later edition is available, check the edition number on the book's spine and then go to Nolo's online Law Store at www.nolo.com or call Nolo's Customer Service Department at 800-728-3555.

Next, even if you have a current edition, you need to be sure it's fully up to date. The law can change overnight. At www.nolo.com, we post notices of major legal and practical changes that affect the latest edition of a book. To check for updates, find your book in the Law Store on Nolo's website (you can use the "A to Z Product List" and click the book's title). If you see an "Updates" link on the left side of the page, click it. If you don't see a link, that means we haven't posted any updates. (But check back regularly.)

Finally, we believe accurate and current legal information should help you solve many of your own legal problems on a cost-efficient basis. But this text is not a substitute for personalized advice from a knowledgeable lawyer. If you want the help of a trained professional, consult an attorney licensed to practice in your state.

10th edition

How to File for
Chapter 7
Bankruptcy

by Attorneys Stephen Elias, Albin Renauer,

Robin Leonard & Kathleen Michon

TENTH EDITION	SEPTEMBER 2002
Editor	LISA GUERIN
Illustrations	MARI STEIN
Cover Design	TONI IHARA
Book Design	TERRI HEARSH
Proofreading	ROBERT WELLS
Index	THÉRÈSE SHERE
Printing	BERTLESMANN SERVICES INC.

How to file for Chapter 7 bankruptcy / by Stephen Elias ... [et al.].--10th ed.
    p. cm.
   Includes index.
   ISBN 0-87337-827-X
    1. Bankruptcy—United States—Popular works.   I. Elias, Stephen.

KF1524.6 .E4 2002
346.7307'8--dc21   2002019858

Dedications

To mom and dad, who gave me what money can't buy, and to whom I'm forever indebted.

—A.R.

To everyone who uses this and other Nolo books, for their courage and for having the good sense to take the law into their own hands.

—S.R.E., R.L. and A.R.

Acknowledgments

For their support and creative contributions to the early editions of this book, the authors gratefully acknowledge the following people:

Jake Warner, Mary Randolph, Terri Hearsh, Toni Ihara, Lisa Goldoftas, Marguerite Kirk, Susan Levinkind, Mike Mansel, Kim Wislee, Jess Glidewell, Les Peat, Lee Ryan, Marian Shostrom, Bobbe Powers, Virginia Simons, Jim Snyder and the late A. Richard Anton.

The current edition would not have been possible without the assistance of:

Deanne Loonin, who updated several chapters of this edition and acted as a valuable sounding board throughout.

Leslie Kane, who graciously reviewed many sections of this edition, bringing her knowledge and experience as a bankruptcy attorney to those pages.

Ella Hirst, who tackled several large and difficult research projects with proficiency and good cheer.

Table of Contents

4 Handling Your Case in Court

5 Life After Bankruptcy

6 Your House

7 Secured Debts

8 Nondischargeable Debts

9 Help Beyond the Book

Appendices

A1 Appendix 1: State and Federal Exemption Tables

A2 Appendix 2: Exemption Glossary

A3 Appendix 3: Addresses of Bankruptcy Courts

A4 Appendix 4: Tear-Out Forms

Index

1

How to Use This Book

This book shows you how to file for Chapter 7 bankruptcy, a legal remedy that provides a fresh financial start to consumers and businesses by canceling all or many of their debts. In the vast majority of cases, Chapter 7 bankruptcy is a routine process that requires no special courtroom or analytical skills. Usually, all you have to do is:

- fill in and file a packet of official forms with a federal bankruptcy court
- attend a five minute out-of-court meeting with a bankruptcy court official (called a trustee), and
- wait for three to six months for your bankruptcy to become final.

You may be thinking, "If this process is so simple, why is this book so big?" The answer is that very few people will need the whole book—most will only use a few chapters. However, the more property you have and the more debts you owe, the more information you'll need to fully understand your options. This book is designed for both the simple cases (most Chapter 7 bankruptcies fit into this category) and for cases that have one or more complicating twists.

A. Quick Answers to Your Bankruptcy Concerns

This section will help you find the information you may need to consider before deciding to file for Chapter 7 bankruptcy. If you've already decided to file, proceed directly to Chapter 3 for step-by-step instructions on how to fill in and file the bankruptcy forms.

- **I need help in deciding whether my economic situation justifies filing a Chapter 7 bankruptcy.**
  Read Ch. 1, Sections C and D.
- **I want an overview of how Chapter 7 bankruptcy works.**
  Read Ch. 1, Section B.
- **I want an overview of how Chapter 13 bankruptcy works (Chapter 13 bankruptcy involves paying some or all your debts off over time).**
  Read Ch. 1, Section F.
- **I want information on the most common alternatives to filing for bankruptcy.**
  Read Ch. 1, Section F.
- **I want to know which items of my property may be affected when I file for Chapter 7 bankruptcy.**
  Read Ch. 2, Section A.
- **I want to know what will happen to my car if I file for bankruptcy.**
  If it is all paid off, read Ch. 2, Section B.
  If you still owe money on the car, read Ch. 7, Section B.
- **I want to know what will happen to my house if I file for bankruptcy.**
  Read Ch. 6, Sections A and C.
- **I want to know what property I risk losing if I file for bankruptcy.**
  Read Ch. 2, Section B, and Appendix 1.
- **I want information on how to hang on to property that I might otherwise lose in a Chapter 7 bankruptcy.**
  Read Ch. 2, Section C.
- **I want to know if I have debts that won't be cancelled in a Chapter 7 bankruptcy.**
  Read Ch. 8, Section A.
- **I want to know whether I can get my student loan cancelled or reduced in a Chapter 7 bankruptcy.**
  Read Ch. 8, Section B.2.
- **I want to know if my tax debt can be canceled (discharged) in Chapter 7 bankruptcy.**
  Read Ch. 8, Section B.3.
- **I want to know whether I will need an attorney to handle my Chapter 7 bankruptcy.**
  Read Section D, below.
- **I have a cosigner for a debt and want to know what effect my Chapter 7 bankruptcy will have on that person.**
  Read Ch. 1, Section C.
- **I want to know what will happen if I give away property to friends or relatives shortly before filing a Chapter 7 bankruptcy or if I don't list certain property on my bankruptcy papers.**
  Read Ch. 1, Section C, and Ch. 2, Section A.
- **I want information on how a Chapter 7 bankruptcy will affect debts I owe because of my divorce.**
  Read Ch. 8, Sections B.4 and C.4.

B. What This Book Doesn't Cover

This book explains routine Chapter 7 bankruptcy procedures. You must be an individual, married couple or small business person with personal liability on your business debts to use this book. If your situation proves to be complicated, you may need more help than we can provide here. Throughout the book, we alert you to potential problems that might merit seeking some assistance. (See Ch. 9, *Help Beyond the Book*.)

This book doesn't cover the following situations:

- **Chapter 13 bankruptcies (repayment plans):** Chapter 13 allows people to repay a portion of their debts, with court supervision. Whether you are eligible to file a Chapter 13 bankruptcy depends on the type of debt you have and how much income you can devote to repaying the debt over a three- to five-year period. This book doesn't tell you how to file a Chapter 13 bankruptcy. However, it does help you figure out whether you might qualify to file a Chapter 13 bankruptcy and how to choose between that and Chapter 7, if both are available to you. The forms you must complete for a Chapter 7 bankruptcy are also used in a Chapter 13 bankruptcy, so any work you do to prepare for a Chapter 7 bankruptcy won't be wasted if you later decide to file a Chapter 13 bankruptcy instead.

- **Bankruptcies for people in business partnerships:** If you're a partner in a business (other than a husband-wife partnership), filing for a personal bankruptcy will affect your business; we don't address that situation in this book. However, if you are partners with your spouse and are filing jointly, then this book will work just fine.

- **Bankruptcies for people who are major stockholders in privately held corporations:** If you are a major owner of a privately held corporation, filing for bankruptcy could affect the corporation's legal and tax status. This book doesn't cover your situation.

- **Business reorganizations:** This book doesn't cover procedures under Chapter 11 of the bankruptcy laws, which allow a business to continue operating while paying off all or a portion of its debts under court supervision.

- **Farm reorganizations:** A special set of bankruptcy statutes, called Chapter 12, lets family farmers continue farming while paying off their debts over time. Unfortunately the program has been in and out of effect over the past several years; as of

the date of this edition, Chapter 12 is not an available remedy. Pending legislation is likely to reauthorize the program and allow farmers who have filed another type of bankruptcy to convert to a Chapter 12. In the meantime, most family farmers can file a Chapter 11 or Chapter 13 instead. This book doesn't cover Chapter 12 bankruptcies or the potentially complex question of whether a farmer is better off filing for a Chapter 7, Chapter 12, Chapter 11 or Chapter 13 bankruptcy. If you're a farmer, check with a bankruptcy professional. If you decide to file for Chapter 7 bankruptcy, this book should do the job.

C. Icons

We do our best to steer you toward the parts of the book you need and away from the parts that don't apply to you.

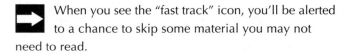 When you see the "fast track" icon, you'll be alerted to a chance to skip some material you may not need to read.

Information following this icon is for married couples only.

This icon cautions you about potential problems.

Suggested references for additional information follow this icon.

This icon suggests ways to save time while preparing the forms.

D. Getting Additional Help

If you need help with your bankruptcy, you have a number of options. Getting help may be as simple as using a bankruptcy petition preparation service to provide you with clerical and filing assistance. Or it may involve consulting a bankruptcy attorney for advice or representation or hitting the law library and figuring things out for yourself. In Ch. 9, we explain how to find the kind of help you need. Throughout the book, we do our best to point out where you may need assistance, although only you can judge whether you're in over your head.

Geographical Variation in Bankruptcy Law

Bankruptcy law comes from the federal Congress and is meant to be uniform across the country. But when disputes arise about those laws, bankruptcy courts must decide what the laws mean—and they don't all decide the issues in the same way. As a result, bankruptcy law and practice vary significantly from court to court and from region to region. This book can't possibly address every variation. When you need a bankruptcy professional, find someone who's familiar with your local bankruptcy court.

Here are some common situations in which you may require the assistance of a bankruptcy lawyer:

- You want to hold on to a house or motor vehicle and the chapters we devote to these subjects don't adequately address your situation or answer your questions.
- You want to get rid of a large debt that won't be wiped out in bankruptcy unless you convince a court that it should be discharged (examples of these types of debts include student loans, income taxes child support and alimony, and fines, penalties and restitution ordered by a court).
- A creditor files a lawsuit in the bankruptcy court claiming that a specific debt should survive your bankruptcy because you incurred it through fraud or other misconduct.
- The bankruptcy trustee (the court official in charge of your case) seeks to have your whole bankruptcy dismissed because of your misconduct.
- You have recently given away or sold valuable property for less than it is worth.
- You went on a recent buying spree with your credit card (especially if you charged more than $1,075 on luxury goods within the past 60 days).

- You want help negotiating with a creditor or the bankruptcy court, and the amount involved justifies hiring a bankruptcy lawyer to assist you.

Bankruptcy Law May Change for the Worse

In early 2001, the United States Congress passed legislation that makes sweeping changes to bankruptcy law. However, the Senate and House versions differ—and these differences have not yet been reconciled as of this writing. Since the bill was passed, the events of September 11 occurred and the economy officially entered a recession. Also, the Senate and House are engaged in a pitched battle over a provision that would prohibit debtors from discharging debts for monetary penalties imposed on them for interfering with a person's access to abortion clinics. For these reasons, the bill may never become law.

But if it does, bankruptcy will become considerably harder for many people. Among other things, the bill would:

- prohibit some people from filing for bankruptcy
- for those who qualify to file, make the procedure more complex and therefore harder to do without a lawyer (and more expensive if you hire one)
- add to the list of debts that people cannot get rid of in bankruptcy
- make it harder for people to come up with manageable repayment plans (if they opt to file a Chapter 13 bankruptcy), and
- limit the protection from collection efforts for those who file for bankruptcy.

At the time this book is published, the legislation may have already become law. To learn about its status and provisions, check Legal Updates on Nolo's website (www.nolo.com). The websites of the American Bankruptcy Institute (www.abiworld.org) and Commercial Law League of America (www.clla.org) also have up-to-date information about the legislation.

CHAPTER
1

Should You File for Chapter 7 Bankruptcy?

If you've already decided to file for Chapter 7 bankruptcy, skip ahead to Chapter 2.

A. Bankruptcy in America—The Big Picture

Although you may not care much about the larger bankruptcy picture, it will help you keep a perspective on the choices you will be asked to make in your own bankruptcy case. It should also reassure you if you are feeling isolated or even like a failure.

1. Why People File Bankruptcy

Over one million individuals and couples file for bankruptcy each year. Studies show that the most common reasons for these bankruptcies are:

- job loss, followed by an inability to find work at anywhere near the same income level
- medical expenses that aren't reimbursed by insurance or government programs
- divorce or legal separation, and
- small business failures.

Of course, none of these events would necessarily require bankruptcy if the people who experience them had adequate savings to weather the storm. But for a number of reasons, most of us lack such savings. In fact, most of us are up to our eyeballs in debt—and only one paycheck away from economic disaster. And when a recession hits and the pink slips start flowing, as is the case while this tenth edition is being prepared, many otherwise stalwart citizens find themselves turning to bankruptcy for relief. Let's take a closer look at how we got so financially overextended.

2. Why You Shouldn't Feel Guilty About Filing Bankruptcy

The American economy is based on consumer spending. Roughly 2/3 of the Gross National Product comes from consumers like us spending our hard-earned dollars on goods and services we deem essential to our lives. If you ever had any doubt about how important consumer spending is to our economy, remember that President George W. Bush wasted no time after the events of September 11 in urging Americans to spend more. And many other government leaders told us that spending was our patriotic duty. As Americans, we learn almost from birth that it's a good thing to buy all sorts of goods and services. A highly paid army of persuaders surrounds us with thousands of seductive messages each day that all say "buy, buy, buy."

These sophisticated advertising techniques (that often cross the border into manipulation) convince us to buy. And for those of us who can't afford to pay as we go, credit card companies are relentless in offering credit to even the most deeply indebted of us. In fact, over 3 billion credit card solicitations were mailed to U.S residents in the year 2000—that's ten solicitations for every man, woman and child. And perhaps surprisingly, the largest growth sectors for credit cards were college students and people with bad credit ratings. The college students were targeted because they are customers of the future—and because their parents can be expected to bail them out when they get carried away with their new purchasing power. And the people with bad credit were brought on board in large numbers because creditors discovered that they would pay huge interest rates for debts run up on their cards, which leads to equally huge profits.

The truth is, readily available credit makes it easy to live beyond our means and difficult to resist the siren songs of the advertisers. If for some reason, such as illness, loss of work or just plain bad planning, we can't pay for the goods or services we need, fear and guilt are often our first feelings. But as we've also seen, the American economy depends on our spending—the more the better. In short, much of American economic life is built on a contradiction.

In the age of $50-billion bailouts for poorly managed financial institutions, should you really feel guilt-ridden about the debts you've run up? That's something only you can decide, but remember that large creditors expect defaults and bankruptcies and treat them as a cost of doing business. The reason banks issue so many credit cards is that it is a very profitable business, even though some credit card debt is wiped out in bankruptcies and never repaid.

Bankruptcy is a truly worthy part of our legal system, based as it is on forgiveness rather than retribution. Certainly, it helps keep families together, frees up income and resources for children, reduces suicide and keeps the ranks of the homeless from growing even larger. And perhaps paradoxically, every successful bankruptcy returns a newly empowered person to the ranks of the "patriotic" consumer. If you suddenly find yourself without a job, socked with huge, unexpected medical bills you can't pay or simply snowed under by an impossible debt burden, bankruptcy provides a chance for a fresh start and a renewed positive outlook on life.

3. What About the Down Side?

Bankruptcy can also have its down sides—economically, emotionally and in terms of your future credit rating. Bankruptcy can get intrusive. You are required to disclose your financial activities during the previous two years, as well as your current property holdings. Having your property and previous activities made public in this way can be depressing, especially if you're forced to surrender property you badly want to keep.

Bankruptcy also carries a certain stigma. Otherwise, why would we spend so much time talking you out of feeling bad about it? Some people would rather struggle under a mountain of debt than accept the label of "bankrupt."

If you have a bankruptcy on your record, you will need to convince those who have business dealings with you that you really are trustworthy and did not lightly use the bankruptcy remedy. Whether you are renting or buying a home, buying or leasing a car or seeking financing for a business, your bankruptcy will be counted against you, at least for several years. And while you will be able to get credit cards after bankruptcy, you will have to pay the highest interest rate, at least for awhile.

While these facts may all seem like downsides, they collectively have an upside. For several years you will find it very easy to be debt-free—you will have to pay as you go because it will be tough to get credit. Filing for bankruptcy will throw some cold water in your face that will give you a new perspective on the credit system. A bankruptcy temporarily removes you from the credit hamster wheel which will give you some time and space to learn to live credit-free (or at least, to fashion a saner relationship to the credit industry).

B. An Overview of Chapter 7 Bankruptcy

This book explains how to file for Chapter 7 bankruptcy. Its name comes from the chapter of the federal statutes that contains the bankruptcy law (Chapter 7 of Title 11 of the United States Code). Chapter 7 bankruptcy is sometimes called "liquidation" bankruptcy—it cancels most of your debts, but you have to let the bankruptcy trustee liquidate (sell) your nonexempt property for the benefit of your creditors. By comparison, Chapter 13 bankruptcy is called a "reorganization" bankruptcy because it allows you to restructure your debt and pay some of it off over time.

Here is a brief overview of the Chapter 7 bankruptcy process, from start to finish.

1. What Bankruptcy Costs in Time and Money

The whole Chapter 7 bankruptcy process takes about four to six months, costs $200 in filing fees and commonly requires only one brief out-of-court meeting with the bankruptcy trustee—the official appointed by the bankruptcy judge to process your bankruptcy on behalf of the court.

2. Bankruptcy Forms

To file for Chapter 7 bankruptcy, you fill out a two-page petition and some accompanying forms called "schedules." You then file these documents with the appropriate bankruptcy court—the court that is closest to where you have lived or done business for the largest number of days during the preceding 180-day period. Basically, the schedules accompanying your petition ask you to describe:

- your property
- your current income and its sources
- your current monthly living expenses
- your debts
- property you claim the law allows you to keep through the bankruptcy process (exempt property)
- property you owned and money you spent during the previous two years, and
- property you sold or gave away during the previous two years.

In the course of your bankruptcy, you may want to amend some or all of these forms to correct mistakes you discover or to reflect agreements you reach with the bankruptcy court official in charge of your case (the trustee). Amending these forms is fairly simple—we explain how to do it in Ch. 4, Section B.

What Can You Keep If You File For Bankruptcy?

If you're thinking about bankruptcy, you probably want to know what property you'll be able to keep if you file. Most states let you keep a wide variety of property items, including clothing, household furnishings, Social Security payments you haven't spent and other necessities (such as a car and tools of your trade). You can keep some items regardless of their value. For other items, like a car, you can keep the item only if the value of your ownership interest is below a set limit—for items worth more, you are entitled only to that portion of its value (which might mean that you will lose the property itself). Property that you can keep is called "exempt property," and the laws that specify what specific property is exempt (and up to what value) are called "exemption laws." Chapter 2 explains exemptions in more detail, and Appendix 1 contains a list of exempt property for each state.

3. Bankruptcy's Magic Wand— the Automatic Stay

Often, people filing for bankruptcy have been faced for weeks, months or even years with creditors demanding payment and threatening lawsuits and collection actions. Bankruptcy puts a stop to all this. By filing your bankruptcy petition, you instantly create a federal court order (called an "Order for Relief" and colloquially known as the "automatic stay") that requires your creditors to stop all collection efforts. So, at least temporarily, creditors cannot call you, write dunning letters, legally grab (garnish) your wages, empty your bank account, go after your car, house or other property, or cut off your utility service or welfare benefits. As we explain later, some creditors can get the automatic stay lifted to collect their particular debt, but they have to go to court and get the judge's permission first.

4. Court Control Over Your Financial Affairs

By filing bankruptcy, you are technically placing the property you own and the debts you owe in the hands of the bankruptcy court. You can't sell or give away any of the property that you own when you file, or pay any of your pre-filing debts, without the court's consent. However, with a few exceptions, you can do what you wish with property you acquire and income you earn after you file for bankruptcy.

5. The Trustee

The bankruptcy court exercises control over your property and debts by appointing an official called a "trustee" to manage your case while it is in the court. The trustee (or the trustee's staff) will examine your papers to make sure they are complete and to look for property to sell for the benefit of your creditors. The trustee's primary duty is to see that your creditors are paid as much as possible. The trustee is mostly interested in what you own and what property you claim as exempt, but will also look at your financial transactions during the previous year (in some cases these can be undone and assets freed up for distribution to your creditors). The more assets the trustee recovers for creditors, the more the trustee is paid.

How Trustees Get Paid

In Chapter 7 cases, trustees get paid a flat $60 per case. In addition, trustees are entitled to pocket a percentage of the funds the trustee disburses to the debtor's creditors—25% of the first $5,000 disbursed, 10% of the next $45,000, and so on. Since most Chapter 7 cases involve no disbursements (because there are no nonexempt assets), the trustee usually has to settle for the $60 fee. But these financial incentives make trustees ever vigilant to situations where they can actually grab some property and earn a statutory "commission."

Some courts appoint full-time trustees (standing trustees) to handle all the cases filed there, while other courts appoint trustees on a rotating basis (sometimes called "panel trustees") from the local bankruptcy attorney bar. Full-time trustees and panel trustees have the same responsibilities. However, full-time trustees usually do a better job of scrutinizing bankruptcy papers for possible mistakes, whether intentional or accidental.

The U.S. Trustee

The Office for the U.S. Trustees is a division of the U.S. Attorney's office, which is in the Department of Justice. Each U.S. Trustee oversees several bankruptcy courts. Individual cases within those courts are assigned to Assistant U.S. Trustees, who also employ attorneys, auditors and investigators. U.S. Trustees work closely with their Department of Justice colleagues from the FBI and other federal agencies to ferret out fraud and abuse in the bankruptcy system. The U.S. Trustees (and the Assistant U.S. Trustees) also supervise the work of the panel or standing trustees appointed by the courts.

---

6. The Creditors Meeting

A week or two after you file for bankruptcy, you (and all the creditors you list in your bankruptcy papers) will receive notice from the court that a "creditors meeting" has been scheduled under Section 341a of the bankruptcy code. This meeting is typically held somewhere in the courthouse (but almost never in a courtroom). The trustee runs the meeting and, after swearing you in, may ask you questions about your bankruptcy and the documents you filed. This questioning rarely takes more than a minute or two. Creditors rarely attend this meeting—if they do, they will also have a chance to question you under oath. In the vast majority of Chapter 7 bankruptcies, this is the debtor's only visit to the courthouse. We discuss the creditors meeting in more detail in Ch. 4, Section A.

7. What Happens to Your Property in a Chapter 7 Bankruptcy

If, after the creditors meeting, the trustee determines that you have some nonexempt property, you may be required to either surrender that property or provide the trustee with its equivalent value in cash. If the property isn't worth very much or would be cumbersome for the trustee to sell, the trustee may "abandon" it—which means that you get to keep it even if it's nonexempt. As it turns out, most Chapter 7 debtors only own property that either is exempt or is essentially worthless for purposes of raising money for the creditors. As a result, few debtors end up having to surrender any of their property—unless the property is collateral for a secured debt.

8. How Your Secured Debts Are Treated

If you've pledged property as collateral for a loan, the loan is called a secured debt. The most common examples of collateral are houses and motor vehicles. In most cases, you'll either have to surrender the collateral to the creditor or make arrangements to pay for it during or after bankruptcy. (Ch. 7, *Secured Debts*, explains how to do this.) If a creditor has recorded a lien against your property without your consent (for example because the creditor obtained a judgment against you), that debt is also secured. However, in some cases and with certain types of property (but not real estate), you may be able to wipe out the debt and keep the property. This is also explained in Ch. 7.

9. How Contracts and Leases Are Treated in Bankruptcy

If you're a party to a contract or lease that's still in effect, the trustee may cancel it unless the contract will produce assets for the creditors. If it's canceled, you and the other party to the contract are cut loose from any contractual obligations. For example, suppose you have a two-year lease on some commercial property when you file for bankruptcy. If the trustee thinks he or she could sell the lease to a third party for money to pay your unsecured creditors, the trustee will assume the lease and sell it to the highest bidder. However, if the trustee doesn't think selling the lease is worth the trouble (as is usually the case), the trustee will cancel the lease.

What If You Change Your Mind About Bankruptcy After Filing?

If you don't want to go through with your Chapter 7 bankruptcy after you file, you can ask the court to dismiss your case. As a general rule, a court will dismiss a Chapter 7 bankruptcy case as long as the dismissal won't harm the creditors. (See Chapter 4, Section D.) You can usually file again if you want to, although you may have to wait 180 days if you requested dismissal after a creditor filed a motion to lift the automatic stay. (See Section C, below.)

10. The Bankruptcy Discharge

At the end of the bankruptcy process, all of your debts are discharged except:

- debts that automatically survive bankruptcy unless the bankruptcy court rules otherwise (child support, most tax debts and student loans are examples), and

- debts that the court has declared nondischargeable as a result of an action brought by the creditor.

11. After Bankruptcy

Once you receive your bankruptcy discharge, you are free to resume your economic life without reporting your activities to the bankruptcy court—unless you receive an inheritance, insurance proceeds or proceeds from a divorce settlement within 180 days of your filing date.

After bankruptcy, you may not be discriminated against by public or private employers solely because of the bankruptcy, although this ban on discrimination has exceptions (discussed in Ch. 5). You can start rebuilding your credit almost immediately, but it will take several years before you can get decent interest rates on a credit card, mortgage or car note. You can't file for a Chapter 7 bankruptcy until six years has passed since your filing date. However, you can file a Chapter 13 bankruptcy at any time (see Section F, below).

C. When Chapter 7 Bankruptcy May Not Be Appropriate

Filing for Chapter 7 bankruptcy is one way to solve debt problems—but it's not the only way. In several common situations, bankruptcy is either unwise or legally impossible.

1. You Previously Received a Bankruptcy Discharge

You cannot file for Chapter 7 bankruptcy if you obtained a bankruptcy discharge of your debts under Chapter 7 or Chapter 13 in a case begun within the past six years. (11 U.S.C. § 727.) However, if you obtained a Chapter 13 discharge in good faith after paying at least 70% of your unsecured debts, the six-year bar does not apply.

The six-year period runs from the date you filed for the earlier bankruptcy, not the date you received your discharge.

EXAMPLE: Brenda Apfel filed a Chapter 7 bankruptcy case on January 31, 1999. She received a discharge on April 20, 1999. Brenda files another Chapter 7 bankruptcy on February 1, 2005. The second bankruptcy is allowed because six years have passed since the date the earlier bankruptcy was filed (even though less than six years have passed since Brenda received a discharge in the earlier case).

2. A Previous Bankruptcy Was Dismissed Within the Previous 180 Days

You cannot file for Chapter 7 bankruptcy if your previous Chapter 7 or Chapter 13 case was dismissed within the past 180 days because:

- you violated a court order, or
- you requested the dismissal after a creditor asked for relief from the automatic stay. (11 U.S.C. §109(g).)

3. A Friend or Relative Cosigned a Loan and You Don't Want Them Subjected to Collection Efforts

A friend, relative or anyone else who cosigns a loan or otherwise takes on a joint obligation with you can be held wholly responsible for the debt if you don't pay it. If you receive a Chapter 7 bankruptcy discharge, you may no longer be liable for the debt, but your cosigners will be left on the hook. If you don't want this to happen, you'll need to use one of the alternatives to Chapter 7 bankruptcy that are outlined in Section F, below. By arranging to pay the debt over time, you can keep creditors from going after your cosigners for payment.

4. You Clearly Qualify for a Chapter 13 Bankruptcy

If you qualify to file a Chapter 13 bankruptcy, the bankruptcy court may dismiss your Chapter 7 bankruptcy on the ground that granting a Chapter 7 discharge would be a "substantial abuse" of the bankruptcy laws.

(11 U.S.C. § 707(b).) The Court can only do this if your debts are primarily consumer debts (not business debts). Usually, this kind of issue only comes before a judge if a bankruptcy trustee raises it. Section F, below, provides a quick and dirty test you can use to determine whether you are eligible to file for a Chapter 13 bankruptcy.

On their face, the bankruptcy laws appear to allow consumers to choose whether to file under Chapter 7 or Chapter 13. In many parts of the country, however—especially in the South—the courts prefer that debtors file for Chapter 13 bankruptcy. These courts do all they can to discourage people who have the means to repay some of their debts from canceling these debts entirely in a Chapter 7 bankruptcy. If you file for a Chapter 7 bankruptcy in one of these states and the judge decides that you should have filed under Chapter 13, the judge may give you the opportunity to convert your case to a Chapter 13. Conversion saves you from repaying the filing fee and preserves the automatic stay intact. You'll need the help of an attorney if you want (or are required) to convert your Chapter 7 case to a Chapter 13 (see Ch. 9 for information on finding and working with a bankruptcy attorney).

There are no hard and fast rules as to when a bankruptcy judge will dismiss a Chapter 7 case on this ground or force you to convert to a Chapter 13 bankruptcy. If you earn a high salary, have lots of luxury expenses (such as maintenance or payments on three cars and ballet lessons for your kids) and could pay off 50% or more of your debts in a Chapter 13, a dismissal is likely. But some courts have also dismissed Chapter 7 bankruptcies filed by debtors with modest incomes who could only pay off a small portion of their debts in Chapter 13. Some of the factors courts consider in making this decision include:

- the amount of your disposable income each month
- whether your income is steady
- whether you lied, included false information or failed to list all of your income on your bankruptcy papers
- the percentage of your unsecured debts (debts not secured by property) you could repay in a Chapter 13 bankruptcy, and
- whether you have a simple or extravagant lifestyle.

One thing a court cannot consider in deciding whether you have enough disposable income to file for Chapter 13 bankruptcy is your past or continuing contributions to churches or charity, as long as they don't exceed 15% of your income.

Even if a bankruptcy judge wouldn't throw out your Chapter 7 case, you may be better off negotiating with your creditors or filing for Chapter 13 bankruptcy if you can repay a healthy portion of your debts over time.

5. You Defrauded Your Creditors

Bankruptcy is geared towards the honest debtor who got in too deep and needs a fresh start. A bankruptcy court will not help someone who has played fast and loose with her creditors.

Certain activities are red flags to the courts and trustees. If you have engaged in any of them, do not file for bankruptcy until you consult with a bankruptcy lawyer. These no-nos are:

- unloading assets to your friends or relatives just before filing (But see Ch. 2, Section C, for information on how you may be able to legally convert nonexempt property to exempt property)
- incurring debts for luxury items when you were clearly broke, and
- concealing property or money from your spouse during a divorce proceeding.

6. You Recently Incurred Debts for Luxuries

Creditors are getting fairly aggressive about crying "fraud." Credit card issuers reportedly lose several billion dollars a year from people who file for bankruptcy. In an effort to minimize the number of debts that are discharged, many credit card issuers routinely challenge bankruptcy cases filed by people who charged large luxury items or got cash advances shortly before filing.

If you've recently run up large debts for a vacation, hobby or entertainment, filing for bankruptcy probably won't help you. Most luxury debts incurred just before filing are not dischargeable if the creditor objects. And

the objection may cause the court to suspect fraud in your entire bankruptcy case and dismiss it entirely.

Last-minute debts presumed to be nondischargeable include:

- debts of $1,150 or more to any one creditor for luxury goods or services made within 60 days before filing, and
- debts for cash advances in excess of $1,150 obtained within 60 days of filing for bankruptcy.

But keep in mind that a judge can still question (and ultimately refuse to discharge) debts for less than $1,150 or debts you incurred more than 60 days ago if she feels that you incurred them without intending to pay them back. To discharge luxury debts, you will have to prove that extraordinary circumstances required you to make the charges and that you really weren't trying to put one over on your creditors. It's an uphill job. Judges often assume that people who incur last-minute charges for luxuries were on a final buying binge before going under and had no intention of paying. In this regard, some courts have held that each use of a credit card carries with it an implied representation that you will pay that charge—evidence showing that you knew you wouldn't be able to pay it is sufficient proof of fraud to make the debt nondischargeable. (*In re Mercer,* 246 F.3d 391 (5th Cir. 2001).)

7. You Are Attempting to Defraud the Bankruptcy Court

Just as a bankruptcy court won't tolerate a debtor who is shown to have played fast and loose with his creditors, the court will toss (and possibly attempt to jail) anyone who deliberately misleads the court itself. If you lie, cheat or attempt to hide assets, it may ultimately harm you more than your current debt crisis.

You must sign your bankruptcy papers under "penalty of perjury," swearing that everything in them is true. If you get caught deliberately failing to disclose property, omitting material information about your financial affairs during the previous two to seven years or using a false Social Security number (to hide your identity as a prior filer), your case will be dismissed and you may be prosecuted for perjury or fraud on the court. On the other hand, you are allowed to make innocent mistakes. If you accidentally leave something off your papers or incorrectly state something on your forms, you can correct your papers or explain the mistake to the trustee. Fraud is very different. It is an intentional act designed to pull the wool over the court's eyes.

While prosecution for fraud is rare, it's on the rise. A debtor in Massachusetts went to jail for failing to list on his bankruptcy papers his interest in a condominium and $26,000 worth of jewelry. Another Massachusetts debtor is serving time for listing her home on her bankruptcy papers as worth $70,000 when it had been appraised for $116,000. An Alaska debtor was jailed for failing to disclose buried cash and diamonds. A Pennsylvania debtor omitted from her papers $50,000 from a divorce settlement and was sentenced to some time in prison. And a debtor in Ohio was imprisoned for using a false Social Security number.

Some courts, most notably the Central District of California (Los Angeles), have developed highly so-phisticated programs for locating fraudulent filers. They scrutinize bankruptcy papers, dismiss cases when the debtor fails to file all papers within 15 days after filing the petition and issue orders barring a debtor from re-filing for 180 days after a case has been dismissed.

Finally, consider this statement taken from the website maintained by the bankruptcy judge for the Northern California District, Santa Rosa Division:

Open Letter to Debtors and Their Counsel

I have noticed a disturbing trend among debtors and their counsel to treat the schedules and statement of affairs as "working papers" which can be freely amended as circumstances warrant and need not contain the exact, whole truth.

Notwithstanding execution under penalty of perjury, debtors and their counsel seem to think that they are free to argue facts and values not contained in the schedules or even directly contrary to the schedules. Some debtors have felt justified signing a statement that they have only a few, or even a single creditor, in order to file an emergency petition, knowing full well that the statement is false.

Whatever your attitude is toward the schedules, you should know that as far as I am concerned they are the sacred text of any bankruptcy filing. There is no excuse for them not being 100% accurate and complete. Disclosure must be made to a fault. The filing of false schedules is a federal felony, and I do not hesitate to recommend prosecution of anyone who knowingly files a false schedule.

I have no idea where anyone got the idea that amendments can cure false schedules. The debtor has an obligation to correct schedules he or she knows are false, but amendment in no way cures a false filing. Any court may properly disregard subsequent sworn statement at odds with previous sworn statements. I give no weight at all to amendments filed after an issue has been raised.

As a practical matter, where false statements or omissions have come to light due to investigation by a creditor or trustee, it is virtually impossible for the debtor to demonstrate good faith in a Chapter 13 case or entitlement to a discharge in a Chapter 7 case. I strongly recommend that any of you harboring a cavalier attitude toward the schedules replace it with a good healthy dose of paranoia.

Dated: September 10, 1997

Alan Jaroslovsky

Alan Jaroslovsky
U.S. Bankruptcy Judge

D. Does Chapter 7 Bankruptcy Make Economic Sense?

If you are inclined to file for Chapter 7 bankruptcy, take a moment to decide whether it makes economic sense. You need to consider two questions:

- Will bankruptcy discharge enough of your debts to make it worth your while?
- Will you have to give up property you desperately want to keep?

If you are married, consider the debts and property of both spouses as you read this section. In Chapter 2, you will have an opportunity to decide whether you are better off filing jointly or filing alone.

1. Will Bankruptcy Discharge Enough of Your Debts?

Certain categories of debts may survive Chapter 7 bankruptcy, depending on the circumstances. These are commonly referred to as nondischargeable debts—and it may not make much sense to file for Chapter 7 bankruptcy if your primary goal is to get rid of them.

There are two categories of nondischargeable debts—debts that automatically survive bankruptcy unless the bankruptcy court rules that a particular exception applies, and debts that only survive bankruptcy if the bankruptcy court says that they should. If most of your debts are the kind that automatically survive bankruptcy unless a particular exception applies, hold off on filing your Chapter 7 bankruptcy until you have at least read Ch. 8 and learned what is likely to happen to these debts in your particular case. In particular, you should be concerned about:

- back child support and alimony
- student loans
- government fines, penalties or court-ordered restitution
- tax arrearages, and
- court judgments for injuries or death resulting from your drunk driving.

The following types of debts can survive bankruptcy only if the creditor mounts a successful challenge to them in the bankruptcy court:

- debt incurred on the basis of fraud, such as lying on a credit application or writing a bad check
- debt for luxury items that you recently bought on credit with no intention of paying for them
- debt from willful and malicious injury to another or another's property, including assault, battery, false imprisonment, libel and slander
- debt from larceny (theft), breach of trust or embezzlement, and
- debt arising out of a marital settlement agreement or divorce decree that doesn't qualify as support or alimony (which are automatically nondischargeable), such as credit card debts you agree to pay or payments you owe to an ex-spouse to even up the property division.

These types of nondischargeable debts are covered in detail in Ch. 8.

If your debt load consists primarily of debts that will be discharged unless a creditor convinces the court that they shouldn't be, it may make sense to file bankruptcy and hope that the creditor doesn't challenge the discharge. Many creditors don't—mounting a challenge to the discharge of a debt usually requires a lawyer, and lawyers don't come cheap. Also, many lawyers advise their clients to write off the debt rather than throw good money after bad in a bankruptcy court challenge.

2. How Much Property Will You Have to Give Up?

Chapter 7 bankruptcy essentially offers this deal: If you are willing to give up your nonexempt property to be sold for the benefit of your creditors, the court will erase some or all of your debt. If you can keep most of the things you care about, Chapter 7 bankruptcy can be a tremendous remedy for your debt problems. But if Chapter 7 bankruptcy would force you to part with treasured property, you may need to look for another solution.

The laws that control what property you can keep in a Chapter 7 bankruptcy are called exemptions. Each state's legislature produces a set of exemptions for use by people who file bankruptcy in that state. In 15 states (and the District of Columbia), debtors can choose between their state's exemptions or another set of exemptions created by Congress (known as federal bankruptcy exemptions). States that currently allow debtors this choice are Arkansas, Connecticut, Hawaii, Massachusetts, Michigan, Minnesota, New Hampshire, New Jersey, New Mexico, Pennsylvania, Rhode Island, Texas, Vermont, Washington and Wisconsin.

As it does in so many things, California has adopted its own unique exemption system. Rather than using the federal exemptions, California offers two sets of state exemptions for people filing bankruptcy. As in the 15 states that have the federal bankruptcy exemptions,. people filing bankruptcy in California must choose one or the other set of California's state exemptions.

Property that is not exempt can be sold by a bankruptcy court official (the trustee) to pay your creditors. You can avoid this result by finding some cash to pay the trustee what the property is worth or convincing the trustee to accept some exempt property of roughly equal value as a substitute. Also, if the property lacks sufficient value to produce money at a public sale, the trustee may decide to let you keep it. For instance, few trustees bother to take well-used furniture or second-hand electronic gadgets or appliances. These items generally aren't worth what it would cost to sell them.

As you've no doubt figured out, the key to getting the most out of the bankruptcy process is to use exemptions to keep as much of your property as possible while erasing as many debts as you can. To make full and proper use of your exemptions, you'll want to:

- understand how exemptions work generally
- become familiar with the exemptions available to you in your state, and
- choose the exemptions most appropriate to your circumstances.

In Ch. 2, Section B, we provide step-by-step instructions for figuring out whether your property is exempt. Here, we provide a brief overview of what you can generally expect to keep under most state exemption systems.

a. Property That Is Typically Exempt

Certain kinds of property are exempt in almost every state, including:

- equity in motor vehicles to a certain value (usually between $1,000 and $5,000)

- reasonably necessary clothing (no mink coats)
- reasonably needed household furnishings and goods (the second TV may have to go if it has any value)
- household appliances
- jewelry, to a certain value
- personal effects
- life insurance (cash or loan value, or proceeds), to a certain value
- pensions
- equity in your home to a certain value (commonly called the homestead exemption)
- tools of your trade or profession, to a certain value
- a portion of unpaid but earned wages, and
- public benefits (welfare, Social Security, unemployment compensation) accumulated in a bank account.

Many states also provide a "wildcard" exemption, an exemption for a set dollar amount that you can apply to any property that would otherwise not be exempt (see Ch. 2, Section B). Also, if you are using the federal exemptions or the California "System 2" exemptions and you don't need to protect equity in a home, you can use some or all of the homestead exemption as a wildcard.

b. Property That Is Typically Nonexempt

In most states, you will have to give up or pay the trustee for the following types of property (in legal terms, these items are "nonexempt"):

- expensive musical instruments (unless you're a professional musician)
- computers and peripherals (unless they qualify as tools of your trade)
- cameras, camcorders and personal digital assistants
- stamp, coin and other collections
- valuable family heirlooms
- cash, bank accounts, stocks, stock options, bonds, royalties and other investments
- business assets
- non-residential real estate
- boats, planes and off-road vehicles
- a second car or truck, and
- a second or vacation home.

If it appears that you have a lot of nonexempt property, read Chapter 2 before deciding whether or not to file for bankruptcy. That chapter helps you determine exactly how much of your property is not exempt and suggests ways to:

- buy it from the trustee (if you really want to hold on to it)
- use exempt property to barter with the trustee, or
- retain the value of your nonexempt property by selling some of it and buying exempt property with the proceeds before you file.

If Chapter 7 Bankruptcy Won't Let You Keep Treasured Property

If it looks like Chapter 7 bankruptcy is destined to come between you and property that you really want to keep, consider filing for Chapter 13 bankruptcy (or using one of the other alternatives discussed in Section E, below). Chapter 13 bankruptcy lets you keep your property regardless of its exempt status, as long as you will have sufficient income over the next three to five years to pay off all or a portion of your unsecured debts and to pay any priority debts you have (such as back child support, alimony and taxes) in full.

EXAMPLE 1: Several years ago, John and Louise inherited a genuine Chinese jade vase, their most prized possession. It's worth $10,000. They don't want to give it up, but are in desperate financial shape, with debts of more than $60,000.

If they file for Chapter 7 bankruptcy, their debts will be discharged, but they will probably lose the vase because it's not exempt in their state (and there's no wildcard exemption available). In Chapter 13 bankruptcy, they could keep the vase and pay their debts out of their income over the next three to five years. After several anguished days, John and Louise decide to file for Chapter 7 bankruptcy and give up the vase.

John and Louise might be tempted to hide the vase and hope the trustee doesn't discover it. That would be a crime (perjury), for which they could be

fined or jailed. It's also an abuse of the bankruptcy process that could get their petition dismissed and prevent them from filing again for six months. A much safer (but still risky) alternative would be to sell the vase before they file and use the proceeds to buy exempt property (see Ch. 2 for information on how to do this). Or, John and Louise might offer the trustee exempt property in place of the jade vase.

EXAMPLE 2: Over the years, Mari has carefully constructed an expensive computer system that she uses primarily for hobbies, but also as a work tool for her marginal desktop publishing business. Over a substantial period of time, Mari has also amassed a debt of $100,000, consisting primarily of ten bank credit cards, medical bills and department store charge accounts.

If Mari files for Chapter 7 bankruptcy, she can discharge all of her debts because they are unsecured debts and she did not incur them fraudulently. However, unless a wildcard exemption applies, Mari must either surrender most of the computer equipment (though she can keep the pieces essential to her desktop publishing business) or find a way to replace it with exempt property of equivalent value to be sold for the benefit of her creditors. Mari decides that canceling her debts is far more important to her than hanging on to the entire system and proceeds to file for Chapter 7 bankruptcy.

E. Will the Automatic Stay Help?

In Section B, we introduced you to the automatic stay. When you file for bankruptcy, the automatic stay immediately stops any lawsuit filed against you and virtually all actions against your property and income by a creditor, collection agency or government entity. The automatic stay may provide a powerful reason to file for bankruptcy if you are at risk of

- eviction or foreclosure
- being found in contempt of court for failing to pay child support, or
- losing such basic resources as utility services, welfare, unemployment benefits, your driver's

license or your job (because of a raft of wage garnishments).

Here is how the automatic stay affects some common emergencies:

- **Utility disconnections.** If you're behind on a utility bill and the company is threatening to disconnect your water, electric, gas or telephone service, the automatic stay will prevent the disconnection for at least 20 days. (11 U.S.C. § 366.) Bankruptcy will probably discharge the past due debts for utility service. Although the amount of a utility bill alone rarely justifies a bankruptcy filing, preventing electrical service cutoff in January in New England might give you a pretty good incentive.

- **Foreclosure.** If your home mortgage is in foreclosure, the automatic stay temporarily stops the proceedings. However, the creditor will often be able to proceed with the foreclosure sooner or later. If you are facing foreclosure and want to keep your home, Chapter 13 bankruptcy is almost always a better remedy. (See Section F, below.)

- **Eviction.** If you are being evicted from your home, the automatic stay can usually buy you a few days or a few weeks. But if the landlord asks the court to lift the stay and let the eviction proceed—which landlords usually do—the court will probably allow it. Despite the attractiveness of even a temporary delay, it is seldom a good idea to file for bankruptcy solely because you're being evicted. You'll probably be better off spending your time looking for a new place to live or fighting the eviction in state court, if you have a defense.

- **Enforcement of child support or alimony.** If you owe child support or alimony, bankruptcy will not interrupt your obligation to make current payments. And the automatic stay does not stop proceedings to establish, modify or collect the back support. Also, these debts will survive bankruptcy intact, which means that you will have to pay them once the case is closed. If you file for Chapter 13 bankruptcy, however, you can pay off the back support over a three- to five-year period. See Section F, below.

- **Public benefit overpayments.** If you receive public benefits and were overpaid, the agency is generally entitled to collect the overpayment out of your future checks. The automatic stay prevents this collection; furthermore, the debt (the overpayment you owe) is dischargeable unless the agency convinces the court it resulted from fraud on your part. Whether the threatened collection of an overpayment justifies bankruptcy depends on how severely you'll be affected by the proposed reduction in benefits, your property situation and your other debts.

- **Loss of driver's license because of liability for damages.** In some states, your driver's license may be suspended until you pay a court judgment for damages resulting from an automobile accident. The automatic stay can prevent this suspension if it hasn't already occurred. If you are absolutely dependent on your ability to drive for your livelihood and family support, keeping your driver's license can be a strong incentive to file for bankruptcy.

- **Multiple wage garnishments.** No more than 25% of your wages may be taken to satisfy a court judgment unless it is for child support or alimony. Up to 50% can be garnished if the judgment is for child support or alimony and you currently support children, up to 60% if you don't, and even more if you are more than 12 weeks in arrears. However, many people file for bankruptcy if more than one wage garnishment is threatened. For some people, any loss of income is devastating; also, some employers get angry at the expense and hassle of facilitating a succession of garnishments and take it out on their employees. Although federal law prohibits you from being fired for one garnishment, an employer can fire you for garnishments on multiple debts. (15 U.S.C. § 1674 (a).) Filing for bankruptcy stops garnishments dead in their tracks. Not only will you take home a full salary (although this effect may not be immediate), but you may also be able to discharge the debt in bankruptcy and recover the amounts that the sheriff collected before you filed, as long as they have not yet been turned over to the creditor.

Do You Qualify for Chapter 13 Bankruptcy?

Here are seven easy steps that will give you a rough idea as to whether your income and debt situation qualify you to file a Chapter 13 bankruptcy:

Step 1: Does your total secured debt exceed $871,550? If so, you don't qualify.

Step 2: Does your total unsecured debt exceed $290,522? If so, you don't qualify.

Step 3: Compute your gross monthly income from all sources, less mandatory deductions such as federal and state taxes, child support wage attachments, union dues and FICA. This is your monthly net income. If you want a more accurate figure for your net income, complete Schedule I (see Ch. 3, Section F.9).

Step 4: From your monthly net income computed in Step 3, *subtract* your monthly expenses. As part of your expenses, include any payments you are making on your home and car but don't include the monthly payments you are making on your credit card debts, medical bills and other unsecured debts (debts for which you haven't pledged property as collateral). The difference is your monthly disposable income. (If you want more accurate figures, complete Schedule J (see Ch. 3, Section F.10).

Step 5: Multiply your monthly disposable income by 36—this is how much disposable income you'll have over a three-year period.

Step 6: From the amount computed in Step 5, subtract the full amount of any back taxes, back child or spousal support or other priority debts you owe (for a complete list of priority debts, see Schedule E (Ch. 3, Section 5). The result is the amount of disposable income you will have available for repayment of your other unsecured debts over the next three years.

Step 7: Figure out your unsecured debt by turning to Ch. 3 and filling in a rough draft of Schedule F. The percentage of your unsecured debt that you can repay generally determines your eligibility for a Chapter 13. Some courts allow plans that require you to repay only a small percentage of your unsecured debts, while other courts require you to pay upwards of 50%.

⚠ This little test is not meant to give you a final determination of whether you qualify for Chapter 13 bankruptcy. Rather, it's a "quick and dirty" way for you to decide whether Chapter 13 may be a viable option for you. If you want more complete instructions on how to determine your eligibility for Chapter 13, get a copy of *Bankruptcy: Is It the Right Solution to Your Debt Problems?* by Robin Leonard (Nolo).

> ### Bankruptcy Doesn't Affect a Wage Attachment for Child Support
>
> People who owe child support or alimony often have the current support payments taken directly out of their paycheck. This type of wage attachment is not affected by bankruptcy and will continue as before. In contrast, if your wages have been garnished to collect support arrearages, the automatic stay created by your bankruptcy filing will apply and cause the garnishment to be lifted. However, you will still owe the back support after bankruptcy and the support that has already been collected through the garnishment will not be returned to you.

If the primary reason you file is to get the benefit of the automatic stay, you don't need to file all of your papers at once. The stay goes into effect once you file the two-page petition and a mailing list of your creditors. If you don't file the rest of your papers within 15 days, however, the case will be dismissed and you may be prevented from refiling for 180 days. Ch. 3, Section J, explains emergency filings.

F. Alternatives to Chapter 7 Bankruptcy

In many situations, filing for Chapter 7 bankruptcy is the best remedy for debt problems. In others, however, another course of action makes more sense. This section outlines your main alternatives.

1. Do Nothing

Surprisingly, the best approach for some people who are deeply in debt is to take no action at all. If you're living simply (that is, with little income and property), and look forward to a similar life in the future, you may be what is known as "judgment proof." This means that anyone who sues you and obtains a court judgment won't be able to collect simply because you don't have anything they can legally take. (As a famous song of the 1970s said, "Freedom's just another word for nothing left to lose.") Except in highly unusual situations (for example, if you are a tax protester or willfully refuse to pay child support), you can't be thrown in jail for failing to pay your debts.

Normally, a creditor cannot take your property or income without first suing you and obtaining a court judgment (except for taxing authorities and student loan collectors). However, even if the creditor is armed with a court judgment, the law prevents creditors (except for the IRS, of course) from taking your exempt property, including food, clothing, personal effects and furnishings. (See Section D.2, above). And creditors won't go after your nonexempt property unless it is worth enough to cover the creditor's costs of seizure and sale.

Before taking property, creditors usually try to go after your wages and other income. But a creditor can only take 25% of your net wages to satisfy a court judgment unless it is for child support or alimony. Often, you can keep more than 75% of your wages if you can demonstrate that you need the extra amount to support yourself and your family. Income from a pension or other retirement benefit is usually treated like wages. Creditors cannot touch public benefits such as welfare, unemployment insurance, disability insurance or Social Security.

To sum up, if you don't have a steady job or other source of income that a creditor can snatch, or you can live on 75% of your wages (or perhaps a little more), you needn't fear a lawsuit. Similarly, if most of your property is exempt, there is little the creditor can seize to repay the debt. In these situations, most creditors don't bother trying to collect the debt at all.

Now that you have the good news, here's some bad. Judgments usually last for five to ten years, and they can be renewed for longer periods. In the age of computers, credit reporting bureaus and massive databases that track our every activity, you may have to live with your decision to do nothing for a long, long time. And in many cases, interest on your debt will continue to accrue which means the $10,000 you owe today could become a $100,000 debt in the future.

Even if you are judgment proof, you may be better off dealing with your debt situation now, either through bankruptcy or through one of the other alternatives discussed below.

2. Negotiate With Your Creditors

If you have some income, or you have assets you're willing to sell, you may be a lot better off negotiating with your creditors than filing for bankruptcy. Through negotiation, you may be able to come up with a new payment plan that allows you to get back on your feet. Or you may be able to settle your debt for less than you owe.

 Negotiating with creditors. How to negotiate with your creditors is covered in detail in *Money Troubles: Legal Strategies to Cope With Your Debts*, by Robin Leonard & Deanne Loonin (Nolo). That book covers how to deal with creditors when you owe money on a variety of debts, including credit cards, mortgage loans, car loans, child support and alimony.

3. Get Outside Help to Design a Repayment Plan

Many people have trouble negotiating with creditors, either because they don't have the skills and negotiating experience to do a good job or because they find the whole process exceedingly unpleasant. Indeed, because the ability to negotiate is an art, many people benefit from outside help.

If you don't want to negotiate with your creditors, you can turn to a lawyer or a credit counseling agency. These agencies come in two basic varieties: nonprofit and for-profit. They all work on the same basic principal —a repayment plan is negotiated with all your unsecured creditors. You make one monthly payment to the agency and they distribute the payment to your creditors as provided in the plan. As long as you make the payments, the creditors will not take any action against you. And if you succeed in completing the plan, one or more of your creditors may be willing to extend you new credit on reasonable terms. The nonprofit agencies tend to be funded primarily by the major creditors (in the form of a commission for each repayment plan they negotiate) and by moderate fees charged the user (roughly $20–$25 per plan negotiated). The for-profit agencies are funded by the same sources, but tend to charge much higher fees than the nonprofit agencies.

The big downside to entering into one of the repayment plans is that if you fail to make a payment, the creditors may pull the plug on the deal and come after you, regardless of how faithful you've been in the past. If and when that happens, you may find that you would have been better off filing for bankruptcy in the first place. For more on the pros and cons of repayment plans, see *Money Troubles*, by Robin Leonard & Deanne Loonin (Nolo).

 Doing nothing or negotiating with your creditors could cost you. The IRS treats certain forgiven debts (debts for which a creditor agrees to take less than is owed or nothing) and debts written off (debts that the creditor has stopped trying to collect, declared uncollectible and reported as a tax loss to the IRS) as taxable income to you. (26 U.S.C. § 108.) Specifically, any bank, credit union, savings and loan or other financial institution that forgives or writes off all or part of a debt for $600 or more must send you and the IRS a Form 1099-C at the end of the tax year. When you file your tax return, you must report the write-off as income, and pay taxes on it.

The Internal Revenue Code provides three exceptions to this rule for consumers: Even if the financial institution issues a Form 1099-C, you do not have to report the income if:

- the forgiveness or write-off is intended as a gift (this would be unusual)
- you discharge the debt in bankruptcy, or
- you were insolvent before the creditor agreed to waive the debt or wrote off the debt.

The Internal Revenue Code does not define "insolvent." Generally, it means that your debts exceed the value of your assets. To figure out whether or not you are insolvent, you will have to total up your assets and your debts, including the debt that was forgiven or written off. If you conclude that you are insolvent, you will need to attach an explanatory letter to your tax return listing your assets and debts.

4. Pay Over Time With Chapter 13 Bankruptcy

Chapter 13 bankruptcy lets you enter into a court-approved plan to deal with your debts over three to five years. Some debts must be paid in full (back taxes and child support are the most common examples), while others may be paid only in part. The basic idea is that you must devote all of your disposable income to whatever plan is approved by the bankruptcy court. With a few exceptions, Chapter 13 doesn't require you to give up any property—for that reason, it's the bankruptcy of choice for folks who have significant amounts of nonexempt property.

If you do file for a Chapter 13 bankruptcy, the minimum amount you will have to pay is roughly equal to the value of your nonexempt property. Since very few prospective Chapter 7 bankruptcy filers have much nonexempt property, this won't be an issue for most people.

In addition, you must pledge your disposable income (net income less reasonable expenses) over the life of your plan. This income need not come from wages. You can use benefits, investment income or receipts earned as an independent contractor or businessperson.

To file for Chapter 13 bankruptcy, you fill out the same forms as in a Chapter 7 bankruptcy, listing your money, property, expenses, debts and income, and file them with the bankruptcy court along with a filing fee of $185. In addition, you must file a plan to repay your debts, based on your income and expenses. With the possible exception of your mortgage and car note, you make payments under the plan directly to the bankruptcy trustee, who in turn distributes the money to your creditors. When you complete your plan, any remaining unpaid balance on the unsecured debts is wiped out.

As in Chapter 7 bankruptcy, the act of filing for Chapter 13 immediately stops your creditors from taking further action against you. Also as in Chapter 7 bankruptcy, certain debts cannot be discharged in Chapter 13 bankruptcy. This means that if they are not paid in full through your plan, you must pay the balance after your case ends. The debts that are considered nondischargeable in Chapter 13 bankruptcy are the same ones that are automatically nondischargeable in a Chapter 7 bankruptcy. (See Section D.1, above.) But the other Chapter 7 nondischargeable debts—those that are discharged unless the creditor successfully objects—can be wiped out at the end of a Chapter 13

bankruptcy even if they are not paid in full by the plan. This is known as Chapter 13 bankruptcy's "super discharge."

You can file for Chapter 13 bankruptcy at any time, even if you got a Chapter 7 bankruptcy discharge the day before or just completed another Chapter 13 repayment plan. But if you file more than one Chapter 13 case, you'll be required to pay back a larger percentage of your debts.

If you start but are not able to finish a Chapter 13 repayment plan—for example, you lose your job six months into the plan and can't make the payments—the trustee may modify your plan. The trustee may give you a grace period (if the problem seems temporary), reduce your total monthly payments or extend the repayment period. As long as it looks like you're acting in good faith, the trustee will try to be accommodating and help you across rocky periods. If it's clear you won't be able to complete the plan because of circumstances beyond your control, the court might let you discharge your debts on the basis of hardship. Examples of hardship would be a sudden plant closing in a one-factory town or a debilitating illness.

If the bankruptcy court won't let you modify your plan or give you a hardship discharge, you still have two options:

- you can convert your case to a Chapter 7 bankruptcy (unless you received a Chapter 7 discharge in a case filed within the previous six years), or
- you can ask the bankruptcy court to dismiss your Chapter 13 petition, which would leave you in the same position you were in before you filed, except you'll owe less because of the payments you made on your debts. If your Chapter 13 bankruptcy is dismissed, your creditors may add to their debts any interest that was abated during your Chapter 13 petition case.

Filing for Chapter 13 bankruptcy. For information on Chapter 13 bankruptcy—including instructions on how to complete the forms—see *Chapter 13 Bankruptcy: Repay Your Debts*, by Robin Leonard (Nolo). ■

Your Property and Bankruptcy

This chapter explains what happens to your property when you file for Chapter 7 bankruptcy. Section A explains what property is subject to the reach of the bankruptcy court. Section B introduces the Worksheet, which will help you inventory your property and determine which of it is exempt—that is, which of it you will be able to keep despite filing for bankruptcy. Happily, most people find that they can keep virtually all their property through the bankruptcy process. There is one major exception: a creditor can repossess property that serves as security for a debt (collateral) if you are behind on the payments when you file your Chapter 7 bankruptcy. And even if you are current on the payments, the creditor may repossess the property unless you

- agree to continue owing the underlying debt
- pay the creditor the fair market value of the property, or
- in some states, continue making payments even though the underlying debt is wiped out.

In Ch. 7, we explain collateral in more detail.

Once you have figured out what property you can keep through bankruptcy, you may be able to exchange some of your nonexempt property for exempt items before you file. Section C offers suggestions—and important cautions—if you want to try this.

A. Property in Your Bankruptcy Estate

When you file for Chapter 7 bankruptcy, everything you own when you file becomes subject to the bankruptcy court's authority. This property is collectively called your "bankruptcy estate." With a few exceptions (discussed below), property you acquire after you file for Chapter 7 bankruptcy isn't included in your bankruptcy estate. If you originally filed for Chapter 13 bankruptcy and now want to convert your case to a Chapter 7 bankruptcy, everything you owned on the date you filed your Chapter 13 petition is the property of your Chapter 7 bankruptcy estate. (11 U.S.C. § 348(f)(1)(A).)

These categories of property make up your bankruptcy estate.

Using the Information in This Chapter

This chapter will help you:

- **Decide whether bankruptcy is appropriate.** Knowing what you own and how much you can get for it will help you decide whether or not to file for Chapter 7 bankruptcy. It may be easier simply to sell off some property (especially property that you would have to give up anyway if you filed for bankruptcy) and pay creditors directly than to go through bankruptcy.
- **Determine what property you can keep.** You'll be able to keep some types of property no matter how high their value. However, your right to keep property in bankruptcy often depends on what it is worth. For instance, many states allow you to keep a car, but only if your equity is less than a certain amount ($1,500 is a common limit). If you own considerably more equity, you will have to turn the car over to the trustee to be sold (or find a way to pay the trustee the equivalent value in cash or other exempt property). After the sale, you'll get $1,500 from the proceeds (in this example) and your creditors will get the rest.
- **Summarize information about your property before you file.** If you decide to file for bankruptcy, you'll need to fill out forms to indicate what property you own, how much it's worth and what you claim as exempt. The work you do in this chapter can be transferred to those forms.

---

1. Property You Own and Possess

Property that you own and possess—for example, clothing, books, computers, cameras, TV, stereo system, furniture, tools, car, real estate, boat, artworks and stock certificates—are included in your bankruptcy estate.

Property that belongs to someone else is not part of your bankruptcy estate—even if you control the property—because you don't have the right to sell it or give it away. Here are some examples:

EXAMPLE 1: A parent establishes a trust for her child and names you as trustee to manage the money in the trust until the child's 18th birthday. You possess and control the money, but it's solely for the child's benefit under the terms of the trust; you cannot use it for your own purposes. It isn't part of your bankruptcy estate.

EXAMPLE 2: Your sister has gone to Zimbabwe for an indefinite period and has loaned you her computer system while she's gone. Although you might have use of the equipment for years to come, you don't own it. It isn't part of your bankruptcy estate.

EXAMPLE 3: You are making monthly payments on a leased car. You are entitled to possess the car as long as you make the monthly payments, but you don't own it. It is not part of your bankruptcy estate (but the lease itself is).

2. Property You Own But Don't Possess

Any property you own is part of your bankruptcy estate, even if you don't have physical possession of it. For instance, you may own a share of a vacation cabin in the mountains, but never go there yourself. Or you may own furniture or a car that someone else is using. Other examples include a deposit held by a stockbroker, stock options, contractual rights to a royalty or commission or a security deposit held by your landlord or the utility company.

3. Property You Have Recently Given (or Had Taken) Away

People contemplating bankruptcy are often tempted to unload their property on friends and relatives or pay favorite creditors before they file. Don't bother. Property given away or paid out shortly before you file for bankruptcy is still part of your bankruptcy estate—and

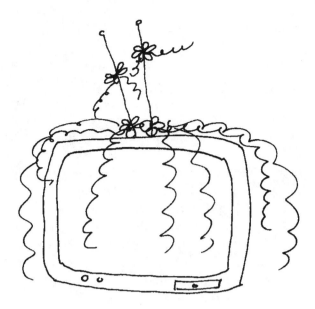

the trustee has the legal authority to take it back. Be sure to include this property on the Worksheet in Section B, below.

a. Giving Away Property

You might be thinking about signing over the title certificate to an item of property to a relative or the person you live with, then not listing it in your bankruptcy papers. This is both dishonest and foolhardy. On your bankruptcy forms, you must list all property transactions made within the previous year. Failure to report a transaction is perjury—a felony. And if the unreported transfer is discovered, the trustee can seize the item from whoever has it and sell it to pay your creditors if

- the transfer occurred within the year before you filed
- you didn't receive a reasonable amount for the item—selling an item for less than it's worth is the same as giving a gift for bankruptcy purposes, or
- the transfer either left you insolvent or greatly pushed you towards that state.

Even worse, if you transfer property with the intent to defraud your creditors, the court may refuse to discharge *any* of your debts. (11 U.S.C. § 727(a)(2).)

b. Paying Off a Favorite Creditor

You can't pay a favorite creditor, such as a relative or friend, before you file for bankruptcy, then leave your other creditors with less than they would have otherwise received. Bankruptcy law calls payments and repossessions made shortly before filing for bankruptcy "preferences." The trustee can sue the creditor for the amount of the preference and make it a part of the bankruptcy estate, so that it can be distributed among your creditors. In general, a preference exists when you pay or transfer property worth more than $600 to a creditor

- within 90 days before filing for bankruptcy, or
- within one year before filing if the creditor was close to you—for example, a friend, relative, business partner or corporation owned by you. (11 U.S.C. § 547.)

4. Property You Are Entitled to Receive but Don't Yet Possess When You File

Property to which you are legally entitled at the time you file for bankruptcy is included in your bankruptcy estate, even if you haven't actually received it yet. The most common examples are wages you have earned but have not yet been paid and tax refunds that are legally owed to you. Here are some other examples:

- Vacation or severance pay earned before you filed for bankruptcy.
- Property you've inherited, but not yet received, from someone who has died. If you're a beneficiary in the will or revocable living trust of someone who is alive, you don't have to list that on your bankruptcy papers—he could change his will or trust before he dies. If he has already died, however, you have a legal right to receive the property and you must list it.
- Property you will receive from a trust. If you receive periodic payments from a trust but aren't entitled to the full amount of the trust yet, the full amount of the trust is considered property of your bankruptcy estate and should be listed on the Worksheet and your bankruptcy papers. Although the bankruptcy trustee may not be able to get the money (depending on the type of trust), you don't want to be accused of hiding it.

- Proceeds of an insurance policy, if the death, injury or other event that triggers payment has occurred. For example, if you were the beneficiary of your father's life insurance policy, and your father has died but you haven't received your money yet, that amount is part of your bankruptcy estate.
- A legal claim to monetary compensation (sometimes called a legal "cause of action"), even if the value of the claim hasn't yet been determined. For example, if you have a claim against someone for injuring you in a car accident, you must include this potential source of money in your bankruptcy papers, even if the amount has not yet been determined in a lawsuit, settlement agreement or insurance claim.
- Accounts receivable (money owed you for goods or services you've provided). Even if you don't think you'll be paid, that money is considered part of your bankruptcy estate. It's the trustee's job to go after the money; leaving it off the bankruptcy forms can get you into trouble.
- Money earned (but not yet received) from property in your bankruptcy estate. This includes, for example, rent from commercial or residential real estate, royalties from copyrights or patents, and dividends earned on stocks.

5. Proceeds From Property of the Bankruptcy Estate

If property in your bankruptcy estate earns income or otherwise produces money after you file for bankruptcy, this money is also part of your bankruptcy estate. For example, suppose a contract to receive royalties for a book you have written is part of your bankruptcy estate. Any royalties you earn under this contract after you file for bankruptcy are also property of the estate. The one exception to this rule is money you earn from providing personal services after filing for bankruptcy, which isn't part of your bankruptcy estate. Continuing our example, work on a new edition of the book after you file for bankruptcy would be considered personal services. The royalties you earn for that new work would not be part of your bankruptcy estate.

Are Stock Options Part of Your Bankruptcy Estate?

Whether stock options are part of your bankruptcy estate depends on when you received them and when they vest.

If you own stock options, you have the right to purchase stock at a specific price that is assigned at the time the stock options are granted. Making such a purchase is called "exercising your stock options." As a general rule, stock options that you own when you file for bankruptcy are part of your bankruptcy estate. In addition, any stock you purchase by exercising your stock options is also part of the estate, even if you exercise those options after you file for bankruptcy. Courts treat these stock purchases as proceeds earned on property of the estate (as explained in this Section.)

Sometimes, your stock options do not vest (that is, they cannot be exercised) until you have been with your company for a certain period of time. In that case, only those stock options that have already vested on the date you file for bankruptcy will be included in your bankruptcy estate.

To calculate the value of your stock options, multiply the number of vested stock options you own by the difference between your option price and the fair market value of the stock. [Value of options = (number of vested stock options) x (fair market value – option price).] Even if the potential value of your options is very uncertain, they are still part of your bankruptcy estate and the trustee will take them if they are marketable.

6. Certain Property Acquired Within 180 Days After You File for Bankruptcy

Most property you acquire—or become entitled to acquire—after you file for bankruptcy isn't included in your bankruptcy estate. But there are exceptions. If you acquire (or become entitled to acquire) certain items within 180 days after you file, you must report them to the bankruptcy court—and the bankruptcy trustee may take them. (11 U.S.C. § 541(a)(5).)

The 180-day rule applies to:

- property you inherit during the 180-day period
- property from a marital settlement agreement or divorce decree that goes into effect during the 180-day period, and
- death benefits or life insurance policy proceeds that become owed to you during the 180-day period.

You must report these items on a supplemental form, even if your bankruptcy case is over. You can find instructions for filing the supplemental form in Ch. 4, Section B.

7. Your Share of Marital Property

How much of your marital property—the property you and your spouse own together—is included in your bankruptcy estate depends on two factors: (1) whether you file jointly or alone, and (2) the laws of your state regarding marital property.

If you file jointly, all marital property that fits into any of the above five categories (Sections 1 through 5) belongs to your bankruptcy estate.

However, if you are married and you file for bankruptcy alone, some marital property may not be part of your bankruptcy estate. Whether property is part of the estate depends on whether you live in a community property, tenancy by the entirety or common law property state.

a. Community Property States

These are the community property states: Alaska, Arizona, California, Idaho, Louisiana, Nevada, New Mexico, Texas, Washington and Wisconsin.

In these states, the general rule is that all property either spouse earns or receives during the marriage is community property and is owned jointly by both spouses. Exceptions are made for gifts and inheritances received specifically by one spouse, and property owned by one spouse before the marriage or acquired after permanent separation—these are the separate property of the spouse who acquired or received them.

If you are married, live in a community property state and file for bankruptcy, all the community property you and your spouse own is considered part of your bankruptcy estate, even if your spouse doesn't file.

This is true even if the community property might not be divided 50-50 if you were to divorce.

> **EXAMPLE:** Paul and Sonya live in California, a community property state. Sonya contributed $20,000 of her separate property toward the purchase of their house. All the rest of the money used to pay for the house is from community funds, and the house is considered community property. If Paul and Sonya were to divorce and split the house proceeds, Sonya would be entitled to $20,000 more than Paul as reimbursement for her down payment. But they aren't divorced, and Paul files for bankruptcy without Sonya. Their house is worth $250,000. Paul must list that entire value on his bankruptcy papers—that is, he can't subtract the $20,000 Sonya would be entitled to if they divorced.

The separate property of the spouse filing for bankruptcy is also part of the bankruptcy estate. But the separate property of the spouse *not* filing for bankruptcy is not part of the bankruptcy estate.

> **EXAMPLE:** Paul owns a twin-engine Cessna as his separate property (he owned it before he married Sonya). Sonya came to the marriage owning a grand piano. Because only Paul is filing for bankruptcy, Paul's aircraft will be part of his bankruptcy estate, but Sonya's piano won't be.

You may need to do some research into your state's property laws to make sure you understand which of your property is separate and which is community. See Ch. 9 for tips on research.

b. Tenancy by the Entirety States

States that recognize some form of tenancy by the entirety include Delaware, the District of Columbia, Florida, Hawaii, Indiana, Maryland, Massachusetts, Michigan, Missouri, North Carolina, Ohio, Pennsylvania, Tennessee, Vermont, Virginia and Wyoming.

In these states, the general rule is that property spouses own as "tenants by the entirety" is part of the bankruptcy estate. However, if one spouse owes most of the debts and files for bankruptcy alone, this property is exempt—that is, neither the trustee nor any creditor can seize it to pay debts. The reasoning behind this rule is simple: because the property belongs to the marriage (rather than to one spouse or the other), neither spouse can give it away or encumber it with debts on his or her own.

There are many variations on this general rule. For example, some states recognize tenancy by the entirety as a form of ownership that applies only to real estate. Some states presume that spouses who own property together own it as tenants by the entirety, while others require spouses to specify how they hold the property. Space restrictions prohibit us from going into greater detail on this tenancy by the entirety exemption. It's potentially a very powerful tool for debtors who declare bankruptcy: if your property falls within this rule, it is entirely exempt, regardless of its value. This means that you might be able to keep your house, for example, even if your equity well exceeds your state's homestead exemption.

If you live in a state that recognizes this form of ownership, you should certainly do some research or talk to a lawyer to find out whether and how it applies to you. (See Ch. 9 for more information on research and lawyers.)

c. Common Law Property States

If your state is not listed above as a community property or tenancy by the entirety state, it is a common law property state. When only one spouse files for bankruptcy in a common law property state, all of that spouse's separate property plus half of the couple's jointly owned property go into the filing spouse's bankruptcy estate.

The general rules of property ownership in common law states are:

- Property that has only one spouse's name on a title certificate (such as a car, house or stocks), even if bought with joint funds, is that spouse's separate property.
- Property that was purchased or received as a gift or inheritance by both for the use of both spouses is jointly owned, unless title is held in only one spouse's name (which means it belongs to that spouse separately, even if both spouses use it).

• Property that one spouse buys with separate funds or receives as a gift or inheritance for that spouse's separate use is that spouse's separate property (unless, again, a title certificate shows differently).

B. Property You Can Keep

As we have seen, your property is everything you own. If you own your own home (or you have any ownership interest in real estate of any kind), you are the proud owner of what is called "real property." If you don't own any real estate, everything you own is considered personal property.

When filing for Chapter 7 bankruptcy, you may be able to keep your home. However, you will probably have to give up any other real estate you own to be sold for the benefit of your creditors. You will also be able to keep some or all of your personal property. How much you get to keep will depend on whether the property is considered exempt under your state's exemption statute (or under the federal exemption statute if your state allows it to be used).

After we explain the exemption system, we assist you in completing the Worksheet. The purpose of this worksheet is to help you figure out exactly what property you own—and how much of it you would get to keep if you decide to file a Chapter 7 bankruptcy. If you do decide to file, the information you provide here can be easily transferred to the official forms you'll need to file with your bankruptcy Petition. A blank copy of the Worksheet is in Appendix 4. Tear it out (or make a copy) now and keep it handy.

1. Understanding the Property Exemption System

Figuring out exactly what property you're legally entitled to keep if you file for bankruptcy takes some work, but it's very important. It's your responsibility—and to your benefit—to claim all exemptions to which you're entitled. If you don't claim property as exempt, you could lose it to your creditors unnecessarily.

Exempt property is the property you can keep during and after bankruptcy. Nonexempt property is the property that the bankruptcy trustee is entitled to take to use to pay your creditors. Therefore, the more you can claim as exempt, the better off you are.

In Ch. 1 we explained that each state's legislature produces a set of exemptions for use by people who file bankruptcy in that state. Fifteen states (and the District of Columbia) allow debtors to choose between their state's exemptions or another set of exemptions created by Congress (called federal bankruptcy exemptions). States that currently allow debtors this choice are Arkansas, Connecticut, Hawaii, Massachusetts, Michigan, Minnesota, New Hampshire, New Jersey, New Mexico, Pennsylvania, Rhode Island, Texas, Vermont, Washington and Wisconsin.

Remember also that California has adopted its own unique exemption system. Although California doesn't allow debtors to use the federal exemptions, California offers two sets of state exemptions for people filing bankruptcy. As in the 15 states that have the federal bankruptcy exemptions, people filing bankruptcy in California must choose one or the other set of California's state exemptions.

You might be able to keep your nonexempt property. You won't have to surrender a specific item of nonexempt property to the trustee if you pay her the property's value in cash, or if she is willing to accept exempt property of roughly equal value instead. Also, the trustee might reject or "abandon" the item if it would be too costly or cumbersome to sell. In that case, you also get to keep it. So when we say that you have to give up property, remember that you still might be able to barter with the trustee to keep it.

a. Types of Exemptions

Both state and federal exemptions come in several basic flavors. Some exemptions protect the value of your ownership in a particular item only up to a set dollar limit. For instance, the New Mexico state exemptions allow you to keep $4,000 of equity in a motor vehicle. If you were filing Chapter 7 bankruptcy in that state and using the state exemption list, you could keep your car if it was worth $4,000 or less. You could also keep the car if selling it would not raise enough money to pay what you still owe on it and give you the full value of your $4,000 exemption. For example, if you own a car worth $20,000 but still owe $16,000 on it, selling it would raise $16,000 for the lender and $4,000 for you (thanks to the exemption). Since there would be nothing left over to pay your other creditors, the trustee wouldn't take the car. Instead, you would be allowed to keep it as long as you are—and remain—current on your payments.

However, if your equity in the car exceeded the $4,000 exemption, the trustee might sell the car to raise money for your other creditors. To continue our example, let's say you only owe $10,000 on that car. Selling the car for $20,000 would pay off the lender in full, pay your $4,000 exemption and leave a portion of the remaining $6,000 (after the costs of sale are deducted) to be distributed to your other creditors. In this scenario, you are entitled to the full value of your exemption—$4,000—but not to the car itself.

Another type of exemption allows you to keep specified property items regardless of their value. For instance, the Utah state exemptions allow you to keep a refrigerator, freezer, microwave, stove, sewing machine and carpets with no limit on their value. For comparison purposes, another Utah state exemption places a $500 limit on "heirlooms, sofas, chairs, and related furnishings." Go figure.

Some states (and the federal exemption list) also provide a general-purpose exemption, called a "wildcard" exemption. This exemption gives you a dollar amount that you can apply to any type of property. If you play poker, you undoubtedly have played a game where a particular card is designated a wildcard, which means you can use it as a queen of diamonds, a two of spades, or any other card you want to make the most of the other cards in your hand. The same principle applies here. For example, suppose you own a $3,000 boat in a state that doesn't exempt boats but does have a wildcard of $5,000. You can take $3,000 of the wildcard and apply it to the boat, which means the boat will now be considered exempt. And if you have other nonexempt property, you can apply the remaining $2,000 to that property.

You can also use a wildcard exemption to increase an existing exemption. For example, if you have $5,000 worth of equity in your car but your state only allows you to exempt $1,500 of its value, you will likely lose the car. However, if your state has a $5,000 wildcard

exemption, you could use the $1,500 motor vehicle exemption and $3,500 of the wildcard exemption to exempt your car entirely. And you'd still have $1,500 of the wildcard exemption to use on other nonexempt property.

b. Why State Exemptions Vary So Much

Each state's exemptions are unique. The property you can keep therefore varies considerably from state to state. Why the differences? State exemptions are used not only for bankruptcy purposes but also to shelter property that otherwise could be taken by creditors who have obtained court judgments. The exemptions reflect the attitudes of state legislators about how much property, and which property, a debtor should be forced to part with when a judgment is being collected. These attitudes are rooted in local values and concerns. But in many cases there is another, more pressing reason why state exemptions differ. Some state legislatures have raised exemption levels in recent times, while other states last looked at their exemptions many decades ago. In states that don't reconsider exemption amounts very often, you can expect to find lower exemptions.

c. If You Are Married and Filing Jointly

If the federal bankruptcy exemptions are available in your state and you decide to use them, you may double all of the exemptions if you are married and filing jointly (for more on whether to file jointly, see Section A.7, above). This means that you and your spouse can each claim the full amount of each exemption. If you decide to use your state's exemptions, you may be able to double some exemptions but not others. For instance, in the California exemption System 1 list, the $1,900 limit for motor vehicles may not be doubled, but the $5,000 limit on tools of the trade may be doubled in some circumstances. In order for you to double for a single piece of property, title to the property must be in both of your names. In Appendix 1, we've noted whether a court or state legislature has expressly allowed or prohibited doubling. If the chart doesn't say one way or the other, it is probably safe to double. However, keep in mind that this area of the law changes rapidly—legislation or court decisions issued after the publication date of this book will not be reflected in the chart. (See Ch. 9 for information on doing your own legal research.)

2. Real Estate You Can Keep: Worksheet, Part A

Referral Note: Part A of the Worksheet is only for people who own their own home. If you own real estate that you do not use as your home, you will still need to identify it in your bankruptcy papers (should you choose to file). However, we don't address that sort of property here because no state offers an exemption for non-residential real estate. Because the purpose of the Worksheet is to help you decide what property you can keep, we only deal with real estate used as a home. If you don't own your home, skip to Part B (Personal Property).

⚠ You might lose your home. If you are behind on your mortgage payments when you file, you will probably lose your home if you file a Chapter 7 bankruptcy. You may want to consider filing a Chapter 13 bankruptcy instead, assuming you qualify (see Ch. 1, Section F). If this is your situation, there is no need for you to complete Part A of the worksheet unless you have a plan to bring your mortgage up-to-date. Ch. 6 gives you detailed information to help you figure out what is likely to happen to your home in a Chapter 7 bankruptcy.

The amount of actual dollar ownership you have in your home (your equity) will determine whether you can keep it or whether the trustee will sell it for the benefit of your creditors. Part A of the Worksheet will help you compute your equity, then compare this equity against the homestead exemption allowed in your state. If your equity is less than the homestead, you will probably get to keep your home. If your equity is equal to or higher than your state's homestead allowance, you will most likely lose your home (although you will be paid for your equity, up to the homestead amount).

Unlimited Homestead States

If you live in Arkansas, District of Columbia, Florida, Iowa, Kansas, Louisiana (for some types of debts only), Oklahoma, South Dakota or Texas, you will be able to keep your home regardless of its value—as long as it fits the description provided in those states' homestead allowances. See Ch. 6 for more on how to read these statutes.

⚠ This section is not for everyone. The following discussion assumes that you fit into one of the following categories.
- you are not married and you are the only owner of the property
- you are married, own the property with your spouse and would be filing for Chapter 7 bankruptcy jointly, or
- you are married, own the property with your spouse in a community property state and would be filing for Chapter 7 bankruptcy alone.

If you are not married but own the real estate jointly with another individual, you'll need to read Ch. 6 to determine how bankruptcy will affect your home. The same is true if you are married, filing separately and live in a common law property or tenancy by the entirety state.

a. Completing Worksheet, Part A

Line 1: Provide a brief description of your home, including its address and type of structure. Most commonly this will be a street address and one of the following: single family home, condo or mobile home.

Line 2: Enter your home's fair market value. You can get this value from any local real estate agent or appraiser. For most homes, the fair market value will be based on what similar homes in the same neighborhood have recently been sold for on the open market.

Line 3: List all mortgages, home equity loans and liens recorded against the property. Add them up and write the total on Line 3.

Line 4: From the fair market value on Line 2, subtract the dollar value of all liens recorded against the property from Line 3 and enter the difference here. This is your equity.

Line 5: Enter the homestead exemption for your state (or the federal homestead exemption, if it's larger and you are allowed to use it). To find the appropriate homestead exemption, follow these steps:

1. Turn to the Exemption Appendix (Appendix 1).
2. Locate the page with your state's exemptions.
3. Check the top item (labeled homestead).
4. If you live in one of the states with an "unlimited" homestead exemption, your exemption will be measured by the size of your lot. If you live in any other state, your exemption will have a dollar limit. If you are married and filing jointly, check to see whether your state allows you to double the exemption (you can find this information on your state's exemption page).
5. If your state's homestead amount is less than the federal homestead exemption (currently $17,425, or $34,850 for married couples), check at the top of the page to see whether your state allows federal exemptions. If it does, and your equity is above your state's homestead level, you may wish to use the federal homestead exemption.

Line 6: Subtract your homestead exemption (Line 5) from your equity (Line 4) and enter the difference. If your equity is larger than your exemption, the result will be a positive number and you will probably lose your home. If your equity is smaller than your exemption, you will have a negative number and you will probably be able to keep your home. For more information on how this works, see Ch. 6.

Here are two examples that illustrate how to complete Part A of the Worksheet:

EXAMPLE 1: Tim Klyven is a single man who lives in Ohio. He owns a home with a fair market value of $100,000. He enters the address and a brief description of the house on Line 1 and the fair market value on Line 2. He owes about $80,000 on a mortgage and has borrowed an additional $18,000 against the home as part of a home equity loan. He puts $98,000 on Line 3. He subtracts this from the amount on Line 2 and enters the difference ($2,000) on Line 4. This is his equity. Tim next locates Appendix 1 and find the page with the Ohio exemptions. The first entry on the page sets out the Ohio homestead amount. Tim learns that in Ohio you can keep any property used as a residence up to $5,000 in value. He lists this amount on Line 5. As we've seen, exemptions that impose dollar limits on specific items refer to the amount the debtor can keep, not the actual value of the property. Tim subtracts the exemption ($5,000) from his equity ($2,000) and enters negative $3,000 on Line 6. Since this is a negative number, Tim will be able to hold on to the house if he is—and remains—current on the payments to the secured creditors.

EXAMPLE 2: Suppose now that Tim's home is worth $110,000, which means that his equity is $15,000 instead of $5,000. When Tim subtracts his exemption from the equity, he gets $10,000, which he enters on Line 6. Since the number is positive, Tim will probably lose the home if he files a Chapter 7 bankruptcy.

Incidentally, if the federal bankruptcy exemptions were available in Ohio, Tim could keep the home after all, since the federal homestead exemption ($17,425) is higher than Tim's equity ($15,000). Unfortunately, at the very top of the Ohio exemption page, Tim learns that the federal bankruptcy exemptions aren't available in Ohio.

3. Personal Property You Can Keep: Personal Property Checklist and Worksheet, Part B

Part B of the Worksheet will help you figure out what personal property you own and whether you will get to keep it if you file for bankruptcy. You also can use this information to complete the official forms that accompany your bankruptcy petition, if you later decide to file.

Personal Property Checklist

In Appendix 4, you'll find a blank copy of the Personal Property Checklist. Check the box in front of each item you currently own.

Worksheet, Part B

Column 1: Using your completed checklist as a guide, describe each item of property and its location.

For personal property, identify the item (for example, 1994 Ford Mustang) and its location (for example, residence). For cash on hand and deposits of money, indicate the source of each, such as wages or salary, insurance policy proceeds or the proceeds from selling an item of property. Although cash on hand is usually not exempt, you may be able to exempt all or some of it if you can show that it came from an exempt source, such as unemployment insurance.

Column 2: Enter the value of each item of property in Column 1.

It's easy to enter a dollar amount for cash, bank deposits, bonds and most investment instruments. For items that are tougher to value, such as insurance, annuities, pensions and business interests, you may need to get an appraisal from someone who has some financial expertise.

For your other property, estimate its market value—that is, what you could sell it for at a garage sale or through a classified ad. As long as you have a reasonable basis for your estimates, the lower the value you place on property, the more of it you will probably be allowed to keep through the bankruptcy process. Trustees have years of experience and a pretty good sense of what property is worth. Be honest. It's okay to be wrong as long as you do your best to estimate the fair market value and briefly explain any uncertainties. If you can't estimate—for example, if you have an unusual asset such as a future interest, life estate or a lease—leave this column blank.

Here are some tips for valuing specific items:

- **Cars.** Start with the low *Kelley Blue Book* price. If the car needs substantial repair, reduce the value by the amount it would cost you to fix the car. If the car is worth less than the *Blue Book* value, be prepared to show why. You can find a copy of the *Blue Book* at the public library, or on the Web at www.kbb.com.
- **Older goods.** Want ads in a local flea market or penny-saver newspaper are a good place to look for prices. If the item isn't listed, use the garage sale value—that is, begin with the price you paid and then deduct about 20% for each year you've owned the item. For example, if you bought a camera for $400 three years ago, subtract $80 for the first year (down to $320), $64 for the second year (down to $256) and $51 for the third year (down to $205).
- **Life insurance.** List the current cash surrender value. (Call your insurance agent to find out what it is.) Term life insurance has a cash surrender value of zero. Don't list the amount of benefits the policy will pay, unless you're the beneficiary of an insurance policy and the insured person has died.

- **Stocks and bonds.** Check the listing in a newspaper business section. If you can't find the listing, or the stock isn't traded publicly, call your broker and ask what it's worth. If you have a brokerage account, use the value from your last statement. For information on how to calculate the value of any stock options you own, see "Are Stock Options Part of Your Bankruptcy Estate?" above.
- **Jewelry, antiques and other collectibles.** Any valuable jewelry or collections should be appraised.

Add up the amounts in Column 4 and enter the total in the space provided on the last page.

Ignore liens against your personal property when computing the property's value. If you owe money to a major consumer lender such as Beneficial Finance, the lender may have taken a lien on some or all of your personal property. You can usually remove this lien in the course of your bankruptcy. Similarly, you may have a lien against your personal property if a creditor has obtained a court judgment against you. These liens too can frequently be removed. See Ch. 7 to find out more about personal property liens and your options for dealing with them.

Columns 3 and 4. Identify exemptions for your personal property.

You can find every state's exemptions in Appendix 1. If your state allows you to choose the federal exemptions instead of your state's exemptions, you can find these listed directly after Wyoming.

Focus on the property you really want to keep. If you have a lot of property and get bogged down in exemption jargon and dollar signs, start with the property you would feel really bad about losing. After that, if you are so inclined, you can search for exemptions that would let you keep property that is less important to you.

a. If You Can Only Use Your State's Exemptions

Unless you live in Arkansas, Connecticut, Hawaii, Massachusetts, Michigan, Minnesota, New Hampshire, New Jersey, New Mexico, Pennsylvania, Rhode Island, Texas, Vermont, Washington or Wisconsin, you must use your state's exemptions.

Step 1: In Column 3, list the amount of the exemption or write "no limit" if the exemption is unlimited. In Column 4, list the number of the statute identified in Appendix 1 for the exemption that may reasonably be applied to the particular property item. Use the notes at the beginning of Appendix 1 and the definitions in Appendix 2: *Exemption Glossary,* if you need more information or an explanation of terms. In evaluating whether or not your cash on hand and deposits are exempt, look to the source of the money, such as welfare benefits, insurance proceeds or wages.

Err on the side of exemption. If you can think of a reason why a particular property item might be exempt, list it even if you aren't sure that the exemption applies. If you later decide to file for Chapter 7 bankruptcy, you will only be expected to do your best to fit the exemptions to your property. Of course, if you do misapply an exemption and the bankruptcy trustee or a creditor files

a formal objection within the required time, you may have to scramble to keep the property that you mistakenly thought was exempt.

Step 2: If a particular exemption has no dollar limit, then apply that exemption to all property items that seem to fall into that category. If there is a limit (for instance, $1,000 worth of electronic products), total the value of all property items you wish to claim under that exemption. Then compare the total with the exemption limit. If the total is less than the limit, then there is no problem. However, if the total is more than the limit, you may have to either give the trustee enough of the property to bring your total back under the limit, or apply a wildcard exemption to the extra property, if your state has one.

b. If You Live in California or a State That Allows You to Choose the Federal Exemptions

If your state allows you to use the federal bankruptcy exemptions or you live in California, you'll need to decide which exemption system to use. If you own a home in which you have equity, your choice will often be dictated by which system gives you the most protection for that equity. In California, for example, the homestead exemption in System 1 protects up to $125,000 in equity, while the System 2 list only protects $17,425. Most homeowners in California end up choosing System 1, for obvious reasons.

Unless your choice of exemption lists is dictated by your home equity you'll be best served by going through Part B of the Worksheet twice. The first time through, use your state's exemption (or System 1 in California). The second time, use the federal bankruptcy exemptions (or System 2 in California).

After you apply both exemption lists to your property, compare the results and decide which exemption list will do you the most good. You may find federal exemptions that don't exist in your state's exemption list, or that are more generous than your state's exemptions. Or vice versa. You may be sorely tempted to pluck some exemptions out of one list and add them to the other list. Can't be done. You'll either have to use your state's exemption list or the federal bankruptcy exemptions—you can't mix and match them.

EXAMPLE: Paula Willmore rents a condo in Albuquerque, New Mexico. Other than clothing, household furniture and personal effects, the only property Paula owns is a vintage 1967 Chevy Camaro Rally Sport. Paula often checks out local car magazines and knows that the model she owns typically sells for about $10,000, although this price varies by several thousand dollars based on the car's condition. Paula wants to know what will happen to her car if she files Chapter 7 bankruptcy.

Paula's first step is to locate the exemptions for New Mexico in Appendix 1. At the bottom of the New Mexico exemption listings for personal property, Paula finds an entry for motor vehicles and sees that the exemption is $4,000. Paula begins to worry that she may lose her car, since it is worth more than double the exemption limit.

Paula's next step is to search the New Mexico state exemptions for a wildcard exemption. (See Section B.1 above for an explanation of wildcard exemptions.) Paula discovers (at the bottom of the list) that she has a $2,500 wildcard exemption that she can apply to any property, including the Camaro. Add that to the $4,000 regular motor vehicle exemption and Paula now has $6,500. This amount still doesn't cover the Camaro's fair market value, which means the trustee would probably sell it, give Paula her $6,500 exemption and distribute the rest of the sales proceeds to Paula's unsecured creditors.

Paula's next step is to see whether New Mexico allows debtors to use the federal bankruptcy exemptions. She looks at the top of the exemption page and sees a note that the federal bankruptcy exemptions are available in her state. Hoping that the federal bankruptcy exemptions will give her a higher exemption limit for her Camaro, she turns to the end of Appendix 1 (right after Wyoming) and finds the federal bankruptcy exemption list. Under personal property she sees a listing for motor vehicles in the amount of $2,775. Oops. That's going in the wrong direction.

Paula next examines the federal bankruptcy exemptions to see whether they provide a wildcard exemption. She discovers that the federal bankruptcy exemptions let you use one half of the $17,425 homestead exemption as a wildcard. Since Paula has no home equity to protect, she can apply $8,725 worth of wildcard to the Camaro, in addition to the federal exemption for motor vehicles of $2,775. And further, Paula sees that she can get an additional wildcard exemption of $925 under the federal exemption system, just in case she has other non-exempt property.

Because Paula is most concerned about keeping her car, and because the federal bankruptcy exemptions let her keep her car while the state exemptions don't, Paula decides to use the federal bankruptcy exemption list.

Five Steps to Applying Exemptions to Your Personal Property

1. Check your state's exemptions for specific property items that you want to keep.
2. If your state exemptions don't cover the property you want to keep (either because they don't exempt that property at all or because they exempt less than your property is worth), look for a wildcard exemption in the state exemption list.
3. If your state also lets you use the federal bankruptcy exemptions (or you live in California), see whether a specific federal exemption (or a System 2 exemption in California) covers your property.
4. If the federal bankruptcy exemptions are available to you but don't seem to cover your property, see whether the federal bankruptcy wildcard exemption will work.
5. If you have the choice of two exemption systems, decide which exemption list you want to use. Don't mix and match.

Tip # 1: Double your exemptions if you're married and filing jointly, unless the state exemption list prohibits it. If you're using the federal bankruptcy exemptions, you may double all exemptions.

Tip #2: While you're figuring out which of your property is exempt, write down in Column 4 the numbers of the statutes that authorize each exemption. (You can find these in Appendix 1.) You will need this information when you fill out Schedule C of your bankruptcy papers.

Special Exemption Rules for Retirement Plans

If your retirement plan is covered by a federal law called ERISA (Employee Retirement Income Security Act—ask the pension plan administrator, benefits coordinator or personnel manager at your job), pay special attention to these rules.

Rule 1: Your ERISA retirement plan is exempt in its entirety if you use the federal bankruptcy exemption system.

Rule 2: Your ERISA retirement plan is exempt in its entirety if you use a state exemption system, even if your state exemption list doesn't refer to ERISA retirement plans. The reason is somewhat complex, involving both ERISA law and bankruptcy law. But the upshot for you is that you don't even need to list your ERISA retirement plan in Schedule C, because it's not considered to be part of your bankruptcy estate. (*Patterson v. Shumate*, 504 U.S. 753 (1992).)

If your retirement plan is not covered by ERISA, it is still exempt if:

- you use your state's exemptions, and
- the retirement plan is listed in either your state exemption list or the federal non-bankruptcy exemption list.

If your retirement plan isn't covered by ERISA or isn't specifically listed in your state exemptions, don't give up yet. Many courts have ruled that certain non-ERISA retirement accounts are exempt under state or federal law. For example, bankruptcy courts in many states have held that Individual Retirement Accounts (IRAs) are exempt. If it looks like you might lose your retirement plan in bankruptcy, talk to a lawyer before filing.

Using Federal Non-Bankruptcy Exemptions

If you are using your state exemptions (or System 1 in California), you are also entitled to use a handful of exemptions called Federal Non-Bankruptcy exemptions (you can find these listed at the end of Appendix 1). These primarily refer to federal benefits of limited application, such as CIA employee retirement benefits and Klamath Indian tribe benefits for Indians residing in Oregon. Still, you may as well check to see if any apply to you.

You cannot combine your exemptions if the federal non-bankruptcy exemptions duplicate your state's exemptions.

EXAMPLE: You're using your state's exemptions. Both your state and the federal non-bankruptcy exemptions let you exempt 75% of unpaid wages. You cannot combine the exemptions to claim 100% of your wages; 75% is all you can exempt.

C. Selling Nonexempt Property Before You File

If you want to reduce the amount of nonexempt property you own before you file for bankruptcy, you can sell the nonexempt property and use the proceeds to buy exempt property. Or you can use the proceeds to pay certain types of debts. But be careful: if the court thinks you sold this property in order to defraud creditors, you'll be in trouble (see Section 2, below).

Talk to a lawyer first. Before you sell nonexempt property, consult a bankruptcy attorney. Your local bankruptcy court may consider these kinds of transfers an attempt to defraud your creditors. (See Section 2, below.) The only sure way to find out what is and isn't permissible in your area is to ask an attorney familiar with local bankruptcy court practices. A consultation on this sort of issue should not run more than $100, and is well worth the cost if it will help you hold on to the value of your nonexempt property.

1. How to Proceed

Here are some ways to use the proceeds from the sale of your nonexempt property.

a. Replace Nonexempt Property With Exempt Property

There are several ways to replace your nonexempt property items with exempt property:

- Sell a nonexempt asset and use the proceeds to buy an asset that is completely exempt. For example, you can sell a nonexempt coin collection and purchase clothing, which in most states is exempt without regard to value.
- Sell a nonexempt asset and use the proceeds to buy an asset that is exempt up to the amount received in the sale. For example, you can sell a nonexempt coin collection worth $1,200 and purchase a car that is exempt up to $1,200 in value.
- Sell an asset that is only partially exempt and use the proceeds to replace it with a similar asset of lesser value. For example, if a television is exempt up to a value of $200, you could sell your $500 television and buy a workable second-hand one for $200, putting the remaining cash into other exempt assets such as clothing or appliances.
- Use cash (which isn't exempt in most states) to buy an exempt item, such as furniture or work tools.

b. Pay Debts

If you choose to reduce your nonexempt property by selling it and using the proceeds to pay debts, keep the following points in mind:

- **Don't pay off a debt that could be discharged in bankruptcy.** Many debts (such as credit card bills) can be completely discharged in bankruptcy. The only reasons you should consider paying a dischargeable debt are:
  - to keep good relations with a valued creditor, such as a doctor on whom you rely for necessary medical treatment, or
  - to pay a debt for which a relative or friend is a co-signer, so that the friend or relative is not stuck paying the whole debt after your liability is discharged.
- **If you pay more than $600, wait to file for bankruptcy.** If you pay a creditor over $600, you should wait at least 90 days before you file for bankruptcy. Otherwise, the payment will be considered a "preference," and the trustee can get the money back and add it to your bankruptcy estate. (11 U.S.C. §§ 547(b), (c)(7) and (f).) If the creditor you pay is a relative, close friend or company in which you are an officer, you should wait at least one year before filing. (See Section A.3, above for further explanation.)
- **You can pay regular bills.** You can pay regular monthly bills right up until you file for bankruptcy. So keep paying your phone bills, rent and mortgage.
- **Think twice before paying secured debts.** If you want to use the proceeds from nonexempt property to pay off a debt secured by collateral, read Ch. 7 first. If the collateral for the debt isn't exempt, paying off the debt won't do you much good, because the trustee will take the collateral anyway when you file for bankruptcy. If the collateral is exempt, you may be able to keep it even if you don't pay off the debt before you file for bankruptcy.

2. Fraudulent Transactions

There's one major limitation on selling nonexempt property and using it to purchase exempt property: you can't do it to defraud your creditors. If a creditor or the trustee complains about a pre-bankruptcy transaction, and the court concludes that your primary motive was greed rather than gaining a fresh start, the court may let the trustee take the new property and sell it to pay your creditors. In extreme cases, the court may even deny you a bankruptcy discharge.

There are two main factors a judge looks at:

- **Your motive.** The bankruptcy court will probably go along with your sale and purchase if the exempt property you end up with is a necessity, or will clearly help you make a fresh start. For example, it's probably fine to sell a second (and usually nonexempt) car and buy some tools needed for your cabinetmaking business, or school clothing or books for your children. But if you sell your second car and buy a $3,000 diamond ring with the proceeds, a court might consider it a greedy attempt to cheat your creditors, even if the ring is exempt under your state's laws. Put a little differently, if the court thinks that you're trying to preserve the value of your nonexempt property for use after bankruptcy rather than really acquiring useful property, your conversion attempt will probably fail.

- **The amount of property involved.** If the amount of nonexempt property you get rid of before you file is enough to pay most of your debts, the court may dismiss your case.

Here are five important guidelines for staying out of trouble when you're making these kinds of pre-bankruptcy transactions.

1. **Accurately report all your transactions** on Form 7, the Statement of Financial Affairs. If the subject comes up with the trustee, creditors or the court, freely admit that you tried to arrange your property holdings before filing for bankruptcy so that you could better get a fresh start. Courts see frankness about your pre-bankruptcy activities as a sign of honorable intentions. If you lie or attempt to conceal what you did or why you did it, the bankruptcy trustee or court may conclude that you had fraudulent intentions and either disallow the transaction or—even worse—deny you a bankruptcy discharge.

2. **Sell and buy for equivalent value.** If you sell a $500 nonexempt item and purchase an exempt item obviously worth $500, you shouldn't have a problem. If, however, you sell a $500 nonexempt item and purchase a $100 exempt item, be prepared to account for the $400 difference. Otherwise, the court will probably assume that you're trying to cheat your creditors and either force you to cough up the $400 (if you still have it) or, possibly, dismiss your bankruptcy case.

3. **Sell and buy property at reasonable prices.** When you sell nonexempt property with an eye towards purchasing exempt property, make the price as close to the item's market value as possible. This is especially true if the sale is made to a friend or relative. If you sell your brother a $900 stereo system for $100, a creditor or the trustee may cry foul, and the judge may agree.

At the other end of the transaction, if you pay a friend or relative significantly more for exempt property than it is apparently worth, suspicions may be raised that you're just trying to transfer your assets to relatives to avoid creditors.

4. **Don't make last minute transfers or purchases.** The longer you can wait to file for bankruptcy after making these kinds of property transfers, the less likely the judge is to disapprove. For example, judges frequently rule that a hasty transaction on the eve of filing shows an intent to cheat creditors. The open, deliberate and advance planning of property sales and purchases, however, is usually considered evidence that you didn't intend to defraud. But even this isn't foolproof. One court ruled that the debtor's deliberate planning over a year before filing was evidence of an intent to cheat creditors. This conflict reinforces our earlier warning: You must find out your bankruptcy court's approach before you sell nonexempt property. (See *In re Carey*, 938 F.2d 1073 (10th Cir. 1991); *In re Holt*, 894 F.2d 1005 (8th Cir. 1990); *Ford v. Poston*, 773 F.2d 52 (4th Cir. 1985); *In re Swift*, 72 B.R. 563 (W.D. Okla. 1987) and *In re Krantz*, 97 B.R. 514 (N.D. Iowa 1989).)

Moving to a State With More Generous Exemptions May Not Be Allowed

Some debtors take a look at the list of exemptions for their state in Appendix 1 and are horrified to see how short the list is or how low the exemptions are.

One couple tried to get around this problem by selling their assets, moving to Florida, buying a new house with the cash (Florida has an unlimited homestead exemption) and then filing for bankruptcy more than a year after buying the house. The bankruptcy court, however, declared the purchase fraudulent and denied them the homestead exemption. (*In re Coplan*, 156 B.R. 88 (M.D. Fla. 1993).)

So be careful if you plan to move to improve your lot.

5. **Don't just change the form of property ownership.** Simply changing the way property is held from a nonexempt form to an exempt form is usually considered fraud.

EXAMPLE: Jeff owns a house as his separate property. Although he's married, Jeff incurred virtually all of his debts alone, so he plans to file for bankruptcy alone. In Jeff's state, the homestead exemption is only $7,500. Jeff's equity in his home is nearly $30,000. Jeff's state also exempts property held as tenancy by the entirety, so Jeff transfers ownership of the house to himself and his wife as tenants by the entirety. That would normally exempt the house from all debts Jeff incurred solely. But because Jeff merely changed the form of property ownership, rather than buying exempt property or paying off debts to give himself a fresh start, the bankruptcy court would probably find the transfer fraudulent and take Jeff's house. (Jeff would get $7,500 from the sale as his homestead exemption.)

Community property warning. As mentioned earlier, if you're married and live in a community property state (Alaska, Arizona, California, Idaho, Louisiana, Nevada, New Mexico, Texas, Washington or Wisconsin), the trustee can usually take both your share of community property and your spouse's, even if your spouse doesn't file for bankruptcy. So you might be tempted to change all or a portion of the community property into your spouse's separate property. Beware: Creditors or the trustee are apt to cry fraud, and the trustee is likely to take the property anyway.

To give you an idea of what judges consider improper behavior shortly before filing for bankruptcy, here are some transactions that courts found to be fraudulent:

- A debtor bought goods on credit but never paid for them. He then sold those goods and bought property that he tried to exempt.
- A debtor with nonexempt property was forced into involuntary bankruptcy by a creditor. The debtor convinced the creditor to drop the forced bankruptcy. Then the debtor sold the nonexempt property, purchased exempt property and filed for Chapter 7 bankruptcy.
- A debtor sold nonexempt property that was worth enough to pay off all her debts (but didn't pay them off).
- A debtor sold nonexempt items for amounts well below what they were worth.
- A debtor sold valuable property to a non-filing spouse for one dollar.
- A debtor transferred nonexempt property the day after a creditor won a lawsuit against him, then filed for bankruptcy.
- A debtor in a state with an "unlimited" homestead exemption sold all her nonexempt property and used the proceeds to pay off a large portion of her mortgage.
- A debtor bought a piano and harpsichord and a whole life insurance policy, all exempt in his state. He didn't play either instrument, and he had no dependents who needed insurance protection.

Taking Out Loans to Pay Nondischargeable Debts

Some people are tempted to borrow money to discharge debts that aren't dischargeable—for instance, a student loan—and then list the new loan as a dischargeable unsecured debt. Be careful if you do this. A court could consider your actions fraudulent and dismiss your bankruptcy. If the court doesn't dismiss your case, the creditor may ask the court to declare the debt nondischargeable. If you take out the loan while you're broke and file for bankruptcy soon after, you probably will be penalized. And if you borrow money or use your credit card to pay off a nondischargeable tax debt, you will not be able to discharge the loan or credit card charge. (11 U.S.C. § 523(a)(14).)

Filling in and Filing the Bankruptcy Forms

This chapter shows you how to fill out and file the forms for a Chapter 7 bankruptcy. For the most part, it's very simple—just a matter of putting the right information in the right blanks and shipping the papers off to the right bankruptcy court.

A. Finding the Right Bankruptcy Court

Because bankruptcy is a creature of federal, not state, law, you must file for bankruptcy in a special federal court. There are federal bankruptcy courts all over the country.

The federal court system divides the country into judicial districts. Every state has at least one judicial district; most have more. Normally, you file in the bankruptcy court for the federal judicial district where you've lived during the greater part of the previous 180 days (six months). You'll probably file in the nearest sizable city. If you run a business, you can instead file in the district where your principal place of business has been located during the previous 180 days, or where the business's principal assets have been located during that period. (28 U.S.C. § 1408.)

Appendix 3 includes the addresses, phone numbers, fax numbers and websites of the federal bankruptcy courts. If you live in a state with more than one district, call the court in the closest city and ask whether you live in its district. Chances are you do. While we do our best to keep Appendix 3 up-to-date, locations and contact information of bankruptcy courts change. If information in Appendix 3 is wrong, look in the government listings in your white pages or call directory assistance.

> EXAMPLE: For the past two months, you've lived in San Luis Obispo, which is in California's central judicial district. Before that you lived in Santa Rosa, in California's northern judicial district. Because you spent more of the past six months in the northern district than in the central, you should file in the bankruptcy court in the northern district. If it's too inconvenient to file there, you could wait another month, when you would qualify to file in the central district court.

 Emergency Filing. Although people usually file all their bankruptcy forms at once, you don't have to. If you need to stop creditors quickly, you can simply file the two-page Voluntary Petition, together with a form called a Matrix, which lists the name, address and zip code of each of your creditors. The automatic stay, which stops collection efforts and lawsuits against you, will then go into effect. You have 15 days to file the rest of the forms. (Bankruptcy Rule 1007(c).) See Section J, below, for instructions.

B. Before You Begin: Get Some Information From the Court

Although bankruptcy courts operate similarly throughout the country, every bankruptcy court has its own requirements for filing bankruptcy papers. If your papers don't meet these local requirements, the court clerk may reject them. So before you begin preparing your papers, contact your bankruptcy court to find out its requirements.

In urban areas especially, you may get no response to a letter or phone call. You may need to visit the court and get the information in person. Or, the information may be available on the Internet. Several courts have websites that include copies of local forms and local rules. (See Appendix 3.)

1. Fees

Currently, the total fee for filing for a Chapter 7 bankruptcy is $200—$155 filing fee and $45 administrative fee. Fees change, however, so make sure you verify them with the court.

In general, you must pay the fees regardless of your income. If you can't come up with the full amount, you can ask the court for permission to pay the filing fee in installments. (Instructions for making this request are in Section J, below.) You can pay in up to four installments over 120 days. You can't pay an attorney or typing service until you've fully paid your filing fees—the court is entitled to its money first.

If you fall below the national poverty level as established by the Office of Management and Budget (these income levels are very low), the court may waive the $45 administrative fee. If you think you might qualify for this waiver, contact a local legal aid office. Ask the office if your income is below the national poverty level, and, if it is, ask for a blank fee waiver. When you fill out the fee waiver, be sure to note that you are requesting waiver of the $45 administrative fee only. Some legal aid offices might also prepare your bankruptcy forms for you.

2. Local Forms

In addition to the official forms that every bankruptcy court uses (they are in listed Section C, below), your local bankruptcy court may require you to file one or two forms that it has developed. People filing in Southern California in particular must get local forms.

You can get all local forms from your local bankruptcy court, a local stationery store or, as mentioned above, possibly off the court's website. Of course, we can't include all local forms in this book, or tell you how to fill them out. Most, however, are self-explanatory. If you need help in obtaining or understanding them, see a local bankruptcy lawyer. (See Ch. 9, *Help Beyond the Book*.)

3. Local Court Rules

Most bankruptcy courts publish local rules that govern the court's procedures. These rules seldom apply to Chapter 7 bankruptcy cases; instead, they primarily concern Chapter 11 business bankruptcies and adversarial bankruptcy actions. But occasionally, a rule does affect a Chapter 7 bankruptcy. You can get your local rules from the bankruptcy court—possibly on its website—but be prepared to comb through reams of material to find the one or two rules that might apply in your case.

4. Number of Copies

Before filing your papers, be sure you know how many copies your court requires.

Below is a sample letter you can send to the court requesting the information discussed above. (A tear-out copy is in Appendix 4.) Include a large, self-addressed envelope. Call and ask the court if you need to affix return postage. Again, if you live in an urban area, you'll probably have to visit the court to get this information.

Letter to Bankruptcy Court

Sandra Smith
432 Oak Street
Cincinnati, OH 45219
(123) 456-7890

July 2, 20XX

United States Bankruptcy Court
Atrium Two, Room 800
221 East Fourth Street
Cincinnati, OH 45202
Attn: COURT CLERK
TO THE COURT CLERK:
Please send me the following information:

1. Copies of all local forms required by this court for an individual (not corporation) filing a Chapter 7 bankruptcy and for making amendments.
2. The number of copies or sets required for filing.
3. The order in which forms should be submitted.
4. Complete instructions on this court's emergency filing procedures and deadlines.

I would also appreciate answers to three other questions:

1. Do you require a separate creditor mailing list (matrix)? If so, do you have specific requirements for its format?
2. Is the filing fee still $155? Is the administrative fee still $45? If either have changed, please advise.
3. Should I two-hole punch my papers or is that done by the court?

I've enclosed a self-addressed envelope for your reply. Thank you.

Sincerely,
Sandra Smith
Sandra Smith

C. Bankruptcy Forms Checklist

You must file:

- ☐ Form 1—Voluntary Petition, in which you ask the bankruptcy court to discharge your debts.
- ☐ Form 6, which consists of:
  - ☐ Schedule A—Real Property
  - ☐ Schedule B—Personal Property
  - ☐ Schedule C—Property Claimed As Exempt
  - ☐ Schedule D—Creditors Holding Secured Claims
  - ☐ Schedule E—Creditors Holding Unsecured Priority Claims
  - ☐ Schedule F—Creditors Holding Unsecured Nonpriority Claims
  - ☐ Schedule G—Executory Contracts and Unexpired Leases
  - ☐ Schedule H—Codebtors
  - ☐ Schedule I—Current Income
  - ☐ Schedule J—Current Expenditures
  - ☐ Summary Schedules A through J
  - ☐ Declaration Concerning Debtor's Schedules, in which you declare under penalty of perjury that the information you put in the schedules is true and correct.
- ☐ Form 7—Statement of Financial Affairs, in which you provide information about your economic affairs during the past several years.
- ☐ Form 8—Chapter 7 Individual Debtor's Statement of Intention, in which you tell the court and your secured creditors what you plan to do with any property that is collateral for a secured loan.
- ☐ Mailing Matrix—a form on which you list your creditors and their addresses. The court uses this form to prepare mailing labels and mail notice of your bankruptcy filing to your creditors.
- ☐ Required local forms, if any.

Note: Forms 2, 4 and 5 aren't used in Chapter 7 voluntary bankruptcy filings. Form 3 is the Application to Pay the Filing Fee in Installments, which you may or may not need to file.

All together, these forms are usually called your "bankruptcy petition," although technically your petition is only Form 1. Appendix 4 contains a tear-out copy of each form, except for required local forms. As mentioned, you'll have to get these forms from the court (possibly on its website), a local bankruptcy lawyer or a typing service.

Using the Nolo Forms

The content and numbering of the forms are set by the official Bankruptcy Rules, a set of rules issued by the United States Supreme Court. Private publishers, however, are free to modify the format of official forms, as long as each form includes the same questions in the same order.

Courts must accept all forms that:

- contain the questions and answers prescribed by the official forms
- are printed on one side only, and
- have adequate top margins.

Under the Bankruptcy Rules, all courts must accept the forms in this book, even if the court is used to seeing forms published by a different company, with its own unique format. Our forms meet all of the official Bankruptcy Rule requirements. (Bankruptcy Rules 5005, 9009 and 9029.)

D. Tips for Completing Forms

Here are some tips that will make filling in your forms easier and the whole bankruptcy process smoother. A sample completed form accompanies each form's instructions. Refer to it while you fill in your bankruptcy papers.

Use Your Worksheet. If you've completed the Worksheet, you've already done a lot of the work. It will save you lots of time when you prepare your bankruptcy forms, so keep it handy. If you skipped Chapter 2, refer to the Worksheet and the accompanying instructions (Ch. 2) for help in identifying what property you should list in your bankruptcy forms.

Photocopy the Forms Before You Start. You can't tear out and file the forms in Appendix 4 because they are slightly smaller than regulation size, due to bookbinding requirements. Good photocopies of the forms on 8½" by 11" paper will work fine, however. Make at least two photocopies of all the forms in the Appendix. Keep the originals (taken from Appendix 4) for additional copies if you need more. Or, print the forms off of the federal judiciary's website at www.uscourts.gov/bankform.

Start With Drafts. First enter the information in pencil, so you can make corrections along the way. Prepare final forms to file with the court only after you've double-checked your drafts.

Type Your Final Forms. Although you are not required to type your forms, many courts prefer that they be typed. But even if your court doesn't, the court clerk is likely to be friendlier if you show up with neatly typed forms. If you don't have access to a typewriter, many libraries have typewriters available to the public (for a small rental fee), or you can hire a bankruptcy form preparation service to prepare your forms using the information you provide. (See Ch. 9, *Help Beyond the Book.*)

Be Ridiculously Thorough. Always err on the side of giving too much information rather than too little. If you leave information off the forms, the bankruptcy trustee or court may become suspicious of your motives. If you leave creditors off the forms, the debts you owe these creditors probably won't be discharged—hardly the result you want. Even worse, the court could dismiss your bankruptcy case.

If you intentionally or carelessly fail to list all your property, or fail to accurately describe your recent property transactions, the court may rule that you acted with fraudulent intent. It may deny your bankruptcy discharge altogether, and you may lose some property that you could otherwise have kept.

Respond to Every Question. Most of the forms have a box to check if your answer is "none." If a question doesn't have a "none" box and the question doesn't apply to you, type in "N/A" for "not applicable." This will let the trustee know that you didn't overlook the question. Occasionally, a question that doesn't apply to you will have a number of blanks. Put "N/A" in only the first blank if it is obvious that this applies to the other blanks as well. If it's not clear, put "N/A" in every blank.

Don't Worry About Repetition. Sometimes different forms—or different questions on the same form—may ask for the same or overlapping information. Don't worry about providing the same information multiple times—too much information is never a sin in bankruptcy.

Explain Uncertainties. If you can't figure out which category on a form to use for a debt or an item of property, list the debt or item in what you think is the appropriate place and briefly note next to your entry

that you're uncertain. The important thing is to disclose the information somewhere. The bankruptcy trustee will sort it out, if necessary.

Be Scrupulously Honest. You must swear, under penalty of perjury, that you've been truthful on your bankruptcy forms. The most likely consequence of failing to be scrupulously honest is a dismissal of your bankruptcy case, but you could be prosecuted for perjury if it's evident that you deliberately lied.

Use Continuation Pages If You Run out of Room. The space for entering information is sometimes skimpy, especially if you're filing jointly. Most of the forms come with pre-formatted continuation pages if you need more room. But if there is no continuation form in Appendix 4, prepare one yourself, using a piece of regular white 8½" by 11" paper. Put "see continuation page" next to the question you're working on and enter the additional information on the continuation page. Label the continuation pages with your name, the form name and indicate "Continuation Page 1," "Continuation Page 2" and so on. (See the Sample Continuation Page below.) Be sure to attach all continuation pages to their appropriate forms when you file your bankruptcy papers.

Get Help If You Need It. If your situation is complicated, you're unsure about how to complete a form or you run into trouble when you go to file your papers, consult a bankruptcy attorney or do some legal research before proceeding. (See Ch. 9, *Help Beyond the Book.*)

Seek Emotional Support If You Need It

Many people who file for bankruptcy feel a sense of loss. It may be a loss of an old comfortable lifestyle, a loss of identity or a loss of property. They grieve for the way things used to be or could have been.

If you feel this sense of loss, focus on the future before you. Many who have filed for bankruptcy before you are now prosperous.

It may be important for you to discuss your experience with someone who you feel can help you: a counselor, a clergy member, your spouse or another loved one.

Sample Continuation Page

In re: Joshua and Alice Milton, Debtors.

Form 7, Statement of Financial Affairs

Continuation Page 1

11. Closed Financial Accounts: Bank of Iowa, 150 Broadway, Cedar Rapids, IA 52407;
Savings Account
No. 1-23-567-890, final balance of $3,446.18; closed September 11, 20XX.

E. Form 1—Voluntary Petition

Filing your Voluntary Petition gets your bankruptcy started and puts the automatic stay into effect, which stops creditors from trying to collect debts from you.

➡️ **Emergency filing.** If you want to file as quickly as possible (without filling in all the bankruptcy forms) go to Section J for instructions.

⚠️ **Sample forms.** Throughout this chapter, we have included the completed sample forms of Molly and Jonathan Maytag, who live in Ohio. Bear in mind that these are examples only. Even if you live in Ohio, your completed forms will look very different.

A completed sample two-page Voluntary Petition and line-by-line instructions follow.

First Page

Court Name. At the top of the first page, fill in the first two blanks with the name of the judicial district you're filing in, such as the "Central District of California." If your state has only one district, type XXXXXX in the first blank. If your state divides its districts into divisions, type the division after the state name, such as "Northern District of Ohio, Eastern Division." See Appendix 3 for the bankruptcy courts in your state.

Name of Debtor. Enter your full name (last name first), in capital letters, as used on your checks, driver's license and other formal documents.

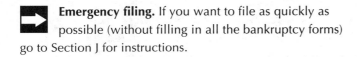 **Are you married and filing with your spouse?** If you and your spouse are filing jointly, you'll have to designate one of you as the debtor and one of you as the spouse. In some states, if a couple has lived together for a period of time and have held themselves out as husband and wife, they may be legally married. Such common law marriages can be created in Alabama, Colorado, Iowa, Kansas, Montana, New Hampshire (for inheritance purposes only), Oklahoma, Pennsylvania, Rhode Island, South Carolina, Texas, Utah and the District of Columbia. If you live in one of these states (or did at a time when you believed that you had a common law marriage), you may be married for purposes of the bankruptcy laws. If you are unsure of your marital status, see a lawyer.

Name of Joint Debtor (Spouse). If you are married and filing jointly with your spouse, put your spouse's name (last name first) in the joint debtor box. Again, use the name that appears on formal documents. If you're filing alone, type "N/A" anywhere in the box.

All Other Names. If you have been known by any other name in the last six years, list it here. If you've operated a business as an individual proprietor during

(Official Form 1) (9/01)

FORM B1	**United States Bankruptcy Court** Northern _____ **District of** _____ Ohio, Eastern Division	**Voluntary Petition**

Name of Debtor (if individual, enter Last, First, Middle): MAYTAG, MOLLY MARIA	Name of Joint Debtor (Spouse) (Last, First, Middle): MAYTAG, JONATHAN
All Other Names used by the Debtor in the last 6 years (include married, maiden, and trade names): Johnson, Molly Maria	All Other Names used by the Joint Debtor in the last 6 years (include married, maiden, and trade names): dba Maytag Delicatessen
Soc. Sec./Tax I.D. No. (if more than one, state all): 999-99-9999	Soc. Sec./Tax I.D. No. (if more than one, state all): 000-00-0000
Street Address of Debtor (No. & Street, City, State & Zip Code): 21 Scarborough Road South Cleveland Heights, OH 41118	Street Address of Joint Debtor (No. & Street, City, State & Zip Code): 21 Scarborough Road South Cleveland Heights, OH 41118
County of Residence or of the Principal Place of Business: Cuyahoga	County of Residence or of the Principal Place of Business: Cuyahoga
Mailing Address of Debtor (if different from street address): N/A	Mailing Address of Joint Debtor (if different from street address): N/A

Location of Principal Assets of Business Debtor
(if different from street address above):
N/A

Information Regarding the Debtor (Check the Applicable Boxes)

Venue (Check any applicable box)

☒ Debtor has been domiciled or has had a residence, principal place of business, or principal assets in this District for 180 days immediately preceding the date of this petition or for a longer part of such 180 days than in any other District.

☐ There is a bankruptcy case concerning debtor's affiliate, general partner, or partnership pending in this District.

Type of Debtor (Check all boxes that apply)	**Chapter or Section of Bankruptcy Code Under Which the Petition is Filed** (Check one box)
☐ Individual(s) ☐ Railroad ☒ Corporation ☐ Stockbroker ☐ Partnership ☐ Commodity Broker ☐ Other_____	☒ Chapter 7 ☐ Chapter 11 ☐ Chapter 13 ☐ Chapter 9 ☐ Chapter 12 ☐ Sec. 304 - Case ancillary to foreign proceeding
Nature of Debts (Check one box) ☒ Consumer/Non-Business ☐ Business	**Filing Fee** (Check one box) ☒ Full Filing Fee attached
Chapter 11 Small Business (Check all boxes that apply) ☐ Debtor is a small business as defined in 11 U.S.C. § 101 N/A ☐ Debtor is and elects to be considered a small business under 11 U.S.C. § 1121(e) (Optional)	☐ Filing Fee to be paid in installments (Applicable to individuals only) Must attach signed application for the court's consideration certifying that the debtor is unable to pay fee except in installments. Rule 1006(b). See Official Form No. 3.

Statistical/Administrative Information (Estimates only)	THIS SPACE IS FOR COURT USE ONLY

☒ Debtor estimates that funds will be available for distribution to unsecured creditors.

☐ Debtor estimates that, after any exempt property is excluded and administrative expenses paid, there will be no funds available for distribution to unsecured creditors.

Estimated Number of Creditors	1-15	16-49	50-99	100-199	200-999	1000-over
	☐	☒	☐	☐	☐	☐

Estimated Assets	$0 to $50,000	$50,001 to $100,000	$100,001 to $500,000	$500,001 to $1 million	$1,000,001 to $10 million	$10,000,001 to $50 million	$50,000,001 to $100 million	More than $100 million
	☐	☐	☒	☐	☐	☐	☐	☐

Estimated Debts	$0 to $50,000	$50,001 to $100,000	$100,001 to $500,000	$500,001 to $1 million	$1,000,001 to $10 million	$10,000,001 to $50 million	$50,000,001 to $100 million	More than $100 million
	☐	☐	☒	☐	☐	☐	☐	☐

the previous six years, include your trade name (fictitious or assumed business name) preceded by "dba" for "doing business as". But don't include minor variations in spelling or form. For instance, if your name is John Lewis Odegard, don't put down that you're sometimes known as J.L. But if you've used the pseudonym J.L. Smith, list it. If you're uncertain, list any name that you think you may have used with a creditor. The purpose of this box is to make sure that when your creditors receive notice of your bankruptcy filing, they'll know who you are. Do the same for your spouse (in the box to the right) if you are filing jointly. If you're filing alone, type "N/A" anywhere in the box to the right.

Soc. Sec./Tax I.D. No. Enter your Social Security number. If you have a taxpayer's I.D. number, enter it as well. Do the same for your spouse (in the box to the right) if you are filing jointly. If you're filing alone, type "N/A" anywhere in the box to the right.

Street Address of Debtor. Enter your current street address. Even if you get all of your mail at a post office box, list the address of your personal residence.

Street Address of Joint Debtor. Enter your spouse's current street address (even if it's the same as yours) if you are filing jointly—again, no post office boxes. If you're filing alone, type "N/A" anywhere in the box.

County of Residence. Enter the county in which you live. Do the same for your spouse if you're filing jointly. Otherwise type "N/A" in the box.

Mailing Address of Debtor. Enter your mailing address if it is different from your street address. If it isn't, put "N/A." Do the same for your spouse (in the box to the right) if you are filing jointly.

Location of Principal Assets of Business Debtor. If you—or your spouse, if you are filing jointly—have been self-employed or operated a business as a sole proprietor within the last two years, you'll be considered a "business debtor." This means you will have to provide additional information on Form 7 (see Section G, below). If your business owns any assets—such as machines or inventory—list their primary location. If they are all located at your home or mailing address, enter that address.

Venue. Check the top box. Here is where you state why you're filing in this particular bankruptcy court. Remember, you must file in the judicial district that has been your residence (for most of the previous 180 days),

the principal place of your business or the location of the principal assets of your business (Section A, above).

Type of Debtor. Check the first box—"Individual(s)"—even if you have been self-employed or operated a sole proprietorship during the previous two years. If you are filing as a corporation, partnership or other type of business entity, you shouldn't be using this book. (See Introduction, *How to Use This Book,* Section A.)

Nature of Debts. Check "Consumer/Non-Business" if you aren't in business and haven't been for the previous two years. If you're self-employed or in business as a sole proprietor, check "Consumer/Non-Business" if most of your debts are owed personally—not by your business. If, however, your business owes the bulk of your debt, check "Business." If you are in doubt, check "Business."

Chapter 11 Small Business. Type "N/A" anywhere in the box.

Chapter or Section of Bankruptcy Code Under Which the Petition is Filed. Check "Chapter 7."

Filing Fee. If you will attach the entire fee, check the first box. If you plan to ask the court for permission to pay in installments, check the second box. (Instructions for applying to the court are in Section J, below.)

Statistical/Administrative Information. In the next four boxes, you estimate information about your debts and assets. If you completed the Worksheet in Ch. 2, you may be able to fill in these sections now. If you didn't complete that worksheet, wait until you've completed the other forms before providing this information. But remember to come back and check the appropriate boxes before filing.

If you plan to make an emergency filing (Section J, below), use the Worksheet to arrive at your best estimates.

Second Page

Name of Debtor(s). Enter your name and your spouse's, if you are filing jointly.

Prior Bankruptcy Case Filed Within Last 6 Years. If you haven't filed a bankruptcy case within the previous six years, type "N/A" in the first box. If you—or your spouse, if you're filing jointly—have, enter the requested information. A previous Chapter 7 bankruptcy bars you from filing another one until six years have passed. And, if you filed a Chapter 7 bankruptcy case which was dismissed for cause within the previous 180 days,

(Official Form 1) (9/01)　　　　　　　　　　　　　　　　　　　　　　　　FORM B1, Page 2

Voluntary Petition *(This page must be completed and filed in every case)*	Name of Debtor(s): 　　Maytag, Molly & Jonathan

Prior Bankruptcy Case Filed Within Last 6 Years (If more than one, attach additional sheet)		
Location Where Filed:　　　N/A	Case Number:	Date Filed:

Pending Bankruptcy Case Filed by any Spouse, Partner or Affiliate of this Debtor (If more than one, attach additional sheet)		
Name of Debtor: 　　　N/A	Case Number:	Date Filed:
District:	Relationship:	Judge:

Signatures

Signature(s) of Debtor(s) (Individual/Joint)

I declare under penalty of perjury that the information provided in this petition is true and correct.

[If petitioner is an individual whose debts are primarily consumer debts and has chosen to file under chapter 7] I am aware that I may proceed under chapter 7, 11, 12 or 13 of title 11, United States Code, understand the relief available under each such chapter, and choose to proceed under chapter 7.

I request relief in accordance with the chapter of title 11, United States Code, specified in this petition.

X *Molly Maytag*
　　Signature of Debtor

X *Jonathan Maytag*
　　Signature of Joint Debtor

　(216) 555-7373
　Telephone Number (If not represented by attorney)

　July 13, 20XX
　Date

Signature of Attorney

X N/A
　Signature of Attorney for Debtor(s)

　Printed Name of Attorney for Debtor(s)

　Firm Name

　Address

　Telephone Number

　Date

Signature of Debtor (Corporation/Partnership)

I declare under penalty of perjury that the information provided in this petition is true and correct, and that I have been authorized to file this petition on behalf of the debtor.

The debtor requests relief in accordance with the chapter of title 11, United States Code, specified in this petition.

X　N/A
　Signature of Authorized Individual

　Printed Name of Authorized Individual

　Title of Authorized Individual

　Date

Exhibit A

(To be completed if debtor is required to file periodic reports (e.g., forms 10K and 10Q) with the Securities and Exchange Commission pursuant to Section 13 or 15(d) of the Securities Exchange Act of 1934 and is requesting relief under chapter 11)

☐　Exhibit A is attached and made a part of this petition.

Exhibit B

(To be completed if debtor is an individual whose debts are primarily consumer debts)

I, the attorney for the petitioner named in the foregoing petition, declare that I have informed the petitioner that [he or she] may proceed under chapter 7, 11, 12, or 13 of title 11, United States Code, and have explained the relief available under each such chapter.

X　N/A
　Signature of Attorney for Debtor(s)　　　Date

Exhibit C

Does the debtor own or have possession of any property that poses or is alleged to pose a threat of imminent and identifiable harm to public health or safety?

☐　Yes, and Exhibit C is attached and made a part of this petition.
☐　No

Signature of Non-Attorney Petition Preparer

I certify that I am a bankruptcy petition preparer as defined in 11 U.S.C. § 110, that I prepared this document for compensation, and that I have provided the debtor with a copy of this document.

　　　　　N/A
　Printed Name of Bankruptcy Petition Preparer

　Social Security Number

　Address
　　　N/A

Names and Social Security numbers of all other individuals who prepared or assisted in preparing this document:

If more than one person prepared this document, attach additional sheets conforming to the appropriate official form for each person.

X
　Signature of Bankruptcy Petition Preparer

　Date

A bankruptcy petition preparer's failure to comply with the provisions of title 11 and the Federal Rules of Bankruptcy Procedure may result in fines or imprisonment or both 11 U.S.C. §110; 18 U.S.C. §156.

you may have to wait to file again or you may not be able to discharge all your debts. (See Ch. 1, Section B. If either situation applies to you, see a bankruptcy lawyer before filing.)

Pending Bankruptcy Case Filed by any Spouse, Partner or Affiliate of this Debtor. "Affiliate" refers to a related business under a corporate structure. "Partner" refers to a business partnership. Again, you shouldn't use this book if you're filing as a corporation, partnership or other type of business entity. If your spouse has a bankruptcy case pending anywhere in the country, enter the requested information. Otherwise, type "N/A" in the first box.

Signature(s) of Debtor(s) (Individual/Joint). You—and your spouse, if you are filing jointly—must sign where indicated. If you are filing singly, type "N/A" on the joint debtor signature line. Include your telephone number and the date. You—and your spouse, if you are filing jointly—declare that you are aware that you may file under other sections of the bankruptcy code and that you still choose to file for Chapter 7 bankruptcy. See "Other Bankruptcy Options," below, for an explanation of other sections of the bankruptcy code.

Signature of Debtor (Corporation/Partnership). Type "N/A" on the first line.

Signature of Attorney. Type "N/A" on the first line.

Exhibit B. Type "N/A" on the signature line.

Exhibit C. If you own or have in your possession any property that might cause "imminent and identifiable" harm to public health or safety (for example, real estate that is polluted with toxic substances or explosive devices such as hand grenades or dynamite), check the yes box, fill in Exhibit C (see the Forms Appendix) and attach Exhibit C to this Petition. If you are unsure about whether a particular piece of property fits the bill, err on the side of inclusion.

Signature of Non-Attorney Petition Preparer. If a Bankruptcy Petition Preparer typed your forms, have that person complete this section. Otherwise, type "N/A" on the first line.

Other Bankruptcy Options

Chapter 13 bankruptcy lets you pay off all or a portion of your debts over a three- to-five-year period without giving up any property. To qualify, you must have steady income in an amount sufficient to pay your unsecured creditors at least the value of your nonexempt property. If you have adequate income left after expenses to pay all or a major portion of your debts over time, the court may force you to file Chapter 13 bankruptcy instead of Chapter 7. For more information on Chapter 13 bankruptcy, see Ch. 1, Section F.4.

Chapter 12 bankruptcy, which is very similar to Chapter 13, is specially designed for family farmers and provides a way to keep the farm while paying off debts over time. Although this option has been unavailable recently, legislation in 2002 is likely to reauthorize the program and allow farmers who have filed another type of bankruptcy to convert to a Chapter 12. In the meantime, most family farmers can file a Chapter 11 or Chapter 13 instead. If you are a farmer, we recommend you speak with a bankruptcy attorney about Chapter 12 bankruptcy before choosing to file a Chapter 7 bankruptcy.

Chapter 11 bankruptcy is usually reserved for corporations and partnerships. Individuals occasionally file for Chapter 11 bankruptcy, however, if their debts exceed either of Chapter 13 bankruptcy's limits of $871,550 (secured debts) or $290,525 (unsecured debts), and they think they'll have enough steady income to pay off a portion of their debts over a several year period. This book doesn't cover Chapter 11 bankruptcies—few bankruptcy attorneys recommend them for individuals.

F. Form 6—Schedules

"Form 6" refers to a series of schedules that provides the trustee and court with a picture of your current financial situation. Most of the information needed for these schedules is included in the Worksheet which—we hope—you completed earlier. Completed sample forms and instructions follow.

1. Schedule A—Real Property

Here you list all the real property you own as of the date you'll file the petition. Don't worry about whether a particular piece of property is exempt. In Schedule C you claim your exemptions. If you filled in the Worksheet in Ch. 2, get it out. Much of that information goes on Schedule A.

A completed sample of Schedule A and line-by-line instructions follow. Even if you don't own any real estate, you still must complete the top of this form.

Real Property Defined

Real property—land and things permanently attached to land—includes more than just a house. It can also include unimproved land, vacation cabins, condominiums, duplexes, rental property, business property, mobile home park spaces, agricultural land, airplane hangars and any other buildings permanently attached to land.

You may own real estate even if you can't walk on it, live on it or get income from it. This might be true, for example, if:

- you own real estate solely because you are married to a spouse who owns real estate and you live in a community property state, or
- someone else lives on property that you are entitled to receive in the future under a trust agreement.

Leases and Time-Shares: If you hold a time-share lease in a vacation cabin or property, lease a boat dock or underground portions of real estate for mineral or oil exploration, or otherwise lease or rent real estate of any description, don't list it on Schedule A. All leases should be listed on Schedule G. (See Section 7, below.)

In re. Type your name and the name of your spouse, if you're filing jointly.

Case No. If you made an emergency filing, fill in the case number assigned by the court. Otherwise, leave this blank.

➡ **If you don't own real estate.** Type "N/A" anywhere in the first column, type "0" in the total box at the bottom of the page and move on to Schedule B.

Description and Location of Property. For each piece of real property you own, list the type of property—for example, house, farm or undeveloped lot—and street address. You don't need to include the legal description (the description on the deed) of the property.

Nature of Debtor's Interest in Property. In this column, you need to provide the legal definition for the interest you (or you and your spouse) have in the real estate. The most common type of interest—outright ownership—is called "fee simple." Even if you still owe money on your mortgage, as long as you have the right to sell the house, leave it to your heirs and make alterations, your ownership is fee simple. A fee simple interest may be owned by one person or by several people jointly. Normally, when people are listed on a deed as the owners—even if they own the property as joint tenants, tenants in common or tenants by the entirety—the ownership interest is in fee simple. Other types of real property interests include:

- **Life estate.** This is the right to possess and use property only during your lifetime. You can't sell the property, give it away or leave it to someone when you die. Instead, when you die, the property passes to whomever was named in the instrument (trust, deed or will) that created your life estate. This type of ownership is usually created when the sole owner of a piece of real estate wants his surviving spouse to live on the property for the rest of her life, but then have the property pass to his children. In this situation, the surviving spouse has a life estate. Surviving spouses who are beneficiaries of A-B, spousal or marital bypass trusts, have life estates.

- **Future interest.** This is your right to own property sometime in the future. A common future interest is owned by a person who—under the terms of a deed, will or trust—will inherit the property when its current possessor dies. Note that until the person who signed the will or living trust dies, you have no future ownership interest in the property—the person making the will or living trust can easily amend the document to cut you out.

- **Contingent interest.** This ownership interest depends upon one or more conditions being fulfilled before it comes into existence. Wills sometimes leave property to people under certain conditions. If the conditions aren't met, the property passes to someone else. For instance, Emma's will leaves her house to John provided that he takes care of her until her death. If John doesn't care for Emma, the house passes to Emma's daughter Jane. Both John and Jane have contingent interests in Emma's home.

- **Lienholder.** If you are the holder of a mortgage, deed of trust, judgment lien or mechanic's lien on real estate, you have an ownership interest in the real estate.

- **Easement holder.** If you are the holder of a right to travel on or otherwise use property owned by someone else, you have an easement.

- **Power of appointment.** If you have a legal right, given to you in a will or transfer of property, to sell a specified piece of someone's property, indicate it.

- **Beneficial ownership under a real estate contract.** This is the right to own property by virtue of having signed a binding real estate contract. Even though the buyer doesn't yet own the property, the buyer does have a "beneficial interest"—that is, the right to own the property once the formalities are completed.

If you have trouble figuring out which of these definitions best fits your type of ownership interest, leave the column blank and let the trustee help you sort it out.

Husband, Wife, Joint, or Community. If you're not married, put "N/A." If you are married, indicate whether the real estate is owned:

- by the husband (H)
- by the wife (W)
- jointly by husband and wife in a common law property state (J), or
- jointly by husband and wife as community property (C).

For more information on ownership of property by married couples, see Ch. 2, *Your Property and Bankruptcy*, Section A.7.

Current Market Value of Debtor's Interest in Property Without Deducting Any Secured Claim or Exemption.

Enter the current fair market value of your real estate ownership interest. If you filled in the Worksheet (Ch. 2), use the amount you entered in Column 2.

Don't figure in homestead exemptions or any mortgages or other liens on the property. Just put the actual current market value as best you can compute it. See Ch. 2, Section B.2, for information on valuing real estate.

If you own the property with someone else who is not filing for bankruptcy, put only your ownership share in this column. For example, if you and your brother own a home as joint tenants (each owns 50%), split the current market value in half.

If your interest is intangible—for example, you are a beneficiary of real estate held in trust that won't be distributed for many years—provide an estimate or put "don't know," and explain why you can't be more precise.

Total. Add the amounts in the fourth column and enter the total in the box at the bottom of the page.

Amount of Secured Claim. List mortgages and other debts secured by the property. If there is no secured claim of any type on the real estate, enter "None." If there is, enter separately the amount of each outstanding mortgage, deed of trust, home equity loan or lien (judgment lien, mechanic's lien, materialman's lien, tax lien or the like) that is claimed against the property. If you don't know the balance on your mortgage, deed of trust or home equity loan, call the lender. To find out the values of liens, visit the land records office in your county and look up the parcel in the records; the clerk can show you how. Or you can order a title search through a real estate attorney or title insurance company. If you own several pieces of real estate and there is one lien on file against all the real estate, list the full amount of the lien for each separate property item. Don't worry if, taken together, the value of the liens on a property item is higher than the value of the property; it's quite common.

How you itemize liens in this schedule won't affect how your property or the liens will be treated in bankruptcy. The idea here is to notify the trustee of all possible liens that may affect your equity in your real estate.

If you can't afford to pay a lawyer or title insurance company to find out any of this information, enter "unknown."

Form B6A
(6/90)

In re **Maytag, Molly and Jonathan** _____ ,   Case No. _____
_____Debtor_____   (If known)

SCHEDULE A—REAL PROPERTY

Except as directed below, list all real property in which the debtor has any legal, equitable, or future interest, including all property owned as a co-tenant, community property, or in which the debtor has a life estate. Include any property in which the debtor holds rights and powers exercisable for the debtor's own benefit. If the debtor is married, state whether husband, wife, or both own the property by placing an "H," "W," "J," or "C" in the column labeled "Husband, Wife, Joint, or Community." If the debtor holds no interest in real property, write "None" under "Description and Location of Property."

Do not include interests in executory contracts and unexpired leases on this schedule. List them in Schedule G—Executory Contracts and Unexpired Leases.

If an entity claims to have a lien or hold a secured interest in any property, state the amount of the secured claim. See Schedule D. If no entity claims to hold a secured interest in the property, write "None" in the column labeled "Amount of Secured Claim."

If the debtor is an individual or if a joint petition is filed, state the amount of any exception claimed in the property only in Schedule C—Property Claimed as Exempt.

DESCRIPTION AND LOCATION OF PROPERTY	NATURE OF DEBTOR'S INTEREST IN PROPERTY	HUSBAND, WIFE, JOINT, OR COMMUNITY	CURRENT MARKET VALUE OF DEBTOR'S INTEREST IN PROPERTY WITHOUT DEDUCTING ANY SECURED CLAIM OR EXEMPTION	AMOUNT OF SECURED CLAIM
House at 21 Scarborough Road South, Cleveland Heights, OH 44118	Fee Simple	J	$95,000	$75,000 mortgage $12,000 second mortgage $2,000 judgment lien
Unimproved lot at 244 Highway 50, Parma, OH 44000	Fee Simple	H	$5,000	none

Total ➡ $ $100,000

(Report also on Summary of Schedules.)

2. Schedule B—Personal Property

Here you must list and evaluate all of your personal property, including property that is security for a debt and property that is exempt. If you didn't fill in the Worksheet, turn to Ch. 2, for explanations and suggestions about what property you should list in each of the schedule's categories.

⚠️ **Be honest and thorough.** Probably the single biggest temptation to cheat in the bankruptcy process arises with your personal property schedule, because once you list an item, the whole world—including the bankruptcy trustee—knows about it. And, if it's non-exempt, it may be sold for the benefit of your creditors. Don't give in to temptation and try to hide an asset. If your omission is discovered, your bankruptcy will most likely be dismissed, and you won't be able to discharge your debts in any subsequent bankruptcy you might file. The failure to disclose even worthless assets has been used as grounds for denying a bankruptcy discharge. (See *In re Calder*, 912 F.2d 454 (10th Cir. 1990).)

A completed sample of Schedule B and line-by-line instructions follow. If you need more room, use an attached continuation page or create a continuation page yourself. (See Section D, above.)

In re and **Case No.** Follow the instructions for Schedule A.

Type of Property. The form lists general categories of personal property. You leave this column as is.

None. If you own no property that fits in a category listed in the first column, enter an "X" in the "None" column.

Description and Location of Property. List specific items that fall in each general category. If you filled out the Worksheet, you already have this information. If not, be sure to review the Worksheet: What Property Can You Keep in Chapter 7 Bankruptcy? (in Appendix 4) which lists types of property to include in each category. Although the categories in the Worksheet correspond to the categories in Schedule B, the Worksheet describes some of them differently (where we felt the Schedule B descriptions weren't clear).

Separately list all items worth $50 or more. Combine small items into larger categories whenever reasonable. For example, you don't need to list every spatula,

colander, garlic press and ice cream scoop; instead, put "kitchen cookware." If you list numerous items in one category (as is likely for household goods and furnishings), you may need to attach a continuation sheet.

Most of your personal property is probably at your residence. If so, write a sentence at the top of the form or column to that effect: "All property is located at my/our residence unless otherwise noted." Indicate specifically when the facts are different. If someone else holds property for you (for example, you loaned your aunt your color TV), put that person's name and address in this column. The idea is to tell the trustee where all your property is located so that it can be taken and sold to pay your creditors if it isn't exempt.

Here are further instructions for answering some of the questions:

Question 1: Include all cash you have on the date you file the petition.

Questions 1 and 2: Explain the source of any cash on hand or money in financial accounts—for example, from wages, Social Security payments or child support. This will help you decide later whether any of this money qualifies as exempt property.

Question 11: Although ERISA-qualified pension plans are not part of the bankruptcy estate, list them here anyway and write: "This is an ERISA-qualified pension plan which is not part of the bankruptcy estate." In the Current Market Value column, enter $0.

Question 12: Include stock options. See "Are Stock Options Part of Your Bankruptcy Estate?," in Ch. 2, Section A.5, for more information.

Question 16: List all child support or alimony arrears—that is, money that should have been paid to you but hasn't been. Specify the dates the payments were due and missed, such as "$250 monthly child support payments for June, July, August and September 20XX."

Question 17: List all money owed to you and not yet paid, other than child support and alimony. If you've obtained a judgment against someone but haven't been paid, list it here. State the defendant's name, the date of the judgment, the court that issued the judgment, the amount of the judgment and the kind of case (such as car accident).

Question 21: State what the patent, copyright, trademark or the like is for. Give the number assigned by the issuing agency and length of time the patent, copyright, trademark or other right will last.

Form B6B

(10/89)

In re ___Maytag, Molly and Jonathan___,   Case No._____

Debtor   (If known)

SCHEDULE B—PERSONAL PROPERTY

Except as directed below, list all personal property of the debtor of whatever kind. If the debtor has no property in one or more of the categories, place an "X" in the appropriate position in the column labeled "None." If additional space is needed in any category, attach a separate sheet properly identified with the case name, case number, and the number of the category. If the debtor is married, state whether husband, wife, or both own the property by placing an "H," "W," "J," or "C" in the column labeled "Husband, Wife, Joint, or Community." If the debtor is an individual or a joint petition is filed, state the amount of any exemptions claimed only in Schedule C—Property Claimed as Exempt.

Do not include interests in executory contracts and unexpired leases on this schedule. List them in Schedule G—Executory Contracts and Unexpired Leases.

If the property is being held for the debtor by someone else, state that person's name and address under "Description and Location of Property."

TYPE OF PROPERTY	NONE	* All property is located at our residence unless otherwise noted. DESCRIPTION AND LOCATION OF PROPERTY	HUSBAND, WIFE, JOINT, OR COMMUNITY	CURRENT MARKET VALUE OF DEBTOR'S INTEREST IN PROPERTY, WITHOUT DEDUCTING ANY SECURED CLAIM OR EXEMPTION
1. Cash on hand.		Cash from wages	J	100
2. Checking, savings or other financial accounts, certificates of deposit, or shares in banks, savings and loan, thrift, building and loan, and homestead associations, or credit unions, brokerage houses, or cooperatives.		Checking account #12345, Ameritrust, 10 Financial Way, Cleveland Hts, OH 44118 (from wages)	J	250
		Savings account #98765, Shaker Savings, 44 Trust Street, Cleveland Hts, OH 44118 (from wages)	J	400
		Checking account #058-118061, Ohio Savings, 1818 Lakeshore Dr., Cleveland, OH 44123	H	100
3. Security deposits with public utilities, telephone companies, landlords, and others.	X			
4. Household goods and furnishings, including audio, video, and computer equipment.		Stereo system	J	300
		Washer/Dryer set	J	150
		Refrigerator	J	250
		Stove	J	150
		Household furniture	J	600
		Minor appliances	J	75
		Antique desk	J	250
		Vacuum	J	30
		Bed & bedding	J	500
		Television	J	135
		VCR	J	75
		Lawnmower	J	100
		Swingset, children's toys	J	180
		Snowblower	J	100
		Oriental rug	J	2,500

Form B6B—Cont.

(10/89)

In re   **Maytag, Molly and Jonathan**   ,   Case No. _____
                 Debtor   (If known)

SCHEDULE B—PERSONAL PROPERTY
(Continuation Sheet)

TYPE OF PROPERTY	NONE	DESCRIPTION AND LOCATION OF PROPERTY	HUSBAND, WIFE, JOINT, OR COMMUNITY	CURRENT MARKET VALUE OF DEBTOR'S INTEREST IN PROPERTY, WITHOUT DEDUCTING ANY SECURED CLAIM OR EXEMPTION
5. Books, pictures and other art objects, antiques, stamp, coin, record, tape, compact disc, and other collections or collectibles.		Books Stamp collection	J J	50 75
6. Wearing apparel.		Clothing	J	625
7. Furs and jewelry.		Wedding rings Diamond necklace Watches	J W J	225 325 50
8. Firearms and sports, photographic, and other hobby equipment.		Mountain bike Camera Sword collection	J J W	165 125 1,485
9. Interests in insurance policies. Name insurance company of each policy and itemize surrender or refund value of each.		Life insurance policy, Lively Ins. Co., 120 Manhattan Street, NY, NY 10012 Policy #14-171136 Life insurance policy, Live-a-long-time Co., 52 Mitchell Ave., Hartford, CT 06434. Policy #33-19195WY17	H W	120 65
10. Annuities. Itemize and name each issuer.	X			
11. Interests in IRA, ERISA, Keogh, or other pension or profit sharing plans. Itemize.		Cleveland Builder's Pension, 100 Chester Way, Cleveland, OH 44114 IRA, Basic Bank, 9712 Smitco Creek Blvd., Columbus, OH 45923	H J	6,612 3,400
12. Stock and interests in incorporated and unincorporated businesses. Itemize.		Trusso Corp. stock, #3711. 50 shares @$20 each Investco Ltd. stock, #1244711, 5 shares @$100 each Rayco Co. stock, #RC53, 20 shares @ $40 each All certificates at Ameritrust, 10 Financial Way, Cleveland Hts, OH 44118	J J J	1,000 500 800
13. Interests in partnerships or joint ventures. Itemize.	X			

Form B6B—Cont.

(10/89)

In re ___Maytag, Molly and Jonathan___ ,   Case No._____
                    Debtor   (If known)

SCHEDULE B—PERSONAL PROPERTY
(Continuation Sheet)

TYPE OF PROPERTY	NONE	DESCRIPTION AND LOCATION OF PROPERTY	HUSBAND, WIFE, JOINT, OR COMMUNITY	CURRENT MARKET VALUE OF DEBTOR'S INTEREST IN PROPERTY, WITHOUT DEDUCTING ANY SECURED CLAIM OR EXEMPTION
14. Government and corporate bonds and other negotiable and non-negotiable instruments.		US Savings Bonds, located at Ameritrust, 10 Financial Way, Cleveland Hts, OH 44118	J	1,000
		Promissory note from Jonathan Maytag's sister, Trini Maytag Ellison, dated 11/3/XX	J	500
15. Accounts receivable.	X			
16. Alimony, maintenance, support, and property settlements to which the debtor is or may be entitled. Give particulars.	X			
17. Other liquidated debts owing debtor including tax refunds. Give particulars.		Wages for 6/XX from Cleveland Builder	H	1,900
		Wages for 6/1/XX to 6/30/XX from Typing Circles	W	100
18. Equitable or future interest, life estates, and rights or powers exercisable for the benefit of the debtor other than those listed in Schedule of Real Property.	X			
19. Contingent and noncontingent interests in estate of a decedent, death benefit plan, life insurance policy, or trust.	X			
20. Other contingent and unliquidated claims of every nature, including tax refunds, counterclaims of the debtor, and rights to setoff claims. Give estimated value of each.	X			
21. Patents, copyrights, and other intellectual property. Give particulars.	X			
22. Licenses, franchises, and other general intangibles. Give particulars.	X			

Form B6B—Cont.

(10/89)

In re ____Maytag, Molly and Jonathan_____,   Case No._____
                    Debtor   (If known)

SCHEDULE B—PERSONAL PROPERTY
(Continuation Sheet)

TYPE OF PROPERTY	NONE	DESCRIPTION AND LOCATION OF PROPERTY	HUSBAND, WIFE, JOINT, OR COMMUNITY	CURRENT MARKET VALUE OF DEBTOR'S INTEREST IN PROPERTY, WITHOUT DEDUCTING ANY SECURED CLAIM OR EXEMPTION
23. Automobiles, trucks, trailers, and other vehicles and accessories.		1988 Honda Motorcycle	W	1,000
24. Boats, motors, and accessories.		Sailboard, docked at Lake Erie Dock, Cleveland, OH	J	1,250
25. Aircraft and accessories.	X			
26. Office equipment, furnishings, and supplies.		Computer (for business)	J	1,100
		Typewriter (for business)	J	125
		Fax Machine (for business)	J	500
27. Machinery, fixtures, equipment, and supplies used in business.		Carpentry tools	J	150
28. Inventory.	X			
29. Animals.		Poodles (2)	J	200
30. Crops—growing or harvested. Give particulars.	X			
31. Farming equipment and implements.	X			
32. Farm supplies, chemicals, and feed.	X			
33. Other personal property of any kind not already listed, such as season tickets. Itemize.	X			
			Total ➡	$ 29,692

____0____ continuation sheets attached

(Include amounts from any continuation sheets attached. Report total also on Summary of Schedules.)

Question 22: List all licenses and franchises, what they cover, the length of time remaining, who they are with and whether you can transfer them to someone else.

Questions 23-25: Include the make, model and year of each item.

Question 30: For your crops, list whether or not they've been harvested, whether or not they've been sold (and if so, to whom and for how much), whether you've taken out any loan against them and whether they are insured.

Husband, Wife, Joint, or Community. If you're not married, put "N/A" at the top of the column.

If you are married and own all or most of your personal property jointly with your spouse, put one of the following on the top or bottom of the form:

- If you live in a common law property state: "All property is owned jointly unless otherwise indicated." Then note when a particular item is owned by only H or W.
- If you live in a community property state: "All property is owned jointly as community property unless otherwise indicated." Then note when a particular item is owned by only H or W.

If you are married and own many items separately, for each item specify:

- husband (H)
- wife (W)
- jointly by husband and wife (J), or
- jointly by husband and wife in a community property state (C).

For more information on ownership of property by married couples, see Ch. 2, Section A.7.

Current Market Value of Debtor's Interest in Property, Without Deducting Any Secured Claim or Exemption. You can take the information requested here from the Worksheet. List the current market value of the property, without regard to any secured interests or exemptions. For example, if you own a car worth $6,000, still owe $4,000 on the car note and your state's motor vehicle exemption is $1,200, put down $6,000 for the market value of the car.

Evaluating Personal Property

As long as your estimates are reasonable, the lower the value you place on property, the more of it you will probably be allowed to keep through the bankruptcy process. Enter the actual values for cash on hand, deposit accounts and assets with actual cash values, such as insurance, annuities, pensions, stocks, partnerships, bonds, accounts receivable and support to which you are entitled. For interests that are difficult to assess, perhaps because their value depends upon future events, seek the help of a property appraiser or state that you can't estimate the value.

Other suggestions for valuing specific items are in Chapter 2, Section B.3.

Total. Add the amounts in this column and put the total in the box at the bottom of the last page. If you used any continuation pages in addition to the preprinted form, remember to attach those pages and include the amounts from those pages in this total.

3. Schedule C—Property Claimed As Exempt

On this form, you claim all property you think is legally exempt from being taken to pay your creditors. In the overwhelming majority of Chapter 7 bankruptcies filed by individuals, all—or virtually all—of the debtor's property is exempt.

If you own a home. Be sure to read Ch. 6, *Your House*, before completing Schedule C.

When you work on this form, you'll need to refer frequently to several other documents. Have in front of you:

- The Worksheet (from Ch. 2)
- your drafts of Schedules A and B
- the list of state or federal bankruptcy exemptions you'll be using, provided in Appendix 1, and
- if you're using your state's exemptions, the additional non-bankruptcy federal exemptions, provided in Appendix 1.

Set out below is a sample completed Schedule C and line-by-line instructions.

Give Yourself the Benefit of the Doubt

When you claim exemptions, give yourself the benefit of the doubt: if an exemption seems to cover an item of property, claim it. You may find that you're legally entitled to keep much of the property you're deeply attached to, such as your home, car and family heirlooms. In fact, in the overwhelming majority of Chapter 7 bankruptcies filed by individuals, all—or virtually all—of the debtor's property is exempt.

Your exemption claims will be examined by the trustee and possibly a creditor or two, although few creditors monitor bankruptcy proceedings. In close cases, bankruptcy laws require the trustee to honor rather than dishonor your exemption claims. In other words, you're entitled to the benefit of the doubt.

If the trustee doesn't allow the exemption, or a creditor successfully challenges it, you've lost nothing by trying. You simply may need to amend Schedule C, an easy process described in Ch. 4, Section B.

In re and **Case No.** Follow the instructions for Schedule A.

Debtor elects the exemptions to which the debtor is entitled under. If you're using the federal exemptions, check the top box. If you're using your state exemptions or live in California (where you must use one of two state systems), check the lower box. See Ch. 2,

Section B.1, for information on how to choose between the federal and state exemption systems.

The following instructions cover one column at a time. But rather than listing all your exempt property in the first column and then completing the second column before moving on to the third column, you might find it easier to list one exempt item and complete all columns for that item before moving on to the next exempt item.

Description of Property. To describe the property you claim as exempt, take these steps:

Step 1: Turn to Ch. 2, Section B.1, to find out which exemptions are available to you and which property to claim as exempt (if you have already used the Worksheet to identify your exempt property, skip this step).

Step 2: Decide which of the real estate you listed on Schedule A, if any, you want to claim as exempt. Use the same description you used in the Description and Location of Property column of Schedule A.

Step 3: Decide which of the personal property you listed on Schedule B you want to claim as exempt. For each item identified, list both the category of property (preprinted in the Types of Property column) and the specific item, from the Description and Location of Property column. Do not include the location of the property.

Specify Law Providing Each Exemption. You'll find citations to the specific laws that create exemptions in the state and federal exemption lists in Appendix 1.

You can simplify this process by typing, anywhere on the form, the name of the statutes you are using. The name is noted at the top of the exemption list you use. For example, you might type "All law references are to the Florida Statutes Annotated unless otherwise noted."

For each item of property, enter the citation (number) of the specific law that creates the exemption, as set out on the exemption list. If you are combining part or all of a "wildcard" exemption with a regular exemption, list both citations. If the wildcard and the regular exemption have the same citation, list the citation twice and put "wildcard" next to one of the citations. If you use any reference other than one found in your state statutes, such as a federal non-bankruptcy exemption

Form B6C

(6/90)

In re ___Maytag, Molly and Jonathan___,   Case No._____

Debtor   (If known)

SCHEDULE C—PROPERTY CLAIMED AS EXEMPT

Debtor elects the exemptions to which debtor is entitled under:

(Check one box)

☐ 11 U.S.C. § 522(b)(1): Exemptions provided in 11 U.S.C. § 522(d). **Note: These exemptions are available only in certain states.**

☒ 11 U.S.C. § 522(b)(2): Exemptions available under applicable nonbankruptcy federal laws, state or local law where the debtor's domicile has been located for the 180 days immediately preceding the filing of the petition, or for a longer portion of the 180-day period than in any other place, and the debtor's interest as a tenant by the entirety or joint tenant to the extent the interest is exempt from process under applicable nonbankruptcy law.

DESCRIPTION OF PROPERTY	SPECIFY LAW PROVIDING EACH EXEMPTION	VALUE OF CLAIMED EXEMPTION	CURRENT MARKET VALUE OF PROPERTY WITHOUT DEDUCTING EXEMPTIONS
Real Property House at 21 Scarborough Road South, Cleveland Hts, OH 44118	2329.66(A)(1)	10,000	95,000
Cash on hand Cash from wages	2329.66(A)(13)	100	100
Money deposits Ameritrust checking account #12345	2329.66(A)(4)(a)	250	250
Shaker Savings account #98765	2329.66(A)(4)(a)	400	400
Ohio Savings account #058-118061	1775.24(A)(4)(a)	100	100
Household goods Stereo System	2329.66(A)(17) (wildcard)	300	300
Washer/Dryer set	2329.66(A)(4)(b)	150	150
Refrigerator	2329.66(A)(3)	250	250
Stove	2329.66(A)(3)	150	150
Household furniture	2329.66(A)(4)(b)	600	600
Minor appliances	2329.66(A)(4)(b)	75	75
Antique desk	2329.66(A)(4)(b)	250	250
Vacuum	2329.66(A)(4)(b)	30	30
Beds & bedding	2329.66(A)(3)	500	500
Television	2329.66(A)(4)	135	135
VCR	2329.66(A)(4)	75	75
Lawnmower	2329.66(A)(4)	100	100
Swingset, children's toys	2329.66(A)(4)	180	180
Snowblower	2329.66(A)(4)	100	100
Books, pictures, etc. Stamp collection	2329.66(A)(4)(b)	75	75
Lithograph	2329.66(A)(4)(b)	50	50

Because we are married, we each claim a full set of exemptions to the extent permitted by law. All references are to Ohio Revised Code unless otherwise noted.

In re <u>Maytag, Molly and Jonathan</u>

SCHEDULE C—PROPERTY CLAIMED AS EXEMPT

(Continuation Sheet)

DESCRIPTION OF PROPERTY	SPECIFY LAW PROVIDING EACH EXEMPTION	VALUE OF CLAIMED EXEMPTION	CURRENT MARKET VALUE OF PROPERTY WITHOUT DEDUCTING EXEMPTIONS
<u>Wearing Apparel</u>			
Clothing	2329.66(A)(3)	625	625
<u>Furs & jewelry</u>			
Wedding rings	2329.66(A)(4)(c)	225	225
Diamond necklace	2329.66(A)(4)(c)	325	325
Watches	2329.66(A)(4)(c)	50	50
<u>Insurance</u>			
Lively Insurance Co., life insurance policy #14-171136	3911.12	120	120
Live-a-long-time Co., life insurance policy #33-19195WY17	3911.14	65	65
<u>IRA, Pensions, Etc.</u>			
Cleveland Builder Pension	2329.66(A)(10)(a)	6,612	6,612
IRA	2329.66(A)(10)(b)	3,400	3,400
<u>Firearms, sports equipment</u>			
Mountain bike	2329.66(A)(4)(b)	165	165
Camera	2329.66(A)(4)(b)	125	125
<u>Other liquidated debts</u>			
Wages from Cleveland Builder	2329.66(A)(13)	1,900	1,900
Wages from Typing Circles	2329.66(A)(13)	100	100
<u>Vehicles</u>			
1988 Honda motorcycle	2329.66(A)(2)	1,000	1,000
<u>Animals</u>			
2 Poodles	2329.66(A)(4)(b)	200	200
<u>Office equipment</u>			
Computer (for business)	2329.66(A)(5)	1,100	1,100
Typewriter (for business)	2329.66(A)(5)	125	125
Fax (for business)	2329.66(A)(17) (wildcard)	500	500
<u>Tools of trade</u>			
Carpentry tools	2329.66(A)(5)	150	150

or a court case, list the entire reference for the exempt item.

Value of Claimed Exemption. Claim the full exemption amount allowed, up to the value of the item. The amount allowed is listed in Appendix 1.

Bankruptcy rules allow married couples to double all exemptions unless the state expressly prohibits it. That means that each of you can claim the entire amount of each exemption, if you are both filing. If your state's chart in Appendix 1 doesn't say your state forbids doubling, go ahead and double. If you are married and doubling your exemptions, put a note to this effect on the form. (See sample Schedule C.)

If you are using part or all of a wildcard exemption in addition to a regular exemption, list both amounts. For example, if the regular exemption for an item of furniture is $200, and you plan to exempt it to $500 using $300 from your state's wildcard exemption, list $200 across from the citation you listed for the regular exemption, and $300 across from the citation you listed for the wildcard exemption (or across from the term "wildcard").

Limits on exemptions. Don't claim more than you need for any particular item. For instance, if you're allowed household furniture up to a total amount of $2,000, don't inflate the value of each item of furniture, simply to get to $2,000. Use the values as stated on Schedule B.

Current Market Value of Property Without Deducting Exemptions. Enter the fair market value of the item you are claiming as exempt. For most items, this information is listed on Schedules A and B. However, if you listed the item as part of a group in Schedule B, list it separately here and assign it a separate fair market value.

4. Schedule D—Creditors Holding Secured Claims

In this schedule, you list all creditors who hold claims secured by your property. This includes:

- holders of a mortgage or deed of trust on your real estate

- creditors who have won lawsuits against you and recorded judgment liens against your property
- doctors or lawyers to whom you have granted a security interest in the outcome of a lawsuit, so that the collection of their fees would be postponed (the expected court judgment is the collateral)
- contractors who have filed mechanic's or materialman's liens on your real estate
- taxing authorities, such as the IRS, that have obtained tax liens against your property
- creditors with either a purchase-money or non-purchase-money security agreement (for definitions, see Ch. 7, *Secured Debts*, Section C), and
- all parties who are trying to collect a secured debt, such as collection agencies and attorneys.

Credit Card Debts

Most credit card debts, whether the card is issued by a bank, gasoline company or department store, are unsecured and should be listed on Schedule F. Some department stores, however, claim to retain a security interest in all durable goods, such as furniture, appliances, electronics equipment and jewelry, bought using the store credit card. Also, if you were issued a bank or store credit card as part of a plan to restore your credit, you may have had to post property or cash as collateral for debts incurred on the card. If either of these exceptions apply to you, list the credit card debt on Schedule D.

Line-by-line instructions and a completed sample of Schedule D follow.

In re and **Case No.** Follow Instructions for Schedule A.

☐ **Check this box if debtor has no creditors holding secured claims to report on this Schedule D.** Check the box at the bottom of the Schedule's instructions if you have no secured creditors, then skip ahead to Schedule E.

Creditor's Name and Mailing Address, Including Zip Code. List all secured creditors, preferably in alphabetical order. For each, fill in the account number, if you know it, the creditor's name and the complete mailing address, including zip code. Call the creditor or the post office to get this information if you don't have it.

If you have more than one secured creditor for a given debt, list the original creditor first followed by the other creditors. For example, if you've been sued or hounded by a collection agency, list the information for the attorney or collection agency after the original creditor.

If, after typing up your final papers, you discover that you've missed a few creditors, don't retype your papers to preserve perfect alphabetical order. Simply add the creditors at the end. If your creditors don't all fit on the first page of Schedule D, make as many copies of the preprinted continuation page as you need to fit them all.

Codebtor. If someone else (other than a spouse with whom you are filing jointly) can be legally forced to pay your debt to a listed secured creditor, enter an "X" in this column and list the codebtor in the creditor column of this Schedule. You'll also need to list the codebtor as a creditor in Schedule F and Schedule H.

The most common codebtors are:

- cosigners
- guarantors (people who guarantee payment of a loan)
- ex-spouses with whom you jointly incurred debts before divorcing
- joint owners of real estate or other property
- co-parties in a lawsuit
- non-filing spouses in a community property state (most debts incurred by a non-filing spouse during marriage are considered community debts, making that spouse equally liable with the filing spouse for the debts), and
- non-filing spouses in states other than community property states, for debts incurred by the filing spouse for basic living necessities such as food, shelter, clothing and utilities.

Husband, Wife, Joint, or Community. Follow the instructions for Schedule A.

Date Claim Was Incurred, Nature of Lien, and Description and Market Value of Property. This column calls for a lot of information for each secured debt. If you list two or more creditors on the same secured claim (such as the lender and a collection agency),

simply put ditto marks (") in this column for the second creditor. Let's take these one at a time.

Date Claim Was Incurred. Enter the date the secured claim was incurred. For most claims, this is the date you signed the security agreement. If you didn't sign a security agreement with the creditor, the date is most likely the date a contractor or judgment creditor recorded a lien against your property, or the date a taxing authority notified you of a tax liability or assessment of taxes due.

Nature of Lien. Here are the possibilities:

- Purchase-money security interest—if the debt was incurred to purchase the property, as with a mortgage or car note. The security interest must have been "perfected" (filed or recorded with the appropriate agency) within 20 days of being created to be valid. (*Fidelity Financial Services, Inc. v. Fink*, 118 S. Ct. 651 (1998).)
- Nonpossessory nonpurchase-money security interest—if the debt was incurred for a purpose other than buying the collateral, as with refinanced home loans, home equity loans or loans from finance companies.
- Possessory nonpurchase-money security interest—if you own property that has been pledged to a pawnshop.
- Judgment lien—if the creditor sued you, obtained a court judgment and recorded a lien against your property.
- Tax lien—if a taxing authority recorded a lien against your property.
- Child support lien—if you owe child support and your child's other parent has recorded a lien against your property.
- Mechanic's or materialman's liens—if someone performed work on real property, a vehicle or other property, wasn't paid and recorded a lien.
- If you don't know what kind of lien you are dealing with, put "Don't know nature of lien" after the date. The bankruptcy trustee will help you figure it out later.

See Ch. 7, Section C, for complete definitions of the different types of liens.

Description of Property. Describe each item of real estate and personal property that is collateral for the secured debt listed in the first column. Use the same

Form B6D

(6/90)

In re __Maytag, Molly and Jonathan__ ,   Case No._____
           Debtor   (If known)

SCHEDULE D—CREDITORS HOLDING SECURED CLAIMS

State the name, mailing address, including zip code, and account number, if any, of all entities holding claims secured by property of the debtor as of the date of filing of the petition. List creditors holding all types of secured interest such as judgment liens, garnishments, statutory liens, mortgages, deeds of trust, and other security interests. List creditors in alphabetical order to the extent practicable. If all secured creditors will not fit on this page, use the continuation sheet provided.

If any entity other than a spouse in a joint case may be jointly liable on a claim, place an "X" in the column labeled "Codebtor," include the entity on the appropriate schedule of creditors, and complete Schedule H—Codebtors. If a joint petition is filed, state whether husband, wife, both of them, or the marital community may be liable on each claim by placing an "H," "W," "J," or "C" in the column labeled "Husband, Wife, Joint, or Community."

If the claim is contingent, place an "X" in the column labeled "Contingent." If the claim is unliquidated, place an "X" in the column labeled "Unliquidated." If the claim is disputed, place an "X" in the column labeled "Disputed." (You may need to place an "X" in more than one of these three columns.)

Report the total of all claims listed on this schedule in the box labeled "Total" on the last sheet of the completed schedule. Report this total also on the Summary of Schedules.

☐   Check this box if debtor has no creditors holding secured claims to report on this Schedule D.

CREDITOR'S NAME AND MAILING ADDRESS INCLUDING ZIP CODE	CODEBTOR	HUSBAND, WIFE, JOINT, OR COMMUNITY	DATE CLAIM WAS INCURRED, NATURE OF LIEN, AND DESCRIPTION AND MARKET VALUE OF PROPERTY SUBJECT TO LIEN	CONTINGENT	UNLIQUIDATED	DISPUTED	AMOUNT OF CLAIM WITHOUT DEDUCTING VALUE OF COLLATERAL	UNSECURED PORTION, IF ANY
ACCOUNT NO. 64-112-1861 Ameritrust 10 Financial Way Cleveland Hts, OH 44118		J	9/12/XX; purchase-money secured debt; mortgage on residence VALUE $ 95,000				75,000	–0–
ACCOUNT NO. 64-112-8423 Ameritrust 10 Financial Way Cleveland Hts, OH 44118		J	8/9/XX; nonpurchase-money secured debt; second mortgage on residence VALUE $ 95,000				12,000	–0–
ACCOUNT NO. N/A Computers for Sale P.O. Box 1183 San Ramon, CA 94000		J	8/12/XX; purchase-money secured interest, computer VALUE $ 1,100				2,000	900
ACCOUNT NO. 521129 Quality Collection Agency 21 Main Drive West Cleveland Hts, OH 44115		"	" VALUE $				"	"

_____1_____   continuation sheets attached

Subtotal ➡ $ 89,000
(Total of this page)

Total ➡ $ N/A
(Use only on last page)

(Report total also on Summary of Schedules)

description you used on Schedule A for real property, or Schedule B for personal property. If a creditor's lien covers several items of property, list all items affected by the lien.

Market Value of Property. The amount you put here must be consistent with what you put on Schedule A or B. If you put only the total value of a group of items on Schedule B, you must now get more specific. For instance, if a department store has a secured claim against your washing machine, and you listed your "washer/dryer set" on Schedule B, now you must provide the washer's specific market value. You may have already done this on the Worksheet. If not, see the instructions for the "Current Market Value" of Schedule B.

Contingent, Unliquidated, Disputed. Indicate whether the creditor's secured claim is contingent, unliquidated or disputed. Check all categories that apply. If you're uncertain of which to choose, check the one that seems closest. If none applies, leave them blank. Briefly, these terms mean:

Contingent. The claim depends on some event that hasn't yet occurred and may never occur. For example, if you cosigned a secured loan, you won't be liable unless the principal debtor defaults. Your liability as cosigner is contingent upon the default.

Unliquidated. This means that a debt may exist, but the exact amount hasn't been determined. For example, say you've sued someone for injuries you suffered in an auto accident, but the case isn't over. Your lawyer has taken the case under a contingency fee agreement— he'll get a third of the recovery if you win, and nothing if you lose—and has a security interest in the final re-covery amount. The debt to the lawyer is unliquidated because you don't know how much, if anything, you'll win.

Disputed. A claim is disputed if you and the creditor do not agree about the existence or amount of the debt. For instance, the IRS says you owe $10,000 and has put a lien on your property, and you say you owe $500. List the full amount of the lien, not the amount you think you owe.

⚠ You're not admitting you owe the debt. You may think you don't really owe a contingent, unliquidated or disputed debt, or you may not want to "admit" that you owe the debt. By listing a debt here, however, you aren't admitting anything. Instead, you are assuring that any debt you do owe gets discharged, assuming it's otherwise dischargeable.

Amount of Claim Without Deducting Value of Collateral. For each secured creditor, put the amount it would take to pay off the secured claim, regardless of what the property is worth. The lender can tell you the amount. In some cases, the amount of the secured claim may be more than the market value of the property.

EXAMPLE: Your original loan was for $13,000 plus $7,000 in interest (for $20,000 total). You've made enough payments so that $15,000 will cancel the debt; you would put $15,000 in this column.

If you have more than one creditor for a given secured claim (for example, the lender and a collection agency), list the debt only for the lender and put ditto marks (") for each subsequent creditor.

Subtotal/Total. Total the amounts in the Amount of Claim column for each page. Do not include the amounts represented by the ditto marks if you listed multiple creditors for a single debt. On the final page of Schedule D, which may be the first page or a pre-printed continuation page, enter the total of all secured claims.

Unsecured Portion, If Any. If the market value of the collateral is equal to or greater than the amount of the claim, enter "0," meaning that the creditor's claim is fully secured. If the market value of the collateral is less than the amount of the claim(s) listed, enter the difference here.

EXAMPLE: If the market value of your car is $5,000 but you still owe $6,000 on your car loan, enter $1,000 in this column ($6,000 − $5,000). This is the amount of the loan that is unsecured by the collateral (your car).

If you list an amount in this column for a creditor, do not list this amount again on Schedule F (where you will list all other creditors with unsecured claims). Otherwise, this unsecured amount will be listed twice.

Form B6D—Cont.

(6/90)

In re ___**Maytag, Molly and Jonathan**___ , Case No._____
　　　　　　　　　　　Debtor 　　　　　　　　　　　　　　　　　　　　　(If known)

SCHEDULE D—CREDITORS HOLDING SECURED CLAIMS
(Continuation Sheet)

CREDITOR'S NAME AND MAILING ADDRESS INCLUDING ZIP CODE	CODEBTOR	HUSBAND, WIFE, JOINT, OR COMMUNITY	DATE CLAIM WAS INCURRED, NATURE OF LIEN, AND DESCRIPTION AND MARKET VALUE OF PROPERTY SUBJECT TO LIEN	CONTINGENT	UNLIQUIDATED	DISPUTED	AMOUNT OF CLAIM WITHOUT DEDUCTING VALUE OF COLLATERAL	UNSECURED PORTION, IF ANY
ACCOUNT NO.　5514　 Fanny's Furniture 14—4th Street Cleveland, OH 44114		J	6/4/XX; purchase-money secured interest, children's bedroom furniture　　VALUE $　450				1,000	550
ACCOUNT NO.　N/A　 Bonnie Johnson 40 Mayfield University Hts, OH 44118	X	"	"　　　VALUE $				"	"
ACCOUNT NO.　834-19-77381 Ohio Savings 100 Chester Way Cleveland, OH 44115		J	9/1/XX; judgment lien on all real property in Cuyahoga county　VALUE $　100,000				2,200	-0-
ACCOUNT NO.　N/A　 George Money, Attorney 10 Main Drive Street Cleveland, OH 44112		"	"　　　VALUE $				"	"
ACCOUNT NO.			VALUE $					
ACCOUNT NO.			VALUE $					

Subtotal ➡ $ 3,200
(Total of this page)

Total ➡ $ 92,200
(Use only on last page)

Sheet no. __1__ of __1__ continuation sheets attached to
Schedule of Creditors Holding Secured Claims

(Report total also on Summary of Schedules)

5. Schedule E—Creditors Holding Unsecured Priority Claims

Schedule E identifies certain creditors who may be entitled to be paid first—by the trustee—out of your nonexempt assets.

Set out below are a sample completed Schedule E and line-by-line instructions.

In re and **Case No.** Follow the instructions for Schedule A.

☐ **Check this box if debtor has no creditors holding unsecured priority claims to report on this Schedule E.** Priority claims are claims that must be paid first in your bankruptcy case. The most common examples are unsecured income tax debts and past due alimony or child support. There are several other categories of priority debts, however. Read further to figure out whether or not you can check this box.

Examine each of the following categories. Check a box if you owe a debt in that category.

☐ **Extensions of credit in an involuntary case.** Don't check this box. You are filing a voluntary, not an involuntary, case.

☐ **Wages, salaries, and commissions.** If you own a business and owe a current or former employee wages, vacation pay or sick leave which was earned within 90 days before you file your petition or within 90 days of the date you ceased your business, check this box. If you owe money to an independent contractor who did work for you which was earned within 90 days before you file your petition or within 90 days of the date you ceased your business, check this box only if, in the 12 months before you file for bankruptcy, this independent contractor earned at least 75% of his or her total

independent contractor receipts from you. Only the first $4,650 owed per employee or independent contractor is a priority debt.

☐ **Contributions to employee benefit plans.** Check this box if you own a business and you owe contributions to an employee benefit fund for services rendered by an employee within 180 days before you file your petition or within 180 days of the date you ceased your business.

☐ **Certain farmers and fishermen.** Check this box only if you operate or operated a grain storage facility and owe a grain producer, or you operate or operated a fish produce or storage facility and owe a U.S. fisherman for fish or fish products. Only the first $4,650 owed per person is a priority debt.

☐ **Deposits by individuals.** If you took money from people who planned to purchase, lease or rent goods or services from you which you never delivered, you may owe a priority debt. For the debt to qualify as a priority, the goods or services had to have been planned for personal, family or household use. Only the first $2,100 owed (per person) is a priority debt.

☐ **Alimony, Maintenance, or Support.** Check this box if you are behind on your payments to a spouse, former spouse or child for alimony or child support pursuant to a marital settlement agreement or court order, such as a divorce decree or paternity order.

☐ **Taxes and Certain Other Debts Owed to Governmental Units.** Check this box if you owe unsecured back taxes or if you owe any other debts to the government, such as fines imposed for driving under the influence of drugs or alcohol. Not all tax debts are unsecured priority claims. For example, if the IRS has recorded a lien against your real property, and the equity in your property fully covers the amount of your tax debt, your debt is a secured debt. It should be on Schedule D, not on this schedule.

☐ **Commitments to Maintain the Capital of an Insured Depository Institution.** Don't check this box. It is for business bankruptcies.

If you checked none of the priority debt boxes, go back and check the first box, showing you have no unsecured priority claims to report. Then go on to Schedule F.

If you checked any of the priority debt boxes, make as many photocopies of the continuation page as the number of priority debt boxes you checked. You will

B6E
(Rev. 4/01

In re __Maytag, Molly and Jonathan__ , Case No._____
   Debtor   (If known)

SCHEDULE E—CREDITORS HOLDING UNSECURED PRIORITY CLAIMS

A complete list of claims entitled to priority, listed separately by type of priority, is to be set forth on the sheets provided. Only holders of unsecured claims entitled to priority should be listed in this schedule. In the boxes provided on the attached sheets, state the name and mailing address, including zip code, and account number, if any, of all entities holding priority claims against the debtor or the property of the debtor, as of the date of the filing of the petition.

If any entity other than a spouse in a joint case may be jointly liable on a claim, place an "X" in the column labeled "Codebtor," include the entity on the appropriate schedule of creditors, and complete Schedule H—Codebtors. If a joint petition is filed, state whether husband, wife, both of them, or the marital community may be liable on each claim by placing an "H," "W," "J," or "C" in the column labeled "Husband, Wife, Joint, or Community."

If the claim is contingent, place an "X" in the column labeled "Contingent." If the claim is unliquidated, place an "X" in the column labeled "Unliquidated." If the claim is disputed, place an "X" in the column labeled "Disputed." (You may need to place an "X" in more than one of these three columns.)

Report the total of all claims listed on each sheet in the box labeled "Subtotal" on each sheet. Report the total of all claims listed on this Schedule E in the box labeled "Total" on the last sheet of the completed schedule. Repeat this total also on the Summary of Schedules.

☐ **Check this box if debtor has no creditors holding unsecured priority claims to report on this Schedule E.**

TYPES OF PRIORITY CLAIMS (Check the appropriate box(es) below if claims in that category are listed on the attached sheets)

☐ **Extensions of credit in an involuntary case**

Claims arising in the ordinary course of the debtor's business or financial affairs after the commencement of the case but before the earlier of the appointment of a trustee or the order for relief. 11 U.S.C. § 507(a)(2).

☐ **Wages, salaries, and commissions**

Wages, salaries, and commissions, including vacation, severance, and sick leave pay owing to employees and commissions owing to qualifying independent sales representatives up to $4,650* per person, earned within 90 days immediately preceding the filing of the original petition, or the cessation of business, whichever occurred first, to the extent provided in 11 U.S.C. § 507(a)(3).

☐ **Contributions to employee benefit plans**

Money owed to employee benefit plans for services rendered within 180 days immediately preceding the filing of the original petition, or the cessation of business, whichever occurred first, to the extent provided in 11 U.S.C. § 507(a)(4).

☐ **Certain farmers and fishermen**

Claims of certain farmers and fishermen, up to a maximum of $4,650* per farmer or fisherman, against the debtor, as provided in 11 U.S.C. § 507(a)(5).

☐ **Deposits by individuals**

Claims of individuals up to a maximum of $2,100* for deposits for the purchase, lease, or rental of property or services for personal, family, or household use, that were not delivered or provided. 11 U.S.C. § 507(a)(6).

☐ **Alimony, Maintenance, or Support**

Claims of a spouse, former spouse, or child of the debtor for alimony, maintenance, or support, to the extent provided in 11 U.S.C. § 507(a)(7).

X☐ **Taxes and Certain Other Debts Owed to Governmental Units**

Taxes, customs, duties, and penalties owing to federal, state, and local governmental units as set forth in 11 U.S.C. § 507(a)(8).

☐ **Commitments to Maintain the Capital of an Insured Depository Institution**

Claims based on commitments to the FDIC, RTC, Director of the Office of Thrift Supervision, Comptroller of the Currency, or Board of Governors of the Federal Reserve system, or their predecessors or successors, to maintain the capital of an insured depository institution. 11 U.S.C. § 507 (a)(9).

* Amounts are subject to adjustment on April 1, 2004, and every three years thereafter with respect to cases commenced on or after the date of adjustment.

_____1___ continuation sheets attached

B6E
(Rev. 4/98)

In re ___Maytag, Molly and Jonathan___ ,   Case No._____
                    Debtor   (If known)

SCHEDULE E—CREDITORS HOLDING UNSECURED PRIORITY CLAIMS
(Continuation Sheet)

___Taxes___
TYPE OF PRIORITY

CREDITOR'S NAME AND MAILING ADDRESS INCLUDING ZIP CODE	CODEBTOR	HUSBAND, WIFE, JOINT, OR COMMUNITY	DATE CLAIM WAS INCURRED AND CONSIDERATION FOR CLAIM	CONTINGENT	UNLIQUIDATED	DISPUTED	TOTAL AMOUNT OF CLAIM	AMOUNT ENTITLED TO PRIORITY
ACCOUNT NO. N/A IRS Cincinnati, OH 42111		J	April 15, 20XX, Tax Liability				2,200	2,200
ACCOUNT NO. N/A Ohio Dept. of Tax P.O. Box 1460 Cincinnati, OH 43266-0106		J	April 15, 20XX, Tax Liability				800	800
ACCOUNT NO.								
ACCOUNT NO.								
ACCOUNT NO.								

Subtotal ➡ $ 3,000
(Total of this page)

Sheet no. __1__ of __1__ sheets attached to
Schedule of Creditors Holding Unsecured Priority Claims

Total ➡ $ 3,000
(Use only on last page)

(Report total also on Summary of Schedules)

need to complete a separate sheet for each type of priority debt, as follows:

In re and **Case No.** Follow the instructions for Schedule A.

Type of Priority. Identify one of the types of priority you checked in page 1.

Creditor's Name and Mailing Address, Including Zip Code. List the name and complete mailing address (including zip code) of each priority creditor, as well as the account number if you know it. You may have more than one priority creditor for a given debt. For example, if you've been sued or hounded by a collection agency, list the attorney or collection agency in addition to the original creditor.

Codebtor. If someone else can be legally forced to pay your debt listed to a priority creditor, enter an "X" in this column and list the codebtor in the creditor column of this schedule. You'll also need to list the codebtor as a creditor in Schedule F and Schedule H. Common codebtors are listed in the instructions for Schedule D.

Husband, Wife, Joint, or Community. Follow the instructions for Schedule A.

Date Claim Was Incurred and Consideration for Claim. State the date you incurred the debt—this may be a specific date or a period of time. Also briefly state what the debt is for. For example, "goods purchased," "hours worked for me" or "deposit for my services."

Contingent, Unliquidated, Disputed. Follow the instructions for Schedule D.

Total Amount of Claim. For each priority debt other than taxes, put the amount it would take to pay off the debt in full, even if it's over the priority limit. For taxes, list only the amount that is unsecured (and therefore a priority). The amount that is secured will be listed on Schedule D. If the amount isn't determined, write "not yet determined" in this column.

Subtotal/Total. Total the amounts in the Total Amount of Claim column on each page. If you use continuation pages for additional priority debts, enter the total of all priority debts on the final page.

Amount Entitled to Priority. If the priority claim is larger than the maximum indicated on the first page of Schedule E (for example, $4,300 of wages owed to each employee), put the maximum here. If the claim is less than the maximum, put the amount you entered in the Total Amount of Claim column.

6. Schedule F—Creditors Holding Unsecured Nonpriority Claims

In this schedule, list all creditors you haven't listed in Schedules D or E. For purposes of completing Schedule F, it doesn't matter that the debt might be nondischargeable—such as a student loan. It also doesn't matter if you believe that you don't owe the debt or that you owe only a small amount and intend to pay it off. It's essential that you list every creditor to whom you owe, or possibly owe, money. The only way you can legitimately leave off a creditor is if your balance owed is $0.

Even if you want to repay a particular creditor, list the debt and get it discharged anyway. You can always voluntarily pay the debt out of property or income you receive after you file for bankruptcy, even though the creditor is legally barred from trying to collect the debt.

EXAMPLE: Peter owes his favorite aunt $8,000. When Peter files for bankruptcy he lists the debt, which is discharged when Peter's bankruptcy is over. Peter can voluntarily pay off the $8,000 out of his wages after his bankruptcy discharge. Peter's aunt, however, couldn't sue him or enforce payment of the debt.

Inadvertent errors or omissions on this schedule can come back to haunt you. A debt you owe to a creditor you forget to list might not be discharged in bankruptcy. And leaving a creditor off the schedule might raise suspicions that you deliberately concealed information, perhaps to give that creditor preferential treatment in violation of bankruptcy rules.

Below are a sample completed Schedule F and line-by-line instructions. Use as many preprinted continuation pages as you need.

In re and **Case No.** Follow the instructions for Schedule A.

☐ **Check this box if debtor has no creditors holding unsecured nonpriority claims to report on this Schedule F.** Check this box if you have no unsecured nonpriority debts. This would be very rare.

Creditor's Name and Mailing Address, Including Zip Code. List, preferably in alphabetical order, the name and complete mailing address of each unsecured creditor, as well as the account number if you know it. If you have more than one unsecured creditor for a given debt, list the original creditor first, followed by the

Form B6F

(9/97)

In re ___Maytag, Molly and Jonathan___ ,   Case No._____
                      Debtor   (If known)

SCHEDULE F—CREDITORS HOLDING UNSECURED NONPRIORITY CLAIMS

State the name, mailing address, including zip code, and account number, if any, of all entities holding unsecured claims without priority against the debtor or the property of the debtor as of the date of filing of the petition. Do not include claims listed in Schedules D and E. If all creditors will not fit on this page, use the continuation sheet provided.

If any entity other than a spouse in a joint case may be jointly liable on a claim, place an "X" in the column labeled "Codebtor," include the entity on the appropriate schedule of creditors, and complete Schedule H—Codebtors. If a joint petition is filed, state whether husband, wife, both of them, or the marital community may be liable on each claim by placing an "H," "W," "J," or "C" in the column labeled "Husband, Wife, Joint, or Community."

If the claim is contingent, place an "X" in the column labeled "Contingent." If the claim is unliquidated, place an "X" in the column labeled "Unliquidated." If the claim is disputed, place an "X" in the column labeled "Disputed." (You may need to place an "X" in more than one of these three columns.)

Report the total of all claims listed on this schedule in the box labeled "Total" on the last sheet of the completed schedule. Report this total also on the Summary of Schedules.

☐ Check this box if debtor has no creditors holding unsecured nonpriority claims to report on this Schedule F.

CREDITOR'S NAME AND MAILING ADDRESS INCLUDING ZIP CODE	CODEBTOR	HUSBAND, WIFE, JOINT, OR COMMUNITY	DATE CLAIM WAS INCURRED AND CONSIDERATION FOR CLAIM. IF CLAIM IS SUBJECT TO SETOFF, SO STATE	CONTINGENT	UNLIQUIDATED	DISPUTED	AMOUNT OF CLAIM
ACCOUNT NO. N/A Alan Accountant 5 Green St. Cleveland, OH 44118		J	4/XX, tax preparation				250
ACCOUNT NO. 4189000026113 American Allowance P.O. Box 1 New York, NY 10001		J	1/XX to 4/XX, VISA credit card charges			X	5,600
ACCOUNT NO. Patricia Washington, Esq. Washington & Lincoln Legal Plaza, Suite 1 Cleveland, OH 44114		"	"		"		"
ACCOUNT NO. 845061-86-3 Citibank 200 East North Columbus, OH 43266		J	20XX, student loan charges				10,000

____2____ continuation sheets attached

Subtotal ➡ (Total of this page) $ 15,850

Total ➡ (Use only on last page) $ N/A

(Report total also on Summary of Schedules)

Form B6F—Cont.

(10/89)

In re ___Maytag, Molly and Jonathan___,　　　　Case No._____
　　　　　　　　Debtor　　　　　　　　　　　　　　　　　　　　　　(If known)

SCHEDULE F—CREDITORS HOLDING UNSECURED NONPRIORITY CLAIMS
(Continuation Sheet)

CREDITOR'S NAME AND MAILING ADDRESS INCLUDING ZIP CODE	CODEBTOR	HUSBAND, WIFE, JOINT, OR COMMUNITY	DATE CLAIM WAS INCURRED AND CONSIDERATION FOR CLAIM. IF CLAIM IS SUBJECT TO SETOFF, SO STATE	CONTINGENT	UNLIQUIDATED	DISPUTED	AMOUNT OF CLAIM
ACCOUNT NO. 9816-12HH Cleveland Hospital 19—1st Avenue Cleveland, OH 44115		J	12/XX, surgery and medical treatment				17,450
ACCOUNT NO. Jane Jackson, Esq. 50—2nd Avenue Cleveland, OH 44115		"	"				"
ACCOUNT NO. 4401 Dr. Dennis Dentist 4 Superior Way Cleveland Hts, OH 44118		W	12/XX to 6/XX; dental work				1,050
ACCOUNT NO. 222387941 Illuminating Co. 55 Public Square Cleveland, OH 44115		J	3/XX to 7/XX; electrical work				750
ACCOUNT NO. N/A Bonnie Johnson 40 Mayfield University Hts, OH 44118		W	8/XX; personal loan				5,500

　　　　　　　　　　　　　　　　　　　　　　　　Subtotal ➡ $　24,750
　　　　　　　　　　　　　　　　　　　　(Total of this page)

Sheet no. ___1___ of ___2___ continuation sheets attached to　　　　　Total ➡ $　N/A
Schedule of Creditors Holding Unsecured Nonpriorty Claims　　(Use only on last page)

　　　　　　　　　　　　　　　　　　　(Report total also on Summary of Schedules)

Form B6F—Cont.
(10/89)

In re ___Maytag, Molly and Jonathan___,   Case No._____
                          Debtor   (If known)

SCHEDULE F—CREDITORS HOLDING UNSECURED NONPRIORITY CLAIMS
(Continuation Sheet)

CREDITOR'S NAME AND MAILING ADDRESS INCLUDING ZIP CODE	CODEBTOR	HUSBAND, WIFE, JOINT, OR COMMUNITY	DATE CLAIM WAS INCURRED AND CONSIDERATION FOR CLAIM. IF CLAIM IS SUBJECT TO SETOFF, SO STATE	CONTINGENT	UNLIQUIDATED	DISPUTED	AMOUNT OF CLAIM
ACCOUNT NO. N/A Dr. Helen Jones 11 Marks Way Cleveland, OH 44112		J	4/XX to 8/XX, pediatric care				2,000
ACCOUNT NO. 11210550 Ohio Gas Company East 1717 East 9th St. Cleveland, OH 44115		J	12/XX to 6/XX, gas service				800
ACCOUNT NO. N/A Charlotte Page 900 Grand View Jackson, WY 83001		H	6/XX to 8/XX, settlement for auto accident				1,800
ACCOUNT NO. 487310097 Sears P.O. Box 11 Chicago, IL 60619		J	20XX to 20XY; dept. store and catalogue charges				3,800
ACCOUNT NO. 6007 John White, Esq. 21 Main Street Cleveland, OH 44114		W	2/XX to 6/XX; represented us in lawsuits against us for unpaid bills				3,450

Sheet no. __2__ of __2__ continuation sheets attached to
Schedule of Creditors Holding Unsecured Nonpriorty Claims

Subtotal ➡ $ 11,850
(Total of this page)

Total ➡ $ 52,450
(Use only on last page)

(Report total also on Summary of Schedules)

other creditors. For example, if you've been sued or hounded by a collection agency, list the attorney or collection agency in addition to the original creditor. (But you don't need to list a collection agency that had the debt a while back and has ceased collection efforts.) When you are typing your final papers, if you get to the end and discover that you left a creditor off, don't start all over again in search of perfect alphabetical order. Just add the creditor to the end of the list.

Easy-to-Overlook Creditors

One debt may involve several different creditors. Remember to include:

- your ex-spouse, if you are still obligated under a divorce decree or settlement agreement to pay joint debts, turn any property over to your ex or make payments as part of your property division
- anyone who has cosigned a promissory note or loan application signed by you
- any holder of a loan or promissory note that you cosigned for someone else
- the original creditor, anybody to whom the debt has been assigned or sold and any other person (such as a bill collector or attorney) trying to collect the debt, and
- anyone who may sue you because of a car accident, business dispute or the like.

Codebtor. If someone else can be legally forced to pay your debt to a listed unsecured creditor, enter an "X" in this column and list the codebtor as a creditor in this schedule. Also list the codebtor in Schedule H. The instructions for Schedule D list common codebtors.

Husband, Wife, Joint, or Community. Follow the instructions for Schedule A.

Date Claim Was Incurred and Consideration for Claim. If Claim Is Subject to Setoff, So State. State when the debt was incurred. It may be one date or a period of time. With credit card debts, put the approximate time over which you ran up the charges unless the unpaid charges were made on one or two specific

dates. Then state what the debt was for. You can be general ("clothes" or "household furnishings") or specific ("refrigerator" or "teeth capping").

If you are entitled to a setoff against the debt—that is, the creditor owes you some money, too—list the amount and why you think you are entitled to the setoff. If there is more than one creditor for a single debt, put ditto marks (") in this column for the subsequent creditors.

Contingent, Unliquidated, Disputed. Follow the instructions for Schedule D.

Amount of Claim. List the amount of the debt claimed by the creditor, even if you dispute the amount. That way, it will all be wiped out if it's dischargeable. If there's more than one creditor for a single debt, put the debt amount across from the original creditor and put ditto marks (") across from each subsequent creditor you have listed. Be as precise as possible when stating the amount. If you must approximate, write "approx." after the amount.

Subtotal/Total. Total the amounts in the last column for this page. Do not include the amounts represented by the ditto marks if you listed multiple creditors for a single debt. On the final page (which may be the first page or a preprinted continuation page), enter the total of all unsecured nonpriority claims. On the first page in the bottom left-hand corner, note the number of continuation pages you are attaching.

7. Schedule G—Executory Contracts and Unexpired Leases

In this form, you list every executory contract or unexpired lease to which you're a party. "Executory" means the contract is still in force—that is, both parties are still obligated to perform important acts under it. Similarly, "unexpired" means that the contract or lease period hasn't run out—that is, it is still in effect. Common examples of executory contracts and unexpired leases are:

- car leases
- residential leases or rental agreements
- business leases or rental agreements
- service contracts
- business contracts
- time-share contracts or leases

- contracts of sale for real estate
- copyright and patent license agreements
- leases of real estate (surface and underground) for the purpose of harvesting timber, minerals or oil
- future homeowners' association fee requirements
- agreements for boat docking privileges, and
- insurance contracts.

⚠️ **Contract delinquencies.** If you are delinquent in payments that were due under a lease or executory contract, the delinquency should also be listed as a debt on Schedule D, E or F. The sole purpose of this schedule is to identify existing contractual obligations that you still owe or that someone owes you.

Below are a sample completed Schedule G and line-by-line instructions.

In re and **Case No.** Follow the instructions for Schedule A.

☐ **Check this box if debtor has no executory contracts or unexpired leases.** Check this box if it applies; otherwise, complete the form.

Name and Mailing Address, Including Zip Code, of Other Parties to Lease or Contract. Provide the name and full address (including zip code) of each party—other than yourself—to each lease or contract. These parties are either people who signed agreements or the companies for whom these people work. If you're unsure about whom to list, include the person who signed an agreement, any company whose name appears on the agreement and anybody who might have an interest in having the contract or lease enforced. If you still aren't sure, put "don't know."

Description of Contract or Lease and Nature of Debtor's Interest. State Whether Lease Is for Nonresidential Real Property. State Contract Number of Any Government Contract. For each lease or contract, give:

- a description of the basic type (for instance, residential lease, commercial lease, car lease, business obligation, copyright license)
- the date the contract or lease was signed
- the date the contract is to expire (if any)
- a summary of each party's rights and obligations under the lease or contract, and
- the contract number, if the contract is with any government body.

Executory Contracts and Unexpired Leases Explained

It's up to the trustee to decide whether an executory contract or unexpired lease should be continued in force or terminated (rejected). But don't worry about the trustee terminating your residential lease or car lease against your will.

This provision of the Bankruptcy Code is primarily intended for business bankruptcies. In fact, one subsection was enacted in response to the high number of shopping mall owners going bankrupt. This doesn't mean it has no application in consumer cases, but the power to terminate a lease is rarely invoked by a trustee in a consumer case.

If the lease or contract will produce assets for the creditors, the trustee is likely to terminate it. As a general rule, people filing Chapter 7 bankruptcies are not parties to leases or contracts that would likely add value to their bankruptcy estates. This isn't an absolute rule, however. If the trustee could sell a lease to someone else for a profit (because you're paying less than market rent, for example), the trustee might terminate it and sell it. But this is highly unusual. A trustee doesn't look for ways to put you on the street or penalize you for getting a great rent deal.

It's also possible that you want out of a contract or lease, such as a residential or auto lease or a time-share you can't afford. Be sure to state at the bankruptcy meeting or even on your papers that you would like the trustee to terminate the agreement. But remember this is up to the trustee to decide.

If the lease or contract is terminated, you and the other parties to the agreement are cut loose from any obligations, and any money you owe the creditor will be discharged in your bankruptcy, even if the debt arose after your filing date. For example, say you are leasing a car when you file for bankruptcy. You want out of the lease. The car dealer cannot repossess the car until the trustee terminates the lease, which normally must occur within 60 days of when you file. During that 60-day period, you can use the car without paying for it. The payments you don't make during this period will be discharged as if they were incurred prior to your bankruptcy.

Bankruptcy law has special rules for executory contracts related to intellectual property (copyright, patent, trademark or trade secret), real estate and time-share leases. If you are involved in one of these situations, see a lawyer.

Form B6G

(10/89)

In re _Maytag, Molly and Jonathan_ ,　　　　　Case No._____

Debtor 　　　　　　　　　　　　　　　　　　　　　(If known)

SCHEDULE G—EXECUTORY CONTRACTS AND UNEXPIRED LEASES

Describe all executory contracts of any nature and all unexpired leases of real personal property. Include any timeshare interests.

State nature of debtor's interest in contract, i.e., "Purchaser," "Agent," etc. State whether debtor is the lessor or lessee of a lease.

Provide the names and complete mailing addresses of all other parties to each lease or contract described.

NOTE: A party listed on this schedule will not receive notice of the filing of this case unless the party is also scheduled in the appropriate schedule of creditors.

☐ Check this box if debtor has no executory contracts or unexpired leases.

NAME AND MAILING ADDRESS, INCLUDING ZIP CODE, OF OTHER PARTIES TO LEASE OR CONTRACT	DESCRIPTION OF CONTRACT OR LEASE AND NATURE OF DEBTOR'S INTEREST. STATE WHETHER LEASE IS FOR NONRESIDENTIAL REAL PROPERTY. STATE CONTRACT NUMBER OF ANY GOVERNMENT CONTRACT
Scarborough Road South Homeowners Association 1 Scarborough Road South Cleveland Hts, OH 41118	Homeowner's Association Contract for residential property, signed 10/XX, expires 12/XX. Provides for maintenance, gardening and repairs of property.

8. Schedule H—Codebtors

In Schedules D, E and F, you identified those debts for which you have codebtors—usually, a cosigner, guarantor, ex-spouse, non-filing spouse in a community property state, non-filing spouse for a debt for a necessity, non-marital partner or joint contractor. You must also list those codebtors here.

In Chapter 7 bankruptcy, your codebtors will be wholly responsible for your debts, unless they, too, declare bankruptcy.

Below are a sample completed Schedule H and line-by-line instructions.

In re and **Case No.** Follow instructions for Schedule A.

☐ **Check this box if debtor has no codebtors.** Check this box if it applies; otherwise, complete the form.

Name and Address of Codebtor. List the name and complete address (including zip code) of each codebtor. If the codebtor is a non-filing current spouse, put all names by which that person was known during the previous six years.

Name and Address of Creditor. List the name and address of each creditor (as listed on Schedule D, E or F) to which each codebtor is indebted.

EXAMPLE: Tom Martin cosigned three different loans—with three different banks—for debtor Mabel Green, who is filing for bankruptcy. In the first column, Mabel lists Tom Martin as a codebtor. In the second, Mabel lists each of the three banks.

If you are married and filing alone. If you live in a community property state, your spouse may be a codebtor for most of the debts you listed in Schedules D, E and F. This is because in these states, most debts incurred by one spouse are owed by both spouses. In this event, don't relist all the creditors in the second column, simply write "all creditors listed in Schedules D, E and F, except:" and then list any creditors whom you owe solely.

9. Schedule I—Current Income of Individual Debtor(s)

The bankruptcy trustee screens each filing for possible abuse of the bankruptcy system. Your income and what you spend it on are the primary factors the trustee considers. If you can afford to repay your debts in a reasonable period of time, the bankruptcy court will probably dismiss your bankruptcy petition.

Chapter 7 bankruptcy petitions are rarely dismissed because the debtor's income is too high or because expenditures are too low. But a very high income coupled with an extravagant lifestyle may mean trouble. You should be concerned if you clearly have enough disposable income to pay a substantial majority of your unsecured debts over a three- to five-year period. (See Ch. 1, Sections C.4 and F.4.)

Below are a sample completed Schedule I and line-by-line instructions. If you're married and filing jointly, you must fill in information for both spouses. If you are married but filing alone, only fill in the information for yourself.

In re and **Case No.** Follow the instructions for Schedule A.

Debtor's Marital Status. Enter your marital status. Your choices are single, married, separated (you aren't living with your spouse and plan never to again), widowed or divorced. You are divorced only if you have received a final judgment of divorce from a court.

Dependents of Debtor and Spouse. List the names, ages and relationships of all persons for whom you and your spouse provide at least 50% of support. This may include your children, your spouse's children, your parents, other relatives and domestic partners. It does not include your spouse.

Employment. Provide the requested employment information. If you have more than one employer, enter "See continuation sheet" just below the box containing the employment information and then complete a continuation sheet. If you are retired, unemployed or disabled, put that.

Income. Enter your estimated monthly gross income from regular employment, before any payroll deductions are taken. In the second blank, put your estimated monthly overtime pay. Add them together and enter the subtotal in the third blank.

Form B6H

(6/90)

In re ___Maytag, Molly and Jonathan___,   Case No._____
                    Debtor   (If known)

SCHEDULE H—CODEBTORS

Provide the information requested concerning any person or entity, other than a spouse in a joint case, that is also liable on any debts listed by debtor in the schedules of creditors. Include all guarantors and co-signers. In community property states, a married debtor not filing a joint case should report the name and address of the nondebtor spouse on this schedule. Include all names used by the nondebtor spouse during the six years immediately preceding the commencement of this case.

☐   Check this box if debtor has no codebtors.

NAME AND ADDRESS OF CODEBTOR	NAME AND ADDRESS OF CREDITOR
Bonnie Johnson 40 Mayfield University Hts, OH 44118	Fanny's Furniture 14—4th Street Cleveland, OH 44114

Form B6I

(6/90)

In re ___Maytag, Molly and Jonathan_____ ,   Case No._____
                                Debtor   (If known)

SCHEDULE I—CURRENT INCOME OF INDIVIDUAL DEBTOR(S)

The column labled "Spouse" must be completed in all cases filed by joint debtors and by a married debtor in a Chapter 12 or 13 case whether or not a joint petition is filed, unless the spouses are separated and a joint petition is not filed.

DEBTOR'S MARITAL STATUS:	DEPENDENTS OF DEBTOR AND SPOUSE		
	NAMES	AGE	RELATIONSHIP
Married	Sara Maytag	14	daughter
	Harold Maytag	12	son

Employment:	DEBTOR	SPOUSE
Occupation	Clerk/typist	Construction Worker
Name of Employer	Typing Circles	Cleveland Builder
How long employed	1 1/2 years	4 years
Address of Employer	40 Euclid Drive Cleveland, OH 44112	100 Chester Way Cleveland, OH 44114

INCOME: (Estimate of average monthly income)	DEBTOR	SPOUSE
Current monthly gross wages, salary, and commissions (pro rate if not paid monthly)	$ 1,450	$ 3,000
Estimated monthly overtime	$ 0	$ 0
SUBTOTAL	$ 1,450	$ 3,000
LESS PAYROLL DEDUCTIONS		
a. Payroll taxes and Social Security	$ 350	$ 600
b. Insurance	$ N/A	$ 250
c. Union dues	$ N/A	$ 50
d. Other (Specify: _____)	$ N/A	$ N/A
SUBTOTAL OF PAYROLL DEDUCTIONS	$ 350	$ 900
TOTAL NET MONTHLY TAKE HOME PAY	$ 1,100	$ 2,100
Regular income from operation of business or profession or farm (attach detailed statement)	$ N/A	$ N/A
Income from real property	$ N/A	$ N/A
Interest and dividends	$ 100	$ 100
Alimony, maintenance or support payments payable to the debtor for the debtor's use or that of dependents listed above	$ N/A	$ N/A
Social Security or other government assistance		
(Specify:_____)	$ N/A	$ N/A
Pension or retirement income	$ N/A	$ N/A
Other monthly income	$ N/A	$ N/A
(Specify:_____)	$ N/A	$ N/A
_____	$ N/A	$ N/A
TOTAL MONTHLY INCOME	$ 1,200	$ 2,200

TOTAL COMBINED MONTHLY INCOME $ ____3,400_____   (Report also on Summary of Schedules)

Describe any increase or decrease of more than 10% in any of the above categories anticipated to occur within the year following the filing of this document:

N/A

If you are self-employed or an independent contractor, use the blank labeled "Regular income from operation of business or profession or farm." Also attach a sheet of paper. Call it "Attachment to Schedule I" and include your name (and spouse's name if you're filing jointly) and list your average gross monthly receipts and average monthly expenses.

Payroll Deductions. In the four blanks, enter the deductions taken from your gross salary. The deductions listed are the most common ones, but you may have others to report. Other possible deductions are state disability taxes, wages withheld or garnished for child support, credit union payments or perhaps payments on a student loan or a car.

Subtotal of Payroll Deductions. Add your payroll deductions and enter the subtotal.

Total Net Monthly Take Home Pay. Subtract your payroll deductions subtotal from your income subtotal.

Regular income from operation of business or profession or farm. If you are self-employed or operate a sole proprietorship, enter your monthly income from that source here. If it's been fairly steady for at least one calendar year, divide the amount you entered on your most recent tax return (IRS Schedule C) by 12 for a monthly amount. If your income hasn't been steady for at least one calendar year, enter the average net income from your business or profession for the past three months. In either case you must attach a statement of your income. Use your most recent IRS Schedule C filed with the IRS.

Income from real property. Enter the monthly income from real estate rentals, leases or licenses (such as mineral exploration, oil and the like).

Interest and dividends. Enter the average estimated monthly interest you receive from bank or security deposits and other investments, such as stocks.

Alimony, maintenance or support payments payable to the debtor for the debtor's use or that of dependents listed above. Enter the average monthly amount you receive for your support (alimony, spousal support or maintenance) or your children (child support).

Social Security or other government assistance. Enter the total monthly amount you receive in Social Security, SSI, public assistance, disability payments, veterans' benefits, unemployment compensation, workers' compensation or any other government benefit. If you receive food stamps, include their monthly value. Specify the source of the benefits.

Pension or retirement income. Enter the total monthly amount of all pension, annuity, IRA, Keogh or other retirement benefits you currently receive.

Other monthly income. Specify any other income (such as royalty payments or payments from a trust) you receive on a regular basis and enter the monthly amount here. You may have to divide by 3, 6 or 12 if you receive the payments quarterly, semi-annually or annually.

Total Monthly Income. Add all additional income to the Total Net Monthly Take Home Pay amount and enter the grand total in this blank.

Total Combined Monthly Income. If you are filing jointly, add your total income to your spouse's total income and enter the result here.

Describe any increase or decrease of more than 10% in any of the above categories anticipated to occur within the year following the filing of this document. Identify any changes in your pay or other income—in excess of 10%—that you expect in the coming year. For instance, if recent layoffs at your place of employment mean you probably won't be working overtime, which will reduce your net monthly income by more than 10%, say so.

10. Schedule J—Current Expenditures of Individual Debtor(s)

In this form, you must list your family's total monthly expenditures, even if you're married and filing alone. Be complete and accurate. Your disposable income is computed by subtracting your reasonable expenditures from your net income (on Schedule I). Expenditures for items the trustee considers luxuries won't be considered reasonable, and will be disregarded for the purpose of figuring your disposable income. For instance, payments on expensive cars or investment property may be disregarded by the trustee. Reasonable expenditures for housing, utilities, food, medical care, clothing, education and transportation will be counted. Be ready to prove high amounts with bills, receipts and canceled checks.

EXAMPLE 1: Joe owes $100,000 (excluding his mortgage), earns $4,000 a month and spends $3,600 a month, primarily for necessities, including mortgage payments on a moderately priced family home. Joe would be allowed to proceed with a Chapter 7 bankruptcy because his monthly disposable income ($400) wouldn't let him pay off 70% or more of his debts over three to five years.

EXAMPLE 2: Same facts, except that Joe spends $2,200 a month. In this case, the court might rule that because Joe has $1,800 a month in disposable income, he could pay off most of his debts either informally or under a Chapter 13 repayment plan. The court could dismiss Joe's Chapter 7 bankruptcy petition or pressure him to convert it to Chapter 13 bankruptcy.

EXAMPLE 3: Same facts as Example 2, but Joe is incurably ill and will soon quit working. The court will more than likely allow him to proceed with a Chapter 7 bankruptcy.

Review the sample completed Schedule J and the guidelines below for filling it out.

Once again, be accurate. Creditors sometimes try to use the information on these forms to prove that you committed fraud when you applied for credit. If a creditor can prove that you fraudulently filled in a credit application, the debt may survive bankruptcy. See Ch. 8, *Nondischargeable Debts.* If accuracy on this form will substantially contradict information you previously gave a creditor, see a bankruptcy attorney before filing.

In re and **Case No.** Follow the instructions for Schedule A.

☐ **Check this box if a joint petition is filed and debtor's spouse maintains a separate household. Complete a separate schedule of expenditures labeled "Spouse."** If you and your spouse are jointly filing for bankruptcy, but maintain separate households (for example, you've recently separated), check this box and make sure that you each fill out a separate Schedule J.

Expenditures. For each listed item, fill in your monthly expenses. If you make some payments biweekly, quarterly, semi-annually or annually, prorate them to show your monthly payment. Here are some pointers:

- Do not list payroll deductions you listed on Schedule I.
- Include payments you make for your dependents' expenses in your figures as long as those expenses are reasonable and necessary for the dependents' support.
- Utilities—Other: This includes garbage and cable TV service.
- Installment payments—Other: Write "credit card accounts" on one line and enter your total monthly payments for them. Put the average amount you actually pay, even if it's less than it should be. On the other line put "loans" (except auto loans) and enter your total payments.

Total Monthly Expenses. Total up all your expenses.

For Chapter 12 and 13 Debtors Only. Type "N/A" anywhere in this section.

Form B6J

(6/90)

In re ___Maytag, Molly and Jonathan___,   Case No._____

Debtor   (If known)

SCHEDULE J—CURRENT EXPENDITURES OF INDIVIDUAL DEBTOR(S)

Complete this schedule by estimating the average monthly expenses of the debtor and the debtor's family. Pro rate any payments made bi-weekly, quarterly, semi-annually, or annually to show monthly rate.

☐ Check this box if a joint petition is filed and debtor's spouse maintains a separate household. Complete a separate schedule of expenditures labeled "Spouse."

Rent or home mortgage payment (include lot rented for mobile home)	$ 650
Are real estate taxes included? Yes **X** No _____	
Is property insurance included? Yes **X** No _____	
Utilities: Electricity and heating fuel	$ 245
Water and sewer	$ 40
Telephone	$ 85
Other ___garbage___	$ 15
Home maintenance (repairs and upkeep)	$ 175
Food	$ 550
Clothing	$ 125
Laundry and dry cleaning	$ 50
Medical and dental expenses	$ 400
Transportation (not including car payments)	$ 80
Recreation, clubs and entertainment, newspapers, magazines, etc.	$ 30
Charitable contributions	$ 50
Insurance (not deducted from wages or included in home mortgage payments)	
Homeowner's or renter's	$ 120
Life	$ N/A
Health	$ N/A
Auto	$ 60
Other _____	$ N/A
Taxes (not deducted from wages or included in home mortgage payments)	
(Specify: ___income taxes to IRS & Ohio Dept. of Tax___)	$ 200
Installment payments: (In Chapter 12 and 13 cases, do not list payments to be included in the plan)	
Auto	$ N/A
Other ___credit card accounts___	$ 400
Other ___loans___	$ 550
Alimony, maintenance, and support paid to others	$ 600
Payments for support of additional dependents not living at your home	$ N/A
Regular expenses from operation of business, profession, or farm (attach detailed statement)	$ N/A
Other _____	$ N/A
TOTAL MONTHLY EXPENSES (Report also on Summary of Schedules)	$ 4,425

[FOR CHAPTER 12 AND CHAPTER 13 DEBTORS ONLY]

Provide the information requested below, including whether plan payments are to be made bi-weekly, monthly, annually, or at some other regular interval.

A. Total projected monthly income **N/A**	$ _____
B. Total projected monthly expenses	$ _____
C. Excess income (A minus B)	$ _____
D. Total amount to be paid into plan each _____	$ _____
(interval)	

11. Summary of Schedules

This form helps the bankruptcy trustee and judge get a quick look at your bankruptcy filing. Below is a completed Summary and line-by-line instructions.

Court Name. Copy this information from Form 1—Voluntary Petition.

In re and **Case No.** Follow the instructions for Schedule A.

Name of Schedule. This lists the schedules. Don't add anything.

Attached (Yes/No). You should have completed all of the schedules, so type "Yes" in this column for each schedule.

Number of Sheets. Enter the number of pages you completed for each schedule. Remember to count continuation pages. Enter the total at the bottom of the column.

Amounts Scheduled. For each column—Assets, Liabilities and Other—copy the totals from Schedules A, B, D, E, F, I and J and enter them where indicated. Add up the amounts in the Assets and Liabilities columns and enter their totals at the bottom.

Now, go back and fill in the statistical-administrative information on Form 1—Voluntary Petition.

12. Declaration Concerning Debtor's Schedules

In this form, you are required to swear that everything you have said on your schedules is true and correct. Deliberate lying is a major sin in bankruptcy, and could cost you your bankruptcy discharge, a fine of up to $500,000 and up to five years in prison.

Below is a completed Declaration and instructions.

In re and **Case No.** Follow the instructions for Schedule A.

Declaration Under Penalty of Perjury by Individual Debtor. Enter the total number of pages in your schedules (the number on the Summary plus one). Enter the date and sign the form. Be sure that your spouse signs and dates the form if you are filing jointly.

Certification and Signature of Non-Attorney Bankruptcy Petition Preparer. If a BPP typed your forms, have that person complete this section. Otherwise, type "N/A" anywhere in the box.

Declaration Under Penalty of Perjury on Behalf of Corporation or Partnership. Enter "N/A" anywhere in this blank.

Form B6—Cont.

(6/90)

United States Bankruptcy Court

__Northern__ District of __Ohio, Eastern Division__

In re __Maytag, Molly and Jonathan__ ,   Case No._____

Debtor   (If known)

SUMMARY OF SCHEDULES

Indicate as to each schedule whether that schedule is attached and state the number of pages in each. Report the totals from Schedules A, B, D, E, F, I and J in the boxes provided. Add the amounts from Schedules A and B to determine the total amount of the debtor's assets. Add the amounts from Schedules D, E and F to determine the total amount of the debtor's liabilities.

NAME OF SCHEDULE	ATTACHED (YES/NO)	NUMBER OF SHEETS	AMOUNTS SCHEDULED		
			ASSETS	LIABILITIES	OTHER
A Real Property	Yes	1	$ 100,000		
B Personal Property	Yes	4	$ 29,692		
C Property Claimed as Exempt	Yes	2			
D Creditors Holding Secured Claims	Yes	2		$ 92,200	
E Creditors Holding Unsecured Priority Claims	Yes	2		$ 3,000	
F Creditors Holding Unsecured Nonpriority Claims	Yes	3		$ 52,450	
G Executory Contracts and Unexpired Leases	Yes	1			
H Codebtors	Yes	1			
I Current Income of Individual Debtor(s)	Yes	1			$ 3,400
J Current Expenditures of Individual Debtor(s)	Yes	1			$ 4,425

Total Number of Sheets of All Schedules ➡ 18

Total Assets ➡ $ 129,692

Total Liabilities ➡ $ 147,650

Form B6—Cont.

(12/94)

In re ___Maytag, Molly and Jonathan_____,   Case No._____

         Debtor   (If known)

DECLARATION CONCERNING DEBTOR'S SCHEDULES

DECLARATION UNDER PENALTY OF PERJURY BY INDIVIDUAL DEBTOR

    I declare under penalty of perjury that I have read the foregoing summary and schedules consisting of _____**19**_____

sheets, and that they are true and correct to the best of my knowledge, information, and belief.   (Total shown on summary page plus 1)

Date____**July 3, 20XX**_____   Signature____*Molly Maytag*_____

                                                                    Debtor

Date____**July 3, 20XX**_____   Signature____*Jonathan Maytag*_____

                                                              (Joint Debtor, if any)

[If joint case, both spouses must sign.]

CERTIFICATION AND SIGNATURE OF NON-ATTORNEY BANKRUPTCY PETITION PREPARER (See 11 U.S.C. § 110)

    I certify that I am a bankruptcy petition preparer as defined in 11 U.S.C. § 110, that I prepared this document for compensation, and that I have provided the debtor with a copy of this document.

N/A

_____   _____

Printed or Typed Name of Bankruptcy Petition Preparer   Social Security No.

_____

_____

Address

Names and Social Security numbers of all other individuals who prepared or assisted in preparing this document:

If more than one person prepared this document, attach additional signed sheets conforming to the appropriate Official Form for each person.

X_____   _____

Signature of Bankruptcy Petition Preparer   Date

A bankruptcy petition preparer's failure to comply with the provisions of Title 11 and the Federal Rules of Bankruptcy Procedure may result in fine or imprisonment or both. 11 U.S.C. § 110; 18 U.S.C. § 156.

DECLARATION UNDER PENALTY OF PERJURY ON BEHALF OF CORPORATION OR PARTNERSHIP

N/A

    I, the _____ [the president or other officer or an authorized agent of the corporation or a member or an authorized agent of the partnership] of the _____ [corporation or partnership] named as debtor in this case, declare under penalty of perjury that I have read the foregoing summary and schedules, consisting of _____ sheets, and that they are true and correct to the best of my knowledge, information, and belief.

  (Total shown on summary page plus 1)

Date_____   Signature_____

                                                              _____

                                                              [Print or type name of individual signing on behalf of debtor]

[An individual signing on behalf of a partnership or corporation must indicate position or relationship to debtor.]

Penalty for making a false statement or concealing property: Fine of up to $500,000, imprisonment for up to 5 years, or both. 18 U.S.C. §§ 152 and 3571.

G. Form 7—Statement of Financial Affairs

Congratulations—you're almost through. This form gives information about your recent financial transactions such as payments to creditors, sales or other transfers of property and gifts. Under certain circumstances, the trustee may be entitled to recapture property that you transferred to others prior to filing for bankruptcy, and sell it for the benefit of your unsecured creditors.

The questions on the form are, for the most part, self-explanatory. Spouses filing jointly combine their answers and complete only one form.

If you have no information for a particular item, check the "None" box. If you fail to answer a question and don't check "None," you will have to amend your papers—that is, file a corrected form—after you file. Add continuation sheets if necessary.

⚠️ **Be honest and complete.** Don't give in to the temptation of leaving out a transfer or two, assuming that the trustee won't find or go after the property. Not only must you sign this form under penalty of perjury, but if the trustee or a creditor discovers that you left information out, your bankruptcy will probably be dismissed and you may be prosecuted.

A completed Statement of Financial Affairs and instructions follow.

Court Name. Copy this information from Form 1—Voluntary Petition.

In re and **Case No.** Follow the instructions for Schedule A.

1. Income from employment or operation of business. Enter your gross income for this year and for the previous two years. This means the total income before taxes and other payroll deductions or business expenses are removed.

2. Income other than from employment or operation of business. Include interest, dividends, royalties, workers' compensation, other government benefits and all other money you have received from sources other than your job or business during the last two years. Provide the source of each amount, the dates received and the reason you received the money so that the trustee can verify it if he desires.

3. Payments to creditors. Here you list payments you've recently made to creditors. There are two kinds of creditors—regular creditors and insiders. An insider—defined on the first page of the Statement of Financial Affairs—is essentially a relative or close business associate. All other creditors are regular creditors.

a. **List any payment over $600 made to a regular creditor,** if the payment was made:
   • to repay a loan, installment purchase or other debt, and
   • during the 90 days before you file your bankruptcy petition.

b. **List any payment made to an insider creditor,** if the payment was made within one year before you file your bankruptcy petition. Include alimony and child support payments.

The purpose of these questions is to discover if you have preferred any creditor over others. If you have paid a regular creditor during the 90 days before you file or an insider during the year before you file, the trustee can demand that the creditor turn over the amount to the court, so the trustee can use it to pay your other unsecured creditors. (See Ch. 2, Section A.3.) The trustee may ask you to produce written evidence of any payments you list here, such as copies of canceled checks, check stubs or bank statements.

4. Suits, executions, garnishments and attachments.

a. Include all court actions that you are currently involved in or which you were involved in during the year before filing. Court actions include personal injury cases, small claims actions, contract disputes, divorces, paternity actions, support or custody modification actions and the like. Include:

   • **Caption of the suit and case number.** The caption is the case title (such as *John Jones v. Ginny Jones*). The case number is assigned by the court clerk and appears on the first page of any court-filed paper.
   • **Nature of the proceeding.** A phrase, or even a one-word description, is sufficient. For example, "suit by debtor for compensation for damages to debtor's car caused by accident," or "divorce."
   • **Court and location.** This information is on any Summons you received or prepared.

- **Status or disposition.** State whether the case is awaiting trial, is pending a decision, is on appeal or has ended.

b. If, at any time during the year before you file for bankruptcy, your wages, real estate or personal property was taken from you under the authority of a court order to pay a debt, enter the requested information. If you don't know the exact date, put "on or about" the approximate date.

5. Repossessions, foreclosures and returns. If, at any time during the year before you file for bankruptcy, a creditor repossessed or foreclosed on property you had bought and were making payments on, or had pledged as collateral for a loan, give the requested information. For instance, if your car, boat or video equipment was repossessed because you defaulted on your payments, describe it here. Also, if you voluntarily returned property to a creditor because you couldn't keep up the payments, enter that here.

6. Assignments and receiverships.

a. If, at any time during the 120 days (four months) before you file for bankruptcy, you assigned (legally transferred) your right to receive benefits or property to a creditor to pay a debt, list it here. Examples include assigning a percentage of your wages to a creditor for several months or assigning a portion of a personal injury award to an attorney. The assignee is the person to whom the assignment was made, such as the creditor or attorney. The terms of the assignment should be given briefly—for example, "wages assigned to Snorkle's Store to satisfy debt of $500."

b. Identify all of your property that has been in the hands of a court-appointed receiver, custodian or other official during the year before you file for bankruptcy. If you've made child support payments directly to a court, and the court in turn paid your child's other parent, list those payments here.

7. Gifts. Provide the requested information about gifts you've made in the past year. The bankruptcy court and trustee want this information to make sure you haven't improperly unloaded any property before filing for bankruptcy. List all charitable donations over $100 and gifts to family members over $200.

You don't have to list gifts to family members that are "ordinary and usual," but there is no easy way to identify such gifts. The best test is whether someone outside of the family might think the gift was unusual under the circumstances. If so, list it. Forgiving a loan is also a gift, as is charging interest substantially below the market rate. Other gifts include giving a car or prepaid trip to a business associate.

8. Losses. Provide the requested information. If the loss was for an exempt item, most states let you keep the insurance proceeds up to the limit of the exemption. (See Appendix 1.) If the item was not exempt, the trustee is entitled to the proceeds. In either case, list any proceeds you've received or expect to receive.

9. Payments related to debt counseling or bankruptcy. If you paid an improperly high fee to an attorney, bankruptcy petition preparer, debt consultant or debt consolidator, the trustee may try to get some of it back to be distributed to your creditors. Be sure to list all payments someone else made on your behalf as well as payments you made directly.

10. Other transfers. List all real and personal property that you've sold or used as collateral for a secured debt during the year before you file for bankruptcy. Some examples are selling or abandoning (junking) a car, pledging your house as security (collateral) for a loan, granting an easement on real estate or trading property.

Don't include any gifts you listed in Item 7. Also, don't list property you've parted with as a regular part of your business or financial affairs. For example, if you operate a mail order book business, don't list the books you sold during the past year. Similarly, don't put down payments for regular goods and services, such as your phone bill, utilities or rent. The idea is to disclose transfers of property that legally belongs in your bankruptcy estate.

EXAMPLE 1: Two years before filing for bankruptcy, Jack sold some personal electronic mixing equipment to a friend for a modest sum. Since this sale wasn't made within the previous year, Jack needn't list it here.

EXAMPLE 2: John has accumulated a collection of junked classic cars to resell to restoration hobbyists. Within the past year John has sold three of the cars for a total of $20,000. Since this is part of John's regular business, he needn't report the sales here.

```
Form 7
(9/00)
```

FORM 7. STATEMENT OF FINANCIAL AFFAIRS

UNITED STATES BANKRUPTCY COURT

_____Northern_____ **DISTRICT OF** _Ohio, Eastern Division_____

In re: __Maytag, Molly and Jonathan__ , Case No. _____
        (Name)   (if known)
            Debtor

STATEMENT OF FINANCIAL AFFAIRS

This statement is to be completed by every debtor. Spouses filing a joint petition may file a single statement on which the information for both spouses is combined. If the case is filed under chapter 12 or chapter 13, a married debtor must furnish information for both spouses whether or not a joint petition is filed, unless the spouses are separated and a joint petition is not filed. An individual debtor engaged in business as a sole proprietor, partner, family farmer, or self-employed professional, should provide the information requested on this statement concerning all such activities as well as the individual's personal affairs.

Questions 1 - 18 are to be completed by all debtors. Debtors that are or have been in business, as defined below, also must complete Questions 19 - 25. **If the answer to an applicable question is "None," mark the box labeled "None."** If additional space is needed for the answer to any question, use and attach a separate sheet properly identified with the case name, case number (if known), and the number of the question.

DEFINITIONS

"In business." A debtor is "in business" for the purpose of this form if the debtor is a corporation or partnership. An individual debtor is "in business" for the purpose of this form if the debtor is or has been, within the six years immediately preceding the filing of this bankruptcy case, any of the following: an officer, director, managing executive, or owner of 5 percent or more of the voting or equity securities of a corporation; a partner, other than a limited partner, of a partnership; a sole proprietor or self-employed.

"Insider." The term "insider" includes but is not limited to: relatives of the debtor; general partners of the debtor and their relatives; corporations of which the debtor is an officer, director, or person in control; officers, directors, and any owner of 5 percent or more of the voting or equity securities of a corporate debtor and their relatives; affiliates of the debtor and insiders of such affiliates; any managing agent of the debtor. 11 U.S.C. § 101.

_____

1. Income from employment or operation of business

None
☐

State the gross amount of income the debtor has received from employment, trade, or profession, or from operation of the debtor's business from the beginning of this calendar year to the date this case was commenced. State also the gross amounts received during the **two years** immediately preceding this calendar year. (A debtor that maintains, or has maintained, financial records on the basis of a fiscal rather than a calendar year may report fiscal year income. Identify the beginning and ending dates of the debtor's fiscal year.) If a joint petition is filed, state income for each spouse separately. (Married debtors filing under chapter 12 or chapter 13 must state income of both spouses whether or not a joint petition is filed, unless the spouses are separated and a joint petition is not filed.)

AMOUNT		SOURCE (if more than one)
$6,000	(1/1/XX–7/3/XX)	Wife's employment
$18,000	(1/1/XX–7/3/XX)	Husband's employment
$14,000	(20XY)	Wife's employment
$29,000	(20XY)	Husband's employment
$11,000	(20XZ)	Wife's employment
$16,000	(20XZ)	Husband's employment

2

2.   Income other than from employment or operation of business

None ☐   State the amount of income received by the debtor other than from employment, trade, profession, or operation of the debtor's business during the **two years** immediately preceding the commencement of this case. Give particulars. If a joint petition is filed, state income for each spouse separately. (Married debtors filing under chapter 12 or chapter 13 must state income for each spouse whether or not a joint petition is filed, unless the spouses are separated and a joint petition is not filed.)

AMOUNT	SOURCE
$300	20XX, stock dividends (J)
$740	20XY, stock dividends (J)
$4,000	20XX, worker's comp benefits (H)

3.   Payments to creditors

None ☐   a.   List all payments on loans, installment purchases of goods or services, and other debts, aggregating more than $600 to any creditor, made within **90 days** immediately preceding the commencement of this case. (Married debtors filing under chapter 12 or chapter 13 must include payments by either or both spouses whether or not a joint petition is filed, unless the spouses are separated and a joint petition is not filed.)

NAME AND ADDRESS OF CREDITOR	DATES OF PAYMENTS	AMOUNT PAID	AMOUNT STILL OWING
Ameritrust	4/17/XX	$650	$87,000
10 Financial Way	5/17/XX	$650	
Cleveland Hts, OH 44118	6/17/XX	$650	

None ☐   b.   List all payments made within **one year** immediately preceding the commencement of this case to or for the benefit of creditors who are or were insiders. (Married debtors filing under chapter 12 or chapter 13 must include payments by either or both spouses whether or not a joint petition is filed, unless the spouses are separated and a joint petition is not filed.)

NAME AND ADDRESS OF CREDITOR AND RELATIONSHIP TO DEBTOR	DATE OF PAYMENT	AMOUNT PAID	AMOUNT STILL OWING
Ellen Rogers	8/XX to 5/XY	$600/month	$600/month since 6/XY
900 Grand View			
Jackson, WY 83001			
(ex-wife, mother of husband's 2 children)			

4.   Suits and administrative proceedings, executions, garnishments and attachments

None ☐   a.   List all suits and administrative proceedings to which the debtor is or was a party within **one year** immediately preceding the filing of this bankruptcy case. (Married debtors filing under chapter 12 or chapter 13 must include information concerning either or both spouses whether or not a joint petition is filed, unless the spouses are separated and a joint petition is not filed.)

CAPTION OF SUIT AND CASE NUMBER	NATURE OF PROCEEDING	COURT OR AGENCY AND LOCATION	STATUS OR DISPOSITION
Cleveland Hospital v. Jonathan Maytag (H)	Suit for doctor's fee and medical bills	Cleveland Municipal Ct., Cleveland, OH	trial set 9/7/XX
Dennis Dentist v. Molly M. Maytag, #91-8080 (W)	Suit for dentist's fees	Cleveland Hts Small Claims Court, Cleveland, OH	*open*
Freedom Financial v. Jonathan & Molly Maytag #90-9101 (J)	Suit for unpaid American Express bill	Cleveland Municipal Ct., Cleveland, OH	open
American Allowance v. Jonathan & Molly Maytag #90-7400 (J)	Suit for unpaid VISA bill	Cleveland Municipal Ct., Cleveland, OH	open

3

None ☐ b. Describe all property that has been attached, garnished or seized under any legal or equitable process within **one year** immediately preceding the commencement of this case. (Married debtors filing under chapter 12 or chapter 13 must include information concerning property of either or both spouses whether or not a joint petition is filed, unless the spouses are separated and a joint petition is not filed.)

NAME AND ADDRESS OF PERSON FOR WHOSE BENEFIT PROPERTY WAS SEIZED	DATE OF SEIZURE	DESCRIPTION AND VALUE OF PROPERTY
Quality Collection Agency 21 Main Street Cleveland, OH 44115	on or about 2/XX	(J) bank account levy — $650
Quality Collection Agency 21 Main Street Cleveland, OH 44115	4/10/XX to 6/30/XX	(H) wage garnishment $850

5. Repossessions, foreclosures and returns

None ☐ List all property that has been repossessed by a creditor, sold at a foreclosure sale, transferred through a deed in lieu of foreclosure or returned to the seller, within **one year** immediately preceding the commencement of this case. (Married debtors filing under chapter 12 or chapter 13 must include information concerning property of either or both spouses whether or not a joint petition is filed, unless the spouses are separated and a joint petition is not filed.)

NAME AND ADDRESS OF CREDITOR OR SELLER	DATE OF REPOSSESSION, FORECLOSURE SALE, TRANSFER OR RETURN	DESCRIPTION AND VALUE OF PROPERTY
Ameritrust 10 Financial Way Cleveland Hts, OH 44118	6/18/XX repossessed	(J) 1987 Honda Civic, approximate value $4,500
Shaker Savings 44 Trust St. Cleveland Hts, OH 44118	6/30/XX repossessed	(J) 1985 Buick Skylark, approximate value $3,000

6. Assignments and receiverships

None a. Describe any assignment of property for the benefit of creditors made within **120 days** immediately preceding the commencement of this case. (Married debtors filing under chapter 12 or chapter 13 must include any assignment by either or both spouses whether or not a joint petition is filed, unless the spouses are separated and a joint petition is not filed.)

NAME AND ADDRESS OF ASSIGNEE	DATE OF ASSIGNMENT	TERMS OF ASSIGNMENT OR SETTLEMENT

None ☒ b. List all property which has been in the hands of a custodian, receiver, or court-appointed official within **one year** immediately preceding the commencement of this case. (Married debtors filing under chapter 12 or chapter 13 must include information concerning property of either or both spouses whether or not a joint petition is filed, unless the spouses are separated and a joint petition is not filed.)

NAME AND ADDRESS OF CUSTODIAN	NAME AND LOCATION OF COURT CASE TITLE & NUMBER	DATE OF ORDER	DESCRIPTION AND VALUE OF PROPERTY

4

7. Gifts

None
☒

List all gifts or charitable contributions made within **one year** immediately preceding the commencement of this case except ordinary and usual gifts to family members aggregating less than $200 in value per individual family member and charitable contributions aggregating less than $100 per recipient. (Married debtors filing under chapter 12 or chapter 13 must include gifts or contributions by either or both spouses whether or not a joint petition is filed, unless the spouses are separated and a joint petition is not filed.)

NAME AND ADDRESS OF PERSON OR ORGANIZATION	RELATIONSHIP TO DEBTOR, IF ANY	DATE OF GIFT	DESCRIPTION AND VALUE OF GIFT

---

8. Losses

None
☐

List all losses from fire, theft, other casualty or gambling within **one year** immediately preceding the commencement of this case **or since the commencement of this case.** (Married debtors filing under chapter 12 or chapter 13 must include losses by either or both spouses whether or not a joint petition is filed, unless the spouses are separated and a joint petition is not filed.)

DESCRIPTION AND VALUE OF PROPERTY	DESCRIPTION OF CIRCUMSTANCES AND, IF LOSS WAS COVERED IN WHOLE OR IN PART BY INSURANCE, GIVE PARTICULARS	DATE OF LOSS
Mountain bike; $165	Daughter Sara's bicycle was stolen. Insurance covered replacement. We purchased new bike on 12/17/XY.	10/5/XX

---

9. Payments related to debt counseling or bankruptcy

None
☐

List all payments made or property transferred by or on behalf of the debtor to any persons, including attorneys, for consultation concerning debt consolidation, relief under the bankruptcy law or preparation of a petition in bankruptcy within **one year** immediately preceding the commencement of this case.

NAME AND ADDRESS OF PAYEE	DATE OF PAYMENT, NAME OF PAYOR IF OTHER THAN DEBTOR	AMOUNT OF MONEY OR DESCRIPTION AND VALUE OF PROPERTY
John White, Esq. 21 Main St. Cleveland, OH 44114	2/11/XX	(J) $500 retainer fee paid

---

10. Other transfers

None

List all other property, other than property transferred in the ordinary course of the business or financial affairs of the debtor, transferred either absolutely or as security within **one year** immediately preceding the commencement of this case. (Married debtors filing under chapter 12 or chapter 13 must include transfers by either or both spouses whether or not a joint petition is filed, unless the spouses are separated and a joint petition is not filed.)

NAME AND ADDRESS OF TRANSFEREE, RELATIONSHIP TO DEBTOR	DATE	DESCRIBE PROPERTY TRANSFERRED AND VALUE RECEIVED

5

11. Closed financial accounts

None
☐

List all financial accounts and instruments held in the name of the debtor or for the benefit of the debtor which were closed, sold, or otherwise transferred within **one year** immediately preceding the commencement of this case. Include checking, savings, or other financial accounts, certificates of deposit, or other instruments; shares and share accounts held in banks, credit unions, pension funds, cooperatives, associations, brokerage houses and other financial institutions. (Married debtors filing under chapter 12 or chapter 13 must include information concerning accounts or instruments held by or for either or both spouses whether or not a joint petition is filed, unless the spouses are separated and a joint petition is not filed.)

NAME AND ADDRESS OF INSTITUTION	TYPE AND NUMBER OF ACCOUNT AND AMOUNT OF FINAL BALANCE	AMOUNT AND DATE OF SALE OR CLOSING
Ohio Savings 1818 Lakeshore Avenue Cleveland, OH 44123	(H) Checking account #058-118061 final balance $84.12	12/2/XY

12. Safe deposit boxes

None
☐

List each safe deposit or other box or depository in which the debtor has or had securities, cash, or other valuables within **one year** immediately preceding the commencement of this case. (Married debtors filing under chapter 12 or chapter 13 must include boxes or depositories of either or both spouses whether or not a joint petition is filed, unless the spouses are separated and a joint petition is not filed.)

NAME AND ADDRESS OF BANK OR OTHER DEPOSITORY	NAMES AND ADDRESSES OF THOSE WITH ACCESS TO BOX OR DEPOSITORY	DESCRIPTION OF CONTENTS	DATE OF TRANSFER OR SURRENDER, IF ANY
Ameritrust 10 Financial Way Cleveland Hts., OH 44118	Molly Maytag Jonathan Maytag 21 Scarborough Rd. So. Cleveland Hts, OH 41118	stock certificates for Trusso Corp., Investco Ltd., and Rayco Co.	N/A

13. Setoffs

None

List all setoffs made by any creditor, including a bank, against a debt or deposit of the debtor within **90 days** preceding the commencement of this case. (Married debtors filing under chapter 12 or chapter 13 must include information concerning either or both spouses whether or not a joint petition is filed, unless the spouses are separated and a joint petition is not filed.)

NAME AND ADDRESS OF CREDITOR	DATE OF SETOFF	AMOUNT OF SETOFF

14. Property held for another person

None
☐

List all property owned by another person that the debtor holds or controls.

NAME AND ADDRESS OF OWNER	DESCRIPTION AND VALUE OF PROPERTY	LOCATION OF PROPERTY
Paul & Bonnie Johnson 40 Mayfield University Hts, OH 44118	Poodle — Binkie $100	residence
Felicia Maytag 8 Superior Rd Cleveland, OH 44114	20XW Ford Pickup $750	residence

6

15. Prior address of debtor

None

If the debtor has moved within the **two years** immediately preceding the commencement of this case, list all premises which the debtor occupied during that period and vacated prior to the commencement of this case. If a joint petition is filed, report also any separate address of either spouse.

ADDRESS   NAME USED   DATES OF OCCUPANCY

16. Spouses and Former Spouses

None

If the debtor resides or resided in a community property state, commonwealth, or territory (including Alaska, Arizona, California, Idaho, Louisiana, Nevada, New Mexico, Puerto Rico, Texas, Washington, or Wisconsin) within the **six-year period** immediately preceding the commencement of the case, identify the name of the debtor's spouse and of any former spouse who resides or resided with the debtor in the community property state.

NAME

17. Environmental Information.

For the purpose of this question, the following definitions apply:

"Environmental Law" means any federal, state, or local statute or regulation regulating pollution, contamination, releases of hazardous or toxic substances, wastes or material into the air, land, soil, surface water, groundwater, or other medium, including, but not limited to, statutes or regulations regulating the cleanup of these substances, wastes, or material.

"Site" means any location, facility, or property as defined under any Environmental Law, whether or not presently or formerly owned or operated by the debtor, including, but not limited to, disposal sites.

"Hazardous Material" means anything defined as a hazardous waste, hazardous substance, toxic substance, hazardous material, pollutant, or contaminant or similar term under an Environmental Law

None

a.   List the name and address of every site for which the debtor has received notice in writing by a governmental unit that it may be liable or potentially liable under or in violation of an Environmental Law. Indicate the governmental unit, the date of the notice, and, if known, the Environmental Law:

SITE NAME   NAME AND ADDRESS   DATE OF   ENVIRONMENTAL
AND ADDRESS   OF GOVERNMENTAL UNIT   NOTICE   LAW

None

b.   List the name and address of every site for which the debtor provided notice to a governmental unit of a release of Hazardous Material. Indicate the governmental unit to which the notice was sent and the date of the notice.

SITE NAME   NAME AND ADDRESS   DATE OF   ENVIRONMENTAL
AND ADDRESS   OF GOVERNMENTAL UNIT   NOTICE   LAW

7

None

c. List all judicial or administrative proceedings, including settlements or orders, under any Environmental Law with respect to which the debtor is or was a party. Indicate the name and address of the governmental unit that is or was a party to the proceeding, and the docket number.

NAME AND ADDRESS   DOCKET NUMBER   STATUS OR
OF GOVERNMENTAL UNIT   DISPOSITION

18 . Nature, location and name of business

None

a. If the debtor is an individual, list the names, addresses, taxpayer identification numbers, nature of the businesses, and beginning and ending dates of all businesses in which the debtor was an officer, director, partner, or managing executive of a corporation, partnership, sole proprietorship, or was a self-employed professional within the **six years** immediately preceding the commencement of this case, or in which the debtor owned 5 percent or more of the voting or equity securities within the **six years** immediately preceding the commencement of this case.

If the debtor is a partnership, list the names, addresses, taxpayer identification numbers, nature of the businesses, and beginning and ending dates of all businesses in which the debtor was a partner or owned 5 percent or more of the voting or equity securities, within the **six years** immediately preceding the commencement of this case.

If the debtor is a corporation, list the names, addresses, taxpayer identification numbers, nature of the businesses, and beginning and ending dates of all businesses in which the debtor was a partner or owned 5 percent or more of the voting or equity securities within the **six years** immediately preceding the commencement of this case.

              TAXPAYER   BEGINNING AND ENDING
NAME   I.D. NUMBER   ADDRESS   NATURE OF BUSINESS   DATES

None

b. Identify any business listed in response to subdivision a., above, that is "single asset real estate" as defined in 11 U.S.C. § 101.

NAME   ADDRESS

The following questions are to be completed by every debtor that is a corporation or partnership and by any individual debtor who is or has been, within the **six years** immediately preceding the commencement of this case, any of the following: an officer, director, managing executive, or owner of more than 5 percent of the voting or equity securities of a corporation; a partner, other than a limited partner, of a partnership; a sole proprietor or otherwise self-employed.

*(An individual or joint debtor should complete this portion of the statement **only** if the debtor is or has been in business, as defined above, within the six years immediately preceding the commencement of this case. A debtor who has not been in business within those six years should go directly to the signature page.)*

N/A

8

19. Books, records and financial statements

None ☐ a. List all bookkeepers and accountants who within the **two years** immediately preceding the filing of this bankruptcy case kept or supervised the keeping of books of account and records of the debtor.

NAME AND ADDRESS   DATES SERVICES RENDERED

_____

None ☐ b. List all firms or individuals who within the **two years** immediately preceding the filing of this bankruptcy case have audited the books of account and records, or prepared a financial statement of the debtor.

NAME   ADDRESS   DATES SERVICES RENDERED

_____

None ☐ c. List all firms or individuals who at the time of the commencement of this case were in possession of the books of account and records of the debtor. If any of the books of account and records are not available, explain.

NAME   ADDRESS

_____

None ☐ d. List all financial institutions, creditors and other parties, including mercantile and trade agencies, to whom a financial statement was issued within the **two years** immediately preceding the commencement of this case by the debtor.

NAME AND ADDRESS   DATE ISSUED

_____

20. Inventories

None ☐ a. List the dates of the last two inventories taken of your property, the name of the person who supervised the taking of each inventory, and the dollar amount and basis of each inventory.

                                                         DOLLAR AMOUNT OF INVENTORY
DATE OF INVENTORY   INVENTORY SUPERVISOR   (Specify cost, market or other basis)

_____

None ☐ b. List the name and address of the person having possession of the records of each of the two inventories reported in a., above.

                                                         NAME AND ADDRESSES OF CUSTODIAN
DATE OF INVENTORY   OF INVENTORY RECORDS

9

21 . Current Partners, Officers, Directors and Shareholders

None ☐   a.   If the debtor is a partnership, list the nature and percentage of partnership interest of each member of the partnership.

NAME AND ADDRESS   NATURE OF INTEREST   PERCENTAGE OF INTEREST

None ☐   b.   If the debtor is a corporation, list all officers and directors of the corporation, and each stockholder who directly or indirectly owns, controls, or holds 5 percent or more of the voting or equity securities of the corporation.

NAME AND ADDRESS   TITLE   NATURE AND PERCENTAGE OF STOCK OWNERSHIP

22 . Former partners, officers, directors and shareholders

None ☐   a.   If the debtor is a partnership, list each member who withdrew from the partnership within **one year** immediately preceding the commencement of this case.

NAME   ADDRESS   DATE OF WITHDRAWAL

None ☐   b.   If the debtor is a corporation, list all officers, or directors whose relationship with the corporation terminated within **one year** immediately preceding the commencement of this case.

NAME AND ADDRESS   TITLE   DATE OF TERMINATION

23 . Withdrawals from a partnership or distributions by a corporation

None ☐   If the debtor is a partnership or corporation, list all withdrawals or distributions credited or given to an insider, including compensation in any form, bonuses, loans, stock redemptions, options exercised and any other perquisite during **one year** immediately preceding the commencement of this case.

NAME & ADDRESS
OF RECIPIENT,   DATE AND PURPOSE
RELATIONSHIP TO DEBTOR   OF WITHDRAWAL

AMOUNT OF MONEY
OR DESCRIPTION
AND VALUE OF PROPERTY

10

24. Tax Consolidation Group.

None
☐

If the debtor is a corporation, list the name and federal taxpayer identification number of the parent corporation of any consolidated group for tax purposes of which the debtor has been a member at any time within the **six-year period** immediately preceding the commencement of the case.

NAME OF PARENT CORPORATION   TAXPAYER IDENTIFICATION NUMBER

25. Pension Funds.

None
☐

If the debtor is not an individual, list the name and federal taxpayer identification number of any pension fund to which the debtor, as an employer, has been responsible for contributing at any time within the **six-year period** immediately preceding the commencement of the case.

NAME OF PENSION FUND   TAXPAYER IDENTIFICATION NUMBER

*   *   *   *   *   *

[If completed by an individual or individual and spouse]

I declare under penalty of perjury that I have read the answers contained in the foregoing statement of financial affairs and any attachments thereto and that they are true and correct.

Date   __July 3, 20XX__   Signature   *Molly Maytag* _____
                                  of Debtor

Date   __July 3, 20XX__   Signature   *Jonathan Maytag* _____
                                  of Joint Debtor
                                  (if any)

_____

[If completed on behalf of a partnership or corporation]

I, declare under penalty of perjury that I have read the answers contained in the foregoing statement of financial affairs and any attachments thereto and that they are true and correct to the best of my knowledge, information and belief.

                                     N/A

Date _____   Signature _____

                                     _____
                                     Print Name and Title

[An individual signing on behalf of a partnership or corporation must indicate position or relationship to debtor.]

_____ continuation sheets attached

Penalty for making a false statement: Fine of up to $500,000 or imprisonment for up to 5 years, or both. 18 U.S.C. § 152 and 3571

CERTIFICATION AND SIGNATURE OF NON-ATTORNEY BANKRUPTCY PETITION PREPARER (See 11 U.S.C. § 110)

I certify that I am a bankruptcy petition preparer as defined in 11 U.S.C. § 110, that I prepared this document for compensation, and that I have provided the debtor with a copy of this document.
                                   N/A

_____   _____
Printed or Typed Name of Bankruptcy Petition Preparer   Social Security No.

_____

_____
Address

Names and Social Security numbers of all other individuals who prepared or assisted in preparing this document:

If more than one person prepared this document, attach additional signed sheets conforming to the appropriate Official Form for each person.

X _____   _____
    Signature of Bankruptcy Petition Preparer   Date

A bankruptcy petition preparer's failure to comply with the provisions of title 11 and the Federal Rules of Bankruptcy Procedure may result in fines or imprisonment or both. 18 U.S.C. § 156.

EXAMPLE 3: Within a year previous to filing for bankruptcy, Louise, a nurse, sold a vintage Jaguar e-type for $17,000. Since this isn't part of her business, Louise should list this sale here.

11. Closed financial accounts. Provide information for each account in your name or for your benefit that was closed during the past year or transferred to someone else.

12. Safe deposit boxes. Provide information for each safe deposit box you've had within the past year.

13. Setoffs. A setoff is when a creditor, often a bank, uses money in a customer's account to pay a debt owed to the creditor by that customer. Here, list any setoffs your creditors have made during the last 90 days.

14. Property held for another person. Describe all property you've borrowed from, are storing for or hold in trust for someone. Examples are funds in an irrevocable trust controlled by you and property you're holding as executor or administrator of an estate.

If you list valuable items, the trustee will likely want more details. Some people have described all of their property as being in trust or otherwise belonging to someone else, hoping to escape giving it to the trustee. The tactic doesn't work. Include only property you truly hold for others.

EXAMPLE: You are renting an unfurnished apartment owned by a friend. The friend has left a valuable baby grand piano in your care. If and when you decide to move you have agreed to place the piano in storage for your friend. Since you don't own the piano but rather are taking care of it for your friend, you would describe it here.

15. Prior addresses. If you have moved within the two years before you file for bankruptcy, list all of your residences within those two years.

16. Spouses and Former Spouses. If you lived in a community property state within six years prior to filing for bankruptcy, list the name of your spouse and of any former spouses who lived with you in the community property state.

17. Environmental Information. This is self-explanatory. Read the questions carefully and provide the requested information, if applicable.

18. Nature, location and name of business. Provide the information requested in question "a." If the majority of your business income for any one business comes from renting, leasing or otherwise operating a single piece of real property (other than an apartment building with less than four units), include your business name and the address of the property in "b."

➡️ **Business debtors.** Only business debtors must complete questions 19–25. A business debtor is anyone who operated a profession or business, or who was otherwise self-employed, any time during the six years before filing for bankruptcy. If you are not a business debtor, type "N/A" right before question 19 and skip to the signature page.

19. Books, records and financial statements.

a. Identify every person other than yourself—usually a bookkeeper or accountant—who was involved in the accounting of your business during the previous two years. If you were the only person involved in your business's accounting, check "None."

b. If your books weren't audited during the past two years, check "None." Otherwise, fill in the requested information.

c. Usually, you, your bookkeeper, accountant, ex-business associate or possibly an ex-mate will have business records. If any are missing, explain. The more the loss of your records was beyond your control, the better off you'll be.

d. You may have prepared a financial statement if you applied to a bank for a loan or line of credit for your business or in your own name. If you're self-employed and applied for a personal loan to purchase a car or house, you probably submitted a financial statement as evidence of your ability to repay. Such statements include:

- balance sheets (which compare assets with liabilities)
- profit and loss statements (which compare income with expenses), and
- financial statements (which provide an overall financial description of a business).

20. Inventories. If your business doesn't have an inventory because it's a service business, check "None." If your business does deal in products, but you were primarily the middle person or original manufacturer, put "no inventory required" or "materials purchased for each order as needed." If you have an inventory, fill in the information requested in items "a" and "b."

21. Current Partners, Officers, Directors and Share-holders. Check "None" for "a" and "b."

22. Former partners, officers, directors and share-holders. Check "None" for "a" and "b."

23. Withdrawals from a partnership or distributions by a corporation. Check "None."

24. Tax Consolidation Group. Check "None."

25. Pension Funds. Check "None."

If completed by an individual or individual and spouse. Sign and date this section. If you're filing jointly, be sure your spouse dates and signs it as well.

If completed on behalf of a partnership or corporation. Type "N/A."

Certification and Signature of Non-Attorney Bank-ruptcy Petition Preparer. If a BPP typed your forms, have that person complete this section. Otherwise, type "N/A" anywhere in the box.

Be sure to insert the number of continuation pages, if any, you attached.

H. Form 8—Chapter 7 Individual Debtor's Statement of Intention

This form is very important if you owe any secured debts. All property that is security for a debt may end up in the creditor's hands, even if it's exempt, unless you use this form to describe how you plan to deal with the collateral in your bankruptcy. Briefly, you may reaffirm the debt (agree to repay it despite your bank-ruptcy), redeem the debt by buying the collateral at its fair market value, voluntarily surrender the collateral, or (in many states) get rid of the debt but retain the collateral by continuing to keep your payments current.

⚠ Each of these options is described in detail in Ch. 7, *Secured Debts.* Make sure to read that chapter carefully before you complete this form.

👫 **If you are married.** If you're filing jointly, complete only one form, even though it says "Individual Debtor's Statement of Intention."

Below is a completed Statement of Intention and instructions.

Court Name. Copy this information from Form 1—Voluntary Petition.

In re and **Case No.** Follow the instructions for Schedule A.

Chapter. Type in "7."

If you have no secured debts, type "N/A" after statement 1 and skip ahead to the signature section of the form.

Section a, Property to Be Surrendered. If you've decided to give up any (or all) property you've pledged as collateral for a secured debt, or the property has already been taken and you don't want to get it back, complete Section a. (If you need more space, use a continuation page.) If you plan to retain all property tied to your secured debts, type "N/A."

Section b, Property to Be Retained. If you will surrender all property tied to your secured debts, type "N/A." If you want to hold on to any of the property you've pledged as collateral for a secured debt, read Ch. 7, *Secured Debts*, and Ch. 6, *Your House* (if applicable), to understand your options. Then come back to this form and fill in Section b as follows:

Description of Property. Identify the collateral, such as "20XX Volvo" or "house at 316 Maiden Lane, Miami Beach, Florida."

Creditor's Name. List, on a separate line, the name of each creditor with a lien on the property listed in the first column.

Property is claimed as exempt; Property will be re-deemed; Debt will be reaffirmed. Check the appropriate column, for each creditor with a lien, based on what you read in Ch. 7, *Secured Debts,* and Ch. 6, *Your House.*

If your district lets you keep your property by stay-ing current on your payments (without reaffirming or redeeming) and you want to use this method (described in Ch. 7), fill in a description of the property in the first column. In the second column, fill in the creditor's name, followed by the words, "intend to retain property by keeping payments current on contract with creditor." Do not check any of the last three columns. If your district doesn't specifically allow this method but the creditor has informally agreed to let you retain the property by keeping your payments current, complete Section 2a, *Property to Be Surrendered*, by following the above instructions.

Form B8 (Official Form 8)
(9/97)

Form 8. INDIVIDUAL DEBTOR'S STATEMENT OF INTENTION

UNITED STATES BANKRUPTCY COURT
_____Northern_____ **DISTRICT OF** ___Ohio, Eastern Division___

In re Maytag, Molly and Jonathan,
     Debtor

Case No. _____

Chapter _____7_____

CHAPTER 7 INDIVIDUAL DEBTOR'S STATEMENT OF INTENTION

1. I have filed a schedule of assets and liabilities which includes consumer debts secured by property of the estate.
2. I intend to do the following with respect to the property of the estate which secures those consumer debts:

   a. *Property to Be Surrendered.*

Description of Property	**Creditor's name**
N/A	

   b. *Property to Be Retained*   *[Check any applicable statement.]*

Description of Property	Creditor's Name	Property is claimed as exempt	Property will be redeemed pursuant to 11 U.S.C. § 722	Debt will be reaffirmed pursuant to 11 U.S.C. § 524(c)
Residence	Ameritrust (mortgage)	X		
	Ameritrust (2nd mortgage)	X		
	Ohio Savings (judgment lien)			X
Computer	Computers for Sale		X	
Bedroom furniture	Fanny's Furniture		X	

Date: July 3, 20XX

Molly Maytag/Jonathan Maytag
Signature of Debtor

CERTIFICATION OF NON-ATTORNEY BANKRUPTCY PETITION PREPARER (See 11 U.S.C. § 110)

I certify that I am a bankruptcy petition preparer as defined in 11 U.S.C. § 110, that I prepared this document for compensation, and that I have provided the debtor with a copy of this document.

  N/A
Printed or Typed Name of Bankruptcy Petition Preparer   Social Security No.

Address

Names and Social Security Numbers of all other individuals who prepared or assisted in preparing this document.

If more than one person prepared this document, attach additional signed sheets conforming to the appropriate Official Form for each person.

X_____   _____
Signature of Bankruptcy Petition Preparer   Date

A bankruptcy petition preparer's failure to comply with the provisions of title 11 and the Federal Rules of Bankruptcy Procedure may result in fines or imprisonment or both. 11 U.S.C. § 110; 18 U.S.C. § 156.

Credit Card Debts

If you owe on a bank or department store credit card and want to keep the card through bankruptcy, contact the bank or store before you file. If you offer to "reaffirm" the debt, some banks or stores may let you keep the credit card. If you do reaffirm it, list it on the Statement of Intention, even though technically it isn't a secured debt. But think twice before you do this. If you don't reaffirm the debt, it will be discharged in bankruptcy—giving you the fresh start that is, after all, the point of the process.

Signature. Date and sign the form. If you're married and filing jointly, your spouse must also date and sign the form.

Certification of Non-Attorney Bankruptcy Petition Preparer. If a BPP typed your forms, have that person complete this section. Otherwise, type "N/A" anywhere in the box.

I. Mailing Matrix

As part of your bankruptcy filing, you are required to submit a list of all the creditors whom you want to get official notice of your bankruptcy. Called the mailing "matrix," this list must be prepared in a specific format prescribed by your local bankruptcy court. In a few courts, the form consists of boxes on a page in which you enter the names and addresses of your creditors. This is an artifact from the time when the trustee would use the form to prepare mailing labels. Now, however, most courts ask you to submit the list on a computer disk in a particular word processing format, or at least submit a computer printout of the names so that they may be scanned. You should check with the bankruptcy court clerk or the court's local rules to find out the precise format. Once you have the format down, take these steps:

Step 1: Make a list of all your creditors, in alphabetical order. You can copy them off of Schedules D, E, F and H. Be sure to include cosigners and joint debtors. If you and your spouse jointly

incurred a debt and are filing jointly, however, don't include your spouse. Also, include collection agencies or attorneys, if you've been sued. And if you're seeking to discharge marital debts you assumed during a divorce, include both your ex-spouse and the creditors.

Step 2: Make several copies of the Mailing Matrix form.

Step 3: If you are using the "box" format, enter your name and address in the top left-hand box on the sheet you designate as the first page. Then enter the names and addresses of each creditor, one per box and in alphabetical order (or in the order required by your local bankruptcy court). Use as many sheets as you need.

It is very important to be complete when preparing the matrix. If you leave a creditor off the matrix and the creditor does not find out about your bankruptcy by some other means, that debt may survive your bankruptcy —and you will have to pay it down the line.

J. How to File Your Papers

Filing your papers should be simple. Here's how to do it.

1. Basic Filing Procedures

Step 1: Make sure you have the following information:
- the specific order in which your court papers should be layered (the clerk will have a demonstration set of papers that shows you the correct order)
- the number of copies you'll need (typically four copies are required), and
- the amount of filing fees (currently $200).

Step 2: Put all your bankruptcy forms in the proper order.

Step 3: Check that you, and your spouse if you're filing a joint petition, have signed and dated each form where required.

Step 4: Make the number of copies required by the court (sometimes as many as four), plus:

- two additional copies of all forms (except the Statement of Intention)—one set for the clerk to file-stamp and give or send back to you when you file the papers, and one set for you to keep just in case your papers are lost in the mail (if you file by mail)
- one extra copy of the Statement of Intention for each person listed on that form, and
- one extra copy of the Statement of Intention for the trustee.

Step 5: Unless the court clerk will hole punch your papers when you file them, use a standard two-hole punch (copy centers have them) to punch the top/center of all your bankruptcy papers. Don't staple any forms together.

Step 6: If you plan to mail your documents to the court, address a 9" by 12" envelope to yourself. Although most people prefer to file by mail, you can take your papers to the bankruptcy court clerk. Going to the court will let you correct minor mistakes on the spot.

Step 7: If you can pay the filing and administrative fees when you file, clip or staple a money order (courts do not usually accept checks), payable to "U.S. Bankruptcy Court," to your original set of papers. If you want to pay in installments, attach a filled-in Application and Order to Pay Filing Fee in Installments, plus any additional papers required by local rules. Although you can pay the filing fee ($155) in installments, the administrative fee ($45) must be paid in full when you file your petition. Instructions for paying in installments are in Section 2, below.

Step 8: Take or mail the original and copies of all forms to the correct bankruptcy court (see Section A, above). Include either (1) payment of the full fee, or (2) payment of the administrative fee (currently $45) and an Application to Pay Filing Fee in Installments.

Step 9: In some courts, you may be required to send the Statement of Intention to your creditors. If you must, ask the court clerk for the name and address of the trustee assigned to your case. Then have a friend or relative (other than your spouse, if you are filing jointly) over the age of 18 mail, by first class, a copy of your Statement

of Intention to the bankruptcy trustee and to all the creditors listed on that form. Be sure to keep the original. You must do this within 30 days of filing your papers, but you should do it sooner.

Step 10: On a Proof of Service by Mail (a copy is in Appendix 4), enter the name and complete address of the trustee and all creditors to whom your friend or relative sent your Statement of Intention. Have that person sign and date the Proof of Service.

Step 11: Make a copy of the original Statement of Intention and of the Proof of Service your friend or relative signed. Staple the original Proof of Service to the original Statement of Intention, and send or take the originals to the bankruptcy clerk.

2. Paying in Installments

You must pay the $45 administrative fee in full when you file your petition. You can pay the $155 filing fee in up to four installments over 120 days. (Bankruptcy Rule 1006(b)(1).) To do so, you must file a completed Application to Pay Filing Fee in Installments when you file your petition. A blank copy of this form is in Appendix 4.

You cannot apply for permission to pay in installments if you've paid an attorney or BPP to help you with your bankruptcy.

The Application is easy to fill out. At the top, fill in the name of the court (this is on Form 1—Voluntary Petition), your name and your spouse's name if you're filing jointly, and "7" following the blank "Chapter." Leave the Case No. space blank. Then enter:

- the total filing fee you must pay: $200 (item 1)
- the amount you propose to pay when you file the petition: at least $45 (item 4, first blank)
- the number of additional installments you need: three maximum, and
- the amount and date you propose for each installment payment (item 4, second, third and fourth blanks).

You (and your spouse, if you're filing jointly) must sign and date the Application. If you use a BPP, have that person complete the second section. On the second page of the form, fill in the top of the form just as you did with the first page (name of court, debtor, Chapter "7"). Leave the rest blank. The judge will either approve the Application or modify it. The court will notify you of the judge's decision.

3. Emergency Filing

If you want to file for bankruptcy in a hurry to get an automatic stay, you can accomplish that in most places by filing Form 1—Voluntary Petition and a Mailing Matrix. Some courts also require that you file a cover sheet and an Order Dismissing Chapter 7 Case, which will be processed if you don't file the rest of your papers within 15 days. (Bankruptcy Rule 1007(c).) If the bankruptcy court for your district requires this form, you can get it from the court (possibly on its website), a local bankruptcy attorney or BPP.

If you don't follow up by filing the additional documents within 15 days, your bankruptcy case will be dismissed. You can file again, if necessary. If your case was dismissed when you opposed a creditor's request to lift the stay, you'll have to wait 180 days to refile.

For an emergency filing:

Step 1: Check with the court to find out exactly what forms must be submitted for an emergency filing.

Step 2: Fill in Form 1—Voluntary Petition. (See Section E, above.)

Step 3: On a Mailing Matrix (or whatever other form is required by your court), list all your creditors, as well as collection agencies, sheriffs, attorneys and others who are seeking to collect debts from you. (See Section I, above.)

Step 4: Fill in any other papers the court requires.

Step 5: File the originals and required number of copies, accompanied by your fee (or an application for payment of fee in installments) and a self-addressed envelope with the bankruptcy court. Keep copies of everything for your records.

Step 6: File all other required forms within 15 days. If you don't, your case will probably be dismissed.

K. Effect of Filing

Once you file your bankruptcy papers, your property is under the supervision of the bankruptcy court. Don't throw out, give away, sell or otherwise dispose of any property unless and until the bankruptcy trustee says otherwise. You can however, make day-to-day purchases such as groceries, personal effects and clothing with the income you earn after filing. If you have any questions about this, ask the bankruptcy trustee. ■

Handling Your Case in Court

For most people, the Chapter 7 bankruptcy process is straightforward and proceeds pretty much on automatic pilot. The bankruptcy trustee decides whether or not your papers pass muster and if not, what amendments you need to file. Ordinarily, you have few decisions to make.

This chapter tells you how to handle the routine procedures that move your bankruptcy case along, and how to deal with unexpected complications that may arise if:

- you or the trustee discover an error in your papers
- a creditor asks the court to lift the automatic stay
- you decide to object to a creditor's claim
- a creditor objects to the discharge of a particular debt
- a creditor objects to your claim that an item of property is exempt, or
- you decide to dismiss your case.

Some of these problems—fixing a simple error in your papers, for example—you can handle yourself. For more complicated problems, such as fighting a creditor in court about the discharge of a large debt, you'll need a lawyer's help.

A. Routine Bankruptcy Procedures

A routine Chapter 7 bankruptcy case takes three to six months from beginning to end and follows a series of predictable steps.

1. The Court Schedules the Meeting of Creditors

Shortly after you file for bankruptcy, the court sends an official notice to all the creditors listed in your mailing matrix. This notice contains several crucial pieces of information:

a. Your Filing Date and Case Number

This information puts the creditors on notice that you have filed for bankruptcy and gives them a reference number to use when seeking information about your case.

b. Whether the Case Is an Asset Case or a No-Asset Case

When you filled in the bankruptcy petition, you had to check one of the following two boxes:

- ☐ Debtor estimates that funds will be available for distribution to unsecured creditors.
- ☐ Debtor estimates that, after any exempt property is excluded and administrative expenses paid, there will be no funds available for distribution to unsecured creditors.

Your choice of these boxes determines the type of notice the court sends to your creditors. If you check the first box, your case is known as an "asset case" and your creditors will be advised to file a claim describing what you owe them. If you check the second box, your case will be known as a "no-asset" case and your creditors will be told to not file a claim. However, they will also be informed that they will have an opportunity to file a claim later if it turns out that there are funds available after all.

c. The Date for the Creditors Meeting

The notice also sets a date for the meeting of creditors (also called the "341 meeting"), usually several weeks later. Mark this date carefully—it is very important because:

- You must attend the creditors meeting; if you don't, your case can be dismissed
- Your creditors must file their claims (if it is an asset case) within 60 days after this meeting, and
- Your creditors must file any objections they have to the discharge of their debts within 60 days after this meeting.

2. You Notify Problem Creditors of the Stay

When the trustee mails your creditors official notice of your filing, the automatic stay goes into effect. The automatic stay prohibits virtually all creditors from taking any action to collect the debts you owe them until the court says otherwise. In general, creditors cannot:

- undertake any collection activities, such as writing letters or calling
- file lawsuits

How a Routine Bankruptcy Proceeds		
Step	**Description**	**When It Happens**
1. You notify problem creditors of your bankruptcy filing.	Call or send your own notice to any creditors whom you want to stop bothering you. A tear-out copy of such a notice is in Appendix 4.	As soon as you file your initial papers.
2. The court appoints a trustee.	The trustee's role is to examine your papers and manage your property.	Within a week or two after you file.
3. The court sets a date for the meeting of creditors.	The trustee sends notice of your bankruptcy and the date of the meeting to the creditors listed in your bankruptcy papers.	Shortly after you file.
4. You attend the meeting of creditors.	The meeting of creditors is the only court appearance most people make. The judge is not there and creditors seldom attend. The trustee and any creditors who show up can ask you about the information in your papers.	20–40 days after you file. (Bankruptcy Rule 2003; however, in many districts, the meetings are routinely held 45–90 days after you file.)
5. You and the trustee deal with your nonexempt property.	The trustee may collect your nonexempt property and sell it to pay your creditors. Or you may keep the property if you pay the court its market value in cash or give up exempt property of the same value.	Shortly after the meeting of creditors.
6. You deal with secured property.	If, on your Statement of Intention, you said you would surrender or redeem the collateral securing a debt, or reaffirm a secured debt, you must do so now.	Within 45 days of the date you file the Statement of Intention. (It is usually filed with your initial papers.)
7. The court grants your discharge.	If you reaffirm a debt, the court may schedule a brief final court appearance called a "discharge hearing." It doesn't require preparation on your part. Otherwise, you'll be mailed formal notice of your discharge.	Three to six months after you file.
8. Your case is closed.	The trustee distributes any remaining property to your creditors.	A few days or weeks after the discharge.

- terminate utility service or public benefits (such as welfare or food stamps)
- proceed with a pending lawsuit—all lawsuits are put on hold pending the outcome of your bankruptcy case
- withhold money in their possession as a setoff for a debt (although a creditor can cut off your access to money by freezing your account), or
- record liens against property. (11 U.S.C § 362(a).)

If a creditor takes any of these steps with knowledge that you filed for bankruptcy, you can take the creditor to court and recover damages and possibly attorney's fees. If the creditor had no knowledge of your bankruptcy, you may not be able to recover enough damages to justify going after the creditor in court, but whatever action the creditor took will be considered invalid and you can get it "undone." For instance, if a lawsuit is filed after you file for bankruptcy, the lawsuit will be dismissed.

There are some notable exceptions to the automatic stay, however. Even if you file for bankruptcy, the following proceedings can continue:

- a criminal case against you
- a case to establish paternity or to establish, modify or collect child support or alimony, and
- a tax audit, the issuance of a tax deficiency notice, a demand for a tax return, the issuance of a tax assessment and the demand for payment of such an assessment—the IRS cannot, however, record a lien or seize your property after you file for bankruptcy. (11 U.S.C. § 362(b).)

In addition, the bankruptcy court can lift the automatic stay for a particular creditor—that is, allow the creditor to continue collection efforts. (Lifting the automatic stay is covered in Section D, below.)

Creditors won't know that they have to stop their collection efforts until they receive notice of your bankruptcy filing. The notice sent by the court may take several weeks to reach your creditors. If you want quicker results, send your own notice to creditors (and bill collectors, landlords or sheriffs) whom you want to stop harassing you. A sample letter notifying your creditors is shown below. A tear-out form notice, which you can adapt to your own situation, is in Appendix 4. You can also call your creditors. Be prepared to give your bankruptcy case number, the date you filed and the name of the court in which you filed.

Notice to Creditor of Filing for Bankruptcy

Lynn Adams
18 Orchard Park Blvd.
East Lansing, MI 48823

June 15, 20XX

Cottons Clothing Store
745 Main Street
Lansing, MI 48915

Dear Cottons Clothing:

On June 14, 20XX, I filed a voluntary petition under Chapter 7 of the U.S. Bankruptcy Code. The case number is 43-6736-91. I filed my case *in pro per*; no attorney is assisting me. Under 11 U.S.C. § 362(a), you may not:

- take any action against me or my property to collect any debt
- enforce any lien on my real or personal property
- repossess any property in my possession
- discontinue any service or benefit currently being provided to me, or
- take any action to evict me from where I live.

A violation of these prohibitions may be considered contempt of court and punished accordingly.

Very truly yours,
Lynn Adams
Lynn Adams

If a creditor tries to collect a debt in violation of the automatic stay, you can ask the bankruptcy court to hold the creditor in contempt of court and to award you money damages. The procedures for making this request are beyond the scope of this book.

3. Attend the Meeting of Creditors

For most people, the creditors' meeting is brief. Very few, if any, creditors show up, and the trustee asks some questions about information in your forms.

If you don't show up, you may be fined by the judge. Even worse, your case may be dismissed. If you know in advance that you can't attend the creditors' meeting, call or visit the court clerk and try to reschedule the meeting.

 If you're married and filing jointly. Both you and your spouse must attend the meeting of creditors.

The meeting of creditors is the place where the trustee gets information from the debtor. Some trustees question a debtor more closely about items in the bankruptcy papers than others.

a. Preparing for the Creditors' Meeting

Before the meeting, call or visit the bankruptcy court clerk. Explain that you're proceeding without a lawyer ("in pro per") and ask what records you're required to bring. You should take a copy of every paper you've filed with the bankruptcy court. Also, bring copies of all documents that describe your debts and property, such as bills, deeds, contracts and licenses. Some courts also require you to bring financial records, such as tax returns and checkbooks.

If the clerk refuses to tell you what documents to bring, get the clerk's name. If you bring the wrong documents to the creditors' meeting, explain to the bankruptcy trustee what happened. Remember, you have a right to represent yourself. Although the clerks can't give legal advice, they're required to give you general information about the court's requirements.

Some people become anxious at the prospect of answering a trustee's questions and consider having an attorney accompany them. But if you were forthright with your creditors and honest in preparing your bankruptcy papers, there's no reason to have an attorney with you at the creditors' meeting. If you think you've been dishonest with a creditor or the court, or you have specific questions, see a lawyer before you go to court—or better yet, before you file. You can visit the bankruptcy court and watch other meetings of creditors if you think that might help alleviate some anxiety. Just call the clerk and ask when these meetings are held.

The night before the creditors' meeting, thoroughly review the papers you filed with the bankruptcy court. If you discover mistakes, make careful note of them.

You'll probably have to correct your papers after the meeting, an easy process. (Instructions are in Section B, below.)

After reviewing your papers, go over the list of questions the trustee is likely to ask you (below). Be sure you can answer them by the time of the meeting.

At the beginning of the meeting, the trustee may ask you whether you have read the Statement of Information required by 11 U.S.C. Section 341. If you read Chapters 1 and 2, you have learned all the information on this form. However, we set the form out here so you will be able to answer "yes" to the trustee's question.

Before you go to the creditors' meeting, make sure you have a photo ID (such as a driver's license, passport or identification card) and proof of your Social Security number. If you don't have a Social Security card or a standard photo ID, check with the court to see what it will accept.

b. The Routine Creditors' Meeting

Most creditors' meetings are quick and simple. You appear in the bankruptcy courtroom at the date and time stated on the bankruptcy notice. A number of other people who have filed for bankruptcy will be there too, for their own creditors' meetings. When your name is called, you'll be asked to sit or stand near the front of the courtroom. The court clerk will swear you in and ask your name, address and other identifying information. Then the trustee will briefly go over your forms with you, asking many of the questions listed below. Your answers to all questions should be truthful and consistent with your bankruptcy papers. The trustee is likely to be most interested in:

• anticipated tax refunds

STATEMENT OF INFORMATION REQUIRED BY U.S.C. § 341

Introduction

Pursuant to the Bankruptcy Reform Act of 1994, the office of the United States Trustee, United States Department of Justice, has provided this information to help you understand some of the possible consequences of filing a bankruptcy petition under Chapter 7 of the Bankruptcy Code. This information is intended to make you aware of—

1. The potential consequences of seeking a discharge in bankruptcy, including the effects on credit history
2. The effect of receiving a discharge of debts
3. The effect of reaffirming a debt
4. Your ability to file a petition under a different chapter of the Bankruptcy Code.

There are many other provisions of the Bankruptcy Code that may affect your situation. This information contains only general principles of law and is not a substitute for legal advice. If you have questions or need further information as to how the bankruptcy laws apply to your specific case, you should consult with an attorney.

What Is a Discharge?

The filing of a Chapter 7 petition is designed to result in a discharge of most of the debts listed on bankruptcy schedules. A discharge is a court order that says you do not have to repay your debts, but there are a number of exceptions. Debts which may not be discharged in a Chapter 7 case include:

Most taxes, child support, alimony, student loans, court-ordered fines and restitution, debts obtained through fraud and deception, and personal injury debts caused by driving while intoxicated or under the influence of drugs.

Your discharge may be denied entirely if you, for example, destroy or conceal property, destroy, conceal or falsify records or make a false oath. Creditors cannot compel you to pay any debts which have been discharged. You can only receive a Chapter 7 discharge once every six years.

What Are the Potential Effects of a Discharge?

The fact that you filed bankruptcy can appear on your credit record for as long as 10 years. Thus filing a bankruptcy petition may affect your ability to obtain credit in the future. Also, you may not be excused from repaying any debts that were not listed on your bankruptcy schedules or that you incurred after you filed bankruptcy.

What Are the Effects of Reaffirming a Debt?

After you file your petition, a creditor may ask you to reaffirm a certain debt or you may seek to do so on your own. Reaffirming a debt means that you sign and file with the court a legally enforceable document, which states that you promise to repay all or a portion of the debt that may otherwise have been discharged in a bankruptcy case.

Reaffirmation agreements are strictly voluntary. REAFFIRMATION AGREEMENTS ARE NOT REQUIRED BY THE BANKRUPTCY CODE OR OTHER STATE OR FEDERAL LAW. You can voluntarily repay any debt instead of signing a reaffirmation agreement, but there may be valid reasons for wanting to reaffirm a particular debt.

Reaffirmation agreements must not impose an undue burden on you or your dependents and must be in your best interest. If you decide to sign a reaffirmation agreement, you may cancel it at any time before the court issues your discharge order or within 60 days after the reaffirmation agreement is filed with the court, whichever is later. If you reaffirm a debt and fail to make the payments required in the reaffirmation agreement, the creditor can take action against you to recover any property that was given as security for the loan and you may remain personally liable for any remaining debt.

Other Bankruptcy Options

You have a choice in deciding what chapter of the Bankruptcy Code will best suit your needs. Even if you have already filed for relief under Chapter 7, you may be eligible to convert your case to a different chapter. (See the various chapters under bankruptcy which are included in the Notice to Individual Consumer Debtor in the packet of documents, B201.)

AGAIN, PLEASE CONSULT AN ATTORNEY IF YOU NEED FURTHER INFORMATION OR EXPLANATION, INCLUDING HOW THE BANKRUPTCY LAWS RELATE TO YOUR SPECIFIC CASE.

_____   _____

Debtor's Signature   Date

- any possible right that you have to sue someone because of a recent accident or business loss, and
- recent large payments to creditors or relatives.

If your answer to a trustee's question is different than what you said in your bankruptcy papers, the trustee will have reason to suspect your entire case— and your bankruptcy may change from a routine procedure to an uphill battle. If you have made mistakes, you should call them to the trustee's attention before he or she raises the issue. If you are caught in a contradiction, immediately explain how it happened. But this may prove difficult. For instance if someone else prepared your papers for you, you can't use that as an excuse. You are responsible for the information in your papers—which is why you should thoroughly review them before appearing.

When the trustee is finished questioning you, he or she will offer any creditors who have appeared an opportunity to ask you questions. Most often, no creditors show up. If any do appear, they will probably be secured creditors who want to clarify your intentions regarding the collateral securing the debt. Also, if you obtained any cash advances or ran up credit cards debts shortly before filing for bankruptcy, the credit card issuers may show up to question you about the circumstances and about what you did with the proceeds. And finally, a creditor might also ask for explanations if information in your bankruptcy papers differs from what was on your credit application. (See Ch. 3.) When the creditors are through asking questions, you're dismissed.

Except in highly unusual situations, the trustee and any creditors should be finished questioning you in five minutes or less. In busy courts, creditors' meetings often last no more than 90 seconds. When the trustee and creditors are done, you'll be dismissed—that is, told you can leave. If you have no secured debts or are reaffirming the ones you have, and your property is exempt, your case will effectively be over. No one will come to your house to inventory your property. No one will call your employer to confirm the information on your papers. Your bankruptcy case turns into a waiting game—waiting for the court to send you your notice of discharge and case closure. That should happen within six months after you originally filed your papers.

Common Questions at the Creditors Meeting

1. What is your full name and your current address?
2. Do you own or rent your home?
3. What is your spouse's name?
4. When were you married?
5. Have you made any voluntary or involuntary transfers of real or personal property within the last year?
6. Are any of your debts from credit card use?
7. Have you returned or destroyed your credit cards?
8. Are your schedules complete or do you want to make any changes?
9. Are you suing anyone?
10. Are you currently expecting a tax refund?
11. What caused your financial difficulties?
12. Have those difficulties ended?
13. How did you get the money to pay the filing fees for your bankruptcy case?

Hold Your Head High

No matter how well you prepare for the creditors' meeting, you may feel nervous and apprehensive about coming face to face with the trustee and possibly your creditors, to whom you've disclosed the intimate details of your finances over the last several years. You may feel angry with yourself and your creditors at having to be there. You may be embarrassed. You may think you're being perceived as a failure.

Nonsense. It takes courage to face your situation and deal firmly with it. Bankruptcy, especially when you're handling your own case without a lawyer, isn't an easy out. Let yourself see this as a turning point at which you're taking positive steps to improve your life. Go to the creditors' meeting proud that you've chosen to take control over your life and legal affairs.

c. Potential Problems at the Creditors' Meeting

If you or your papers give any indication that you own valuable nonexempt property, the trustee may question you vigorously. Or a creditor who's owed a lot of money may grill you about the circumstances of the debt, hoping to show that you incurred the debt without intending to pay it or by lying on a credit application, and that therefore it should survive bankruptcy. (See Ch. 8.)

You may also be closely questioned about why you claimed certain property as exempt. For some reason, some bankruptcy trustees, who are usually attorneys, believe that claiming exemptions requires legal expertise. If this happens to you, simply describe the process you went through in selecting your exemptions from Appendix 1. All the trustee can do if she disagrees is to object to your exemptions. (See Section D.2, below.)

4. Deal With Nonexempt Property

After the meeting of creditors, the trustee is supposed to collect all of your nonexempt property and have it sold to pay off your creditors. Normally, the trustee accepts the exemptions you claim on Schedule C and only goes after property you haven't claimed as exempt. If, however, the trustee or a creditor disagrees with an exemption you claimed and files a written objection with the bankruptcy court, the court will schedule a hearing. After listening to both sides, the judge will decide the issue. (See Section D, below.)

If you really want to keep certain nonexempt items and can borrow money from friends or relatives, or you've come into some cash since you filed for bankruptcy, you may be able to trade cash for the item. The trustee, whose sole responsibility at this stage is to maximize what your creditors get paid, is interested simply in what cash your property can produce, not in any particular item. So the trustee shouldn't mind taking cash in place of nonexempt property you want to keep.

EXAMPLE: Maura files for Chapter 7 bankruptcy and claims her parlor grand piano as exempt. The trustee disagrees, and the judge rules the piano to be non-exempt. To replace the piano on the open market might cost Maura $7,000. The trustee determines that the piano would probably sell for $4,500 at an auction,

and is willing to let Maura keep the piano for that amount.

The trustee may also be willing to let you keep non-exempt property if you volunteer to trade exempt property of equal value. For instance, the trustee might be willing to let Maura keep her nonexempt piano if she gives up her car, even though Maura could claim it as exempt in her state. Again, the trustee is interested in squeezing as many dollars as possible from the estate, and usually won't care whether the money comes from exempt or nonexempt assets.

5. Deal With Secured Property

When you filed your Statement of Intention, you told the trustee and your creditors whether you wanted to keep property that is security for a debt or give it to the creditor in return for cancellation of the debt. (Ch. 7, *Secured Debts,* discusses your options.) The law says you must carry out your intentions within 45 days of the date you filed the Statement.

For instance, if you have photography equipment that's security for a debt, and on the Statement of Intention you said that you wanted to redeem it by paying its fair market value to the creditor, the payment is supposed to be made within the 45-day period. Similarly, if you stated your intention to reaffirm a car note (by agreeing to have the debt survive bankruptcy) and continue making payments as before, you're supposed to sign a reaffirmation agreement within 45 days. If you planned to file a motion to avoid a lien on the property, the motion should be filed within 45 days.

Courts, however, have no practical way to enforce the 45-day deadline and generally will let you and the creditor work matters out. This means that you have some flexibility in dealing with your secured property. For instance, if you stated your intention to reaffirm a car note, but later discover that you can raise the cash to redeem the car, you can change your mind, amend your Statement of Intention and then arrange the redemption. If you stated your intention to redeem property but the 45-day period passes before you can raise the cash, you'll still be able to redeem the property if the creditor agrees to hold off.

But if you don't honor your intentions within the 45-day period, the creditor can ask the court for permission to take the collateral. And the court will probably grant it.

To avoid a sticky situation, do your best to honor the 45-day deadline. This means you should:

- sign a reaffirmation agreement if you said you were going to reaffirm the debt
- pay a creditor the property's fair market value if you want to redeem the property, or
- file the necessary court papers to eliminate the lien, or reduce it and informally pay it off.

You can find instructions for all these procedures in Ch. 7.

6. Attend the Discharge Hearing

You may have to attend a brief court hearing called a discharge hearing. At the hearing, the judge explains the effects of discharging your debts in bankruptcy and lectures you about staying clear of debt. You should receive a discharge order from the court within four weeks of the hearing. If you don't, call the trustee.

Most courts don't schedule a discharge hearing unless you stated on your Statement of Intention that you intended to reaffirm a debt. At the hearing, the judge warns you of the consequences of reaffirmation: you'll continue to owe the full debt, you may lose the collateral and the creditor can sue you if you default on your payments.

Whether or not you must attend a discharge hearing, you'll receive a copy of your discharge order from the court. The order will not specify which debts were discharged. It simply says that those debts which qualified for discharge were discharged. Nevertheless, you should make several photocopies of the order and keep them in a safe place. If it's necessary, be ready to send copies to creditors who attempt to collect their debt after your case is over or to credit bureaus that still list you as owing a discharged debt. A sample discharge order is below.

B. Amending Your Bankruptcy Papers

One of the outstanding aspects of bankruptcy procedure is that you can amend any of your papers at any time before your final discharge. This means that if you made a mistake on papers you've filed, you can correct it easily.

There may be a few exceptions to this rule. For instance, some courts will not let you amend your exemption schedule after the deadline for creditors to object to the exemptions has passed. Bankruptcy rules state clearly, however, that you have a right to amend any time before your case is closed. (Bankruptcy Rule 1009.) If you run into a judge who rules to the contrary, consult a bankruptcy attorney.

Some courts will require you to pay $20 to amend your bankruptcy papers. In others, you will only have to pay to amend if, as a result of your amendment, the court has to send a new notice to your creditors.

If you amend your schedules to add creditors before the meeting of creditors, you'll usually be required to provide the newly listed creditors with notice of the meeting and notice of your amendment. (Instructions are in Section B.2, below.)

If you become aware of debts or property that you should have included in your papers, amending your petition will avoid any suspicion that you're trying to conceal things from the trustee. If you don't amend your papers after discovering this kind of information, your bankruptcy petition may be dismissed or one or more of your debts may not be discharged.

Even if your bankruptcy case is already closed, you may be allowed to amend your papers to add an omitted creditor who tries to collect the debt. (See Ch. 5.)

Don't over-amend your papers. It's important to make changes, corrections, additions and deletions in as few amendments as possible. If you file amendments too many times, the court may not let you back into court until you get help from an attorney. The court's action may be illegal, but virtually impossible to challenge as a practical matter.

1. Common Amendments

Even a simple change in one form may require changes in several other forms. Here are some of the more common reasons for amendments and the forms that you may need to amend. Exactly what forms you'll have

Form 18. DISCHARGE OF DEBTOR
IN A CHAPTER 7 CASE

UNITED STATES BANKRUPTCY COURT

_____ DISTRICT OF _____

In re _____ ,   Case No. _____
           (Name)   (If known)

              Debtor

                                       Chapter _____

DISCHARGE OF DEBTOR

It appearing that the debtor is entitled to a discharge, **IT IS ORDERED**: The debtor is granted a discharge under section 727 of title 11, United States Code (the Bankruptcy Code).

Dated: _____

BY THE COURT

_____

United States Bankruptcy Judge

SEE THE BACK OF THIS ORDER FOR IMPORTANT INFORMATION.

EXPLANATION OF BANKRUPTCY DISCHARGE IN A CHAPTER 7 CASE

This court order grants a discharge to the person named as the debtor. It is not a dismissal of the case and it does not determine how much money, if any, the trustee will pay to creditors.

<u>Collection of Discharged Debts Prohibited</u>

The discharge prohibits any attempt to collect from the debtor a debt that has been discharged. For example, a creditor is not permitted to contact a debtor by mail, phone, or otherwise, to file or continue a lawsuit, to attach wages or other property, or to take any other action to collect a discharged debt from the debtor. *[In a case involving community property:]* [There are also special rules that protect certain community property owned by the debtor's spouse, even if that spouse did not file a bankruptcy case.] A creditor who violates this order can be required to pay damages and attorney's fees to the debtor.

However, a creditor may have the right to enforce a valid lien, such as a mortgage or security interest, against the debtor's property after the bankruptcy, if that lien was not avoided or eliminated in the bankruptcy case. Also, a debtor may voluntarily pay any debt that has been discharged.

<u>Debts That are Discharged</u>

The Chapter 7 discharge order eliminates a debtor's legal obligation to pay a debt that is discharged. Most, but not all, types of debts are discharged if the debt existed on the date the bankruptcy case was filed. (If this case was begun under a different chapter of the Bankruptcy Code and converted to Chapter 7, the discharge applies to debts owed when the bankruptcy case was converted.)

<u>Debts that are Not Discharged</u>.

Some of the common types of debts which are <u>not</u> discharged in a Chapter 7 bankruptcy case are:

a. Debts for most taxes.

b. Debts that are in the nature of alimony, maintenance, or support.

c. Debts for most student loans.

d. Debts for most fines, penalties, forfeitures, or criminal restitution obligations.

e. Debts for personal injuries or death caused by the debtor's operation of a motor vehicle while intoxicated.

f. Some debts which were not properly listed by the debtor.

g. Debts that the bankruptcy court specifically has decided or will decide in this bankruptcy case are not discharged.

h. Debts for which the debtor has given up the discharge protections by signing a reaffirmation agreement in compliance with the Bankruptcy Code requirements for reaffirmation of debts.

This information is only a general summary of the bankruptcy discharge. There are exceptions to these general rules. Because the law is complicated, you may want to consult an attorney to determine the exact effect of the discharge in this case.

to change depends on your court's rules. (Instructions for making the amendments are in Section B.2, below.)

a. Add or Delete Exempt Property on Schedule C

If you want to add or delete property from your list of exemptions, you must file a new Schedule C. You may also need to change:

- Schedule A, if the property is real estate and you didn't list it there
- Schedule B, if the property is personal property and you didn't list it there
- Schedule D and Form 8—Chapter 7 Individual Debtor's Statement of Intention, if the property is collateral for a secured debt and isn't already listed
- Form 7—Statement of Financial Affairs, if any transactions regarding the property weren't described on that form, or
- Mailing Matrix, if the exempt item is tied to a particular creditor.

b. Add or Delete Property on Schedules A or B

You may have forgotten to list some of your property on your schedules. Or, you may have received property after filing for bankruptcy. The following property must be reported to the bankruptcy trustee if you receive it, or become entitled to receive it, within 180 days after filing for bankruptcy:

- property you inherit or become entitled to inherit
- property from a marital settlement agreement or divorce decree, or
- death benefits or life insurance policy proceeds. (See Ch. 2, Section A.)

If you have new property to report for any of these reasons, you may need to file amendments to:

- Schedule A, if the property is real estate
- Schedule B, if the property is personal property
- Schedule C, if the property was claimed as exempt or you want to claim it as exempt
- Schedule D and Form 8—Chapter 7 Individual Debtor's Statement of Intention, if the property is collateral for a secured debt
- Form 7—Statement of Financial Affairs, if any transactions regarding the property haven't been described on that form, or

- Mailing Matrix, if the item is tied to a particular creditor.

If your bankruptcy case is already closed, see Ch. 5, Section A.

c. Change Your Plans for Secured Property

If you've changed your plans for dealing with an item of secured property, you must file an amended Form 8—Chapter 7, Individual Debtor's Statement of Intention.

d. Correct Your List of Creditors

To correct your list of creditors, you may need to amend:

- Schedule C, if the debt is secured and you plan to claim the collateral as exempt
- Schedule D, if the debt is a secured debt
- Schedule E, if the debt is a priority debt (as defined in Ch. 3)
- Schedule F, if the debt is unsecured
- Form 7—Statement of Financial Affairs, if any transactions regarding the property haven't been described on that form, or
- Mailing Matrix, which contains the names and addresses of all your creditors.

If your bankruptcy case is already closed, see Ch. 5.

e. Add an Omitted Payment to a Creditor

If you didn't report a payment to a creditor made within the year before you filed for bankruptcy, you must amend your Form 7—Statement of Financial Affairs.

2. How to File an Amendment

To make an amendment, take these steps:

Step 1: Fill out the Amendment Cover Sheet in Appendix 4, if no local form is required. Otherwise, use the local form. If you use our form, put *your* name, address and phone number in the upper left. In the "In re" box, put your name (and your spouse's name, if you are filing jointly).

Step 2: Make copies of the forms affected by your amendment.

Step 3: Check your local court rules or ask the court clerk whether you must retype the whole form to make the correction or if you can just type the new information on another blank form. If you can't find the answer, ask a local bankruptcy lawyer or non-attorney bankruptcy petition preparer. If it's acceptable to just type the new information, precede the information you're typing with "ADD:," "CHANGE:" or "DELETE:" as appropriate. At the bottom of the form, type "AMENDED" in capital letters.

Step 4: Call or visit the court and ask what order the papers must be in and how many copies are required.

Step 5: Make the required number of copies, plus one copy for yourself, one for the trustee and one for any creditor affected by your amendment.

Step 6: Have a friend or relative mail, first class, a copy of your amended papers to the bankruptcy trustee and to any creditor affected by your amendment.

Step 7: Enter the name and complete address of every new creditor affected by your amendment on the Proof of Service by Mail (a copy is in Appendix 4). Also enter the name and address of the bankruptcy trustee. Then have the person who mailed the Amendment to the trustee and new creditors sign and date the Proof of Service.

Step 8: Mail or take the original Amendment and Proof of Service and copies to the bankruptcy court. Enclose or take a money order for the filing fee, if required. If you use the mail, enclose a prepaid self-addressed envelope so the clerk can return a file-stamped set of papers to you.

If the meeting of creditors occurred before you file your amendment, the court is likely to schedule another one.

C. Filing a Change of Address

If you move while your bankruptcy case is still open, you must give the court, the trustee and your creditors your new address. Here's how to do it:

Step 1: Make one or two photocopies of the blank Notice of Change of Address and Proof of Service forms in Appendix 4.

Step 2: Fill in the Change of Address form.

Step 3: Make one photocopy for the trustee, one for your records and one for each creditor listed in Schedules D, E and F or the Mailing Matrix.

Step 4: Have a friend or relative mail a copy of the Notice of Change of Address to the trustee and to each creditor.

Step 5: Have the friend or relative complete and sign the Proof of Service by Mail form, listing the bankruptcy trustee and the names and addresses of all creditors to whom the Notice was mailed.

Step 6: File the original Notice of Change of Address and original Proof of Service with the bankruptcy court.

D. Special Problems

Sometimes, complications arise in a bankruptcy—usually when a creditor files some type of motion or objects to the discharge of a debt or the entire bankruptcy. If a creditor does this, the court will notify you by sending you a Notice of Motion or Notice of Objection. (See sample copy, below). At that point, you may need to go to court yourself or get an attorney to help you. Here are some of the more common complications that may crop up.

1. A Creditor Asks the Court to Lift the Automatic Stay

Your automatic stay lasts from the date you file your papers until the date you receive your bankruptcy discharge or the date your bankruptcy case is closed, whichever happens first. For example assume you receive a discharge but the trustee keeps your case open because she is waiting to collect your tax refund or an inheritance you are due to receive in the future. In this situation, the automatic stay would not be in effect after your discharge, even though your case would still be open.

As long as the stay is in effect, a creditor must get permission from a judge to take any action against you or your property that might affect your bankruptcy estate. To get this permission, the creditor must file a

Form 20A. Notice of Motion or Objection

UNITED STATES BANKRUPTCY COURT

_____ DISTRICT OF _____

In re _____ ,   Case No. _____
                        (Name)   (If known)
                                  Debtor

                                                          Chapter _____

NOTICE OF [MOTION TO   ] [OBJECTION TO   ]

_____ has filed papers with the court to [relief sought in motion or objection].

Your rights may be affected. You should read these papers carefully and discuss them with your attorney, if you have one in this bankruptcy case. (If you do not have an attorney, you may wish to consult one.)

If you do not want the court to [relief sought in motion or objection], or if you want the court to consider your views on the [motion] [objection], then on or before (date), you or your attorney must:

File with the court a written request for a hearing [or, _if the court requires a written response_, an answer, explaining your position] at:

[address of the bankruptcy clerk's office]

If you mail your [request] [response] to the court for filing, you must mail it early enough so the court will **receive** it on or before the date stated above.

You must also mail a copy to:

[movant's attorney's name and address]

[names and addresses of others to be served]

[Attend the hearing scheduled to be held on   (date) , (year) , at ___ a.m./p.m. in Courtroom _____, United States Bankruptcy Court, [address].]

[Other steps required to oppose a motion or objection under local rule or court order.]

If you or your attorney do not take these steps, the court may decide that you do not oppose the relief sought in the motion or objection and may enter an order granting that relief.

Date: _____   Signature: _____

                                                        Name:_____

                                                        Address: _____

request in writing, called a Motion to Lift Stay. The court will schedule a hearing on this motion and send you written notice. You will have a certain period of time to file a written response. Even if you decide not to file a response, you may still be able to appear in court to argue that the stay shouldn't be lifted. Check your local rules on this point.

If you don't show up for the hearing—even if you filed a written response—the stay will probably be lifted as requested by the creditor, unless lifting the stay would potentially harm other creditors. For instance, if the creditor is seeking permission to repossess your car, and your equity in the car would produce some income for your unsecured creditors if sold by the trustee, the court may refuse to lift the stay, whether or not you show up.

After hearing the motion, the judge will either decide the issue a decision then and there ("from the bench") or "take it under submission" and mail a decision in a few days. A creditor can ask a judge to lift the stay within a week or two after you file, but a delay of several weeks to several months is more common.

a. Grounds for Lifting the Stay

The bankruptcy court may lift the automatic stay for several reasons:

- The activity being stayed is not a legitimate concern of the bankruptcy court. For instance, the court may let a child custody hearing proceed, because its outcome won't affect your economic situation.
- The activity being stayed is going to happen, no matter what the bankruptcy court does. For instance, if a lender shows the court that a mortgage foreclosure will ultimately occur, regardless of the bankruptcy filing, the court will usually lift the stay and let the foreclosure proceed. (If you want to keep your house, you may be better off filing for Chapter 13 bankruptcy. See Ch. 6.)
- The creditor's interest in property you own or possess is being harmed by the stay. For instance, if you've stopped making payments on a car and it's losing value, the court may lift the stay. That would allow the creditor to repossess the car now, unless you're willing and able to periodi-

cally pay the creditor an amount equal to the ongoing depreciation until your case is closed.
- You have no ownership interest in property sought by the creditor. If you don't own some interest in property that a creditor wants, the court isn't interested in protecting the property—and won't hesitate to lift the stay.

Do You Have an Ownership Interest in the Property?

There are many kinds of ownership interests. You can own property outright. You can own the right to possess it sometime in the future. You can co-own it with any number of other owners. You can own the right to possess it, while someone else actually owns legal title.

For most kinds of property, there's an easy way to tell if you have an ownership interest: If you would be entitled to receive any cash if the property were sold, you have an ownership interest.

For intangible property, however—property you can't see or touch—it may be harder to show your ownership interest. For instance, if you have a one-year lease on your home, most bankruptcy courts would consider it an ownership interest in the property and would not lift the stay to let a landlord go ahead with eviction. But if the lease has expired, a court would probably rule that you have no ownership interest in the property and would lift the stay, allowing the eviction to go forward.

Another example of an unlikely ownership interest is the contractual right to continued coverage an insured person has under an insurance policy, which means the automatic stay prevents insurance companies from canceling insurance policies.

b. Opposing a Request to Lift the Stay

Generally, a court won't lift the stay if you can show that it's necessary to preserve your property for yourself (if it's exempt) or for the benefit of your creditors (if it's not), or to maintain your general economic condition. You may also need to convince the court that the creditor's investment in the property will be protected while the bankruptcy is pending.

Here are some possible responses you can make if a creditor tries to get the stay lifted.

- **Repossession of cars or other personal property:** If the stay is preventing a creditor from repossessing personal property pledged as collateral, such as your car, furniture or jewelry, the creditor will probably argue that the stay should be lifted because you might damage the collateral, or because the property is depreciating (declining in value) while your bankruptcy case is pending. Your response should depend on the facts. If the property is still in good shape, be prepared to prove it to the judge.

  If the property is worth more than you owe on it, you can argue that depreciation won't hurt the creditor, because the property could be repossessed later and sold for the amount of the debt or more. But if, as is common, you have little or no equity in the property, you'll need to propose a way to protect the creditor's interest while you keep the property—assuming you want it. One way to do this is to pay the creditor a cash security deposit that would offset the expected depreciation.

If you intend to keep secured property (see Ch. 7), you can argue that lifting the stay would deprive you of your rights under the bankruptcy laws. For example, if you intend to redeem a car by paying its fair market value, the court should deny the motion to lift the stay until you have an opportunity to do so.

- **Utility disconnections:** For 20 days after you file your bankruptcy petition, a public utility—electric, gas, telephone or water company—may not alter, refuse or discontinue service to you, or discriminate against you in any other way, solely on the basis of an unpaid debt or your bankruptcy filing. (11 U.S.C. § 366(a).) If your service was disconnected before you filed, the utility company must restore it within 20 days after you file for bankruptcy—without requiring a deposit—if you so request it.

  After 20 days, the utility is entitled to discontinue service unless you provide adequate assurance that your future bills will be paid. (11 U.S.C. § 366(b).) Usually, that means you'll have to come up with a security deposit.

  If you and the utility can't agree on the size of the deposit, the utility may cut off service, which

means you'll need to get a lawyer and ask the bankruptcy court to have it reinstated. If the utility files a motion to lift the stay, argue at the hearing that your deposit is adequate.

- **Evictions:** If you rely on the automatic stay to stop an eviction, expect the landlord to come barreling into court to have the stay lifted. Filing for bankruptcy has become a favorite tactic for some eviction defense clinics, who file a bare-bones bankruptcy petition to stop evictions even if the tenant's debts don't justify bankruptcy. In response, many bankruptcy courts are willing to grant landlords immediate relief from the stay without looking too closely at the case. This is true even if you have a legitimate bankruptcy.

2. The Trustee or a Creditor Disputes a Claimed Exemption

After the meeting of creditors, the trustee and creditors have 30 days to object to the exemptions you claimed. If the deadline passes and the trustee or a creditor wants to challenge an exemption, he is out of luck, even if the claimed exemption isn't supported by the exemption statutes. (*Taylor v. Freeland and Kronz,* 503 U.S. 638 (1992).) The objections must be in writing and filed with the bankruptcy court. Copies must be served on (personally handed or mailed to) the trustee, you and, if you have one, your lawyer. (Bankruptcy Rule 4003.)

Make Sure the Creditors' Meeting Is Closed

The 30-day period in which the trustee and creditors must file objections to exemptions starts running when the creditors' meeting is finished or "closed." But some trustees never officially "close" or "adjourn" the meeting. If this happens, the 30-day period to file objections never starts to run. Check the court file to make sure the trustee closed (or adjourned) the meeting of creditors. Otherwise, the trustee and creditors will have unlimited time to file objections.

a. Reasons for Objecting

The most common grounds for the trustee or a creditor to object are:

- The claimed item isn't exempt under the law. For example, a plumber who lives in New Jersey and selects his state exemptions might try to exempt his plumbing tools under the "goods and chattels" exemption. The trustee and creditors are likely to object on the ground that these are work tools rather than goods and chattels, and that New Jersey has no "tools of trade" exemption.
- Shortly before you filed for bankruptcy, you sold nonexempt property and purchased exempt property to cheat your creditors. (Ways to avoid this accusation are discussed in Ch. 2.)
- Property you claimed as exempt is worth more than you say it is. If the property's true value is higher than the exemption limit for that item, the item should be sold and the excess over the exemption limit distributed to your creditors.

   EXAMPLE: In Connie's state, clothing is exempt to a total of $2,000. Connie values her mink coat at $1,000 and her other clothes at $1,000, bringing her within the $2,000 exemption. A creditor objects to the $1,000 valuation of the coat, claiming that such mink coats routinely sell for $3,000 and up. If the creditor prevails, Connie would have to surrender the coat to the trustee. She'd get the first $1,000 (the exempt amount of the coat's sale price). Or, Connie could keep the coat if she gave the trustee $2,000 or other property of equivalent value.

- You and your spouse have doubled an exemption where doubling isn't permitted.

   EXAMPLE: David and Marylee, a married couple, file for bankruptcy using California's System 1 exemptions. Each claims a $1,900 exemption in their family car, for a total of $3,800. California bars a married couple from doubling the System 1 automobile exemption. They can only claim $1,900.

b. Responding to Objections

When objection papers are filed, the court schedules a hearing. The creditor or trustee must prove to the bankruptcy court that the exemption is improper. You don't have to prove anything. In fact, you don't have to respond to the objection or show up at the hearing unless the bankruptcy court orders—or local rules require—that you do so. Of course, you can—and probably should—either file a response or show up at the hearing to defend your claim of a legitimate exemption.

3. A Creditor Objects to the Discharge of a Debt

There are two possible reasons that a creditor may object to the discharge of a debt:
- the creditor claims that the debt is not dischargeable, or
- the creditor claims that the debt is secured and therefore, that you must reaffirm the debt, redeem the property or abandon the property.

a. Claims That the Debt Is Nondischargeable

Several types of debts can survive bankruptcy. (See Ch. 8.) Most of these debts are automatically nondischargeable. Others, however, survive bankruptcy only if the creditor successfully raises an objection in the bankruptcy court within 60 days after the meeting of creditors. Briefly, they are:
- debts incurred on the basis of fraud, such as lying on a credit application
- debts from willful and malicious injury to another or another's property, including assault, battery, false imprisonment, libel and slander
- debts from larceny, breach of trust or embezzlement, and
- debts arising from a marital settlement agreement or divorce decree (other than child support or alimony, which are automatically nondischargeable).

To object formally to the discharge of a debt, the creditor must file a document called a Complaint to Determine Dischargeability of a Debt. A copy of the complaint must be delivered to you and the trustee.

To defend against the objection, you must file a written response within a specified time limit and be prepared to argue your case in court.

If the creditor's debt is one of the first three types listed above, the creditor has the burden of proving that the debt fits within the specified category. For instance, if the debt is alleged to arise from a "willful and malicious injury" you caused, the creditor will have to prove the willful and malicious nature of your acts. Similarly, if the creditor is arguing that a particular debt arose from your fraudulent acts, the creditor will have to prove that all the required elements of fraud were present. Absent this proof, the bankruptcy court will reject the creditor's lawsuit.

The fact that the creditor has the burden of proof doesn't mean that you should sit back and do nothing. You should be prepared with proof of your own to show that the creditor's allegations in the complaint are not true.

If the debt fits within the fourth category (debts—other than child support or alimony—that arise from a divorce decree or marital settlement agreement), the burdens of proof are a little different. Once the creditor establishes the core facts—that is, that the debt arose from a divorce decree or marital settlement agreement—you will have the burden of showing that:
- based on your assets, income and other obligations, you will not be able to pay the debt after your bankruptcy case is over, or
- even if you can afford to pay the debt after your bankruptcy case, the benefit you would receive from the discharge outweighs any detriment your ex-spouse or child would suffer because of the discharge.

i. Credit Card Fraud

Increasingly, the creditors most likely to object to the discharge of a debt are credit card issuers. Except for the situations outlined in Ch. 8, Section C, there are no specific rules about what constitutes credit card fraud in bankruptcy. But courts are increasingly looking to the following factors to determine fraud:
- a short time between incurring the charges and filing for bankruptcy

- incurring more debt after consulting an attorney
- recent charges over $1,150
- many charges under $50 (to avoid pre-clearance of the charge by the credit card issuer) when you've reached your credit limit
- charges after the card issuer has ordered you to return the card or sent several "past due" notices
- changes in your pattern of use of the card (for instance, much travel after a sedentary life)
- charges made when you were clearly insolvent and wouldn't be able to make the required minimum payment (for instance, you had lost your job and had no other income or savings)
- charges for luxuries, and
- multiple charges on the same day.

Banks claim that insolvency is evidenced by any of the following:

- A notation in the customer's file that the customer has met with an attorney.
- A rapid increase in spending, quickly followed by 60–90 days of quiet.
- The date noted on any attorneys' fee statement, if the customer consults a lawyer for help with a bankruptcy. Thus, if you pay a bankruptcy professional for help and submit a fee statement, be sure to put the date of your filing on that form. If you use an earlier date, your creditors may claim you knew you were insolvent at that earlier date and that all subsequent purchases should be declared nondischargeable.

Of course, the mere fact that a creditor challenges your discharge of a credit card debt doesn't mean the creditor is right. In most of these cases, the creditor files a standard 15- to 20-paragraph form complaint, which states conclusions without supporting facts. The creditor rarely attaches statements for the account, but only a printout of the charges to which it is objecting.

Some very sophisticated debtors may be able to represent themselves in this type of case. If you decide to do this, you'll need lots of time to familiarize yourself with general litigation procedures and strategies, as well as the bankruptcy cases in your district that deal with this issue. Start by getting a copy of *Represent Yourself in Court*, by Paul Bergman and Sara Berman-Barrett (Nolo). That book shows you how to file and serve papers, gather evidence through a formal procedure called discovery, make and respond to motions

and try your own case. Engaging in formal discovery can be very helpful in this kind of case. For example, you may want to send the credit card issuer a set of questions (called interrogatories) to answer under oath, asking the following:

- You have alleged that the debtor obtained funds from you by false pretenses and false representations. Please state with particularity the nature of the false pretenses and false representations.
- State all steps taken by you to determine the creditworthiness of the debtor.
- Identify all means you used to verify the debtor's income, expenses, assets or liabilities. Identify any documents obtained in the verification process.
- Identify your general policies concerning the decision to grant credit and how those policies were applied to the debtor.
- You have alleged that at the time the debtor obtained credit from you he/she did not intend to repay it. State all facts in your possession to support this allegation.
- Identify all credit policies you allege were violated by the debtor. State how such policies were communicated to the debtor and identify all documents which contained those policies.
- Identify the dates on which you claim any of the following events occurred:
  ○ The debtor consulted a bankruptcy attorney.
  ○ The debtor had a reduction in income.
  ○ The debtor formed the intent not to repay this debt.
  ○ The debtor violated the terms of the credit agreement.
- State whether you believe that every user of a credit card who does not later repay the debt has committed fraud.
- If the answer to the preceding question is no, state all facts that give rise to fraud in this debtor's use of the card.

After receiving a list of questions like these, the credit card issuer is likely to conclude that you are serious about defending yourself. There is a good chance that it will withdraw its complaint.

If you want to read cases supporting the debtor's position where a credit card issuer claimed fraud, visit a law library or search the Internet for any of the following:

- *In re Hearn*, 211 B.R. 774 (N.D. Ga. 1997)
- *In re Etto*, 210 B.R. 734 (N.D. Ohio 1997)
- *In re Hunter*, 210 B.R. 212 (M.D. Fla. 1997)
- *In re Davis*, 176 B.R. 118 (W.D. N.Y. 1994)
- *In re Kitzmiller,* 206 B.R. 424 (N.D. W.Va. 1997)
- *In re McDaniel,* 202 B.R. 74 (N.D. Tex. 1996)
- *In re Christensen*, 193 B.R. 863 (N.D. Ill. 1996)
- *In re Chinchilla*, 202 B.R. 1010 (S.D. Fla. 1996)
- *In re Grayson*, 199 B.R. 397 (W.D. Mo. 1996)
- *In re Vianese*, 195 B.R. 572 (N.D. N.Y. 1995).

Bankruptcy Resource. An excellent resource is *Discharging Credit Card Debts in Bankruptcy,* by James P. Caher (LRP Publications). You can contact LRP Publications at: 800-341-7874 (phone) or 215-784-9639 (fax) or 215-658-0938 (TYY) or custserve@LRP.com (email). The cost of the book is about $30.

b. Claims That the Debt Is Secured

Some creditors object to the discharge of a debt by claiming that the debt is secured and that the debtor must therefore reaffirm the debt, redeem the property or abandon the property. (These options are discussed in Ch. 7.)

If you believe the debt is not secured, you must respond to the creditor's claim. Usually, this means filing a complaint or motion and asking the court to decide the claim in a separate proceeding. To do this, you'll probably have to consult with a bankruptcy attorney.

Often, a debtor's argument that a piece of property is not secured is based on one of two grounds:

- The security interest itself is invalid. This might be the case if the creditor didn't comply with certain requirements, like describing the property in the security agreement or properly notifying the debtor of the security interest (for example, by "burying" the notice of security interest in the fine print of a sales receipt).
- The value of the collateral is much lower than the amount of the debt. In this situation, the court may find that the debt is no longer secured or is only "nominally" secured and wipe out the debt.

If the creditor is correct and the debt is secured, you then must decide whether to surrender the property, redeem the property or reaffirm the debt. (These options, and how to pursue them, are discussed in Ch.7.)

4. You Want to Get Back Exempt Property Taken by a Creditor

You may have filed bankruptcy after a creditor:

- repossessed collateral (such as a car) under a security agreement, or
- seized some of your property as part of a judgment collection action.

If so, you should have described the event in your Statement of Financial Affairs, which you filed along with your bankruptcy petition and schedules. Repossessions are difficult to undo because they occur under a contract that you voluntarily entered into. However, property seized to satisfy a judgment can be pulled back into your bankruptcy estate if the seizure occurred within the three months before you filed. If the property is not exempt (or at least some of it is not exempt), the trustee may go after it so that it can be sold for the benefit of your unsecured creditors. If the property is exempt (meaning you are entitled to keep it), you can go after it yourself. However, you'll have to file a formal complaint in the bankruptcy court against the creditor.

The process for getting the bankruptcy judge to order property returned to you is a complex one; you'll probably need the assistance of an attorney. Given the cost of attorneys, it's seldom worth your while to go after this type of property unless it's valuable or an irreplaceable family heirloom. Keep in mind that most property is only exempt up to a certain value—for example, a car may be exempt up to $1,200, furnishings up to $1,000. Thus, even if you get the property back, it may still be sold by the trustee, in which case you'll receive only the exempt amount from the proceeds.

5. You Want to Dismiss Your Case

If you change your mind after you file for bankruptcy, you can ask the court to dismiss your case.

Common reasons for wanting to dismiss your case include the following:

- You discover that a major debt you thought was dischargeable isn't. You don't have enough other debts to justify your bankruptcy case.
- You realize that an item of property you thought was exempt isn't. You don't want to lose it in bankruptcy.
- You come into a sum of money and can afford to pay your debts.
- You realize that you have more property in your estate than you thought and decide that you don't have to file for bankruptcy after all.
- Your bankruptcy case turns out to be more complex than you originally thought. You need a lawyer, but you don't have the money to hire one.
- The emotional stress of bankruptcy is too much for you.

It is within the court's discretion to dismiss your case. That means the court can grant or refuse the dismissal. What the court does may vary from district to district. In some districts, dismissing a case is next to impossible, if your bankruptcy estate has assets that can be sold. However, if yours is a no-asset case and no creditor objects to the dismissal, you may have better luck dismissing it.

If you want to dismiss your case, you must file a request with the court. Instructions on how to do this follow. Depending on how receptive your local bankruptcy court is to dismissal, you may need the help of a lawyer.

Step 1: Refer to your court's local rules for time limits, format of papers and other requirements for voluntary dismissals. If you can't find the precise information you need from reading your local rules, ask the court clerk, the trustee assigned to your case, a local bankruptcy petition preparer or a bankruptcy lawyer for help.

Step 2: Make at least three copies of the blank, line-numbered legal paper in Appendix 4 (to allow for mistakes). Type from line number 1 to line 14 as follows (see samples, below):

Line 1: Your name, and that of your spouse if you're filing jointly.

Line 1.5: Your address.

Line 2: Your city, state and zip code.

Line 2.5: Your phone number.

Line 3: Type: Debtor in Pro Per.

Line 8: Center and type UNITED STATES BANKRUPTCY COURT, in capital letters.

Line 9: Center and type the judicial district and state you are in. Get this information from your bankruptcy petition.

Lines 10-14: Type as shown in the example.

Step 3: Make a few photocopies of the page with the information you have typed so far. This will save you typing later, because you can use this same heading for both forms.

Step 4: Using one of the copies that you just made, start typing again at line 16. Prepare a PETITION FOR VOLUNTARY DISMISSAL, as shown in the sample. In paragraph three, describe your reason for dismissing your bankruptcy case.

Step 5: Using another of your copies, start typing again at line 16. This time, prepare an ORDER GRANTING VOLUNTARY PETITION, as shown in the sample.

Step 6: Make at least three copies of each form.

Step 7: Take your originals and copies to the bankruptcy court clerk. When you get to the court clerk, explain that you are filing a petition to dismiss your case. The clerk will take your originals and one or more of your copies. Ask the clerk the following:

- What notice to your creditors is required?
- If there is a problem, will you be contacted? If not, how will you learn of the problem?
- If the judge signs the Order, when can you expect to get it?
- Once you have a signed order, who sends copies to your creditors—you or the court? If you send the copies, do you also have to file a Proof of Service?

Step 8: Once you receive the signed order, put it away for safekeeping if you don't have to notify your creditors. If you do, make copies and send one to each.

Step 9: If you have to file a Proof of Service, follow the instructions in Ch. 8, Section B.2.

Petition for Voluntary Dismissal

1 John Doe
   1111 Any Street
2 Berkeley, CA 94700
   (510) 555-1223
3 Debtor in Pro Per

4

5

6

7

8   UNITED STATES BANKRUPTCY COURT

9   NORTHERN DISTRICT OF CALIFORNIA

10

   In re:)   Case No. 12-34567 NS
11 John Doe,   )
)
12   )   PETITION FOR VOLUNTARY DISMISSAL
)
13   Debtor(s)   )
   _____)

14

15   The debtor in the above-mentioned case hereby moves to dismiss his bankruptcy case for the following reasons:

16   1. Debtor filed a voluntary petition under Chapter 7 of the Bankruptcy Code on September 12, 20xx.

17   2. No complaints objecting to discharge or to determine the dischargeability of any debts have been filed in

18 the case.

19   3. Debtor realizes that filing a Chapter 7 bankruptcy petition was erroneous. Debtor now realizes that a

20 particular debt may not be dischargeable. Debtor would have to litigate this matter, and Debtor does not feel he

21 has the ability to do so on his own nor the resources to hire an attorney to do it for him. Debtor intends to pursue

22 other means of handling his debts.

23   4. No creditor has filed a claim in this case.

24   5. No creditor has requested relief from the automatic stay.

25   WHEREFORE, Debtor prays that this bankruptcy case be dismissed without prejudice.

26 Date: _____   _____
27   Signature of Debtor

28 Date: _____   _____
                                       Signature of Debtor's Spouse

Order Granting Voluntary Dismissal

1 John Doe
   1111 Any Street
2 Berkeley, CA 94700
   (510) 555-1223
3 Debtor in Pro Per

4

5

6

7

8   UNITED STATES BANKRUPTCY COURT

9   NORTHERN DISTRICT OF CALIFORNIA

10

   In re:)   Case No. 12-34567 NS
11 John Doe,   )
)
12   )   ORDER GRANTING VOLUNTARY DISMISSAL
)
13 _____ Debtor(s) _____)

14

15

16   AND NOW, this _____ day of _____, 20____, the Court having found

17 that the voluntary dismissal of this case is in the best interests of the debtor and does not prejudice the rights of

18 any of his creditors, it is hereby ordered that the petition for voluntary dismissal is approved.

19

20 Dated: _____   _____

21   U.S. Bankruptcy Judge

22

23

24

25

26

27

28

Life After Bankruptcy

Congratulations! After you receive your final discharge and your case is closed, you can get on with your life and enjoy the fresh start that bankruptcy offers. You may, however, want to rebuild your credit, and you may still need to deal with one or more of the following events:

- You receive or discover new nonexempt property.
- A creditor tries to collect a nondischargeable debt.
- A creditor tries to collect a debt that has been discharged.
- A creditor or the trustee asks the court to revoke your discharge.
- A government agency or private employer discriminates against you because of your bankruptcy.

A. Newly Acquired or Discovered Property

If you omit property from your bankruptcy papers, or you acquire certain kinds of property soon after you file, the trustee may reopen your case after your discharge (if the trustee learns about property). The trustee probably won't reopen it, however, unless the property is nonexempt and is valuable enough to justify the expense of reopening the case, seizing and selling the property and distributing the proceeds among your creditors. If the after-discharge property you acquire or discover is of little value, however, tell the trustee about it, even if you think the assets don't justify reopening the case. That is the trustee's decision, not yours.

1. Notifying the Trustee

It's your legal responsibility to notify the bankruptcy trustee if:

- within 180 days of filing for bankruptcy, you receive or become entitled to receive property that belongs in your bankruptcy estate, or
- you failed to list some of your nonexempt property in your bankruptcy papers.

a. Newly Acquired Property

If you receive or become entitled to receive certain property within 180 days after your bankruptcy filing

date, it must be reported to the trustee, even if you think the property is exempt or your case is already closed. If you don't report it and the trustee learns of your acquisition, the trustee could ask the court to revoke the discharge of your debts. (See Section E, below.) You must report:

- an inheritance (property you receive or become entitled to receive because of someone's death)
- property from a divorce settlement, or
- proceeds of a life insurance policy or death benefit plan. (11 U.S.C. § 541(a)(5).)

These categories of property are discussed in more detail in Ch. 2, Section A.

To report this property to the trustee, use the form called Supplemental Schedule for Property Acquired After Bankruptcy Discharge. A blank copy is in Appendix 4. The form is self-explanatory. When you've filled it out, follow these steps:

Step 1: Photocopy a Proof of Service by Mail (a blank copy is in Appendix 4) and fill it out, but don't sign it.

Step 2: Make two photocopies of the Supplemental Schedule and the Proof of Service.

Step 3: Have a friend or relative mail the original Supplemental Schedule and a copy of the Proof of Service to the trustee and then sign the original Proof of Service.

Step 4: File a copy of the Supplemental Schedule and the original Proof of Service with the bankruptcy court. No additional filing fee is required.

Step 5: Keep a copy of the Supplemental Schedule and the Proof of Service for your records.

In some areas, the court may require you to file amended bankruptcy papers. If that happens, follow the instructions in Ch. 4, Section B.

b. Property Not Listed in Your Papers

If, after your bankruptcy case is closed, you discover some nonexempt property that you should have listed in your bankruptcy papers, you don't need to file any documents with the court. You must, however, notify the trustee. A sample letter is shown below.

Letter to Trustee

> 1900 Wishbone Place
> Wilkes-Barre, PA 18704
>
>
> October 22, 20XX
>
> Francine J. Chen
> Trustee of the Bankruptcy Court
> 217 Federal Building
> 197 S. Main St.
> Wilkes-Barre, PA 18701
>
> Dear Ms. Chen:
>
> I've just discovered that I own some property I didn't know of while my bankruptcy case was open. Apparently, when I was a child I inherited a bank account from my uncle, the proceeds of which were supposed to be turned over to me when I turned 21. Although I turned 21 eight years ago, for some unknown reason I never got the money.
>
> The account, #2424 5656-08 in the Bank of New England, 1700 Minuteman Plaza, Boston, MA 02442, has a balance of $4,975.19. As you know, I opted for the federal exemptions in my case and do not own a home. I believe this property would be exempt under 11 U.S.C. § 522(d)(5). Please let me know how you intend to proceed.
>
> Sincerely,
> *Ondine Wallace*
> Ondine Wallace

2. Reopening Your Bankruptcy Case

If any of the new property or newly discovered property is valuable and nonexempt, the trustee may try to reopen your case, take the property and have it sold to pay your creditors. The trustee will probably opt to do this if it looks like the profit from selling the property will be large enough to offset the cost of reopening your bankruptcy case and administering the sale.

To reopen a case, the trustee files a complaint with the court, asking for authorization to sell the new assets and distribute the proceeds. The request will be refused if the bankruptcy judge believes that too much time has passed or that the assets aren't worth enough to justify reopening the case. But it's almost impossible to predict how a judge will decide. In two cases involving the same type of property with approximately the same value, one judge reopened a case 14 months after the discharge, while the other refused to reopen a case just eight months after the discharge, stating that too much time had passed. (*In re Podgorski*, 18 B.R. 889 (N.D. Ind. 1982) and *In re Tyler*, 27 B.R. 289 (E.D. Va. 1983).)

⚠ Get Help if the Situation Merits It. If the trustee reopens your case, and either your bankruptcy discharge or valuable property is at stake, find a bankruptcy lawyer to defend your interests in court. If, however, the amount at stake is something you can stand to lose, you'll probably be better off by simply consenting to what the trustee wants. A third alternative is to oppose the reopening in court, but represent yourself rather than hire a lawyer. For this you'll need to do a heap of legal research. (See Ch. 9.)

B. Newly Discovered Creditors

If you failed to list a creditor in your bankruptcy papers, you may be able to reopen your case, amend your petition and discharge the debt. Remember, if a creditor is not listed in your papers, its debt is not discharged unless: (1) it knew you filed for bankruptcy and intended to discharge the debt and (2) it had an opportunity to file a claim or object to the discharge of its debt.

Whether you can reopen your case to add the creditor depends on whether you had an asset or no-asset case.

- In an asset case, the trustee sells your nonexempt property and pays your unsecured creditors part of what you owed them.
- In a no-asset case, there is no nonexempt property and so your unsecured creditors get nothing.

If your bankruptcy was an asset case, the court probably won't allow you to reopen it to add a creditor. To do otherwise would be unfair to the new creditor. Your nonexempt assets have already been paid to your other unsecured creditors. If added to your case, the new creditor wouldn't get anything.

No-asset cases are another story. Because unsecured creditors don't get anything in no-asset cases, adding a creditor to the case would not be unfair. For this reason, many courts (but not all) will allow you to reopen a no-asset case to add an omitted creditor.

If you think you may be able to discharge the debt of an omitted creditor this way, first check with the court to see if your case has actually been closed. If it's still open, simply follow the steps for amending your bankruptcy papers outlined in Ch.4, Section B. If your case is closed, you'll have to file a motion asking the court to re-open your case. Usually, you'll need to consult with a lawyer to do this. Once the court re-opens your case, you can file an amendment.

If yours is a no-asset case, you probably don't need to go to the trouble of reopening your case and filing an amendment. If the court told your creditors not to file a proof of claim because there were no assets to divide, then an omitted creditor would have nothing to gain by getting notice of your bankruptcy (because it would not have filed a claim anyway). For this reason, debts to creditors in no-asset cases are usually discharged, even if they aren't listed in your papers.

C. Post-Bankruptcy Attempts to Collect Debts

After bankruptcy, creditors whose debts haven't been discharged are entitled to be paid; creditors whose debts have been discharged are not. But it isn't always clear into which category a creditor falls. The reason there's room for argument about which debts have been discharged is that the bankruptcy court doesn't give you a list of your discharged debts. Your final discharge merely says all debts that are legally dischargeable have been discharged.

How do you know which debts have been discharged and which debts must still be paid? Here's the general rule: All the debts you listed in your bankruptcy papers are discharged unless a creditor successfully objected to the discharge of a particular debt in the bankruptcy court, or the debt falls in one of the following categories:

- student loans (unless the court ruled it would be an undue hardship for you to repay them)
- taxes that became due within the past three years or that were assessed within the previous 240 days
- child support or alimony
- fines and penalties or court fees
- debts related to personal injury or death caused by your intoxicated driving
- debts not discharged in a previous bankruptcy because of fraud or misfeasance, or
- certain condominium and cooperative fees.

Ch. 8 discusses all of these categories.

In addition, if only one spouse files in a community property state, the other spouse's share of the community debts (debts incurred during the marriage) is also discharged. The community property states are Alaska, Arizona, California, Idaho, Louisiana, New Mexico, Nevada, Texas, Washington and Wisconsin.

Even if you think some of your debts weren't discharged in bankruptcy, the creditors may never try to collect. Many creditors believe that bankruptcy cuts off their rights, period; even attorneys often don't understand that some debts can survive bankruptcy.

If a creditor does try to collect a debt after your bankruptcy discharge, write to the creditor and state that your debts were discharged. Unless you're absolutely certain that the debt wasn't discharged—for example, a student loan for which the court denied your hardship request—this is a justifiable position for you to take.

Letter to Creditor

388 Elm Street
Oakdale, WY 95439

March 18, 20XX

Bank of Wyoming
18th and "J" Streets
Cheyenne, WY 98989

To Whom It May Concern:

I've received numerous letters from your bank claiming that I owe $6,000 for charges between September of 1997 and September of 1999. I received a bankruptcy discharge of my debts on February 1, 20XX. I enclose a copy of the discharge for your reference.

Sincerely,

Brenda Woodruff

Brenda Woodruff

If the creditor ignores your letter and continues collection efforts, there are other ways to respond.

- **Amend your bankruptcy papers.** If a debt wasn't discharged simply because you forgot to list it on your bankruptcy papers, you may be able to get it discharged after your case is closed by reopening your case and amending your papers to include the debt. See Section B, above.
- **Do nothing.** The creditor knows you've just been through bankruptcy, have little or no nonexempt property and probably have no way to pay the debt, especially all at once. Thus, if you don't respond to collection efforts, the creditor may decide to leave you alone, at least for a while. But if the creditor has sued you and won a court judgment, the creditor may try to collect sometime down the line. In most states a judgment may be collected for ten or 20 years, and usually may be renewed beyond that.
- **Negotiate.** Try to negotiate for a lower balance or a payment schedule that works for you. Again, the creditor knows you've just been through bankruptcy and may be willing to compromise.
- **Defend in court.** If the creditor sues you for the debt, you can raise any defenses you have to the debt itself.

   EXAMPLE: Edna was sued by the Department of Education for failing to pay back a student loan she received. Edna refused to make the payments because the trade school she gave the money to went out of business before classes even began. Because this is a valid defense to the collection of a student loan, Edna should respond to the lawsuit and assert her defense.

- **Protest a garnishment or other judgment collection effort.** A creditor who has sued you and won a court judgment for a nondischargable debt is likely to try to take (garnish) your wages or other property to satisfy the judgment. But the creditor can't take it all. What was exempt during bankruptcy is still exempt. (Appendix 1 lists exempt property.) Nonetheless, the creditor can still request that 25% of your wages be taken out of each paycheck. If the debt was for child support or alimony, the creditor can take even more—up to 60% if you don't currently support anyone and up to 50% if you do. Those amounts may increase by 5% if you haven't paid child support in over 12 weeks.

   Soon after the garnishment—or in some states, before—the state court must notify you of the garnishment, what's exempt under your state's laws and how you can protest. Grounds for protest are that the garnishment isn't justified or that it causes you hardship. To protest, you'll have to file a document in the state court; it goes by different names in different states. In New York, for example, it's called a Discharge of Attachment; in California, it's a Claim of Exemption. If you do protest, the state court must hold a hearing within a reasonable time, where you can present evidence as to why the court should nullify the garnishment. The court may not agree, but it's certainly worth a try.

   Protesting a wage garnishment is usually a relatively straightforward procedure. Because states are required to tell you how to proceed, you'll probably be able to handle it without the assistance of a lawyer.

Most states also have procedures for objecting to other types of property garnishments, such as a levy of a bank account. You'll have to do a bit of research at a law library to learn the exact protest procedure, which is similar to the one for protesting a wage garnishment. (See Ch. 9)

Help in Dealing With Your Debts After Bankruptcy

For some debts, such as taxes, child support or alimony, exempt property may be taken, and a garnishment protest will do little good. Don't be surprised if the U.S. Treasury Department garnishes nearly 100% of your wages to pay back federal income taxes. The best strategy here is to attempt to negotiate the amount down.

Debt Resources. For tips on "doing nothing," negotiating with your creditors, defending against a lawsuit or protesting a garnishment, see *Money Troubles: Legal Strategies to Cope With Your Debts*, by Robin Leonard & Deanne Loonin (Nolo). For specific help in dealing with tax debts, see *Stand Up to the IRS*, by Frederick W. Daily (Nolo); for help in dealing with student loans, see *Take Control of Your Student Loan Debt*, by Deanne Loonin & Robin Leonard (Nolo).

D. Attempts to Collect Clearly Discharged Debts

If a creditor tries to collect a debt that clearly was discharged in your bankruptcy, you should respond at once with a letter like the one shown below. Again, you can assume a debt was discharged if you listed it in your bankruptcy papers, the creditor didn't successfully object to its discharge and it isn't in one of the nondischargeable categories cited in Section C, above. If you live in a community property state and your

spouse filed singly, your share of the community debts is also discharged.

If a debt was discharged, the law prohibits creditors from filing a lawsuit, sending you collection letters, calling you, withholding credit, threatening to file or actually filing a criminal complaint against you. (11 U.S.C. § 524.)

Letter to Creditor

1905 Fifth Road
N. Miami Beach, FL
35466

March 18, 20XX

Bank of Miami
2700 Finances Hwy
Miami, FL 36678

To Whom It May Concern:

I've been contacted once by letter and once by phone by Rodney Moore of your bank. Mr. Moore claims that I owe $4,812 on Visa account number 1234 567 890 123.
As you're well aware, this debt was discharged in bankruptcy on February 1, 20XX. Thus, your collection efforts violate federal law, 11 U.S.C. § 524. If they continue, I won't hesitate to pursue my legal rights, including bringing a lawsuit against you for harassment.

Sincerely,
Dawn Schaffer
Dawn Schaffer

If the collection efforts don't immediately stop, you'll likely need the assistance of a lawyer to write the creditor again and, if that doesn't work, to sue the creditor for harassment. If the creditor sues you over the debt, you'll want to raise the discharge as a defense and sue the creditor yourself to stop the illegal collection efforts. The court has the power to hold the creditor in contempt of court. The court may also fine the creditor for the humiliation, inconvenience and anguish you suffered and order the creditor to pay your attorney's fees. (See, for example, *In re Barbour*, 77 B.R. 530 (E.D. N.C. 1987), where the court fined a creditor $900 for attempting to collect a discharged debt.)

You can bring a lawsuit to stop collection efforts in state court or in the bankruptcy court. Bankruptcy courts are often more familiar with the prohibitions against collection and may be more sympathetic to you. If the creditor sues you (almost certainly in state court), you or your attorney can file papers requesting that the case be transferred (removed) to the bankruptcy court.

E. Attempts to Revoke Your Discharge

In rare instances, a trustee or creditor may ask the bankruptcy court to revoke the discharge of *all* your debts. If the trustee or a creditor attempts to revoke your discharge, consult a bankruptcy attorney. (See Ch. 9.)

Your discharge can be revoked only if the creditor or trustee proves that:

- you obtained the discharge through fraud that the trustee or creditor discovered after your discharge
- you intentionally didn't tell the trustee that you acquired property from an inheritance, a divorce settlement or a life insurance policy or death benefit plan within 180 days after you filed for bankruptcy, or
- before your case was closed, you refused to obey an order of the bankruptcy court or for a reason other than the privilege against self-incrimination, you refused to answer an important question asked by the court.

For the court to revoke your discharge on the basis of fraud, the trustee or creditor must file a complaint within one year of your discharge. For the court to revoke your discharge on the basis of your fraudulent failure to report property or your refusal to obey an order or answer a question, the complaint must be filed either within one year of your discharge or before your case is closed, whichever is later. You're entitled to receive a copy of the complaint, and the court must hold a hearing on the matter before deciding whether to revoke your discharge.

If your discharge is revoked, you'll owe your creditors. Any payment your creditors received from the trustee, however, will be credited against what you owe.

F. Post-Bankruptcy Discrimination

Although declaring bankruptcy has serious consequences, it might not be as bad as you think. There are laws that will protect you from most types of post-bankruptcy discrimination by the government and by private employers.

1. Government Discrimination

All federal, state and local governmental units are prohibited from denying, revoking, suspending or refusing to renew a license, permit, charter, franchise or other similar grant solely because you filed for bankruptcy. (11 U.S.C. § 525(a).) This part of the Bankruptcy Code provides important protections, but it does not insulate debtors from all adverse consequences of filing for bankruptcy. Lenders, for example, can consider a debtor's bankruptcy filing when reviewing an application for a government loan or extension of credit. (See, for example, *Watts v. Pennsylvania Housing Finance Co.*, 876 F.2d 1090 (3rd Cir. 1989) and *Toth v. Michigan State Housing Development Authority*, 136 F.3d 477 (6th Cir. 1998).) Still, under this provision of the Bankruptcy Code, the government cannot:

- deny you a job or fire you
- deny you or terminate your public benefits
- evict you from public housing (although if you have a Section 8 voucher, you may not be protected)
- deny you or refuse to renew your state liquor license
- withhold your college transcript
- deny you a driver's license, or
- deny you a contract, such as a contract for a construction project.

In addition, the Bankruptcy Code bars a lender from excluding you from participating in a government-guaranteed student loan program (11 U.S.C. §525(c)).

In general, once any government-related debt has been discharged, all acts against you that arise out of that debt also must end. If, for example, you lost your driver's license because you didn't pay a court judgment that resulted from a car accident, once the debt is discharged, you must be granted a license. If your license was also suspended because you didn't have insurance, you may not get your license back until you meet the requirements set forth in your state's financial responsibility law.

If, however, the judgment wasn't discharged, you can still be denied your license until you pay up. If you and the government disagree about whether or not the debt was discharged, see Section C, above.

Keep in mind that only post-bankruptcy government denials based on your bankruptcy are prohibited. You may be denied a loan, job or apartment for reasons unrelated to the bankruptcy or for reasons related to your future creditworthiness—for example, because the government concludes you won't be able to repay a Small Business Administration loan.

2. Non-Government Discrimination

Private employers may not terminate your employment or otherwise discriminate against you solely because you filed for bankruptcy. (11 U.S.C. § 525(b).) While the Bankruptcy Act expressly prohibits employers from firing you, it is unclear whether or not the act prohibits employers from not hiring you because you went through bankruptcy.

Unfortunately, however, other forms of discrimination in the private sector aren't illegal. If you seek to rent an apartment and the landlord does a credit check, sees your bankruptcy and refuses to rent to you, there's not much you can do other than try to show that you'll pay your rent and be a responsible tenant. Or, if an employer refuses to hire you because of a poor credit history—not because you filed for bankruptcy—you may have little recourse.

If you suffer illegal discrimination because of your bankruptcy, you can sue in state court or in the bankruptcy court. You'll probably need the assistance of an attorney.

G. Rebuilding Credit

Although a bankruptcy filing can remain on your credit record for up to ten years from the date of your discharge, you can probably rebuild your credit in about three years to the point that you won't be turned down for a major loan. Most creditors look for steady employment and a history, since bankruptcy, of making and paying for purchases on credit. And many creditors disregard a bankruptcy completely after about five years.

Rebuilding Your Credit

For more information on rebuilding your credit, see *Credit Repair*, by Deanne Loonin & Robin Leonard (Nolo).

Should You Rebuild Your Credit?

Habitual overspending can be just as hard to overcome as excessive gambling or drinking. If you think you may be a compulsive spender, one of the worst things you might do is rebuild your credit. Instead, you need to get a handle on your spending habits.

Debtors Anonymous is a 12-step support program similar to Alcoholics Anonymous. It has programs nationwide. If a Debtors Anonymous group or a therapist recommends that you stay out of the credit system for a while, follow that advice. Even if you don't feel you're a compulsive spender, paying as you spend may still be the way to go.

Debtors Anonymous meets all over the country. To find a meeting near you, call directory assistance or send a self-addressed stamped envelope to Debtors Anonymous, General Services Board, P.O. Box 888, Needham, MA 02492-0009. Or call and speak to a volunteer or leave a message at 781-453-2743.

Daily Expenses

Date:

Item	Cost

Date:

Item	Cost

Date:

Item	Cost

Date:

Item	Cost

1. Create a Budget

The first step to rebuilding your credit is to create a budget. Making a budget will help you control impulses to overspend and help you start saving money—an essential part of rebuilding your credit.

Before you put yourself on a budget that limits how much you spend, take some time to find out exactly how much money you spend right now. Make copies of the Daily Expenses form in Appendix 4 and fill it out for 30 days. Write down every cent you spend—50¢ for the paper, $2 for your morning coffee and muffin, $5 for lunch, $3 for the bridge or tunnel toll, and so on. If you omit any money spent, your picture of how much you spend, and your budget, will be inaccurate.

At the end of the 30 days, review your sheets. Are you surprised? Are you impulsively buying things, or do you tend to buy the same types of things consistently? If the latter, you'll have an easier time planning a budget than if your spending varies tremendously from day to day.

Think about the changes you need to make to put away a few dollars at the end of every week. Even if you think there's nothing to spare, try to set a small goal—even $5 a week. It will help. If you spend $2 per day on coffee and a muffin, that adds up to $10 per week and at least $40 per month. Eating breakfast at home might save you most of that amount. If you buy the newspaper at the corner store every day, consider subscribing. A subscription doesn't involve extending credit; if you don't pay, they simply stop delivering.

Once you understand your spending habits and identify the changes you need to make, you're ready to make a budget. At the top of a sheet of paper, write down your monthly net income—that is, the amount you bring home after taxes and other mandatory deductions. At the left, list everything you spend money on in a month. Include any bank or other deposit accounts you use or plan to use for saving money and any nondischarged, reaffirmed or other debts you make payments on. To the right of each item, write down the amount of money you spend, deposit or pay each month. Finally, total up the amount. If it exceeds your monthly income, make some changes—by eliminating or reducing expenditures for non-necessities—and start over. Once your budget is final, stick to it.

Avoiding Financial Problems

These nine rules, suggested by people who have been through bankruptcy, will help you stay out of financial hot water.

1. **Create a realistic budget and stick to it.**
2. **Don't impulse buy.** When you see something you hadn't planned to purchase, go home and think it over. It's unlikely you'll return to the store and buy it.
3. **Avoid sales.** Buying a $500 item on sale for $400 isn't a $100 savings if you didn't need the item in the first place.
4. **Get medical insurance.** Because you can't avoid medical emergencies, living without medical insurance is an invitation to financial ruin.
5. **Charge items only if you could pay for them now.** Don't charge based on future income—sometimes future income doesn't materialize.
6. **Avoid large house payments.** Obligate yourself only for what you can now afford and increase your mortgage payments only as your income increases. Again, don't obligate yourself based on future income that you might not have.
7. **Think long and hard before agreeing to cosign or guarantee a loan for someone.** Your signature obligates you as if you were the primary borrower. You can't be sure that the other person will pay.
8. **Avoid joint obligations with people who have questionable spending habits**—even your spouse or significant other. If you incur a joint debt, you're probably liable for it all if the other person defaults.
9. **Avoid high-risk investments,** such as speculative real estate, penny stocks and junk bonds. Invest conservatively in things such as certificates of deposit, money market funds and government bonds. And never invest more than you can afford to lose.

2. Keep Your Credit File Accurate

Rebuilding your credit requires you to keep incorrect information out of your credit file.

Start by obtaining a copy of your file from one of the "big three" credit reporting agencies:

- Equifax, P.O. Box 740241, Atlanta, GA 30374; 800-685-1111; www.equifax.com
- Experian, P.O. Box 2104, Allen, TX 75013-2104; 888-EXPERIAN; www.experian.com
- Trans Union, Consumer Disclosure Center, P.O. Box 2000, Chester, PA 19022; 800-888-4213; www.tuc.com.

You will need to send the agency your name and any previous names, addresses for the last two years, telephone number, year or date of birth, employer and Social Security number.

You are entitled to a free copy of your report if you were denied credit because of an item in your credit report. You must request your file within 60 days after you were denied credit. Also, you are entitled to a free copy of your report if you receive public assistance, are unemployed and plan to look for work in the next 60 days or believe your file contains errors due to someone's fraudulent use of your name, credit history, Social Security number or the like. Finally, you are entitled to an annual free copy of your report if you live in Colorado, Georgia, Maryland, Massachusetts, New Jersey or Vermont. If you are not entitled to a free copy of your report, expect to pay no more than $8.50 for a copy.

In addition to your credit history, your credit report will contain the sources of the information and the names of people who have received your file within the last year, or within the last two years if those people sought your file for employment reasons.

Credit files can contain negative information for up to seven years, except for bankruptcy filings, which can stay for ten. You will want to challenge outdated entries, as well as incorrect or incomplete information. The bureau must investigate the accuracy of anything you challenge within 30 days, and either correct it or, if it can't verify the item, remove it.

If, after the investigation, the bureau keeps information in your file that you still believe is wrong, you are entitled to write a statement of up to 100 words giving your version, to be included in your file. Be sure the statement is tied to a particular item in your file. When the item eventually is removed from your file, the statement will be also. If you write a general "my life was a mess and I got into debt" statement, however, it will stay for a full seven years from the date you place it, even if the negative items come out sooner. An example of a statement is shown below.

Letter to Credit Bureau

74 Ash Avenue
Hanover, NH 03222

March 18, 20xx

Credit Reporters of New England
4118 Main Blvd.
Manchester, NH 03101

To Whom It May Concern:

Your records show that I am unemployed. That's incorrect. I am a self-employed cabinetmaker and carpenter. I work out of my home and take orders from people who are referred to me through various sources. My work is known in the community and that's how I earn my living.

Sincerely,
Denny Porter
Denny Porter

The statement, or a summary of it, must be given to anyone who receives your credit file. In addition, if you request it, the bureau must pass on a copy or summary of your statement to any person who received your report within the past year, or two years if it involved employment.

You also want to keep new negative information out of your file. To do this, remain current on your bills. What you owe, as well as how long it takes you to pay, will show up in that file.

In addition to information about credit accounts, credit reports also contain information from public records, including criminal records. After receiving your bankruptcy discharge, be sure to modify public records to reflect what occurred in the bankruptcy, so wrong information won't appear in your credit file. For example, if a court case was pending against you at the time you filed for bankruptcy and, as part of the bankruptcy, the potential judgment against you was discharged, be sure the court case is formally dismissed. You may need the help of an attorney. (See Ch. 9.)

Avoid Credit Repair Agencies

You've probably seen ads for companies that claim they can fix your credit, qualify you for a loan and get you a credit card. Stay clear of these companies. Their practices are almost always deceptive and sometimes illegal. Some steal the credit files or Social Security numbers of people who have died or live in places like Guam or the U.S. Virgin Islands, then replace your file with these other files. Others create new identities for debtors by applying to the IRS for a taxpayer I.D. number and telling debtors to use it in place of their Social Security number.

But even the legitimate companies can't do anything for you that you can't do yourself. If items in your credit file are correct, these companies cannot get them removed. About the only difference between using a legitimate credit repair agency and doing it yourself is the money you will save by going it alone.

---

3. Negotiate With Some Creditors

If you owe any debts that show up as past due on your credit file (perhaps the debt wasn't discharged in bankruptcy, was reaffirmed in bankruptcy or was incurred after you filed), you can take steps to make them current. Contact the creditor and ask that the item be removed in exchange for either full or partial payment. On a revolving account (such as a department store), ask the creditor to "re-age" the account—that is,

to make the current month the first repayment month and show no late payments on the account.

4. Stabilize Your Income and Employment

Your credit history is not the only thing lenders will consider in deciding whether to give you credit. They also look carefully at the stability of your income and employment. Plus, if you start getting new credit before you're back on your feet financially, you'll end up in the same mess that led you to file for bankruptcy in the first place.

5. Get a Credit Card

Once you have your budget and some money saved, you can begin to get some positive information in your credit file. One way to do this is by getting a secured credit card.

Some banks will give you a credit card and a line of credit if you deposit money into a savings account. In exchange, you cannot remove the money from your account. Because it's difficult to guarantee a hotel reservation or rent a car without presenting at least one major credit card, get such a card if you truly believe you'll control any impulses to overuse—or even use—it.

Another reason to have these cards is that in a few years, banks and other large creditors will be more apt to grant you credit if, since your bankruptcy, you've made and paid for purchases on credit. A major drawback with these cards, however, is that they often have extremely high interest rates. So use the card only to cash checks or to buy inexpensive items you can pay for when the bill arrives. Otherwise, you're going to pay a bundle in interest and may end up back in financial trouble.

Be sure to shop around before signing up for a secured credit card. Even though you just filed for bankruptcy, you'll probably still get lots of offers for unsecured cards in the mail. Often, these cards have better terms than do secured cards. If you do choose a secured credit card, be sure it isn't secured by your home.

⚠ **Avoid credit card look alikes.** Some cards allow you to make purchases only from the issuing company's own catalogues. The items in the catalogue tend to be overpriced and of mediocre (if not poor) quality. And your use of the card isn't reported to credit bureaus, so you won't be rebuilding your credit.

6. Work With a Local Merchant

Another step to consider in rebuilding your credit is to approach a local merchant (such as a jewelry or furniture store) about purchasing an item on credit. Many local stores will work with you in setting up a payment schedule, but be prepared to put down a deposit of up to 30%, pay a high rate of interest or find someone to cosign the loan.

7. Borrow From a Bank

Bank loans provide an excellent way to rebuild credit. A few banks offer something called a passbook savings loan. But in most cases, you'll have to apply for a standard bank loan. You probably won't qualify for a standard bank loan unless you bring in a cosigner, offer some property as collateral or agree to a very high rate of interest.

The amount you can borrow will depend on how much the bank requires you to deposit (in the case of a passbook loan) or its general loan term limits.

Banks that offer passbook loans typically give you one to three years to repay the loan. But don't pay the loan back too soon—give it about six to nine months to appear on your credit file. Standard bank loans are paid back on a monthly schedule.

Before you take out any loan, be sure to understand the terms:

- **Interest rate.** The interest rate on your loan will probably be between two and six percentage points over what the bank charges its customers with the best credit.
- **Prepayment penalties.** Usually, you can pay the loan back as soon as you want without incurring any prepayment penalties. Prepayment penalties are fees banks sometimes charge if you pay back a loan early and the bank doesn't collect as much interest from you as it had expected. The penalty is usually a small percentage of the loan amount.
- **Whether the bank reports the loan to a credit bureau.** This is key; the whole reason you take out the loan is to rebuild your credit, which means you want the loan to appear in your file. You may have to make several calls to find a bank that reports the loan. ■

CHAPTER

6

Your House

I f you own a home, Chapter 7 bankruptcy may not be the best strategy to deal with your debts. Before you decide to file, you must be aware of two important points:

- Chapter 7 bankruptcy won't stop a mortgage foreclosure. Although it may postpone a foreclosure, it will only do so for a short time. If you want to keep your home, you must keep making your mortgage payments before, during and after bankruptcy. If you've already missed mortgage payments, you'll have to make them up to prevent foreclosure. (See Section B, below.)

- If you have nonexempt equity in your home (that is, equity that isn't protected by a homestead or other exemption), you will lose your home if you file for Chapter 7 bankruptcy. (Exempt property is discussed in Ch. 2, Section B, and in Section C of this chapter.) Even if your mortgage payments are current, if you have equity in your home that isn't exempt, the bankruptcy court will take your home and sell it to pay off your creditors. (See Sections C and D, below.)

This chapter explains how filing for Chapter 7 bankruptcy—or pursuing alternative strategies—affects your chances of keeping your home. Of course, your home isn't your only consideration in deciding whether or not to file for bankruptcy, so make sure to read Ch. 1 before making the decision. If you're still uncertain about what to do after reading these chapters, see a bankruptcy lawyer. Chances are, your home is valuable enough to justify the extra expense to save it.

 Be Aware of the Following:
- Some of the procedures discussed in this chapter are complex and require a lawyer. We don't provide step-by-step instructions. If you try to handle them yourself, a mistake could cost you your home.
- If you own two homes, or you want to protect equity in a home that is not your residence, see a bankruptcy lawyer.

A. How Bankruptcy Affects a Typical Homeowner

Here's an overview of how bankruptcy affects you as a homeowner.

1. Mortgage Payments

You must keep making mortgage payments. As you probably know too well, you don't really "own" much of your home—a bank or other lender that has a mortgage or deed of trust on the home probably owns most of it. (Throughout this chapter, we use the term "mortgage" to include deeds of trust.)

Until the mortgage is paid off, the lender has the right to foreclose if you miss mortgage payments. Chapter 7 bankruptcy doesn't change this. (See Section B, below.)

2. Liens on Your House

Bankruptcy won't eliminate most liens on your home. If you've pledged your home as security for loans other than your mortgage—for example, you took out a home equity loan or second mortgage—or a creditor such as the IRS has recorded a lien, those creditors, too, have claims against your home.

Most lienholders have a right to foreclose (force a sale of your house) if the lien isn't paid off within a specified time.

Who Gets What From the Sale of a Home in Bankruptcy

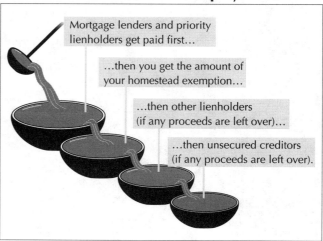

Mortgage lenders and priority lienholders get paid first...

...then you get the amount of your homestead exemption...

...then other lienholders (if any proceeds are left over)...

...then unsecured creditors (if any proceeds are left over).

If there is a judgment lien on your home—that is, if a creditor sued you, obtained a court judgment and recorded a lien at the land records office—you may be able to get rid of the lien entirely without paying a cent to the lienholder. And in some states, if your home is sold in bankruptcy, you will get your homestead amount ahead of secured creditors holding judicial liens.

You can get rid of the lien by filing a motion to avoid a judicial lien. You may also be able to get rid of some liens by filing a separate lawsuit in bankruptcy court. We explain these procedures in Ch. 7.

3. Keeping Your House

Even if you keep up with your mortgage payments, you may still lose your house unless a homestead exemption protects your equity—the difference between what your house is worth and what you owe the mortgage lender and all lienholders. If you were to sell your home today, without filing for bankruptcy, the money raised by the sale would go first to the mortgage lender to pay off the mortgage then to lienholders to pay off the liens and finally to pay off the costs of sale and any taxes due. If anything was left over, you'd get it.

If you file for bankruptcy and the trustee has your house sold, the creditors will get paid in pretty much the same order, with one big difference. In a bankruptcy sale, whatever is left after the mortgages, liens, costs of sale and taxes have been paid goes not to you, but to your unsecured creditors—unless a homestead exemption entitles you to some or all of it.

As a practical matter, if there will be nothing left over for your unsecured creditors, the trustee won't bother to sell your house. Thus, the amount of your homestead exemption often determines whether or not you'll lose your home in bankruptcy.

If the bankruptcy trustee calculates that there would be leftover proceeds from a sale of your home to give to your unsecured creditors, the trustee will, almost always, take your home and sell it to get those proceeds.

Section C of this chapter explains how to figure out whether a homestead exemption will prevent the trustee from selling your home.

How a Homestead Exemption Works: An Example

This chart applies only to those states that use dollar-amount homestead exemptions. If your state bases the homestead exemption on acreage, your lot size will determine whether or not you keep your home. (See Section C, below.)

This example is based on a $100,000 home with a $35,000 homestead exemption.

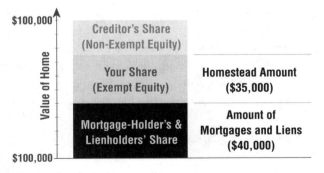

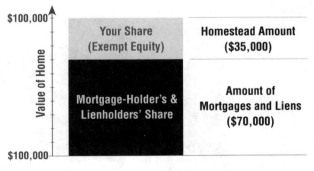

If you have nonexempt equity in your home, the trustee will sell your home. Here, the homeowner's total equity is $60,000 [$100,000 (value of home) – $40,000 (mortgages and liens against home)]. The homeowner's nonexempt equity is $25,000 [$60,000 (total equity) – $35,000 (homestead exemption)]. Because the homeowner has $25,000 in nonexempt equity, the trustee will sell the house and use the nonexempt equity to pay unsecured creditors.

If you don't have any nonexempt equity, the trustee won't sell your home. Here, the homeowner's total equity is $30,000 [$100,000 (value of home) – $70,000 (mortgages and liens against home)]. The homeowner doesn't have any nonexempt equity [$30,000 (total equity) – $35,000 (homestead exemption) = less than zero].

B. If You're Behind on Your Mortgage Payments

If you're behind on your mortgage payments but want to keep your house, your first strategy should be to negotiate with the lender and try other non-bankruptcy alternatives discussed in this section. (This section deals only with secured debts created by agreements. For a discussion of eliminating judicial liens on your home, see Ch. 7, Sections B and C.)

Chapter 7 bankruptcy's automatic stay won't prevent foreclosure if you fall behind on your mortgage payments. At most, it will postpone foreclosure for a month or so.

About the only way Chapter 7 bankruptcy can help you hang on to your home is by discharging your other debts, which will allow you to devote more money to getting current on your mortgage to prevent foreclosure.

⚠️ **If foreclosure is looming.** If you think foreclosure is a real possibility, immediately see a lawyer who is experienced in debt problems. Don't wait until the last minute. The lawyer may need several months to negotiate with the lender or plan for an eventual bankruptcy so that you get the most out of it. The lawyer can also look for other ways to challenge the foreclosure—for example, because the lender didn't give you proper notice of the foreclosure or because of problems with the original mortgage.

1. Negotiating With the Lender

If you've missed a few mortgage payments, most lenders will be willing to negotiate. What the lender agrees to will depend on your credit history, the reason for your missed payments and your financial prospects.

EXAMPLE: Doug misses a few house payments because he had a car accident and couldn't work for two months. It looks like he'll be back to work soon. The bank will probably work out a deal with Doug rather than immediately move to foreclose.

2. Mortgage Workouts

Not all lenders are receptive to informal negotiations. Many will require you to proceed through a more formal process called a "mortgage workout." A workout is an agreement you make with the lender that changes how you pay the delinquency on your mortgage or otherwise keeps you out of foreclosure.

Over the years, lenders have learned that high foreclosure rates can cost them lots of money. As a result, they are often willing to renegotiate payment terms with borrowers in default in order to avoid foreclosure. If you think you have the resources to keep your home by renegotiating the payments, you should consider talking to the lender about a workout.

Here are some workout options your lender might agree to:

- Spread repayment of missed payments over a few months. For example, if your monthly payment is $1,000 and you missed two payments ($2,000), the lender might let you pay $1,500 for four months.
- Reduce or suspend your regular payments for a specified time, then add a portion of your overdue amount to your regular payments later on.
- Extend the length of your loan and add the missed payments at the end.
- For a period of time, suspend the amount of your monthly payment that goes towards the principal, and only require payment of interest, taxes and insurance.

- Refinance your loan to reduce future monthly payments.
- Let you sell the property for less than you owe the lender and waive the rest of the loan. This is called a "short sale."

Before you contact the lender about a workout, you should prepare information about your situation, including:

- An assessment of your current financial situation and a reasonable budget for the future.
- A plan to deal with other essential debts, such as utility bills and car payments.
- A hardship letter explaining why you fell behind on your mortgage. Emphasize the most sympathetic aspects of your situation.
- Information about the property and its value.
- Information about your loan and the amount of the default.

You should also find out if your mortgage is insured by the Federal Housing Administration (FHA) or the U.S. Department of Housing and Urban Development (HUD). Borrowers with these types of mortgages have some special rights that those with "conventional" mortgages don't have.

It's a good idea to look for a nonprofit debt counselor or lawyer who has experience with mortgage workouts to help you. For information on HUD-approved counseling agencies in your area, call 800-569-4287 (TDD 800-877-8339). It's best to start the workout negotiations as early as possible

Be advised that workouts are not for everyone—nor will the lenders always agree to a workout. Be realistic about your situation before you approach the lender. If it is likely that you will lose your house anyway because of your dire financial situation or because you have other pressing financial problems, it doesn't make sense to keep paying your mortgage through a workout.

3. If the Lender Starts to Foreclose

If your debt problems look severe or long-lasting, the lender may take steps toward foreclosure. Again, if you're faced with foreclosure and want to keep your house, consult a lawyer who specializes in debt problems to work out a strategy to save your home.

In most cases, the lender will "accelerate" the debt or "call the loan" before foreclosure actually occurs. This means you must pay the entire balance immediately. If you don't, the lender will foreclose.

EXAMPLE: Don and Louise bought a $100,000 home by putting $20,000 down and getting an $80,000 mortgage. Their monthly house payments are $900. After paying on the mortgage for several years, they've recently missed three consecutive payments. The bank accelerated the loan and is now demanding the entire $76,284 balance. Because they can't pay it, the bank begins foreclosure proceedings.

Foreclosure can take anywhere from three to 18 months, depending on what state you live in and what type of loan you have. During this time, you have several options:

- Sell your house. If you don't get any offers that will cover what you owe your lender, a short sale may be possible.
- Get another lender to give you a loan that pays off all or part of the first loan and puts you on a new schedule of monthly payments. If the original lender has accelerated the loan, you'll need to refinance the entire balance of the loan to prevent foreclosure. If the lender hasn't accelerated the loan, however, you can prevent foreclosure simply by paying the missed payments, taxes and insurance, plus interest. But be careful when deciding whether to refinance. In many cases, refinancing hurts more than it helps. Many lenders have figured out clever ways to hide high costs and fees in refinancing deals.
- File for Chapter 13 bankruptcy if you can't come up with the needed money in a lump sum right away. Chapter 13 bankruptcy allows you to "cure the default"—make up missed payments over time and make the regular payments as they come due. (See Section D.2, below.)

Foreclosure resource. If you live in California and your lender has started to foreclose, get a copy of *Stop Foreclosure Now in California*, by Lloyd Segal (Nolo).

4. Defenses to Foreclosure

You may be able to delay or stop the foreclosure if you have defenses to paying the mortgage or the lender has not properly followed state foreclosure procedures. If you think you might have a defense to foreclosure, contact a lawyer immediately. Some possible defenses are:

- **Violations of the federal Truth in Lending law.** The federal Truth in Lending law requires the lender to give you certain information about your loan before you sign the papers. If the lender failed to provide this information, you may be able to cancel the mortgage. This only applies to loans *not* used to purchase your home.
- **Home improvement fraud.** If you took out a mortgage to finance improvements to your home and got ripped off by the contractor (for example, the work was shoddy or incomplete), you may be able to cancel the loan.
- **Interest rate that violates state or federal law.** Some states limit how much interest can be charged on a loan. Federal law prohibits lenders from making deceptive or false representations about the loan and from charging high closing costs and fees. If your interest is very high or your lender didn't tell you the truth about the terms of your loan, consult a lawyer.
- **Failure to follow foreclosure procedures.** Each state requires lenders to follow specific procedures when foreclosing on a home. If the lender doesn't follow these rules (for example, by not giving proper notice of the foreclosure or failing to inform you of certain rights), you may be able to delay the foreclosure.

Finding defenses to foreclosure is not easy. Nor is raising these defenses in court. If you think you might have a defense to foreclosure, consult an attorney. (See Ch.9 for information on how to find a good lawyer.)

5. If Foreclosure Is Unavoidable

If you've exhausted the suggestions described above and it looks like foreclosure is inevitable, be aware that losing your home in a bankruptcy sale will often be a better deal than losing it in a foreclosure sale, for two reasons.

First, a forced sale of your home in bankruptcy is supervised by the bankruptcy trustee, who will want to sell the house for as much as possible. In a foreclosure sale, the foreclosing creditor will try to get only a high enough price to cover the amount due on the mortgage. If you have a homestead exemption on the house, the more the house is sold for, the more you get for your homestead exemption. (See Section C, below.)

Second, debtors are rarely entitled to the homestead exemption if the house is sold through foreclosure. In a bankruptcy sale, however, you are entitled to your homestead amount in cash, if there are proceeds left over after the secured creditors have been paid off.

In the end, what happens to your home will be up to the bankruptcy trustee. If there is enough equity in your home to produce some money for your unsecured creditors, the trustee will sell it, pay off the mortgage and other lienholders, give you your exemption and distribute the rest. If there is not enough equity to generate money for your unsecured creditors, the trustee will release his authority over the home (called abandonment) and let the mortgage holder pursue any remedies available to it, which will most likely result in foreclosure if you owe an arrearage.

C. Will the Trustee Sell Your Home?

If you file for Chapter 7 bankruptcy, the fact that you've kept up on your house payments may not prevent you from losing it. The trustee will still have your house sold if the sale will produce some cash to pay your unsecured creditors. If the sale won't produce cash, the trustee will not take the house.

Whether you will be able to keep your home depends on two facts:

- whether you have any equity in your home, and
- if so, whether that equity is exempt.

Use the worksheet that follows to figure out the answers to these questions.

Part I: Do You Have Any Equity in Your Home?

Line 1: Estimated market value of your home
If you've already filled out Worksheet 1 in Ch. 2, take the home value from that worksheet.

If you haven't filled out Worksheet 1, estimate how much your home could be sold for in a bankruptcy sale. In a bankruptcy sale, a typical home goes for 10%–30% less than what it would bring in a normal sale. The trustee knows this and will probably take it into account when deciding whether or not to go after your home.

However, the trustee is not required to use this discounted value. He may use the full market value of your home in deciding whether to take it. To be on the safe side, you may want to put the full market value of your home on this line.

To get a rough idea of what your home is worth, ask a realtor what comparable homes in your neighborhood have sold for. Or look in newspaper real estate sections. You can also generate rough home valuation estimates from websites, such as www.eloan.com.

Line 2: Costs of sale

Costs of sale vary, but they tend to be about 5% of the sales price. The trustee does not have to subtract the costs of sale in determining whether to take your home, but many do. If you want to err on the side of caution, put "0" in this blank.

Line 3: Amount owed on mortgages and other loans

Enter the amount needed to pay off your mortgage and any other loans that are secured by the home as collateral. If you can't come up with a reasonably reliable estimate, contact each lender and ask how much is necessary to cancel the debt.

Line 4: Amount of liens

Enter the amount of all liens recorded against your home (other than liens created by mortgages and home equity loans). If you've already figured this amount in Worksheet 1 of Ch. 2, you can use those figures.

If you haven't yet filled out Worksheet 1, read on. Liens are claims against your home that have been recorded with the land records office. The three most common types of liens are tax liens, mechanic's liens and judgment liens. Tax liens can be recorded against your home by the county, state or federal government for failure to pay property, income or other taxes.

People who do work on your home and claim that you didn't pay them what you owed can record mechanic's or materialman's liens against your home. And judgment liens can be recorded by anyone who has sued you and won.

If you think there might be liens on your home, visit the county land records office. Tell the clerk you'd like to check your title for liens. The clerk should direct you to an index (often on microfiche) that lists all property in the county by the owner's last name. Next to your home should be a list of any liens recorded against it.

Line 5 = Line 2 + Line 3+ Line 4

Add up the total costs that would have to be paid if you were to sell your home.

Line 6 (Your Equity) = Line 1 – Line 5

If line 1 is more than line 5, subtract line 5 from line 1, and put the result on line 6. For bankruptcy purposes, this is your equity in the property—that is, the amount the house will sell for, less the amount that will have to be paid to others from the proceeds.

If the amount on line 5 is more than the amount on line 1, you have no equity; you can stop here. There will be no reason for the trustee to take your home in bankruptcy—once all of the liens and mortgage(s) are paid off, there would be nothing left to distribute to your unsecured creditors.

If you do have equity, go on to Part II to determine how much of it is protected in your state.

Legal research note. If you do legal research in this area, pay attention to how bankruptcy court decisions use the term "equity." Courts occasionally divide a homeowner's equity into two types: "encumbered" and "unencumbered." Encumbered equity is your home's value less only the mortgage. Unencumbered equity is your home's value less the mortgage and liens. We use equity to mean unencumbered equity. But some courts use equity to mean encumbered equity. The term often appears in cases discussing whether a state's homestead exemption allows the debtor to be paid before certain lienholders.

Part II: If You Have Equity, Is It Protected by an Exemption?

This part assumes that in Part I, you found that you have some amount of home equity. Here in Part II, we'll determine how much of that equity you can claim as exempt—that is, how much of it you're entitled to keep.

Line 7: Does your state have a homestead exemption that protects your kind of dwelling?

States With No Homestead Exemption

Delaware	Maryland	New Jersey
Pennsylvania		

Only four states do not have a homestead exemption: If you live in one of these four states, enter $0 on line 10.

If your state has a homestead exemption, check the table in Appendix 1 to see if your type of dwelling is protected in your state. Some types of dwellings may not be covered, including:

- **Mobile homes.** Most states specifically include mobile homes in their homestead exemptions. Other states include any "real or personal property used as a residence." This would include a trailer, mobile home or houseboat, as long as you live in it. Some states don't say. If your mobile home does not qualify for a homestead exemption, it would be protected only by the exemption for a "motor vehicle."
- **Co-ops or condominiums.** Some homestead laws specifically cover co-ops, or use language that says the exemption protects "any property used as a dwelling."
- **Apartments.** Most homestead statutes *do not* protect apartments, though a few do.

If your type of dwelling is not covered, enter $0 on line 10.

If it is unclear whether your type of dwelling is covered by your state's homestead exemption, you may need to do some legal research. (See Ch. 9 for help getting started.)

Line 8: Do the laws of your state require you to file a "declaration of homestead" to claim the exemption?

States That Require a Declaration of Homestead

Alabama	Montana	Utah
Idaho	Nevada	Virginia
Massachusetts	Texas	Washington

If you live in one of the states listed above, you are not entitled to your homestead exemption until you record a written "declaration of homestead" with the county land records office.

Requiring you to record a declaration before you can get the benefit of the homestead exemption may violate the bankruptcy laws (*In re Leicht*, 222 B.R. 670 (1st Cir. BAP 1998)). Regardless of the legalities, however, you will be best served by filing your declaration of homestead before you file for bankruptcy.

Other states allow (but do not require) you to file a homestead declaration in certain circumstances. In Texas, for example, you may file a homestead declaration to claim protection for property you own but are not currently living in.

> **EXAMPLE:** John and Doris live in Texas. They have retired and have decided to rent out their spacious country home and live in an apartment closer to town. They can still claim their country home as their homestead by recording a declaration of homestead with county land records office.

Also, if you own more than one piece of real estate, some states allow a creditor to require you to file a declaration of homestead to clarify which property you are claiming as your homestead.

Line 9: Lot Size: does your state's homestead exemption limit the size of the lot you can protect?

Most states place a limit on how much property you can claim as your homestead exemption, but a few states have no such limits. Find out what kind of homestead exemption system your state uses by looking at the lists below.

Worksheet: Will the Trustee Sell Your Home If You File for Bankruptcy?

Part I. Do you have any equity in your home?

1. Market value of your home .... $_____
2. Costs of sale (if unsure, put 5% of market value) .... $_____
3. Amount owed on all mortgages .... $_____
4. Amount of all liens on the property .... $_____
5. Total of lines 2, 3 and 4 .... $_____
6. Your equity (Line 1 minus line 5) .... $_____

If line 6 is less than zero, skip the rest of the worksheet. The trustee will have no interest in selling your home.

Part II. Is your property protected by an exemption?
Refer to the tables in Appendix 1 to complete this part.

7. Does your state have a homestead exemption that protects your kind of dwelling? (See instructions.)
   - ☐ Yes. Go to question 8.
   - ☐ No. Enter $0 on line 10, then continue on to line 11.
8. Does your state require you to file a "declaration of homestead" before you can claim the homestead exemption?
   - ☐ Yes, but I have not filed it yet. (You should. See instructions.)
   - ☐ Yes, and I have already filed it.
   - ☐ No.
9. **Lot Size Limits:** Does your state limit the size of the property you may claim as exempt?
   - ☐ No. My state's exemption has no limit on lot size.
   - ☐ Yes. The exemption is limited to property of _____ acres.

   Is your property smaller than this limit?
   - ☐ Yes.
   - ☐ No. (See instructions.)
10. **Dollar Value Limits:** Does your state limit the dollar value of the homestead exemption?
    - ☐ Yes. Enter the dollar limit here: .... $_____
    - ☐ No dollar limit. (Enter "Unlimited" in line 10 if it is still blank.)

    If line 10 is either "unlimited" or larger than line 6, write "fully exempt." You can skip the rest of this worksheet. Your state's exemption fully protects your equity, so there will be no reason for the trustee to sell your home.

11. **Unprotected Equity:** If line 10 is less than line 6, enter the difference here. This is your unprotected equity. .... $_____

12. **The "Tenancy by the Entirety" Exemption:** Married couples who own property in some states are entitled to a special exemption that protects property owned as "tenancy by the entirety." (See instructions for details.)
    Do you qualify for this exemption? ☐ Yes. ☐ No.

13. **Using the "Wildcard" Exemption:** A few states allow you to apply the so-called wildcard exemption to real estate as well as personal property. (See instructions.)
    Does your state allow this?
    - ☐ No. ☐ Yes. The amount of the wildcard exemption is .... $_____

Unlimited Homestead Exemption

District of Columbia

If you are lucky enough to live in D.C., congratulations: the trustee won't sell your home if you file for bankruptcy. You can skip the rest of this chapter.

Homestead Exemption Based on Lot Size Only

Arkansas	Kansas	Texas
Florida	Oklahoma	
Iowa	South Dakota	

In these states, you can easily determine whether your home is exempt. The homestead exemption is based simply on acreage. Look in Appendix 1 for the acreage limitation in your state.

If your property is less than the maximum allowable acreage, your home is fully protected. You can skip the rest of this chapter

If your property exceeds the maximum allowable acreage, the excess acreage will be sold by the trustee if you have any equity in it. Enter $0 in line 10 of the worksheet.

Homestead Exemption Based on Lot Size and Equity

Alabama	Michigan	Nebraska
Hawaii	Minnesota	Oregon
Louisiana	Mississippi	

These states use the size of your lot and the amount of your equity to determine whether your home is exempt. First look in Appendix 1 for the acreage limitation in your state; enter it on line 9.

If your property exceeds the maximum allowable acreage, the trustee will want to sell the excess acreage if you have enough equity in it.

If your lot size is within the allowed acreage, your exemption is determined by the equity amount limit. Proceed to line 10.

Homestead Exemption Based on Equity Alone

All Other States with Homestead Exemptions (see Appendix 1)
Federal Exemptions

If your state has a homestead exemption but isn't listed in either of the lists above, or if you are using the federal exemptions, your homestead exemption is not based on lot size. Go to Line 10.

Line 10: Amount of equity protected by homestead exemption

On this line, write the amount of equity protected by your state's homestead exemption (or the federal exemption if your state allows it and you plan to use it). See Appendix 1 for these figures. In some states, if you own your home jointly with your spouse, you can each claim the full homestead exemption (this is called "doubling"). Other states limit both spouses to the one exemption. When you check Appendix 1, look carefully to see whether doubling is prohibited. If no mention is made one way or the other, assume that you can double.

Line 11: Is your home fully protected by your state's homestead exemption?

Subtract line 10 from line 6 and enter the total on line 11. If the amount is less than zero, all of your equity is exempt. But remember, this is only an estimate. If your estimate is correct, the trustee won't have your home sold, because the proceeds would go to you and the mortgage-holders and lienholders, not to your unsecured creditors.

But if line 11 is greater than zero—that is, if your equity (line 6) is more than the homestead exemption amount (line 10)—the bankruptcy trustee can force the sale of your home to pay off your creditors. If you can raise the cash, most trustees will let you pay them the difference between your equity and your homestead exemption, then allow you to keep your home. (See Section D.2, below.)

From the proceeds of the sale, your secured creditors will be paid the amounts of their mortgages, liens and so forth. You will get cash in the amount of the homestead exemption and your unsecured creditors will get the rest.

⚠ **This worksheet is for estimate purposes only.** If this worksheet shows that your equity is equal to or near the maximum amount of your state's homestead exemption, take note: The trustee can challenge the value you claim for your home, and may determine that it is worth more than you think. If this happens, the trustee may conclude that your equity exceeds the amount you can claim as exempt in your state, and therefore may seek to sell your home. Accordingly, if your estimate from this worksheet shows that you may be close to exceeding your state's exemption limit, seek the advice of an experienced bankruptcy practitioner in your area.

Line 11: Can you use the "Tenancy by the Entirety" exemption?

If you have determined that some or all of your equity is not protected by a homestead exemption, you may still be in luck: If you are married and live in the right state, you may qualify for the "tenancy by the entirety" exemption.

Tenancy by the entirety (TBE) is a form of ownership available to married couples in about 25 states. Of those 25 states, 16 have laws that prohibit TBE property from being sold to pay debts that are owed by only one spouse. The exemption has no dollar limit. (It also applies to personal property—for example, checking accounts—in some states.)

To qualify for this kind of protection, all five of the following must be true:

1. You are married.
2. You and your spouse own property in one of these states:

Delaware	Massachusetts	Pennsylvania
D.C.	Michigan	Tennessee
Florida	Missouri	Vermont
Hawaii	North Carolina	Virginia
Indiana	Ohio	Wyoming
Maryland		

Note: Unlike all other exemptions, the tenancy by the entirety exemption is based on the law where the property is located, not where you live. For example, if you and your spouse live in Minnesota, but own a condo in Florida as tenants by the entirety, the Florida property is protected under Florida law against debts that are owed by only one spouse, even though Minnesota law offers no such protection.

3. You and your spouse own the residence as "tenants by the entirety." (See below.)
4. The debts you are trying to discharge are yours alone, not debts that you owe jointly with your spouse.
5. You are filing for bankruptcy alone (without your spouse). Note: If you file jointly, this exemption is nullified.

If you think you meet these five criteria, this exemption could be very important to you. You may want to see a bankruptcy specialist to plan the best way to take full advantage of this exemption.

Line 12: Can you increase your exempt amount with a wildcard exemption?

In some states, you can add a wildcard exemption amount to the amount of your homestead exemption. Although these amounts are usually small, they may be enough to make a difference.

Wildcard Exemptions That Can Be Applied to Real Estate	
California, System 2	$800
Connecticut	$1,000
Georgia	$400
Indiana	$4,000
Kentucky	$1,000
Maine	$400
Maryland (this is the only exemption you can use on your home; there is no homestead exemption)	$5,500
Missouri	$1,250
New Hampshire	$8,000
Ohio	$400
Pennsylvania	$300
Vermont	$400
Virginia (if you're a disabled veteran)	$2,000
West Virginia	$800
Federal	$925

Other states have wildcard exemptions, but they apply only to personal property.

Conclusion

If, after completing this worksheet, you find that you have a large amount of nonexempt equity in your home, don't file for Chapter 7 bankruptcy if you want to keep your house. The trustee will almost certainly sell your home. You'll probably fare better, and hold on to your home longer, by using your equity to help pay off your debts. Some of these methods are discussed in Section D.

D. Ways to Prevent the Loss of Your House in Bankruptcy

If you have nonexempt equity in your home and would lose it if you filed for bankruptcy, you probably want to explore options other than bankruptcy. We outline some of them here, but you should ask an experienced bankruptcy lawyer for help.

1. Reduce Your Equity Before Filing for Bankruptcy

If you can reduce your nonexempt equity before you file, you may be able to pay off your other debts and avoid bankruptcy. And if you later file for bankruptcy, you may be able to save your home. But you'll probably have to act at least 91 days to one year before you file.

There are two ways to reduce your equity:
- borrow against the equity, or
- sell part ownership of your house.

You can use the proceeds to buy exempt property or to pay off other debts.

⚠ **Consult a local bankruptcy lawyer before reducing your equity.** If you do file for bankruptcy after reducing your equity, the bankruptcy court in your area might view your actions as an abuse of the bankruptcy process and dismiss your bankruptcy petition. How to stay out of trouble is discussed in Ch. 2, Section C.

a. Borrow Against Your Equity

If you borrow against your equity, you won't reduce your overall debt burden. You may be able to lower your overall monthly bills, however, if you can get a lower interest rate or a longer term equity loan to pay off short-term, high-interest debts. You can also fully deduct the interest you pay on home equity loans from your income taxes.

Be careful when you shop for a loan. Many lenders offer very high rate, unaffordable loans to people in financial trouble. Although you may be desperate to save your home, taking out another loan with very high interest rates or high costs and fees will only get you into deeper financial trouble. Also, be extra cautious about loans with balloon payments. A balloon payment is a large lump sum of money due at the end of the loan term. If you can't pay the balloon payment when it comes due, you will lose your home. Most people can't come up with $25,000, $50,000 or $100,000 all at once. You might be able to refinance your home to pay off the balloon, but don't count on it.

b. Sell Some of Your Equity

Another way to protect your equity is to sell some of your house. By owning your home jointly with someone else, your equity is reduced.

Selling a portion of your equity may appeal to you—after all, what you need now is more cash, not another monthly bill. Perhaps a friend or relative would be willing to buy a half share in your home. If you pursue this strategy, you may need to wait a year after the sale before filing for bankruptcy. Otherwise, the sale might be voided by the bankruptcy trustee, especially if it appears that you gave your friend or relative a bargain on the price.

Even a year may not be sufficient in some courts if the judge views your actions as defrauding your creditors. (See Ch. 2, Section C.) Be sure to consult a local bankruptcy attorney who is aware of local practice before you try this.

Also, think long and hard about whether you want to share ownership of your home. A co-owner can sell his interest, force a sale of the property, die and leave it to someone else and so on. Again, consult a bankruptcy lawyer before you sell. This strategy can be fraught with complications and traps for the uninformed.

2. If You File for Bankruptcy

If you do file for Chapter 7 bankruptcy, you may be able to keep the trustee from selling your house through one of the following methods:

- **Offer to substitute cash for the amount of nonexempt equity.** You may be able to convince the trustee not to sell your house if you can come up with as much cash as would be available from the proceeds to pay unsecured creditors. You may be able to raise the cash by selling exempt property or using income you earn after you file.

  EXAMPLE: The Robertsons have approximately $5,000 of nonexempt equity in their home. All of their home furnishings are exempt. After discussing the matter with the trustee, they sell three pieces of furniture and a camera for a total of $1,800, and scrape together $2,700 extra cash from income earned since they filed for bankruptcy. They offer the cash to the trustee as a substitute for the nonexempt equity. The trustee accepts the money, because the creditors will

end up with almost as much as they would have gotten if the home were sold—and the trustee will be spared the hassle of selling your home.

- **File for or convert to Chapter 13 bankruptcy.** Chapter 13 bankruptcy lets you pay your debts out of your income, rather than by selling your property. If you file for Chapter 13 bankruptcy, you won't have to give up your home, even if you have nonexempt equity. Chapter 13 bankruptcy also permits you to spread out repayments of missed installments, taxes and late charges on a mortgage. Furthermore, if your lender has begun foreclosure proceedings, Chapter 13 bankruptcy can halt them as long as your house hasn't yet been sold. (See Ch. 1, Section F, for more on Chapter 13.)

  You can convert to Chapter 13 bankruptcy any time during a Chapter 7 bankruptcy proceeding. If you miss mortgage payments after you filed for your Chapter 7 bankruptcy, however, some courts won't let you include them in your Chapter 13 repayment plan. So try to make all payments due after you file for Chapter 7. If the lender won't accept them (because it wants to proceed with foreclosure), save the money so you can make up the payments later. ■

Secured Debts

Secured debts are debts linked to specific items of property (sometimes called collateral or security). The property guarantees payment of the debt; if the debt isn't paid, the creditor can take the property or force its sale to pay off the debt. Some secured debts you incur voluntarily—such as a mortgage or car loan. Others are imposed against your will—like tax liens and liens imposed on property to enforce a judgment. If you've ever had property repossessed when you failed to pay a bill or had a creditor force the sale of an item after suing you, obtaining a judgment and recording a lien, you've had some experience with secured debts.

This chapter explains what happens to secured debts in bankruptcy and helps you decide whether or not to try to keep property that is collateral for a debt.

You may be able to skip this chapter. If you have no secured debts, you won't need the information in this chapter. To remind you, secured debts commonly arise when you have agreed, in writing, to surrender property if you fail to make your payments. Examples include mortgages, home equity loans, consumer loans from Beneficial Finance, car loans and major item purchases from Sears. Also, you will need this chapter if, within 90 days of your intended filing date, a lien has been placed on your property because of a court judgment.

A. The Statement of Intention Form

When you file for bankruptcy, you must inform the bankruptcy court and your affected creditors what you plan to do about the property that secures your debts. You tell them by filing a form called the "Chapter 7 Individual Debtor's Statement of Intention" and mailing a copy of the form to each creditor you list on it.

There are line-by-line instructions on how to fill out this form in Ch. 3, Section H. Read this chapter first to gain the necessary background to make the decisions requested on the form.

Although the Statement of Intention is not due until 30 days after you file for bankruptcy, it's commonly filed right after you file the other papers. Thus, you should decide what to do with each item of secured property before you file.

The law says you must carry out your stated intentions within 45 days of the date you file the form. There are no apparent penalties if you don't, however.

If you change your mind after you file, you can amend the form easily using the instructions in Ch. 4, Section B.

How to Use This Chapter

This chapter explains what happens to secured debts in bankruptcy, and your options regarding those debts. You'll learn about the advantages and disadvantages of each option listed on the Statement of Intention, as well as suggested strategies for keeping specific items of property such as automobiles.

To get the most out of this chapter, you should proceed as follows:

Step 1: Read Section B to learn about what happens to secured debts in bankruptcy. A clear understanding of this material is crucial to understanding the rest of the chapter and the options listed on the Statement of Intention.

Step 2: Read or skim Section C to learn about your options.

Step 3: Once you understand how these options work, Section D helps you decide whether a particular item of property is worth keeping and, if so, the best option for keeping it.

Step 4: Once you decide what procedures to use, Section E gives you step-by-step, do-it-yourself instructions for the simple procedures. If you opt for one of the complex procedures, Section E explains the basics, but you'll need the help of a lawyer.

Secured Debts and Bankruptcy

Bankruptcy eliminates your personal liability for secured debts, but the creditor's lien remains. Sometimes you can take further steps in bankruptcy to eliminate or reduce a lien.

Unsecured Debt **Secured Debt** **Secured Debt After Bankruptcy**

B. What Bankruptcy Does to Secured Debts

Bankruptcy has a different effect on secured debts than on other kinds of debts, because a secured debt consists of two parts:

- The first part is no different than an unsecured debt: it is personal liability for the debt, which is what obligates you to pay the debt to the creditor. Bankruptcy wipes out your personal liability if the debt is dischargeable. (See Ch. 8.) Once your personal liability is eliminated, the creditor cannot sue you to collect the debt.

- The second part of a secured debt is the creditor's legal claim (lien or security interest) on the property that is collateral for the debt. A lien gives the creditor the right to repossess the property or force its sale if you do not pay the debt. Bankruptcy, by itself, does not eliminate liens. But during bankruptcy you may be able to take additional steps to eliminate, or at least reduce, liens on secured property.

  EXAMPLE: Mary buys a couch on credit from a furniture store. She signs a contract that states she must pay for the couch over the next year. The contract also states that the creditor (the store) has a security interest in the couch and can repossess it if any payment is more than 15 days late. In this type of secured debt, Mary's

obligation to pay the debt is her personal liability, and the store's right to repossess the couch is the lien.

1. Eliminating Liens in Bankruptcy

As mentioned above, there are several steps you can take during bankruptcy to eliminate or reduce liens. But these procedures are neither automatic nor required —you have to request them.

The most powerful of these procedures lets you eliminate (avoid) some types of liens on certain kinds of exempt property without paying anything to the creditor. (See Ch. 2 for a definition of exempt property.) With the lien eliminated, you get to keep the property free and clear without paying anything more to the creditor.

Other procedures let you eliminate a creditor's lien (and keep the property) by paying the creditor either the amount of the lien or the current value of the property, whichever is less.

Finally, you can rid yourself of a lien by simply surrendering the property to the creditor.

The choice of which procedure to use on each item of secured property is up to you.

2. If You Don't Eliminate Liens

If you take no steps to eliminate a lien during bankruptcy, the lien survives bankruptcy intact. The creditor will be free to take the property or force its sale.

EXAMPLE: Mary (from the example above) successfully goes through bankruptcy and receives her discharge. Her personal liability for the purchase price of her couch is eliminated, but the creditor's lien on her couch remains. The creditor has the right to repossess the couch as soon as the automatic stay is lifted, or possibly even sooner.

If the property is valuable and could be easily resold (an automobile, for example), the creditor will surely repossess the item at the first opportunity unless you agree to keep making payments. (See Sections C.4 and C.5, below.) If, however, the property is of little value and not worth the cost of repossessing (such as Mary's couch), the creditor may do nothing.

If the property is of the type with a "title" or ownership document, such as a house or car, and the creditor does nothing, the lien simply remains on the property until you sell it. At that time, the lien must be paid out of the proceeds of the sale if the buyer wants to have clear title to the property. On the other hand, if the property has no ownership title document, the creditor has no practical way to enforce the lien.

In some cases, if the property is declining in value and it is clear that you aren't going to take steps to keep it, the creditor might request the bankruptcy court's permission to take the property even before the bankruptcy case is over.

C. Ways to Deal With Secured Debts in Bankruptcy

There are seven ways to deal with secured debts in bankruptcy. Some options are included on the Statement of Intention form; others are not. All but the first option allow you to keep property.

You may want to skim through these options for now, then refer back to them as you read Section D. That section indicates which option is best for specific kinds of property, including houses and cars.

1. Surrender Property

Description: Surrendering secured property simply means allowing the creditor to repossess or take the item or foreclose on the lien. It completely frees you from the debt—the lien is satisfied by your surrender of the property and your personal liability is discharged by the bankruptcy.

Advantage: A quick and easy way to completely rid yourself of a secured debt.

Disadvantage: You lose the property.

Restrictions: None. You can surrender any kind of property to get rid of any kind of lien.

When to use it: For property that you don't need or want, or would cost too much to keep.

How it works: You simply list the property as surrendered on your Statement of Intention, and send a copy of the form to the creditor. It's then up to the creditor to contact you to arrange a time to pick up the property. If the creditor never takes the property, it's yours to keep. Section E.1 contains step-by-step instructions.

2. Avoid (Eliminate) Liens

Description: Lien avoidance is a procedure by which you ask the bankruptcy court to "avoid" (eliminate or reduce) liens on your exempt property.

How much of a lien can be avoided depends on the value of the property and the amount of the exemption. If the property is entirely exempt or is worth less than the legal exemption limit, the court will eliminate the entire lien and you'll get to keep the property without paying anything. If the property is worth more than the exemption limit, the lien will be reduced to the difference between the exemption limit and either the property's value or the amount of the debt, whichever is less. (11 U.S.C. § 522(f)(2).)

EXAMPLE: A creditor has a $500 lien on Harold's guitar, which is worth $300. In Harold's state, the guitar is exempt only to $200. He could get the lien reduced to $100. The other $400 of the lien is eliminated (avoided).

$$
\begin{array}{lll}
(\$500 \text{ lien}) & \$300 & = \text{ value of item} \\
& -\ \underline{200} & = \text{ exemption amount} \\
& \underline{\$100} & = \text{ amount of lien remaining after} \\
& & \quad \text{ lien avoidance}
\end{array}
$$

Advantages: Lien avoidance costs nothing, involves only a moderate amount of paperwork and allows you to keep property without paying anything. It is the best and most powerful tool for getting rid of liens.

Disadvantage: Some paperwork is involved.

Also, by trying to avoid a lien on exempt property, you may reopen the issue of whether the property is exempt in the first place. This may happen if the property was deemed exempt by default (that is, the property is exempt because the trustee and creditors failed to timely challenge the debtor's claim of exemption). Some courts have allowed creditors to raise the issue of the property's exempt status at a hearing on a motion to avoid a lien. Other courts have ruled that creditors cannot raise this issue—the property is deemed exempt and the only issue to discuss at the hearing is whether the lien may be avoided.

As a practical matter, however, motions to avoid a lien are rarely contested.

Restrictions: Lien avoidance has several important restrictions:

- You must have owned the property before the lien was "fixed" on it. Exactly when a lien is fixed on property depends on vague state law. For purposes of your bankruptcy filing, assume that if the property had a lien on it when you acquired it, you can't avoid that lien. (See *Farrey v. Sanderfoot*, 500 U.S. 291 (1991).)
- The property must be claimed as exempt.
- The lien must be either:
  - a judicial lien, which can be removed from any exempt property, including real estate and automobiles, or
  - a nonpossessory nonpurchase-money security interest, which can be avoided only on the following exempt property:
  - household furnishings, household goods, clothing, appliances, books and musical instruments or jewelry that are primarily for your personal, family or household use
  - health aids professionally prescribed for you or a dependent
  - animals or crops held primarily for your personal, family or household use—but only the first $5,000 of the lien can be avoided (11 U.S.C. § 522(f)(3)), or
  - implements, professional books or tools used in a trade (yours or a dependent's)—but only the first $5,000 of the lien can be avoided. (11 U.S.C. § 522(f)(3).)

When to use it: Use lien avoidance whenever possible, especially if a lien can be completely wiped out. Even if you don't need the property, you can avoid the lien, sell the property and use the money for things you do need.

To keep things simple, you may want to avoid liens only on property that is completely exempt. Then the lien will be eliminated entirely and you'll own the property free and clear, without paying anything to the creditor.

In theory, even partial lien avoidance can be beneficial, but you'll have to pay the remaining amount of the lien to the creditor either in a lump sum or in installments (if the creditor agrees to it). Many creditors refuse to take installment payments after their liens have been reduced.

How it works: You request lien avoidance by checking the column "Property is claimed as exempt" on the Statement of Intention and typing and filing a document called a "motion." (Complete instructions for preparing and filing a motion to avoid a lien are in Section E.2, below.) Although it may sound complicated, lien avoidance is a routine procedure that involves just a little time.

Special Rules for Liens Arising From Divorce

Because courts place a high priority on protecting the interests of children and former spouses, the Bankruptcy Code prohibits you from avoiding a judicial lien that secures a debt to your ex-spouse or children for alimony or child support. (11 U.S.C. § 522(f)(1)(A).) In some divorces, however, it's not always clear if a lien is for support or is just to pay marital bills. In the latter case, the lien may be avoided.

Also, a Supreme Court case limits your right to avoid liens arising out of a division of property that takes place during a divorce. For example, if you get sole ownership of your marital home and your ex-spouse gets a security interest (such as a promissory note) in the home, the court may not let you avoid the lien. The determining issues are when you alone acquired title to the property and when your ex-spouse's lien affixed. Consult with a bankruptcy practitioner to determine how this case—and subsequent cases—may affect you if you want to avoid a lien arising from a divorce. (The main case is *Farrey v. Sanderfoot*, 500 U.S. 291 (1991).)

Eliminating Liens on Real Estate

You may be able to eliminate some liens on your real estate using two different provisions of the bankruptcy code. Under the first provision, 11 U.S.C. § 522 (f), you can only eliminate judicial liens (liens recorded against your property after a judgment has been entered against you). Under the second provision, 11 U.S.C. § 506(d), you may be able to eliminate both judicial and consensual liens (liens you agreed to, such as mortgages).

As explained in Ch. 6, your homestead exemption protects your equity—that is, the extent to which the value of the property exceeds the total of any consensual liens (mortgages) on the property.

EXAMPLE: Zoe and Bud own a $100,000 house with an $80,000 mortgage; their equity is $20,000. The homestead exemption in their state is $30,000. Although Credo-check has recorded a $200,000 judgment (judicial) lien against Zoe and Bud's home, their equity is fully protected because it's less than the homestead exemption amount.

Eliminating Judicial Liens (11 U.S.C. § 522(f)). If your equity is fully protected by an exemption—that is, no equity remains after the consensual liens and homestead exemption are deducted, as is the case in the example—you may be able to entirely eliminate any judicial liens on the property. (11 U.S.C. § 522(f).) At least that has been the dominant interpretation by bankruptcy trial courts. The first appellate court to rule on the question decided otherwise, however. There, the court said that the debtor could not eliminate the entire lien because that would provide him with a windfall. Instead, the court allowed him to avoid only the portion of the lien that impaired his exemption. (*In re Silveira*, 141 F.3d 34 (1st Cir. 1998); see also *In re Hanger*, 217 B.R. 592 (9th Cir. BAP 1998) aff'd by 196 F.3d 1292 (9th Cir. 1999).)

Eliminating Judicial and Consensual Liens (11 U.S.C. § 506(d)). You may be able to get rid of a consensual lien (or a judicial lien that you are unable to eliminate using the above procedure) under a different provision of the bankruptcy code, 11 U.S.C. § 506(d). This is called a "strip off" of the lien. In order to strip off a lien, you must meet two criteria: (1) there must be other liens on the property that have priority over (are senior to) the lien you want to get rid of, and (2) the combined value of the senior liens must be greater than the fair market value of the property at the time you file for bankruptcy. For instance, assume your home is worth $150,000 when you file, and you have two mortgages (or deeds of trust) on the property—a first mortgage for $160,000 and a second mortgage for $25,000. Since the lien created by the first mortgage is greater than the value of the property, the lien created by the second mortgage is unsecured. According to several courts, because it is unsecured, the second mortgage is void. *Yi v. Citibank*, 219 B.R. 394 (E.D. Va. 1998); *In re Farha*, 246 B.R. 547 (2000). Unfortunately, if you want to strip off a lien, you must file a separate lawsuit in the bankruptcy court. For that reason, it is more difficult to use than lien avoidance and may require a lawyer's help.

Important Definitions: Liens Created by Secured Debts

Various types of liens are created by secured debts. The type of lien on your property often determines which lien-reduction or lien-eliminating procedures you can use.

You may want to skip this list of definitions for now and refer to it when we describe specific kinds of liens.

Security Interests—Liens You Agree to

If you voluntarily pledge property as collateral—that is, as a guarantee that you will pay a debt—the lien on your property is called a security interest. Many written security agreements give the creditor the right to take the property if you miss a payment.

The most common types of security interests are:

Purchase-Money Security Interests: If you purchase an item on credit and pledge it as collateral for the debt, the lien on the collateral is called a purchase-money security interest. Typical purchase-money secured debts are automobile loans and debts for large furniture purchases.

These kinds of liens cannot be eliminated in bankruptcy. You will have to either honor the original contract and continue making payments, or pay the value of the property up front to keep the property. (See Section B.2, above.)

Nonpurchase-Money Security Interests: If you pledge property you already own as collateral for a loan, the lien is called a nonpurchase-money security interest. If you keep the property, for example you borrow from a lending company or credit union, and pledge your car or stereo equipment as security for the loan, the loan is called *nonpossessory*.

These kinds of liens can be eliminated in bankruptcy if the collateral is exempt and meets the criteria described in Section C.2.

If you don't retain possession of the property (for instance, if you turn property over to a pawnshop), the loan is called *possessory*. These liens cannot be eliminated in bankruptcy as described in Section C.2.

Liens Created Without Your Consent

If a creditor gets a lien on your property without your consent, it is called a non-consensual lien. There are three major types of non-consensual liens.

Judicial Liens: A judicial lien is created against your property by somebody who wins a money judgment in a lawsuit against you, then takes the additional steps necessary to record a lien against your property.

If a judicial lien is on exempt property, you can probably eliminate it in bankruptcy unless it arose out of a mortgage foreclosure. (See Section C.2.)

Statutory Liens: Non-consensual liens can also be created automatically by law. For example, in most states, when you hire someone to work on your house, the worker or supplier of materials automatically gets a mechanic's lien or materialman's lien on the house if you don't pay. Liens like these are called statutory liens.

EXAMPLE: Sam's home suffered severe water damage after a pipe burst in the upstairs bathroom. He had the damage repaired at a cost of $4,000. Now, because of unexpected medical bills, he can't pay the plumber and carpenter the last $2,000 he owes them for the work done on the house. The carpenter and plumber have a statutory lien on his house for $2,000.

A statutory lien can be eliminated in bankruptcy if it:
- did not become effective at least 90 days before you filed for bankruptcy
- was not perfected (made official by filing the applicable documents with the land records office) before you filed for bankruptcy, or
- is for rent you owe.

There is no specific provision in the bankruptcy code for eliminating these kinds of liens.

Tax Liens: Federal, state and local governments have the authority to impose liens on your property if you owe delinquent taxes. Tax liens are usually impossible to eliminate in bankruptcy.

3. Redeem Property

Description: You have the right to "redeem" property—that is, to buy it back from the creditor rather than have it taken by the creditor and sold to someone else. You pay the creditor the property's current market value, usually in a lump sum, and in return the lien is eliminated. You then own the property free and clear.

> **EXAMPLE:** Susan and Gary owe $500 on some household furniture now worth $200. They can keep the furniture and eliminate the $500 lien by paying the creditor the $200 within 45 days of filing their Statement of Intention.

Advantage: Redemption is a great option if you owe more than the property is worth. The creditor must accept the current value of the item as payment in full.

Disadvantage: Generally, redemption requires immediate lump-sum payment of the value of the item; it may be difficult to come up with that much cash on short notice. You can try to get the creditor to voluntarily accept your redemption payments in installments, but few courts will require a creditor to accept installment payments.

Restrictions: You can redeem property only if all of the following are true:

- The debt is a consumer debt. This means it was incurred "primarily for a personal, family or household purpose." This includes just about everything except business debts.
- The property is tangible personal property. Tangible property is anything you can touch. For instance, a car, furniture, boat, computer, jewelry and furs are all examples of tangible property. Stocks are intangible. The property must also be personal property, which simply means it can't be real estate.
- The property is either:
  - claimed as exempt (exempt property is explained in Ch. 2), or
  - abandoned by the trustee. A trustee will abandon property that has little or no nonexempt value beyond the amount of the liens. If property is abandoned, you'll receive notice in the mail. You can then redeem the property by paying the secured creditor its current market value.

When you fill out your bankruptcy papers, if you know you'll want to redeem an item of property if the trustee abandons it, check the "redeem" column on Form 8, Statement of Intention. If you haven't done this and the trustee abandons the property, you may have to amend your Statement of Intention. Call the trustee and find out. (See Ch. 4, Section B, for how to amend a form.)

When to use it: Use redemption only if you owe more than the property is worth and lien avoidance is not available.

Redemption usually makes sense for keeping small items of household property, where raising money for the lump-sum payment will not be that difficult and the cost of replacing the property would be much greater.

Redemption can also be used for automobiles, which are not eligible for lien avoidance and are likely to be repossessed if a lien remains after bankruptcy and you don't agree to keep making payments. If the creditor won't agree to installment payments, however, raising the cash necessary to redeem an automobile may be difficult.

How it works: You and the creditor must agree on the value of the property, then draft and sign a redemption agreement. Agreeing on the value may take a little negotiation. Also, sometimes you can get the creditor to agree to accept payments in installments by agreeing to a higher value. Whatever you agree to, put it in the redemption agreement. See Section E.3, below, for sample agreements and full instructions.

4. Reaffirm a Debt

Description: When you reaffirm a debt, both the creditor's lien on the collateral and your personal liability survive bankruptcy intact—as if you never filed for bankruptcy. You and the creditor draw up an agreement that sets out the amount you owe and the terms of the repayment. In return, you get to keep the property as long as you keep current on your payments.

If you default on your payments, the creditor can repossess the collateral. You can also be held liable for the difference between what the property is resold for and the unpaid amount of the agreement. This is called a "deficiency balance." Nearly all states permit deficiency balances for most types of property. About half of the states, however, don't allow them on repossessed personal property if the original purchase price was under a few thousand dollars.

You can cancel a reaffirmation agreement by notifying the creditor before either of the following, whichever occurs later:

- the date of your discharge, or
- 60 days after you filed the reaffirmation agreement with the bankruptcy court (this often happens at the discharge hearing). (11 U.S.C. § 524(c)(2).)

If your case is already closed, however, you will not be able to switch to the other options listed in this chapter.

Advantages: Reaffirmation can be used when lien avoidance or redemption is unavailable or impractical. It provides a sure way to keep property, as long as you abide by the terms of the reaffirmation agreement.

Disadvantages: Because reaffirmation leaves you personally liable, there is no way to "walk away" from the debt, even if the property becomes worthless or you simply decide you no longer want it. You'll still be legally bound to pay the agreed-upon amount even if the property is damaged or destroyed. And because you can't file for Chapter 7 bankruptcy again until six years after the date you filed an earlier bankruptcy that resulted in a discharge, you'll be stuck with the debt.

EXAMPLE: Tasha owns a computer worth $900. She owes $1,500 on it. She reaffirms the debt for the full $1,500. Two months after bankruptcy, she spills a soft drink into the disk drive and the computer is a total loss. Now, she has not only lost the computer, but because she reaffirmed the debt, she still has to pay the creditor $1,500.

Restrictions: Reaffirmation can be used on any kind of property and any kind of lien, but the creditor must agree to the terms of the reaffirmation and the court must approve it. The court can disapprove the agreement if it appears that the creditor is giving you a bum deal, or if you've failed to exercise other options that would be more favorable to you.

When to use it: Because of the disadvantages of reaffirmation, you should use it only if redemption and

lien avoidance are unavailable or impractical. Use it primarily for property you can't live without—and only if you have good reason to believe you'll be able to pay off the balance.

For some types of property, such as automobiles or your home, reaffirmation may be the only practical way to keep the item. Also, reaffirmation can be a sensible way to keep property that is worth significantly more than what you owe on it.

If you do decide to reaffirm, try to get the creditor to accept less than the full amount you owe as full payment of the debt. (This doesn't apply when you reaffirm your mortgage.) As a general rule, you should never reaffirm a debt for more than the property is worth. A creditor will often accept a lower amount because that's all the creditor would get for the property if it were repossessed.

How it works: You and the creditor agree to the terms of the reaffirmation in a written "reaffirmation agreement," which is submitted to, and approved by, the court, sometimes at the discharge hearing. Generally, if you know you want to reaffirm a debt, keep current on your payments to stay on the good side of the creditor. If you're behind, the creditor has the right to demand that you get current before agreeing to a reaffirmation contract, but you usually have some room to negotiate. Complete instructions and sample reaffirmation agreements are in Section E.4, below.

Negotiation note. Negotiating with a creditor can be an intimidating experience. If you want help in negotiating a reaffirmation agreement and you think negotiation could save you a significant amount, consider hiring a good negotiator to deal with the creditor. Or, hire a lawyer to do the negotiating for you. (See Ch. 9.)

5. Retain Property Without Reaffirming or Redeeming

Description: Some bankruptcy courts allow you to keep secured property as long as you remain current on your payments under your contract with the creditor. If you fall behind, the creditor can take the property, but your personal liability for the debt is wiped out by the bankruptcy.

EXAMPLE: Jill owes $1,200 on her computer, which she pledged as security when she bought it. One month after the close of her bankruptcy case, her computer falls out her window and breaks into a million pieces. If Jill simply continued to pay off the lien without reaffirming, she could let the creditor repossess the now-useless property and be free of any liability.

Other courts don't allow you to retain property unless you surrender or redeem the property or reaffirm the debt. In those districts, if you do not use these methods, the creditor may repossess the property at any time, regardless of whether you are current on your payments. It is up to you to find out whether the creditor would be willing to voluntarily forego repossessing the property as long as you keep current on the contract.

If your court has not ruled on this matter, consult a bankruptcy practitioner as to the local custom in your area. Because this is an unsettled and changing area of the law, even if your state or district is listed in our chart, you may want to consult a bankruptcy practitioner to see if there's been a change.

Advantages: Informal repayment can be used when lien avoidance or redemption is not available. It allows you to pay in installments rather than a lump sum. Unlike reaffirmation, it also leaves you the option of walking away from a debt without being personally liable for the balance owed.

Disadvantage: Unless the court allows you to keep secured property by remaining current on the payments (see chart below), if you don't reaffirm or redeem, a creditor can take the property at any time—and probably will if the property can be easily resold. Also, if you pay on a debt without any agreement, the creditor may not report your payments to credit bureaus. If you pay on time for years, your credit may not improve as it would have if the payments had been reported.

Restrictions: Because informal repayment requires an agreement between you and the creditor, it can be used on any kind of property and any kind of lien. Some courts that have formally recognized this tactic, however, require the debtor to fully comply with the original terms of the contract, including any requirements to insure the collateral and pay interest on the principal due.

When to use it: Use this option if lien avoidance or redemption is not available, and you don't want to reaffirm the debt.

If your district does not force creditors to agree to this arrangement and you are worried about losing the property, contact the creditor to see if it will forego repossession as long as your payments are current. If losing the property would not be a major inconvenience, you might simply keep sending payments and gamble that the creditor won't bother to repossess as long as the checks keep coming.

Keep in mind that, because this option leaves the creditor in a vulnerable position, the creditor may be eager to repossess and resell the collateral before it declines in value any further. This is especially true for automobiles, which depreciate fast and can be easily resold. In such cases, your only options may be to reaffirm or redeem.

On the other hand, a creditor probably won't be eager to repossess property that isn't worth much or would be hard to resell. For this kind of property, you can probably get the creditor to agree to let you pay off the lien in installments after bankruptcy without having to reaffirm the debt.

How it works: In the districts that allow it, you indicate on your Statement of Intention that you plan to retain the property by keeping current on your obligations—which may include monthly payments, insurance coverage and more—under the contract.

In the districts that do not allow it, ask the creditor to informally let you keep the property as long as you keep current on the contractual obligations. On the Statement of Intention, however, indicate that you are surrendering the property—which means that the creditor doesn't have to wait for you to default to repossess. Complete instructions are in Section E.5, below.

6. Pay Off the Lien Later in a Follow-Up Chapter 13 Bankruptcy

Description: You can file what some bankruptcy practitioners call a "Chapter 20" bankruptcy—that is, filing for Chapter 13 bankruptcy immediately after completing a Chapter 7 bankruptcy. The Chapter 13 bankruptcy is used to pay off any liens remaining after your Chapter

Can You Keep Secured Property Without Reaffirming or Redeeming?

If your state (or district) is not listed below, your bankruptcy court has not yet ruled on whether or not you can keep secured property by simply staying current on your payments.

State or District	Yes	No	Case
Alabama		✔	*Taylor v. AGE Federal Credit Union*, 3 F.3d 1512 (11th Cir. 1993)
Alaska	✔		*In re Parker*, 139 F.3d 668 (9th Cir. 1998)
Arizona	✔		*In re Parker*, 139 F.3d 668 (9th Cir. 1998)
Arkansas (Eastern District)		✔	*In re Kennedy*, 137 B.R. 302 (E.D. Ark, 1992)
Arkansas (Western District)	✔		*In re Parker*, 142 B.R. 327 (W.D. Ark. 1992)
California	✔		*In re Parker*, 139 F.3d 668 (9th Cir. 1998)
Colorado	✔		*Lowery Federal Credit Union v. West*, 882 F.2d 1543 (10th Cir. 1989)
Connecticut	✔		*In re Boodrow*, 126 F.3d 43 (2nd Cir. 1997)
Florida		✔	*Taylor v. AGE Federal Credit Union*, 3 F.3d 1512 (11th Cir. 1993)
Georgia		✔	*Taylor v. AGE Federal Credit Union*, 3 F.3d 1512 (11th Cir. 1993)
Hawaii	✔		*In re Parker*, 139 F.3d 668 (9th Cir. 1998)
Idaho	✔		*In re Parker*, 139 F.3d 668 (9th Cir. 1998)
Illinois		✔	*In re Edwards*, 901 F.2d 1383 (7th Cir. 1990)
Indiana		✔	*In re Edwards*, 901 F.2d 1383 (7th Cir. 1990)
Kansas	✔		*Lowery Federal Credit Union v. West*, 882 F.2d 1543 (10th Cir. 1989)
Louisiana		✔	*In re Johnson*, 89 F.3d 249 (5th Cir. 1996)
Maine		✔	*In re Burr*, 160 F.3d 843 (1st Cir. 1998)
Maryland	✔		*In re Belanger*, 962 F.2d 345 (4th Cir. 1992)
Massachusetts		✔	*In re Burr*, 160 F.3d 843 (1st Cir. 1998)
Michigan (Western District)		✔	*In re Schmidt*, 145 B.R. 543 (W.D. Mich. 1992)
Mississippi		✔	*In re Johnson*, 89 F.3d 249 (5th Cir. 1996)
Missouri (Western District)		✔	*In re Gerling*, 175 B.R. 295 (W.D. Mo. 1994)
Montana	✔		*In re Parker*, 139 F.3d 668 (9th Cir. 1998)
Nevada	✔		*In re Parker*, 139 F.3d 668 (9th Cir. 1998)
New Hampshire		✔	*In re Burr*, 160 F.3d 843 (1st Cir. 1998)
New Mexico	✔		*Lowery Federal Credit Union v. West*, 882 F.2d 1543 (10th Cir. 1989)
New York	✔		*In re Boodrow*, 126 F.3d 43 (2nd Cir. 1997)
North Carolina	✔		*In re Belanger*, 962 F.2d 345 (4th Cir. 1992)
Ohio (Northern District)	✔		*In re Laubacher*, 150 B.R. 200 (N.D. Ohio 1992)
Ohio (Southern District)		✔	*In re Lock*, 243 B.R. 332 (S.D. Ohio 1999)
Oklahoma	✔		*Lowery Federal Credit Union v. West*, 882 F.2d 1543 (10th Cir. 1989)
Oregon	✔		*In re Parker*, 139 F.3d 668 (9th Cir. 1998)
Pennsylvania (Eastern District)	✔		*In re McNeil*, 128 B.R. 603 (E.D. Penn. 1991)
Pennsylvania (Western District)	✔		*In re Stefano*, 134 B.R. 824 (W.D. Penn. 1991)
Rhode Island		✔	*In re Burr*, 160 F.3d 843 (1st Cir. 1998)
South Carolina	✔		*In re Belanger*, 962 F.2d 345 (4th Cir. 1992)
Tennessee (Eastern District)		✔	*In re Whitaker*, 85 B.R. 788 (E.D. Tenn. 1988)
Tennessee (Western District)	✔		*In re Barriger*, 61 B.R. 506 (W.D. Tenn. 1986)
Texas		✔	*In re Johnson*, 89 F.3d 249 (5th Cir. 1996)
Utah	✔		*Lowery Federal Credit Union v. West*, 882 F.2d 1543 (10th Cir. 1989)
Vermont	✔		*In re Boodrow*, 126 F.3d 43 (2nd Cir. 1997)
Virginia	✔		*In re Belanger*, 962 F.2d 345 (4th Cir. 1992)
Washington	✔		*In re Parker*, 139 F.3d 668 (9th Cir. 1998)
West Virginia	✔		*In re Belanger*, 962 F.2d 345 (4th Cir. 1992)
Wisconsin		✔	*In re Edwards*, 901 F.2d 1383 (7th Cir. 1990)
Wyoming	✔		*Lowery Federal Credit Union v. West*, 882 F.2d 1543 (10th Cir. 1989)

7 case has wiped out your personal liability. And if the lien exceeds the value of the property, you can often get the lien fully discharged by simply paying the current value of the item, rather than the full amount of the lien.

Because this book covers Chapter 7 bankruptcies only, space does not permit us to give a full explanation of how to do a successful follow-up Chapter 13 case. For more information, see *Chapter 13 Bankruptcy: Repay Your Debts*, by Robin Leonard (Nolo).

Advantage: Filing a follow-up Chapter 13 case allows you to pay off remaining liens over time, even if the creditor is demanding immediate payment.

Disadvantage: This strategy requires you to file for Chapter 13 bankruptcy, which means you must fill out another set of bankruptcy forms and pay another filing fee. This strategy also requires you to give up all of your disposable income over the next three to five years to the bankruptcy trustee. Staying involved in the bankruptcy system for three to five more years means that it may take that much longer before you can begin to rebuild your credit.

Restrictions: There are no restrictions on the use of the Chapter 20 technique. To file for Chapter 13 bankruptcy, however, your unsecured debts cannot exceed $290,525 and your secured debts cannot exceed $871,550.

When to use it: This remedy makes sense only if lien avoidance is not available or redemption is not practical. It can be particularly useful for dealing with liens on property you need to keep, if you cannot raise the lump sum necessary to redeem the property.

How it works: You file your Chapter 13 petition as soon as you get your Chapter 7 discharge. This keeps the automatic stay in effect and prevents the creditor from taking steps to take your property. Then you work with the bankruptcy court trustee to set up your three- to five-year Chapter 13 payment plan.

7. Lien-Eliminating Techniques Beyond the Scope of This Book

Deep in the recesses of the Bankruptcy Code are other procedures for eliminating certain kinds of "non-consensual" liens. 11 U.S.C. § 522(h) gives a debtor the power to use a wide range of lien avoidance techniques available to the bankruptcy trustee. The techniques are found in §§ 545, 547, 548, 549, 553 and 724(a) of the Bankruptcy Code. These liens include:

- non-judicial liens securing the payment of penalties, fines or punitive damages and
- non-consensual liens that were recorded or perfected while you were already insolvent or within the 90 days before you filed for bankruptcy.

Eliminating these liens requires the aid of an experienced bankruptcy professional.

D. Choosing the Best Options

Now it's time pick the best option for each of your secured debts. If an item has more than one lien on it, you might use different procedures to deal with each lien. For example, you might eliminate a judicial lien on exempt property through lien avoidance, and redeem the property to satisfy a purchase-money security interest.

The chart titled "Options for Dealing With Secured Property" summarizes the strategies discussed in this section.

Options for Dealing With Secured Property

How to Use This Chart: Answer the questions in columns 1 through 4 to narrow down your options. After you've answered all the questions, follow across from your answer in column 4 to find your options. Read all sections listed in *italics* for more information about each option. (N/A = Not Applicable)

1	2	3	4	
Do you want to keep the property?	Is the property exempt?	Is the property an automobile? (If yes, but it is a tool of your trade, choose "No")	What kind of lien is on the property?	Your options
No	N/A	N/A	N/A	Surrender *(Section C.1)*
Yes	No	No *(Section D.4)*	Any Kind	Informally repay—continue to pay off the lien, but do not reaffirm debt *(Section C.5)* Redeem if the trustee abandons the property *(Section C.3)* Reaffirm *(Section C.4)* Surrender and buy replacement property *(Section C.1)*
	Yes	Yes *(Section D.2)*	Any Kind	Redeem if the trustee abandons the property *(Section C.3)* Reaffirm *(Section C.4)* Surrender and buy replacement property *(Section C.1)*
		No *(Section D.3)*	Purchase-Money Security Interest	Redeem *(Section C.3)* Reaffirm if property is worth more than debt *(Section C.4)* Informally repay—continue to pay off the lien, but do not reaffirm debt *(Section C.5)* File a follow-up Chapter 13 bankruptcy *(Section C.6)*
			Non-purchase-Money Security Interest	Avoid lien *(Subject to limitations described in Section C.2)* Redeem *(Section C.3)* Informally repay—continue to pay off the lien, but do not reaffirm debt *(Section C.5)* File a follow-up Chapter 13 bankruptcy *(Section C.6)* Reaffirm *(Section C.4)*
			Judicial Lien	Avoid lien *(Section C.2)* Redeem *(Section C.3)* Informally repay—continue to pay off the lien, but do not reaffirm debt *(Section C.5)* File a follow-up Chapter 13 bankruptcy *(Section C.6)* Reaffirm *(Section C.4)*
			Statutory Lien	Redeem *(Section C.3)* Reaffirm if property is worth more than debt *(Section C.4)* Informally repay—continue to pay off the lien, but do not reaffirm debt *(Section C.5)* File a follow-up Chapter 13 bankruptcy *(Section C.6)*
		Yes *(Section D.2)*	Security Interest	Redeem *(Section C.3)* Reaffirm if property is worth more than debt *(Section C.4)* Surrender and buy replacement property *(Section C.1)*
			Judicial Lien	Avoid lien *(Section C.2)* Redeem *(Section C.3)* Reaffirm if property is worth more than debt *(Section C.4)*
			Statutory Lien	Redeem *(Section C.3)* Reaffirm if property is worth more than debt *(Section C.4)* Surrender and buy replacement property *(Section C.1)*

No Matter Which Option You Choose Remember This Rule

If the option you're considering requires paying more than the current market value of the property you want to keep, it's a bad deal. There are usually ways you or a lawyer can keep any item of secured property by paying no more than the current value of the property.

---

1. What Property Should You Keep?

Be realistic about how much property you will be able to afford to keep after bankruptcy. Face the fact that you may not be able to keep everything, and decide which items you can do without.

These questions will help you decide whether an item is worth keeping:

- How important is the property to you?
- Will you need the property to help you make a fresh start after bankruptcy?
- How much would it cost to keep the property? (This will depend on the procedure you use.)
- Would it be more expensive to redeem the property or to replace it?
- If you're considering installment payments, will you realistically be able to make the payments after bankruptcy?
- If you're considering surrendering your property and buying a replacement item, will you need a loan to purchase it? If so, will you be able to get such a loan after bankruptcy?

EXAMPLE 1: Fran bought a sports car two years ago for $16,000. Now Fran is unemployed, but is about to start a new job. She still owes $13,000 on the car, and it is currently worth $10,000. Although she likes the car, she can't come up with the $10,000 in cash to redeem it, and she doesn't want to remain personally liable for the $13,000 debt. If Fran is willing to lower her standards a little, she can buy a reliable used car to get her to work and back for about $3,000. She decides to surrender the car. Now she will have to buy the lower-priced car, but she may have difficulty getting a loan for it.

EXAMPLE 2: Joe owns a six-year-old Toyota worth $2,000. It is security for a debt of $2,500. If Joe files for bankruptcy, he will probably be able to keep the car by paying the secured creditor only $2,000 (the value of the car). Joe decides it's worth paying that amount. He knows the car is reliable and will probably last another six years. He also believes it would be a hassle to find a car of comparable quality at that price, and it's his only means of getting to work. And, after some realistic budgeting, Joe concludes that making the payments after bankruptcy will not wreck his budget. He has probably made the right decision.

Keep up with your payments. If you are thinking of using reaffirmation, paying off a lien outside of bankruptcy or redeeming property by paying in installments, staying current on your payments will make negotiations go more smoothly, and may persuade the creditor to cut you some slack.

2. Motor Vehicles or Real Estate

Liens on cars or real estate involve special considerations.

a. Your Home

Filing for bankruptcy when you own a house is discussed in Ch. 6, but a few words about eliminating liens are appropriate here. If you own a home and want to file for bankruptcy, Chapter 13 bankruptcy is almost always the better option. Mortgage liens cannot be eliminated or reduced in Chapter 7 bankruptcy, and Chapter 7 bankruptcy won't stop a foreclosure if you are behind on payments.

If you are current on your mortgage, however, Chapter 7 bankruptcy might help you eliminate other liens on your house. To determine if any liens can be eliminated, total up the amount of your mortgage(s), applicable homestead exemption and other liens on your home. If the total exceeds the value of your home, you can probably eliminate some of the liens.

You can use lien avoidance to get rid of judicial liens if they conflict with your homestead exemption.

And you can do this without a lawyer's help. (Lien avoidance is explained in Section C.2, above; the necessary forms are in Section E.2, below.)

Liens on your home that you might be able to eliminate with the help of a lawyer include "unrecorded" tax liens and liens for penalties, fines or punitive damages from a lawsuit. (See Section C.6, above.)

b. Your Car

Because repossessed motor vehicles can easily be resold, if a lien remains on your car, the creditor will probably act quickly to either repossess it or force its sale. For this reason, if you intend to keep your car, you should deal with liens on it during bankruptcy.

If your automobile is exempt, any judicial liens on it can be eliminated through lien avoidance. (See Section C.2, above.)

The purchase-money security interest held by the seller can be dealt with only through redemption or re-affirmation. Raising the lump-sum amount necessary for a redemption is your best option. (See Section C.3, above.) If that is not possible, your only realistic option is to reaffirm the debt. (See Section C.4, above.) Proposals for informal repayment are likely to be rejected by the creditor. (See Section C.5, above.)

If your automobile falls within the "tool of trade" exemption, you can use lien avoidance for any non-purchase-money liens on the vehicle. (See Section C.2, above.)

3. Exempt Property

Liens on exempt property can be dealt with in four different ways:
- lien avoidance
- redemption
- informal payment of the lien, or
- reaffirmation.

You should use lien avoidance whenever possible to eliminate judicial liens and nonpurchase-money security interests. Use redemption whenever the lien exceeds the value of the property and you can raise the lump sum amount necessary to buy the property back at its current market value.

If you can't raise the lump sum necessary for redemption, you'll have to either reaffirm the debt or pay off the lien outside of bankruptcy. The option you choose will depend on how anxious the creditor is to repossess the item. If the property is of little value, you can probably get away with informally paying off the lien. Property of greater value, however, may require reaffirmation. Remember never to agree to pay more than the property is currently worth.

Even if you can get liens wiped out, you still may not get to keep the property, if the property is worth more than your exemption amount. The trustee will want to sell the property, pay you your exemption amount and distribute the remaining portion among your unsecured creditors.

In this situation, the only way to hold on to the property is to buy it back from the trustee. How much you will have to pay depends on several factors, but keep in mind this basic rule: The amount you offer to the trustee has to leave your secured and unsecured creditors no worse off than they would have been had the trustee sold the property to somebody else.

> **EXAMPLE:** Mindy has a $1,000 asset on which she can claim a $500 exemption. There is a $200 judicial lien on the asset. Mindy cannot avoid the lien because it does not "impair" her exemption. If the trustee sold the property, Mindy would get her $500 exemption, the lienholder would get his $200, and the remaining $300 would go to Mindy's unsecured creditors. If Mindy wanted to buy the property from the trustee, she'd have to offer him $500: $200 for the lienholder, and $300 for her unsecured creditors.

As you can see, the amount you have to offer the trustee will vary from case to case, depending on the amount of the liens, the amount of your exemption and whether you or the trustee can eliminate the liens on the asset. You can consult with the trustee to work out the particulars.

4. Nonexempt Property

If you want to keep nonexempt property, your options are limited. You can:

- redeem the property if the trustee "abandons" it (abandoning property means that the trustee releases it from the bankruptcy estate; a trustee will abandon property when there is not enough value in it to justify selling it to raise money for the unsecured creditors)
- reaffirm the debt, or
- pay off the lien informally outside of bankruptcy.

a. Property Worth More Than the Debt

If your nonexempt property is worth more than the liens on it, you probably won't have a chance to keep it. The trustee is likely to sell the property, pay off the liens and distribute the rest of the proceeds to your unsecured creditors.

> **EXAMPLE:** Elena pledges her $4,000 car as security for a $900 loan. The $900 lien is the only lien on her car, and only $1,200 of the $4,000 is exempt. If Elena files for bankruptcy, the trustee will take the car, sell it, pay off the $900 lien, give Elena her $1,200 exemption and distribute the rest of the proceeds to Elena's creditors.

If the trustee does not take the property and you want to keep it, your best bet is probably to reaffirm the debt. This will prevent the creditor from taking the property. (See Sections C.4, above and E.4, below, for complete instructions.)

b. Property Worth Less Than the Debt

If the property is worth less than the liens on it, the trustee will probably abandon the property.

> **EXAMPLE:** When Stan bought his $500 sofa on credit from the Reliable Furniture Co., he pledged the sofa as security. Since then, the sofa has declined in value to only $100, but he still owes $250 on it. The trustee will abandon the property because selling it would yield no proceeds for the unsecured creditors.

The trustee might also abandon property if the collateral has more than one lien on it, and the combined total of all the liens exceeds the value of the collateral. In this case, the creditors with the lowest priority liens are called "undersecured" creditors. (The priority of liens is determined by state and federal law. Generally, the most recent lien is the lowest priority lien, but certain types of liens always have priority over others.)

> **EXAMPLE:** Aaron's car is currently worth $3,000. He pledged his car as collateral for the loan he used to buy it. That loan has a remaining balance of $2,200. He later pledged his car for two personal loans on which he owes $500 each. In addition, there is a judgment lien against his car for $1,000. The total balance of all liens is $4,200.
>
> In this situation, the original $2,200 purchase-money loan is fully secured, and so is the first personal loan for $500. The other $500 loan is secured only by the remaining $300 in equity, so it is an undersecured claim. And there is nothing securing the $1,000 judgment, so it is undersecured.

When the trustee abandons the property, you have the right to buy it back (redeem it) at its current market value. This is your best option, if you can come up with the lump sum payment or if the creditor will accept redemption in installments. Redemption eliminates all liens on the property. (See Section C.3, above.)

If you can't come up with the lump sum necessary to redeem the property, and the creditor won't agree to installment payments, reaffirmation is the only sure way to keep the property. If you are willing to gamble that the creditor won't take the property as long as you keep up your payments, you always have the option of simply continuing to pay off the lien outside of bankruptcy. Whatever option you choose, just remember not to pay more than the property is worth.

Planning reminder. Once you've filed for bankruptcy, a creditor cannot legally take your property. And, as you now know, it's much easier to hold on to property in the first place than it is to get it back after the creditor repossesses it. So if you have some exempt property that a creditor is about to take, and you haven't filed for bankruptcy yet, you may want to file right away to prevent the seizure.

Getting Back Exempt Property Repossessed Just Before Bankruptcy

If, during the 90 days before you filed for bankruptcy, a secured creditor took exempt property that would qualify for either lien avoidance or redemption, you may be able to get the property back. But you must act quickly, before the creditor resells the property. If the creditor has already resold the property, you probably can't get it back. Repossessed cars are usually resold very quickly, but used furniture may sit in a warehouse for months.

Legally, the creditor must give back such property because the repossession is an illegal "preference," which means that the property is still part of the bankruptcy estate. (11 U.S.C. §§ 542, 543, 547; see Ch. 2, Section A.3.) In practice, however, the creditor won't give it back unless the court orders it (which usually means you'll need the help of a lawyer) or unless you make a reasonable offer of cash for the item.

Assuming you don't want to hire a lawyer, you probably won't be able to get an item back unless you talk the creditor into allowing you to redeem it or reaffirm. The creditor might prefer to have cash in hand rather than used property sitting in a warehouse. If you plan to avoid the lien on the exempt item and not pay anything, however, the creditor probably won't turn over the property unless forced to by court order.

Whether it's worth the expense of a court order to get back an exempt item so you can avoid the lien depends on how badly you need the property and how much you'll save through lien avoidance. Compare how much it would cost to redeem the property or buy replacement property. If those options are cheaper, or you decide you can get along without the property, don't bother with the court order.

E. Step-by-Step Instructions

Once you decide what to do with each item of secured property, you must list your intentions on your Statement of Intention, file that form and then carry out the procedures within 45 days. (See Ch. 3 for instructions.)

1. How to Surrender Property

If you plan to surrender any secured property, here's how to proceed.

Step 1: When you fill out your Statement of Intention, state that you are surrendering the property that secures the debt. (Instructions are in Ch. 3.)

Step 2: The creditor, who will receive a copy of the Statement of Intention, must make arrangements to pick up the property. It's not your responsibility to get the property back to the creditor. If the creditor never comes to pick it up, so much the better for you. If the creditor does pick it up, get a receipt. (See sample receipt, below.)

Receipt for Surrender of Property

1. This receipt certifies that ___*name of repossessor (print)*___ took the following item(s): (List items)

   _____

   _____

   _____

   on ___*date*___, 20__, because of debt owed to *name of creditor (print)*.

2. *Name of repossessor (print)* is an authorized agent of *name of creditor (print)*.

   Signed: ___Your signature___

   Dated: _____

   Signed: ___Repossessor's signature___

   Dated: _____

---

2. How to Avoid Liens on Exempt Property

To avoid a lien, you claim the property as exempt on your Statement of Intention and file a separate request (motion) with the bankruptcy court. Filing a motion to avoid a lien is quite simple and can be done without a lawyer.

What you say in your motion papers depends on the kind of lien you're trying to wipe out. Read subsection a, below, if you're dealing with a nonpossessory nonpurchase-money security interest, and subsection b, below, if you want to avoid a judicial lien.

a. Eliminating Nonpossessory Nonpurchase-Money Security Interests

Before you file a motion to avoid a lien, make sure that:

- you have a nonpossessory nonpurchase-money secured debt (defined in Section C.1, above), and
- the secured property qualifies for lien avoidance (see Section C.2, above).

In most courts, you must file your motion with the court within 30 days after you file for bankruptcy. But some courts require you to file before the creditors' meeting. Check your local rules.

If you miss the deadline for filing this motion, go ahead and file it anyway. As it turns out, most of these motions are uncontested—that is, the creditor doesn't respond—and will be granted by default. If the creditor doesn't show up to argue that you filed late, neither the judge nor the trustee has any interest in enforcing the deadline.

You will need to fill out one complete set of forms for each affected creditor—generally, each creditor holding a lien on that property. Sample forms are at the end of this section. Some courts have their own forms; if yours does, use those forms and adapt these instructions to fit them.

Step 1: If your court publishes local rules, refer to them for time limits, format of papers and other details of a motion proceeding.

Step 2: Make at least five copies of the blank, line-numbered legal paper in Appendix 4 (to allow for mistakes). Use those sheets to type your motion to avoid the lien. Type from line number 1 to line 15 as follows (see samples, below):

  Line 1: Your name, and that of your spouse if you're filing jointly.

  Line 1.5: Your address.

  Line 2: Your city, state and zip code.

  Line 2.5: Your phone number.

  Line 3: Type: Debtor in Pro Per.

  Line 8: Center and type UNITED STATES BANKRUPTCY COURT, in capital letters.

  Line 9: Center and type the judicial district and state you are in. Get this information from your local bankruptcy court or from your bankruptcy petition.

  Lines 10-15: Type as shown in the example. Note: Not all courts have separate "AL" (avoid lien) numbers. Leave that space blank until you file your papers with the court.

Step 3: Make a dozen photocopies of the page with the information you have typed so far. This will save you typing later, because you can use this same heading for all the forms mentioned in this section.

Step 4: Using one of the copies that you just made, start typing again at line 17. Prepare a Motion to Avoid Nonpossessory, Nonpurchase-Money Security Interest, as shown in the example, below.

Step 5: If necessary, call the court clerk and set a hearing.

The local rules of some courts require you to set a time for your motion to be heard by the court. The local rules of other courts do not require you to set the hearing. Rather, a hearing is scheduled only if the creditor responds to your motion. In these courts you are required to include language in your motion that tells the creditor how to proceed if they want to contest it. Assuming, however, that your local rules require you to set the hearing, call the court clerk and give your name and case number. Say you'd like to file a motion to avoid a lien and you need to find out when and where the judge will hear arguments on your motion. The clerk will give you a hearing date; ask for one far enough in advance to give the creditor the notice required by your local rules.

If the clerk will not give you this information over the phone, go to the federal courthouse with a copy of your Motion to Avoid

Motion to Avoid Nonpossessory, Nonpurchase-Money Security Interest

```
 1   John Doe
 2   1111 Any Street
     Berkeley, CA 00000
     (510) 000-0000
 3   Debtor in Pro Per
 4
 5
 6
 7
 8                    UNITED STATES BANKRUPTCY COURT
 9        _____ DISTRICT OF _____
            [name of district]              [your state]
10              [name of division, if any]  DIVISION
11   In re:
12   [your name(s)]        Case No. _____ [Copy from your petition]
13                         Chapter 7
14                         AL [This no. may be assigned by the clerk]
15            Debtor(s)            (No.)
16
17      MOTION TO AVOID NONPOSSESSORY, NONPURCHASE-MONEY SECURITY INTEREST
18   1.  Debtor(s)  [your name(s)]  , filed a voluntary petition for relief under Chapter 7 of
19   Title 11 of the United States Code on  [date you filed for bankruptcy]  .
20   2.  This court has jurisdiction over this motion, filed pursuant to 11 U.S.C. § 522(f), to avoid a
21   nonpossessory nonpurchase-money security interest held by  [Name of lienholder]  on property
22   held by the debtor.
23   3.  On or about  [date you incurred the debt], debtors borrowed $ [amount of loan]  from
24   [Name of creditor] . As security for loan,  [Name of creditor]  insisted upon, and the debtors ex-
25   ecuted, a note and security agreement granting to  [Name of creditor]  a security interest in and on the
26   debtor's personal property, which consisted of  [items held as security as they are listed in your
27   loan agreement], which are held primarily for the family and household use of the debtors and their
28   dependents.
```

```
 1   4.  All such possessions of debtors have been claimed as fully exempt in their bankruptcy case.
 2   5.  The money borrowed from  [name of creditor]  does not represent any part of the purchase
 3   money of any of the articles covered in the security agreement executed by the debtors, and all of the
 4   articles so covered remain in the possession of the debtors.
 5   6.  The existence of  [name of creditor]''s lien on debtor's household and personal goods impairs
 6   exemptions to which the debtors would be entitled under 11 U.S.C. § 522(b).
 7      WHEREFORE, pursuant to 11 U.S.C. § 522(f), debtors pray for an order avoiding the security interest
 8   in their personal and household goods, and for such additional or alternative relief as may be just and
 9   proper.
10
11   Dated: _____
12                                      Debtor in Propria Persona
13   Dated: _____
14                                      Debtor in Propria Persona
15                                      Address
16
17
18
19
20
21
22
23
24
25
26
27
28
```

Nonpossessory, Non-purchase-Money Security Interest form filled out. You can file that form and schedule a hearing. Be sure to write down the information about when and where your motion will be heard by the judge.

Step 6: Prepare a proposed Order to Avoid Non-possessory, Nonpurchase-Money Security Interest for the judge to sign, granting your request. (See sample, below.) Specify exactly what property the creditor has secured in the space indicated in the sample. You can get this information from the security agreement you signed, which should also match what you put on Schedule B. Make two extra copies and take them with you to the hearing.

The court's local rules may require you to file the proposed order with the rest of your motion papers.

Step 7: Prepare a Notice of Motion, putting the place, date and time of the hearing in the places indicated on the sample.

Step 8: Prepare at least two Proofs of Service by Mail, as shown in the sample; one for each affected creditor and one for the trustee. These forms state that a friend or relative of yours, who is at least 18 years old and not a party to the bankruptcy, mailed your papers to the creditor(s) or the trustee. Fill in the blanks with your friend's name, county, state, address and zip code as indicated. Put the creditor's (or trustee's) name on line 21. On line 22, put the city or town of the post office that your friend will mail your papers from.

Have your friend sign and date the form at the end as indicated on the sample.

Step 9: Make at least three extra copies of all forms.

Step 10: Keep both copies of the Proof of Service. Put one copy of the Motion, Notice of Motion and proposed Order in a stamped envelope with sufficient postage, and have your friend mail them to the affected creditor(s) and the trustee.

Step 11: File the original copy of the Notice of Motion, Motion, proposed Order (if required in your area) and Proof of Service with the bankruptcy court. There is no fee.

Step 12: The trustee or creditors affected by your motion may submit a written response. In most areas, they are not required to respond in writing and can simply show up in court to argue their side. In some courts, however, if the trustee or a creditor doesn't file a written response to your motion, it may be automatically granted. Consult your local rules.

Step 13: Attend the hearing, if one is scheduled. The hearing is usually very short, ten minutes or less. Because you filed the motion, you argue your side first. Explain briefly that your property falls within the acceptable categories of exempt property listed in 11 U.S.C. § 522(f)(2) (see Section B.2, above), that the lien on it is a nonpossessory nonpurchase-money security interest and that the lien impairs your exemption.

The Bankruptcy Code states that a lien on exempt property can be eliminated to the extent the lien "impairs" the exemption. (Impairs is defined in 11 U.S.C. § 522(f)(2).)

Then the trustee or creditor (or an attorney) responds. The judge either decides the matter and signs your proposed order, or "takes it under submission" and mails you the order in a few days.

There is rarely a penalty if you lose. If, however, a judge believes that you had no reasonable basis for your motion, or if you don't show up for the hearing, you may be required to pay the creditor's costs and reasonable attorney's fees associated with defending against your motion—often $200 to $300.

b. Eliminating a Judicial Lien

To have a judicial lien eliminated, follow the procedure for filing a motion in subsection a, above, but use the Motion to Avoid Judicial Lien and Order to Avoid Judicial Lien forms. Samples are shown below.

If you are eliminating a judicial lien on your home, use the Motion to Avoid Judicial Lien (on Real Estate) and Order to Avoid Judicial Lien (on Real Estate) in this chapter as samples.

Order to Avoid Nonpossessory, Nonpurchase-Money Security Interest & Notice of Motion to Avoid Nonpossessory, Nonpurchase-Money Security Interest

Notice of Motion form

```
 1  John Doe
 2  1111 Any Street
    Berkeley, CA 00000
    (510) 000-0000
 3  Debtor in Pro Per
 4
 5
 6
 7
 8            UNITED STATES BANKRUPTCY COURT
 9        [name of district]   DISTRICT OF   [your state]
10           [name of division, if any]   DIVISION
11  In re:                              Case No. _____ [Copy from your petition]
12  [your name(s)]                      Chapter 7
13
14                                      AL  [This no. may be assigned by the clerk]
15            Debtor(s)                        (No.)
16           NOTICE OF MOTION TO AVOID NONPOSSESSORY,
17                NONPURCHASE-MONEY SECURITY INTEREST
18
19  Please take notice that debtor(s), _____ [your name(s)], _____ motion to
20  avoid nonpossessory, nonpurchase-money security interest is set for a hearing on: _____ [leave
21  blank] _____, 20 ___ at _____ o'clock ___ .m. at _____ [leave blank—location of
22  bankruptcy court] _____, in courtroom _____ [leave blank] .
23
24  Dated: _____                       Debtor in Propria Persona
25  Dated: _____                       Debtor in Propria Persona
26                                      Address
27
28
```

[Proposed] Order form

```
 1  John Doe
 2  1111 Any Street
    Berkeley, CA 00000
    (510) 000-0000
 3  Debtor in Pro Per
 4
 5
 6
 7
 8            UNITED STATES BANKRUPTCY COURT
 9        [name of district]   DISTRICT OF   [your state]
10           [name of division, if any]   DIVISION
11  In re:                              Case No. _____ [Copy from your petition]
12  [your name(s)]                      Chapter 7
13
14                                      AL  [This no. may be assigned by the clerk]
15            Debtor(s)                        (No.)
16  [PROPOSED] ORDER TO AVOID NONPOSSESSORY, NONPURCHASE-MONEY SECURITY INTEREST
17
18  AND NOW COMES the motion of the above-named debtor(s) _____ [your name(s)]
19  to avoid the lien of the respondent, _____ [name of creditor],
20  It is hereby ORDERED and DECREED that the lien is a nonpossessory, nonpurchase-money lien that
21  impairs the debtor's exemptions in the following property:
22      [list all items held as security as listed in your loan agreement]
23  Unless debtor's bankruptcy case is dismissed, the lien of the respondent is hereby extinguished and
24  the lien shall not survive bankruptcy or affix to or remain enforceable against the aforementioned
25  property of the debtor.
26  _____ [name of creditor] _____ shall take all necessary steps to remove any record of the
27  lien from the aforementioned property of the debtor.
28  Dated: _____                       U.S. Bankruptcy Judge
```

Motion to Avoid Judicial Lien

John Doe
1111 Any Street
Berkeley, CA 00000
(510) 000-0000
Debtor in Pro Per

UNITED STATES BANKRUPTCY COURT

[Name of district] DISTRICT OF _[your state]_

[Name of division, if any] DIVISION

In re:
[your name(s)]

_____
Debtor(s)

Case No. _[Copy from your petition]_

Chapter 7

A[_[This no. may be assigned by the clerk]_
(No.)

MOTION TO AVOID JUDICIAL LIEN

1. Debtor(s) _[your name(s)]_ commenced this case on _[date you filed for bankruptcy]_ by filing a voluntary petition for relief under Chapter 7 of Title 11 of the United States Code.

2. This court has jurisdiction over this motion, filed pursuant to 11 U.S.C. § 522(f) to avoid and cancel a judicial lien held by _[Name of judicial lienholder]_ on property held by the debtor.

3. On _[date judicial lien was recorded]_ creditors recorded a judicial lien against the following items of debtor's property: _[list all exempt property affected by lien]_

This judicial lien is entered of record as follows: _[list judicial lien including date of the lien, amount and court case number]_

4. All such possessions of debtor(s) have been claimed as fully exempt in their bankruptcy case.
///

5. The existence of _[Name of creditor's]_ lien on debtor's household and personal goods impairs exemptions to which the debtor(s) would be entitled under 11 U.S.C. § 522 (b).

WHEREFORE, debtor(s) pray for an order against _[Name of lienholder]_ avoiding and cancelling the judicial lien in the above-mentioned property, and for such additional or alternative relief as may be just and proper.

Dated: _____
Debtor in Propria Persona

Dated: _____
Debtor in Propria Persona

Address

Notice of Motion to Avoid Judicial Lien & Order to Avoid Judicial Lien

---

Order to Avoid Judicial Lien

John Doe
1111 Any Street
Berkeley, CA 00000
(510) 000-0000
Debtor in Pro Per

UNITED STATES BANKRUPTCY COURT

[Name of district] DISTRICT OF [your state]

[Name of division, if any] DIVISION

In re:
[your name(s)]   Case No. [Copy from your petition]

Chapter 7

AL [This no. may be assigned by the clerk]
(No.)

Debtor(s)

[PROPOSED] ORDER TO AVOID JUDICIAL LIEN

AND NOW COMES the motion of the above-named debtor(s), [your name(s)],

to avoid the lien of the respondent, [name of creditor]

It is hereby ORDERED and DECREED that the lien is a judicial lien that impairs the exemption as

follows:

[list all exempt property subject to the judicial lien]

Unless debtor's bankruptcy case is dismissed, the lien of the respondent is hereby extinguished and

the lien shall not survive bankruptcy or affix to or remain enforceable against the aforementioned

property of the debtor.

[Name of creditor] shall take all necessary steps to remove any record of the lien from

the aforementioned property of the debtor.

Dated:

U.S. Bankruptcy Judge

Notice of Motion to Avoid Judicial Lien

John Doe
1111 Any Street
Berkeley, CA 00000
(510) 000-0000
Debtor in Pro Per

UNITED STATES BANKRUPTCY COURT

[Name of district] DISTRICT OF [your state]

[Name of division, if any] DIVISION

In re:
[your name(s)]   Case No. [Copy from your petition]

Chapter 7

AL [This no. may be assigned by the clerk]
(No.)

Debtor(s)

NOTICE OF MOTION TO AVOID JUDICIAL LIEN

Please take notice that debtor(s), [your name(s)] motion to avoid judicial lien

is set for a hearing on: [leave blank] , 20 , at o'clock .m.

at [leave blank —location of bankruptcy court] in courtroom [leave blank] .

Dated:
                Debtor in Propria Persona

Dated:
                Debtor in Propria Persona

                Address

Motion to Avoid Judicial Lien (on Real Estate)

John Doe
1111 Any Street
Berkeley, CA 00000
(510) 000-0000
Debtor in Pro Per

UNITED STATES BANKRUPTCY COURT

[Name of district] DISTRICT OF _[your state]_

[Name of division, if any] DIVISION

In re:

[your name(s)]   Case No. _[Copy from your petition]_

Chapter 7

AL _[This no. may be assigned by the clerk]_
(No.)

_____
Debtor(s)

MOTION TO AVOID JUDICIAL LIEN ON REAL ESTATE

1. Debtor(s) _[your name(s)]_ commenced this case on _[date you filed for bankruptcy]_ by filing a voluntary petition for relief under Chapter 7 of Title 11 of the United States Code.

2. This court has jurisdiction over this motion, filed pursuant to 11 U.S.C. § 522(f) to avoid and cancel a judicial lien held by _[name of judicial lienholder]_ on real property used as the debtor's residence, under 28 U.S.C. § 1334.

3. On _[date judicial lien was recorded]_, creditors recorded a judicial lien against debtor's residence at _[your address, city, state, zip code]_. This judicial lien is entered of record as follows: _[list judicial lien including date of the lien, amount and court case number]_.

4. The debtor's interest in the property referred to in the preceding paragraph and encumbered by the lien has been claimed as fully exempt in their bankruptcy case.

///

5. The existence of _[name of judicial lienholder]_ 's lien on debtor's real property impairs exemptions to which the debtor(s) would be entitled under 11 U.S.C. §522(b).

WHEREFORE, debtor(s) request an order against _[name of judicial lienholder]_, avoiding and cancelling the judicial lien in the above-mentioned property, and for such additional or alternative relief as may be just and proper.

Dated: _____

_____
Debtor in Propria Persona

Dated: _____

_____
Debtor in Propria Persona

_____
Address

Notice of Motion to Avoid Judicial Lien & Order to Avoid Judicial Lien (on Real Estate)

Notice of Motion

1. John Doe
2. 1111 Any Street
   Berkeley, CA 00000
   (510) 000-0000
3. Debtor in Pro Per
4.
5.
6.
7.
8. UNITED STATES BANKRUPTCY COURT
9. _[Name of district]_ DISTRICT OF _[your state]_
10. _[Name of division, if any]_ DIVISION
11. In re:
12. _[your name(s)]_   Case No. _[Copy from your petition]_
13. Chapter 7
14. A1 _[This no. may be assigned by the clerk]_
15. Debtor(s)   (No.)
16. NOTICE OF MOTION TO AVOID JUDICIAL LIEN ON REAL ESTATE
17.
18. Please take notice that debtor'(s), _[your name(s)]_ motion to avoid
19. judicial lien on real estate is set for a hearing on: _[leave blank]_ , 20____
20. at ____o'clock ____m. at _[leave blank—location of bankruptcy court]_ ,
21. in courtroom _[leave blank]_ .
22.
23. Dated: Debtor in Propria Persona
24. Dated:
25. Debtor in Propria Persona
26. Address
27.
28.

[Proposed] Order

1. John Doe
2. 1111 Any Street
   Berkeley, CA 00000
   (510) 000-0000
3. Debtor in Pro Per
4.
5.
6.
7.
8. UNITED STATES BANKRUPTCY COURT
9. _[Name of district]_ DISTRICT OF _[your state]_
10. _[Name of division, if any]_ DIVISION
11. In re:
12. _[your name(s)]_   Case No. _[Copy from your petition]_
13. Chapter 7
14. A1 _[This no. may be assigned by the clerk]_
15. Debtor(s)   (No.)
16. [PROPOSED] ORDER AVOIDING JUDICIAL LIEN ON REAL ESTATE
17.
18. AND NOW COMES the motion of the above-named debtor(s), _[your name(s)]_ , to
19. avoid the lien of the respondent, _[Name of judicial lienholder]_
20. It is hereby ORDERED AND DECREED that the judicial lien held by _[Name of judicial lien-_
21. _holder]_ in debtor's residential real estate at _[your address, city, state and zip]_
22. entered of record at _[describe the lien exactly as it appears on the public record]_ be hereby
23. canceled.
24. It is further ORDERED that unless debtor's bankruptcy case is dismissed, _[Name of judicial_
25. _lienholder]_ shall take all steps necessary and appropriate to release the judicial lien and remove it
26. from the local judgment index.
27.
28. Dated: U.S. Bankruptcy Judge

Proof of Service by Mail

1	John Doe
	1111 Any Street
2	Berkeley, CA 00000
	(510) 000-0000
3	Debtor in Pro Per

8 UNITED STATES BANKRUPTCY COURT

9 _____ *[name of district]* _____ DISTRICT OF _____ *[your state]* _____

10 _____ *[name of division, if any]* _____ DIVISION

11 In re:)

12 *[your name(s)]*   )   Case No. _____ *[Copy from your petition]* _____

)

13   )   Chapter 7

)

14 _____ Debtor(s) _____)   AL _*[This no. may be assigned by the clerk]*_

)   (No.)

15   PROOF OF SERVICE BY MAIL

16 I, _*[friend's name]*_, declare that: I am a resident or employed in the County of __*[the county where*

17 *friend lives or works]*_, State of __*[state where friend lives or works]*__. My residence/business address is

18 _*[friend's address]*_. I am over the age of eighteen years and not a party to this case.

19 On _*[leave blank]*_, 20__, I served the *[include the title of the motion, either Notice or Motion to Avoid*

20 *Nonpossessory, Nonpurchase-Money Security Interest or Notice of Motion to Avoid Judical Lien]* on _*[creditor's*

21 *name]*_, by placing true and correct copies thereof enclosed in a sealed envelope with postage thereon fully

22 prepaid in the United States Mail at _*[city of post office where papers will be mailed]*_, address as follows:

23   _*[address of affected creditor's and trustee]*_

24 I declare under penalty of perjury that the foregoing is true and correct, and that this declaration was

25 executed on

26 Dated: _____ *[leave blank]*_____, 20_____ at _____ *[leave blank]* _____

                                                                  (City and State)

27   _____ *[leave blank]* _____

28   (Signature)

3. How to Redeem Property

If you want to redeem exempt or abandoned property, list the property on your Statement of Intention as property to be retained and check the column that says property will be redeemed. (More instructions are in Ch. 3.) You must pay the creditor the current market value of the property within 45 days after you file.

⚠️ **Explore lien avoidance first.** If lien avoidance (Section C.2, above) is available, you may be able to get rid of a lien on exempt property without paying anything.

a. Agreeing on the Value of the Property

Before you can redeem property, you and the creditor must agree on what the property is worth. If you believe the creditor is setting too high a price for the property, tell the creditor why you think the property is worth less—it needs repair, it's falling apart, it's damaged or stained, or whatever. If you can't come to an agreement, you can ask the bankruptcy court to rule on the matter. But you will probably need an attorney to help you make this request, so it is not worth your while unless you and the creditor are very far apart in your estimates of the property's value.

You and the creditor should sign a redemption agreement that sets forth the terms of your agreement and the amount you are going to pay, in case there is a dispute later. (See the sample forms in subsection d, below.)

b. If the Creditor Won't Cooperate

The creditor may refuse to let you redeem property, because the creditor claims that it isn't one of the types of property described in Section C.3 above or because you can't agree on the value. If so, you will need to file a formal complaint in the bankruptcy court to have a judge resolve the issue. You will need an attorney to help you, so think twice about whether you really want to redeem the property. It may be better just to let the creditor have it.

c. Paying in Installments

If you can't raise enough cash to pay the creditor within 45 days, try to get the creditor to let you pay in installments. Some creditors will agree if the installments are substantial and you agree to pay interest on them. But a creditor is not required to accept installments; it can demand the entire amount in cash.

If the creditor refuses to accept installments, you can ask the bankruptcy court to delay your deadline for making the payment for a month or two. But to do so, you will need to file a formal complaint in the bankruptcy court. Again, you will need an attorney to help you, so it may not be worth it.

d. Paperwork

Below are two sample redemption agreements you can use to type up your agreement with the creditor. Form 1 is for installments and Form 2 is for a lump sum payment. Type the form on legal paper (the blank paper in Appendix 4 with numbers down the left side) and put your bankruptcy case number on it in case you need to file it later. You should fill out one form for every item of property you want to redeem. Have the creditor sign it.

There is no need to file these agreements with the trustee. Keep them with your other bankruptcy papers, in case the trustee or the judge wants to see them.

Agreement for Installment Redemption of Property

1 John Doe
   1111 Any Street
2 Berkeley, CA 00000
   (510) 000-0000
3 Debtor in Pro Per

4

5

6

7

8 UNITED STATES BANKRUPTCY COURT

9 _____ *[name of district]* _____ DISTRICT OF _____ *[your state]* _____

10

11 In re:)   Case No. ___ *[Copy from your petition]* ___
   [your name(s)]   )
12   )   Chapter 7
)
13   )
)   AL *[This no. may be assigned by the clerk]*
14 _____ Debtor(s) _____   )   (No.)

15 AGREEMENT FOR INSTALLMENT REDEMPTION OF PROPERTY

16 _____, (Debtor), and _____, (Creditor) agree that

17   1. Creditor owns a security interest in _____ (Collateral).

18   2. The value of Collateral is $_____.

19   3. Creditor's security interest is valid and enforceable despite the debtor's bankruptcy case.

20   4. If Debtor continues to make payments of $_____ a month on Creditor's security interest,

21 Creditor will take no action to repossess or foreclose its security.

22   5. Debtor's payments will continue until the amount of $_____, plus interest (to be computed

23 at the same annual percentage rate as in the original contract between the parties) is paid.

24   6. Upon being fully paid as specified in paragraph 5, Creditor will take all steps necessary to terminate its

25 security interest in Collateral.

26 Dated: _____   _____

27   Signature

28 Dated: _____   _____
                                              Signature

Agreement for Lump Sum Redemption of Property

1 John Doe
   1111 Any Street
2 Berkeley, CA 00000
   (510) 000-0000
3 Debtor in Pro Per

4

5

6

7

8   UNITED STATES BANKRUPTCY COURT

9 _____ *[name of district]* _____ DISTRICT OF _____ *[your state]* _____

10

11 In re:)
    [your name(s)]   )   Case No. _____ *[Copy from your petition]* _____
)
12   )   Chapter 7
)
13   )
)
14 _____ Debtor(s) _____)

15

16   AGREEMENT FOR REDEMPTION OF PROPERTY

17 _____, (Debtor), and _____, (Creditor) agree that:

18   1. Creditor owns a security interest in _____ (Collateral).

19   2. The value of Collateral is $_____.

20   3. Creditor's security interest is valid and enforceable despite the debtor's bankruptcy case.

21   4. Debtor agrees to pay the full value of the collateral no later than _____.

22   5. Upon receiving the payment specified in paragraph 4, Creditor will take all steps necessary to

23 terminate its security interest in Collateral.

24 Dated: _____   _____

25   Debtor in Propria Persona

26 Dated: _____   _____
                                  Debtor in Propria Persona

27

28

4. How to Reaffirm a Debt

If you decide to reaffirm a debt, you must list it as such on your Statement of Intention. Then, within 45 days of filing your Statement of Intention, you must:

- type and sign a Reaffirmation Agreement (a sample is below)
- prepare an Application for Approval of Reaffirmation Agreement and an Order Approving Reaffirmation Agreement (samples are below), and
- attend the discharge hearing, where the judge will probably warn you against reaffirmation and give you a chance to back out.

In the reaffirmation agreement, put the fair market value of the property as well as the amount you actually owe. The form agreement below lets you reaffirm the debt only for an amount equal to or less than the value of the collateral. It also contains a written promise from the creditor not to take the item in return for your promise to pay the creditor a fixed amount equal to the current value of the property.

A Reaffirmation Agreement Is Not Valid Until Filed

A reaffirmation agreement is not valid until the creditor files it with the court. Don't make payments pursuant to the agreement until you receive a copy with the court's file-stamp. In the past, several large department stores (including Macy's, Montgomery Ward and May Department Stores) frequently failed to file reaffirmation agreements, but collected money from the debtors anyway. Many state attorneys general sued and obtained settlements which nullified the reaffirmation agreements and refunded debtors the money they paid under the agreements.

Reaffirmation Agreement

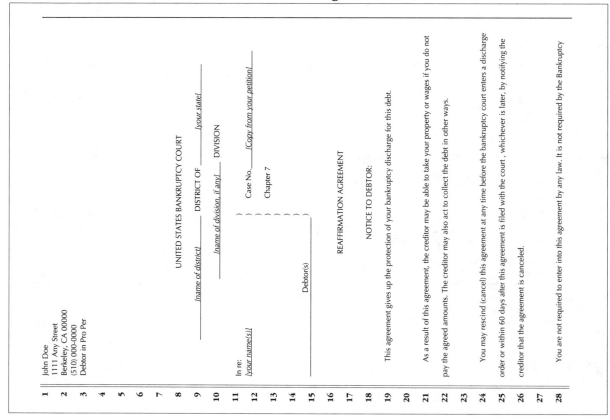

Reaffirmation Agreement (continued)

1 Code, by any other law, or by any contract (except another reaffirmation agreement made in accordance

2 with Bankruptcy Code § 514(c)).

3

4 You are allowed to pay this debt without signing this agreement. However, if you do not sign this

5 agreement and are later unwilling or unable to pay the full amount, the creditor will not be able to

6 collect it from you. The creditor also will not be allowed to take your property to pay the debt unless the

7 creditor has a lien on that property.

8

9 If the creditor has a lien on your personal property, you may have a right to redeem the property

10 and eliminate the lien by making a single payment to the creditor equal to the current value of the

11 property, as agreed by the parties or determined by the court.

12

13 This agreement is not valid or binding unless it is filed with clerk of the bankruptcy court. If you

14 were not represented by an attorney during the negotiation of this reaffirmation agreement, the agree-

15 ment cannot be enforced by the creditor unless 1) you have attended a reaffirmation hearing in the

16 bankruptcy court, and 2) the agreement has been approved by the bankruptcy court. (Court approval is

17 not required if this is a consumer debt secured by a mortgage or other lien on your real estate.)

18

19 AGREEMENT

20 _[Your name(s)]_ the debtor in the above-captioned bankruptcy case, and _[name of creditor]_

21 hereby agree that:

22 1. _[Your name(s)]_ subject to the approval of the bankruptcy court and the statutory right to

23 rescind, reaffirms _[his/her/their]_ debt of _[amount of debt]_ to _[name of creditor]_ secured by

24 _[describe secured property]_ currently valued at _[current value of the secured item]_.

25 2. This debt will be paid in installments of _[amount per month]_ per month, at _[interest rate]_

26 simple interest, until it has been paid in full.

27 3. _[Name of creditor]_ agrees to waive all previous and current defaults on this debt.

28 4. _[Name of creditor]_ further agrees that it will not act to repossess the _[describe secured_

1 _property]_ securing this debt unless the debtor is more than thirty days in default under this agreement.

2 5. _[Name of creditor]_ further agrees that, in the event of any deficiency judgment arising out of

3 this transaction, it will not execute against the debtor's wages.

4

5 DEBTORS' STATEMENT OF EFFECT OF AGREEMENT ON FINANCES

6 6. Debtor's monthly income (take-home pay plus any other income received) is $ _[insert amount of_

7 _take-home pay]_.

8 7. Debtor's monthly expenses total $ _[insert amount of expenses]_, not including any payment due

9 under this agreement or any debt to be discharged in this bankruptcy case.

10 8. Debtor believes this agreement _[will or will not]_ impose an undue hardship on debtor or

11 debtor's dependents.

12

13 DEBTOR'S STATEMENT CONCERNING DECISION TO REAFFIRM

14 9. Debtor agreed to reaffirm this debt because _____

15 _____

16 10. Debtor believes this agreement is in his or her best interest because _____

17 _____ .

18 THIS AGREEMENT MAY BE CANCELLED BY THE DEBTOR ANY TIME BEFORE _[date 60 days after_

19 _filing with the court]_ OR THE DATE OF THE BANKRUPTCY DISCHARGE IF THAT IS AFTER _[same_

20 _date as above]_ BY GIVING NOTICE TO _[name of creditor]_.

21 Debtor is aware that reaffirming this debt is not required by the Bankruptcy Act, by nonbankruptcy

22 law or by any agreement.

23 Debtor was not represented by an attorney during the course of negotiating this agreement.

24

25 Dated: _____   _[sign your name here]_

26   [type your name here]

27 Dated: _____   [creditor's signature]

28   for [type creditor's name here]

Application for Approval of Reaffirmation Agreement Pursuant to 11 U.S.C. § 524(c)

John Doe
1111 Any Street
Berkeley, CA 00000
(510) 000-0000
Debtor in Pro Per

UNITED STATES BANKRUPTCY COURT

[Name of district] DISTRICT OF _[your state]_

[Name of division, if any] DIVISION

In re:
[your name(s)]   Case No. _[Copy from your petition]_

                                    Chapter 7

                    Debtor(s)

APPLICATION FOR APPROVAL OF REAFFIRMATION
AGREEMENT PURSUANT TO 11 U.S.C. § 524(C)

TO THE HONORABLE _____, BANKRUPTCY JUDGE:

The debtor(s) in this case, _[your name(s)]_ hereby apply for approval of their reaffirmation agreement with _[Name of creditor]_. In support of this application we hereby aver that:

1. _[Your name(s)]_, wish to reaffirm _[his/hers/their]_ debt with _[Name of creditor]_ to the extent it is secured by _[describe secured property]_.

2. The _[describe secured property]_ is presently worth _[current value of secured property]_.

3. The reaffirmation agreement, signed by the parties and providing for the payment of _[current value of secured property]_ at _[interest rate]_ interest, in _[number of payments]_ monthly installments, is attached to this application.

///

4. The agreement does not impose a hardship on _[name(s) of debtor's]_ _[for our/my dependents, if any]_ because the debtor(s)' current income is $_____ per month, and expenses are $_____ per month.

WHEREFORE, the debtors pray that the reaffirmation of the aforesaid debt be approved.

Dated: _____   _[sign your name here]_
                            [type your name here]

Order Approving Reaffirmation Agreement

1   John Doe
       1111 Any Street
2   Berkeley, CA 00000
       (510) 000-0000
3   Debtor in Pro Per

4

5

6

7

8   UNITED STATES BANKRUPTCY COURT

9   _____ *[name of district]* _____ DISTRICT OF _____ *[your state]* _____

10   _____ *[name of division, if any]* _____ DIVISION

11   In re:)
     [your name(s)]   )   Case No. ____ *[Copy from your petition]*
12   )
)   Chapter 7
13   )
)
14   )
           Debtor(s)   )
15 _____

16

           [PROPOSED] ORDER APPROVING REAFFIRMATION AGREEMENT
17

18   AND NOW, this _____ day of _____ , 20___, the court having found

19   that the reaffirmation agreement proposed by the debtor(s) is in the best interest of the debtor(s) and does

20   not pose a hardship on the debtor(s) or the debtor(s)'s dependents,

21   IT IS HEREBY ORDERED that the reaffirmation with _____ *[name of creditor]* _____ is approved.

22

23   Dated: _____   _____

24   U.S. Bankruptcy Judge

25

26

27

28

⚠️ **Make sure your reaffirmation agreement isn't for too much.** If the creditor requires you to reaffirm for the full amount owed on the collateral (an amount that is greater than the current market value of the collateral), select another option unless you really, really want the property and won't be able to get similar property after bankruptcy. In general, you should try to avoid staying on the hook for a debt larger than the current value of the property you want to keep.

Your right to cancel reaffirmation agreements. The Bankruptcy Code gives you the right to cancel any reaffirmation agreement by notifying the creditor at any time:

- before you receive your discharge, or
- within 60 days after the reaffirmation agreement is filed with the bankruptcy court,

whichever is later. (11 U.S.C. § 524(c)(2).)

Notice to the creditor should be by certified mail, return receipt requested. This precludes the creditor from later claiming it was not notified.

Canceling your reaffirmation will leave your debt in the same condition as if you had never filed the reaffirmation agreement. That is, your personal liability for debt will be discharged (assuming the debt is dis-

chargeable), and the creditor will be able to enforce its lien on your property by either repossessing it or foreclosing on it. If your bankruptcy case is still open, you can still try other options discussed in this chapter.

Bankruptcy courts frown on reaffirmation agreements because they obligate debtors to make payments after bankruptcy, which contradicts bankruptcy's purpose. If you elect to reaffirm a debt, the trustee may question you about it at the meeting of the creditors. (See Ch. 4, Section A.3.) In addition, your reaffirmation agreement must include a statement that you understand that bankruptcy law does not require you to reaffirm a debt. The agreement must also include a statement that you either were advised by a lawyer of the consequence of reaffirming a debt or were not represented by a lawyer in negotiating the reaffirmation agreement.

5. How to Retain Property Without Reaffirming or Redeeming

In the districts that allow you to retain property without reaffirming or redeeming (noted in Section C.5, above), in the second column after typing the creditor's name, write on your Statement of Intention the following: "I plan to retain the property by keeping current on my obligations under the contract." Remember that this obligation may include monthly payments, insurance coverage and more.

In the districts that do not allow this method of retaining property, ask the creditor to informally let you keep the property as long as you keep current on your contractual obligations. On the Statement of Intention, indicate that you are surrendering the property. If you default, the creditor's only recourse is to repossess the property.

But the creditor doesn't have to wait for you to default to take the property. Because you indicated that you are surrendering your property on the Statement of Intention, the creditor can repossess at any time. Keep making payments and keep a copy of every check or money order you send in.

If the lien was reduced during the bankruptcy, you can stop paying when your payments total the reduced lien amount plus interest. Unless the creditor takes steps to have the lien removed from the property, however, it will remain on public record. If you will

never sell the property, this won't be a problem. But you might have problems several years down the road if you need clear title to the property in order to sell it. You may have to go to court to prove that you've paid off the lien.

6. How to Pay Off Liens in a Follow-Up Chapter 13 Bankruptcy (the "Chapter 20" Strategy)

As you undoubtedly understand by now, certain types of debts survive bankruptcy, either because the law says they do or because the court has so ordered. Also, while Chapter 7 bankruptcy may discharge a particular debt, it won't affect any lien that has been placed on your property—unless the bankruptcy court allows you to avoid it. So, your Chapter 7 bankruptcy may get rid of a lot of your debt but still leave you with large nondischargeable debts and liens on your home or other property. While you won't be able to file another Chapter 7 bankruptcy until six years have passed from the date you filed this one, the law allows you to immediately file a Chapter 13 bankruptcy, get the protection offered by the automatic stay and propose a three- to five-year plan to pay off your nondischargeable debt (and perhaps reduce the amount of the liens), all under the supervision of the bankruptcy court. This one-two punch is known in the trade as a Chapter 20 bankruptcy (Chapter 7 plus Chapter 13). ■

Nondischargeable Debts

Not all debts can be discharged in a Chapter 7 bankruptcy. Some debts survive the bankruptcy process—they remain valid and collectable, just as they were before you filed for bankruptcy. To understand exactly what bankruptcy will do for you, you need to know which, if any, of your debts are likely to survive bankruptcy.

When granting your final discharge, the bankruptcy court won't specify which of your debts have been discharged. Instead, you'll receive a non-specific form from the court. (A copy is in Ch. 4, Section A.6.)

This chapter helps you figure out exactly which of your debts will be discharged and which debts may survive.

A. Overview of Nondischargeable Debts

Under the bankruptcy laws, 12 major categories of debts may turn out to be nondischargeable. Debts in eight of these categories are never discharged unless you prove that the debt fits within a narrow exception to the general rule. Debts in the other four categories are always discharged unless the creditor files an objection in the bankruptcy court and convinces the court that the debt shouldn't be discharged.

1. Debts Not Discharged Unless an Exception Applies

These debts aren't discharged unless you can show the bankruptcy court that the debt comes within an exception to the rule:

- Debts you don't list in your bankruptcy papers (11 U.S.C. § 523(a)(3)).
- Student loans, unless repayment would cause you undue hardship (11 U.S.C. § 523(a)(8)).
- Most federal, state and local taxes (11 U.S.C. § 523(a)(1)) and any money borrowed or charged on a credit card to pay those taxes (11 U.S.C. § 523(a)(14)).
- Child support, alimony and debts in the nature of support (11 U.S.C. §§ 523(a)(5) and 523(a)(18)).

- Fines or restitution (to the court or victim) imposed in a criminal-type proceeding (11 U.S.C. § 523(a)(7); 18 U.S.C. § 3613).
- Fees imposed by a court for filing cases, motions, complaints or appeals or for other costs and expenses assessed with such filing (11 U.S.C. § 523(a)(17)). Although it's unclear from the text of the statute, most experts and all courts that have looked at this provision have stated that it only applies to prisoners.
- Debts resulting from intoxicated driving (11 U.S.C. § 523(a)(9)).
- Debts you couldn't discharge in a previous bankruptcy that was dismissed due to fraud or misfeasance (11 U.S.C. § 523(a)(10)).
- Certain condominium and cooperative fees (11 U.S.C. § 523(a)(16)).

To get a debt in any of these categories discharged, you can take one of two courses of action:

- **Hire a lawyer and ask the bankruptcy court, while your case is open, to rule that a particular debt should be discharged.** You'll have to file a Complaint to Determine Dischargeability of a Debt with the bankruptcy court and then show, in court, that your debt isn't covered by the general rule that these kinds of debts aren't dischargeable. (The grounds for getting such debts discharged are discussed in detail in Section B, below.) If you prove the exception, the court will rule that the debt is discharged, and the creditor won't be allowed to collect it after bankruptcy.

  Filing a Complaint to Determine Dischargeability requires an attorney's help; procedures vary considerably among courts. In a few courts, including the District of Oregon and the Southern District of New York, you can request that the dispute be sent to court-sponsored mediation. The creditor does not have to agree, nor does the judge have to send your case to mediation. However, if everyone agrees, mediation can provide an informal, quick and inexpensive resolution of the dispute.

- **Don't take any action during bankruptcy, and if the creditor attempts to collect after your case is closed, argue that the debt was discharged.** If you don't do anything while your bankruptcy is pending, your next chance to make such an argument is when a creditor sues you over the debt, or if you've already lost a lawsuit, when the creditor sets out to collect. At this point, you can argue that the debt was discharged. The advantage of waiting is that you avoid the hassle of litigating the issue as part of your bankruptcy case. And the problem may never come up again if the creditor doesn't sue you. The down side to this strategy is that questions about the dischargeability of the debt will be left hanging over your head after the bankruptcy case is over.

This strategy of passive resistance will almost certainly fail if your creditor is a federal or state taxing agency. However, your chances of success are much greater if you're up against an individual creditor whose claim is not big enough to justify hiring a lawyer.

2. Debts Discharged Unless the Creditor Objects

The other four categories of nondischargeable debts are in fact discharged if:

- you list them on your bankruptcy petition, and
- the creditor doesn't formally object within the time allowed.

If the creditor doesn't file an objection, the debt will be discharged and the creditor will be barred from trying to collect. The reason a creditor must object for these debts to be nondischargeable is that a court must examine the circumstances closely to determine whether or not the debt should be legally discharged.

These four categories of nondischargeable debts are as follows:

1. Debts incurred on the basis of fraudulent acts (11 U.S.C. § 523(a)(2)).
2. Debts from willful and malicious injury to another or another's property (11 U.S.C. § 523(a)(6)).
3. Debts from embezzlement, larceny or breach of trust (fiduciary duty) (11 U.S.C. § 523(a)(4)).
4. Debts arising from a marital settlement agreement or divorce decree (other than debts for child support or alimony) (11 U.S.C. § 523(a)(15)).

If you have a debt of this type, your best approach is to do nothing and hope the creditor doesn't come forward. If the creditor does object, you must respond if you want the debt to be discharged. If the debt is large enough to justify the fees you'll have to pay, hire a bankruptcy attorney to handle it. If the judge rules in your favor after a creditor has accused you of fraud, the court should make the creditor pay your attorney's fees. See Section C.1, below.

If you can't afford an attorney or don't want to hire one, you'll have to do some legal research yourself. See Ch. 9.

B. Debts Not Discharged Unless an Exception Applies

This section discusses each category of debt that, under the bankruptcy laws, isn't dischargeable in a Chapter 7 bankruptcy unless an exception applies.

1. Debts or Creditors You Don't List

For a debt to be discharged in bankruptcy, you must list the debt and the creditor must know of the bankruptcy proceeding in time to object to the discharge. Creditors usually hear of a bankruptcy from the court, which sends a notice to all creditors listed in your bankruptcy papers. If the official notice fails to reach the creditor for some reason beyond your control—because the post office errs or the creditor moved without leaving a forwarding address, for example—the debt will be discharged.

If you forget to list a creditor on your bankruptcy papers, the creditor won't be notified by the court. If that happens, the debt won't be discharged unless the creditor knew of your bankruptcy and your intention to discharge its debt through other means, such as a letter or phone call from you. (See Ch. 4, Section A.2.)

If at any time during the bankruptcy process you discover that you left a creditor or debt off your bankruptcy papers, you should file an amendment. It's a simple process. See Ch. 4, Section B, for instructions. If you discover the omission after your case ends, you may be able to return to court and get the omitted creditor added. (See Chapter 5, Section B.)

2. Student Loans

Before October 1998, you could get rid of student loans in bankruptcy if your payments had become due more than seven years prior to the bankruptcy or if repaying the loans would be a severe hardship for you. Congress eliminated the seven-year rule in 1998, making it much more difficult for borrowers to use bankruptcy to eliminate student loan debt. Although a few exceptions do exist (described below), bankruptcy will rarely get you off the hook for paying back your loans. Those few exceptions are:

- the loan was not made, insured or guaranteed by a government or nonprofit institution
- the money owed is not for a loan, scholarship, stipend overpayment or other educational benefit, or
- repayment would cause you undue hardship.

But even if bankruptcy can't erase your student loans, it may help you get rid of other debts, leaving you with more money to repay your student loans.

Getting Your Transcript

If you don't pay back loans obtained directly from your college, the school can withhold your transcript. But if you file for bankruptcy and receive a discharge of the loan, the school can no longer withhold your records. (*In re Gustafson*, 111 B.R. 282 (9th Cir. BAP 1990).)

In addition, while your bankruptcy case is pending, the school cannot withhold your transcript even if the court eventually rules your school loan nondischargeable. (*Loyola University v. McClarty*, 234 B.R. 386 (E.D. La. 1999).)

a. Loans Not Connected to the Government or a Nonprofit Institution

Loans that are made, insured or guaranteed by the government, or funded in whole or in part by the government or a nonprofit institution, cannot be discharged in bankruptcy unless one of the other exceptions applies. This rule covers virtually all loans, including Federal Direct Loans, Stafford Loans, Guaranteed Student Loans (GSLs), Federal Insured Student Loans (FISLs), Perkins Loans, National Direct and National Defense Student Loans (NDSLs), PLUS Loans, Supplemental Loans for Students (SLS), Auxiliary Loans to Assist Students (ALAS), Health Education Assistance Loans (HEALs) and Health Professions Student Loans (HPSLs).

So what's left? Not much. At first blush, private loans, particularly those issued to graduate and professional students, look as if they should fall outside the reach of this rule. But that is not what the courts have said. Because private loans, while initially made by for-profit institutions, are sold to nonprofit organizations which collect and process payments and pursue debtors in default, courts have found that this provision of the Bankruptcy Code applies to all loans made under a program in which a nonprofit institution provides funds. (See *In re Hammarstrom*, 95 B.R. 160 (N.D. Cal. 1989) and *In re Pilcher*, 149 B.R. 595 (9th Cir. 1993).)

If you can show that no nonprofit institution was connected to your private loan—as may be the case if it was issued, processed and collected by a for-profit vocational school—you may be able to eliminate the loan in bankruptcy. (See *United Resource Systems v. Meinhart*, 211 B.R. 750 (D. Col. 1997) and *Action Career Training v. McClure*, 210 B.R. 985 (N.D. Tex. 1997).)

b. Debt Did Not Provide an Educational Benefit

The Bankruptcy Code also states that a debt for an educational benefit, scholarship or stipend is not dischargeable unless one of the other exceptions applies. While most who have argued that a debt was not for an educational benefit, scholarship or stipend have failed, some have succeeded. Examples of successful cases include the following:

- Some (but not all) courts have allowed the discharge where the student's debt to the school did not arise from a loan agreement or credit extension. For example, debts for tuition or "room and board" may be dischargeable if they were not part of a loan or credit agreement. (See *In re Renshaw*, 229 B.R. 552 (B.A.P. 2d Cir. 1999).)
- A doctor received a National Health Service Corps, or NHSC, scholarship that required her

either to work for four years at a location NHSC designated or repay the money. Her employer, not one chosen by NHSC, agreed to lend her money to repay NHSC so she could go to work for the employer immediately. She later filed for bankruptcy and included the loan from her employer. The bankruptcy court granted the discharge, ruling that the purpose of the loan was for her employment, not her education. (*In re Segal*, 57 F.3d 342 (3rd Cir. 1995).)

c. Repayment Would Cause You Undue Hardship

If you don't fit into one of the unusual exceptions described above, you'll have to repay your student loan unless you can show the bankruptcy court that it would cause you undue hardship to do so.

Courts rarely allow student loans to be discharged on hardship grounds. They take the position that Congress wants student loans to be repaid absent exceptional circumstances. And sometimes, even if a court finds that it would be a hardship to repay the entire debt, the court allows only a portion of it to be discharged. (This practice has been criticized as not authorized by the Bankruptcy Code. See, for example, *In re Hornsby*, 144 F.3d 433 (6th Cir. 1998); *In re Brown*, 239 B.R. 204 (S.D. Cal. 1999).)

i. Factors Courts Use in Determining Undue Hardship

In determining undue hardship, most bankruptcy courts look to the three factors discussed below. Only if you can show that all of these factors are present will the court grant an undue hardship discharge of your student loan. (The main case establishing these factors is *Brunner v. New York State Higher Education Services Inc.*, 46 B.R. 752 (S.D. N.Y. 1985), *aff'd*, 831 F.2d 395 (2nd Cir. 1987).)

- **Poverty.** Based on your current income and expenses, you cannot maintain a minimal living standard and repay the loan. The court must consider your current and future employment and income (or employment and income potential), education, skills and the marketability of your skills, health and family support obligations.
- **Persistence.** It is not enough that you can't currently pay your loan. You must also demonstrate

to the court that your current financial condition is likely to continue for a significant portion of the repayment period.

- **Good Faith.** The court must conclude that you've made a good-faith effort to repay your debt. Someone who files for bankruptcy immediately after getting out of school or after the pay-back period begins will not fall into good favor with the court. Nor will someone who hasn't looked extensively for employment. And if you haven't made any payments, you should be able to show the court that you thought enough about your obligation to obtain a deferment or forbearance.

Recently, one court suggested that the above factors may no longer apply to student loan discharges in bankruptcy because they were created at a time when there were alternative ways to discharge student loans. (*In re Kopf*, 245 B.R. 731 (Bankr. D. Me. 2000).) This court proposed a new test: the bankruptcy court should examine "the totality of the circumstances" when deciding whether to grant a student loan discharge. Only time will tell whether other courts agree.

Special Rules for HEAL and PLUS Loans

HEAL. The dischargeability of Health Education Assistance Loans (HEAL loans) is governed by the federal HEAL Act, not bankruptcy law. Under the HEAL Act, to discharge a loan, you must show that the loan became due more than seven years prior and that repaying it would not merely be a hardship, but would impose an unconscionable burden on your life. (42 U.S.C. § 292f(g).)

PLUS. Parental Loans for Students (PLUS Loans) are granted to a parent to finance a child's education. Even though the parent does not receive the education, if the parent files for bankruptcy, the loan is treated like any other student loan. The parents must meet the undue hardship test to discharge the loan. (See, for example, *In re Wilcon*, 143 B.R. 4 (D. Mass. 1992) and *In re Salter*, 207 B.R. 272 (Bkrtcy. M.D. Fla. 1997).)

Complaint to Determine Dischargeability of Student Loan

John Doe
1111 Any Street
Berkeley, CA 00000
(510) 000-0000
Debtor in Pro Per

UNITED STATES BANKRUPTCY COURT

[Name of district] DISTRICT OF _[your state]_

[Name of division, if any] DIVISION

[your name(s)]
                Case No. ___ _[Copy from your petition]_

    v.   Chapter 7

[name(s) of creditor(s)]

COMPLAINT TO DETERMINE DISCHARGEABILITY OF STUDENT LOAN

1. Debtor(s) filed this case under Chapter 7 of the Bankruptcy Code on _[insert the date you filed your petition]_. This Court thus has jurisdiction over this action under 28 U.S.C. § 1334. This proceeding is a core proceeding.

2. One of the unsecured debts owing by the Debtor(s) and listed on Schedule F—Creditors Holding Unsecured Nonpriority Claims— is a student loan owing to _[insert the name of the holder of your loan]_.

3. This loan was incurred to pay expenses at _[insert the name of the school(s) you attended]_.

4. Based on the Debtor(s)' current income and expenses, the Debtor(s) cannot maintain a minimal living standard and repay the loan. _[insert information about your current and future employment, your income and income potential, education, skills and the marketability of your skills, health, and family support obligations]_.

5. The Debtor(s)' current financial condition is likely to continue for a significant portion of the repayment period of the loan. _[insert information about your health including any life-threatening, debilitating or chronic conditions you have]_.

6. The Debtor(s) have made a good-faith effort to repay their debt as follows: _[insert information about your payment history or other attempts to pay back the loan]_.

7. The Debtor(s) have filed for bankruptcy for reasons other than just to discharge their student loan.

WHEREFORE, the Debtor(s) ask this court to enter an Order declaring the student loan debt to be dischargeable.

Dated: _____

    Debtor in Propria Persona

Dated: _____

    Debtor in Propria Persona

    Address

Proof of Service by Mail

1 John Doe
2 1111 Any Street
  Berkeley, CA 00000
3 (510) 000-0000
  Debtor in Pro Per

UNITED STATES BANKRUPTCY COURT

[Name of district] DISTRICT OF [your state]

[Name of division, if any] DIVISION

[your name(s)]

v.

[name of creditor]

Case No. [Copy from your petition]

Chapter 7

PROOF OF SERVICE BY MAIL

I, [friend's name] declare that: I am a resident or employed in the County of [county where friend lives or works], State of [state where friend lives or works]. My residence/business address is [friend's address]. I am over the age of eighteen years and not a party to this case.

On [leave blank] 20___ I served the Complaint to Determine Dischargeability of Student Loan on [creditor's name] by placing true and correct copies thereof enclosed in a sealed envelope with postage thereon fully prepaid, in the United States Mail at [city of post office where papers will be mailed], addressed as follows:

[this space for address of affected creditor(s) and trustees]

I declare under penalty of perjury that the foregoing is true and correct, and that this declaration

was executed on

Date: [leave blank], 20___ at [leave blank] (City and State)

_____ [leave blank]
(Signature)

ii. Filing a Complaint to Determine Dischargeability

To seek a discharge of your student loan on the ground of undue hardship, you must file a formal complaint with the bankruptcy court. This is considered an "adversarial proceeding" in bankruptcy. You should look at your local rules to see if any apply to complaints or adversarial proceedings.

In general, you can file your complaint with the court any time after you file for bankruptcy. Some courts may require that adversarial proceedings be filed at a certain time, however, so check your local rules.

You will need to fill out at least two forms, depending on your court's requirements. Sample completed forms are below.

Step 1: Refer to your court's local rules for time limits, format of papers and other details of an adversarial proceeding.

Step 2: Make at least three copies of the blank, line-numbered legal paper in Appendix 4 (to allow for mistakes). Type from line number 1 to line 15 as follows (see samples, below):

Line 1: Your name, and that of your spouse if you're filing jointly.

Line 1.5: Your address.

Line 2: Your city, state and zip code.

Line 2.5: Your phone number.

Line 3: Type: Debtor in Pro Per.

Line 7: Center and type UNITED STATES BANKRUPTCY COURT, in capital letters.

Line 8: Center and type the judicial district and state you are in. Get this information from your bankruptcy petition.

Lines 9-15: Type as shown in the example. Be sure to include all entities connected with your loan on the creditor line, including the Department of Education, a guarantee agency and any collection agency.

Step 3: Make a few photocopies of the page with the information you have typed so far. This will save you typing later, because you can use this same heading for both forms.

Step 4: Using one of the copies that you just made, start typing again at line 16. Prepare a COMPLAINT TO DETERMINE DISCHARGEABILITY OF STUDENT LOAN, as shown in the example, below. When you are done, make at least four copies of the Complaint.

Step 5: Call the bankruptcy court clerk and ask the following:

- Is the fee for filing a Complaint to Determine Dischargeability still $120?
- How much does it cost to make photocopies of papers at the courthouse?
- What is the mailing address of the trustee in your case (if you don't already have it)?
- What is the mailing address of the U.S. trustee? (The U.S. trustee oversees all bankruptcy matters in your district.)

Step 6: Prepare a Proof of Service by Mail, as shown in the sample. This form states that a friend or relative of yours, who is at least 18 years old and not a party to the bankruptcy, mailed your papers. Fill in the blanks with your friend's name, county, state, address and zip code as indicated. On line 23, put the city or town of the post office that your friend will mail your papers from. Starting at line 25, put the names and addresses of the creditor, the trustee in your case and the U.S. trustee.

Step 7: Take your Complaint to the bankruptcy court for filing. Remember to bring your checkbook to pay the filing fee and change to make photocopies. When you get to the court clerk, ask for a Summons, which you will have to fill out before you file your Complaint. A Summons is a paper which lets the creditor know you've filed a Complaint. You can use your pen—you don't have to type the information on the Summons. It asks for your name, the name of the creditor, your case number and some other identifying information. Ask the clerk for help if you don't know what to put in any blank.

In many districts, the court clerk will give you a "status conference date"—a date when you'll meet with the creditor and bankruptcy judge. The date will probably be in a few weeks or months, depending on how busy the judge is. The clerk either will tell you to write the date on the Summons or will give you a separate paper, called an Order, which contains the date.

Step 8: Ask the clerk where a copy machine is located; make four copies of the Summons and any Order.

Step 9: Get back in line and file your Complaint and Summons.

Step 10: Put one copy of the Complaint, any Order and Summons in a stamped envelope with sufficient postage; have your friend mail them to the creditor, your trustee and the U.S. trustee. The creditor gets the original Summons; your trustee and the U.S. trustee each get a copy; keep another for your records.

Step 11: The creditor(s) affected by your Complaint have 30 days to submit a written response.

Step 12: Get a copy of *Represent Yourself in Court: How to Prepare & Try a Winning Case*, by Paul Bergman and Sara Berman-Barrett (Nolo). It contains all the information you need to handle your own case, from start to finish, without a lawyer. Particularly if your case is fairly straightforward—for example, a medical or similar condition is keeping you from working or working enough to pay your student loan—you should be able to proceed on your own. However, some people find it stressful or uncomfortable to discuss their own medical or other problems in court. If you think this might be difficult for you, consider filing your own bankruptcy and then hiring a lawyer to handle only this procedure.

Step 13: From here, your case proceeds like any other trial. If your district requires you to attend a status conference, go. The bankruptcy judge will try to settle the matter. If you can't settle it, the judge will see what plans each side has. Will anyone be filing motions or doing discovery? (All of this is explained in *Represent Yourself in Court*.) The judge will probably also set a trial date.

3. Taxes

As a general rule, recent federal, state and local taxes aren't dischargeable in Chapter 7 bankruptcy. (They can, however, be included in a Chapter 13 bankruptcy repayment plan.) Although there are some exceptions, these exceptions seldom apply in practice. And even if they do, the taxing authority will probably be able to enforce any tax lien that has been placed on your property. Before automatically assuming your tax debt does not qualify for discharge, do some research or see an attorney. One book we recommend is *Stand Up to the IRS,* by Frederick W. Daily (Nolo).

Income taxes. Federal, state and local income taxes cannot be discharged unless they were first owed at least three years before you file for bankruptcy and you properly filed your tax return for the years in question at least two years prior to filing for bankruptcy. If the IRS completes a Substitute for Return on your behalf which you neither sign nor consent to, your return is not considered filed. (See *In re Bergstrom*, 949 F.2d 341 (10th Cir. 1991).)

There's one exception to this three-year/two-year rule, so if you've recently been negotiating with the IRS or state tax agency or have been in a tax court case, and the three-year period has elapsed, don't get too excited. Any income tax liability assessed within 240 days of filing for bankruptcy is nondischargeable. This means that once your negotiation or case is over and your tax liability set, you must wait at least 240 days before filing if you want a chance at having your taxes discharged.

Also, if you borrowed money or used your credit card to pay taxes that would otherwise be nondischargeable, you cannot eliminate the loan or credit card debt in bankruptcy. In other words, you can't turn your nondischargeable tax debt into a dischargeable tax debt by paying it with your credit card.

⚠ **Understand the assessment date.** If you're unsure of the assessment date, consider seeing a tax lawyer—but don't rely on the IRS for the date. If the IRS gives you the wrong date—telling you that the 240 days have elapsed—the IRS won't be held to it if it turns out to be wrong. (See, for example, In re Howell, 120 B.R. 137 (9th Cir. BAP 1990).)

Penalties on taxes that are dischargeable are also dischargeable. If the underlying tax debt is nondischargeable, courts are split as to whether you can discharge the penalties or not.

> **EXAMPLE:** Jill failed to file a tax return for 1993. In 1999, the IRS discovers Jill's failure and in January 2000 assesses tax of $5,000 and penalties and interest of $12,000. Jill files for bankruptcy in January 2001. Because Jill didn't file a return for 1993, she can't discharge the tax, even though it became due more than three years past (and more than 240 days have elapsed since the taxes were assessed). Jill may be able to discharge the IRS penalties for failure to file a tax return and failure to pay the tax. Or course, the IRS is likely to argue that she cannot discharge the penalties, and some courts will agree.

Property taxes. Property taxes aren't dischargeable unless they became due more than a year before you file for bankruptcy and the taxing authority hasn't assessed your liability within the previous 240 days. But even if your personal liability for paying the property tax out of your pocket is discharged, the tax lien on your property is unaffected. From a practical standpoint, this discharge is no discharge at all, because you'll have to pay off the lien before you can transfer clear title to the property.

Other taxes. Other types of taxes that aren't dischargeable are business-related: payroll taxes, excise taxes and customs duties. Sales, use and poll taxes are also probably not dischargeable. If you have any of these types of taxes, see a bankruptcy attorney.

4. Child Support and Alimony

Alimony (also called spousal support or maintenance) and child support obligations are usually not dischargeable, but there are a few exceptions.

a. Dischargeable Alimony and Child Support

Two kinds of alimony or child support debts can be discharged.

- **Support paid under an agreement between unmarried persons.** If an unmarried couple enters into an agreement covering their obligations to each other, as many do, the agreement often covers support (who pays whom) in the event the couple separates. In most states, these agreements are enforceable—the recipient can sue if the other person doesn't pay. But unlike alimony or child support ordered by a court, if the person who must pay files for bankruptcy, the obligation can be discharged unless the person who was supposed to receive support sues and wins a court judgment against the other person.
- **Support owed someone other than a spouse, ex-spouse or child.** If a parent or a child has given (assigned, in legal terms) the right to receive support to someone else, or a creditor has garnished the payments, the debt is dischargeable unless it's owed to the welfare department or another government agency or office, such as a court child support collections unit.

  Be aware, however, that courts are increasingly characterizing debts to people other than parents, but for the benefit of children—such as attorney's fees incurred in a child custody case or hospital delivery costs—as nondischargeable child support. (See, for example, *In re Poe,* 118 B.R. 809 (N.D. Okla. 1990); *In re Jones,* 9 F.3d 878 (10th Cir. 1993); *In re Seibert,* 914 F.2d 102 (7th Cir. 1990).)

b. Nondischargeable Alimony and Child Support

An obligation called child support, alimony or something similar is clearly nondischargeable. However, some debts that go by other names may also be considered nondischargeable child support or alimony. The most common are marital debts—the debts a spouse was ordered to pay when the couple divorced.

Often, the spouse who will pay alimony or child support agrees at the time of the divorce to pay more than half of the marital debts, in exchange for a lower support obligation. If that spouse later files for bankruptcy, a portion of the debt is really support. Consequently, it's considered a nondischargeable debt owed to the other spouse. Similarly, one spouse may have agreed to pay some of the other spouse's or children's future living expenses (shelter, clothing, health insurance, transportation) in exchange for a lower support obligation. The obligations for the future expenses are treated as support owed to the other spouse and aren't dischargeable.

> **EXAMPLE:** When Erica and Tom divorced, they had two young children. Tom offered to pay most of the marital debts in exchange for low child support payments; Erica agreed because she had a good income of her own and felt able to support the children without too much help from Tom. If Tom files for bankruptcy before paying off the marital debts, the bankruptcy judge won't grant a discharge for all the marital debts.

Obligations that are generally considered support and aren't dischargeable include debts that:

- are paid to a spouse who is maintaining the primary residence of the children while there is a serious imbalance of incomes
- terminate on the death or remarriage of the recipient spouse
- depend on the future income of either spouse, or
- are paid in installments over a substantial period of time. (See, for example, *In re Goin,* 808 F.2d 1391 (10th Cir. 1987); *In re Calhoun,* 10 B. Ct. D. 1402 (6th Cir. 1983).)

5. Fines, Penalties and Restitution

You cannot discharge fines, penalties or restitution that a federal, state or local government has imposed to punish you for violating a law. Examples include:

- fines imposed for infractions (most traffic tickets, for example), misdemeanors (petty offenses) or felonies (serious crimes)
- fines imposed by a judge for contempt of court
- fines imposed by a government agency for violating agency regulations (for example, a fine imposed for fraudulently obtaining public benefits)
- some penalties for underpaying taxes or filing a late tax return (see Section 3, above)
- restitution (payment to an economically injured victim) imposed in criminal cases—in some criminal cases, judges give a convicted defendant probation, as long as he makes restitution to the victim; restitution is nondischargeable because it's imposed against the defendant, as rehabilitation, rather than to compensate the victim. (18 U.S.C. § 3613.)

6. Court Fees

You cannot discharge a fee imposed by a court for the filing of a case, motion, complaint or appeal, or for other costs and expenses assessed with respect to such court filing. This provision probably only applies to prisoners. But the law is a bit unclear and very few courts have ruled on this issue.

7. Intoxicated Driving Debts

Debts for the death of, or personal injury to, someone resulting from your driving while illegally intoxicated by alcohol or drugs (under the intoxicated driving laws of your state) aren't dischargeable.

In contrast, debts for property damage resulting from your intoxicated driving are dischargeable.

> **EXAMPLE:** Christopher was in a car accident in which he caused both property damage and personal injury to Ellen. Several months later Christopher filed for bankruptcy and listed Ellen as a creditor. After the

bankruptcy case was over, Ellen sued Christopher, claiming that the debt wasn't discharged because Christopher was driving while intoxicated. If Ellen shows that Christopher was illegally intoxicated under his state's laws, she will be able to pursue her personal injury claim against him. She is barred, however, from trying to collect for any property damage.

8. Debts You Couldn't Discharge in a Previous Bankruptcy

If a bankruptcy court dismissed a previous bankruptcy case because of your fraud or other bad acts (misfeasance), you cannot discharge any debts that would have been discharged in the earlier bankruptcy. This rule doesn't affect debts incurred since the date you filed the earlier bankruptcy case.

9. Condominium and Cooperative Fees

You cannot discharge certain condominium or housing cooperative fees. Only fees assessed during a period in which you physically lived in the condo or received rent from a tenant are nondischargeable.

C. Debts Discharged Unless the Creditor Objects

Four types of nondischargeable debts are in fact discharged unless the creditor objects during the bankruptcy proceedings. Again, the four types of debts are:
- debts incurred by fraudulent acts
- debts from willful and malicious injury to a person or property
- debts from embezzlement, larceny or breach of trust (fiduciary duty), and
- debts (other than alimony or child support) that arise from a marital settlement agreement or divorce decree.

To object to the discharge of this kind of debt, a creditor must file a written complaint with the bankruptcy court and prove in court that the debt fits in one of the categories. The complaint must be filed within 60 days of the first date set by the court for the meeting of creditors. If a creditor gets late notice of the bankruptcy and files a late claim, the court will extend the 60-day period for filing objections.

Because filing a complaint usually requires the help of an attorney, it's expensive. Creditors tend to object only when the debt is substantial—about $1,000 or more. You'll probably need to hire an attorney yourself if you want to respond to the creditor in court. (See Ch. 9.)

1. Debts From Fraud

You cannot discharge certain debts incurred through fraud. There are two main categories of these types of debts, listed below.

If a creditor challenges discharge of a debt by claiming you engaged in fraud, but the judge finds in your favor, the judge may order the creditor to reimburse you for the money you spent on attorney's fees.

a. Debts From Intentionally Fraudulent Behavior

If a creditor can show that a debt arose because of your dishonest act, and that the debt wouldn't have arisen had you been honest, the court will probably not let you discharge the debt. Common examples are as follows:
- You wrote a check for something and stopped payment on it after changing your mind and deciding not to pay.
- You wrote a check against insufficient funds but assured the merchant that the check was good.
- You rented or borrowed an expensive item and claimed it was yours to get a loan.
- You got a loan by telling the lender you'd pay it back, when you had no intention of doing so.

The dishonest act (fraud) can be oral or written. A debt arising from a false written statement about your financial condition is also nondischargeable under another section of the bankruptcy code, discussed below.

Sometimes even silence can be fraudulent rather than golden. For example, one woman obtained an extension of a loan from her mother-in-law without mentioning that she planned to divorce her husband. A court ruled that the omission was fraudulent and the loan nondischargeable. (*In re Verdon*, 95 B.R. 877 (N.D. N.Y. 1989).)

Two types of debts are presumed to be fraud:

- Debts of more than $1,075 to one creditor for luxury goods or services incurred within 60 days before filing for bankruptcy.
- Cash advances totaling more than $1,075 under an open-ended consumer credit plan incurred within 60 days before filing for bankruptcy.

Credit cards and fraud. See Ch. 4, Section D.3, for more information on claims that credit card debts are nondischargeable due to fraud.

b. Debts From a False Written Statement About Your Financial Condition

If a creditor proves that you incurred a debt because of a false written statement you made, it isn't dischargeable. Here are the rules:

- The false statement must be written—for instance, made in a credit application or rental application.
- The false statement must have been "material"— that is, a potentially significant factor in the creditor's decision to extend you credit. The two most common materially false statements are omitting debts and overstating income.
- The false statement must relate to your financial condition or the financial condition of "insiders"— people close to you or a business entity with which you're associated. Specifically, an insider is a relative, a business partner, a partnership in which you're a general partner or a corporation in which you're a director or officer or which you control.
- The creditor must have relied on the false statement, and the reliance must have been reasonable. A creditor is presumed to have relied on any statement you make in a credit application or financial statement. And reliance is normally considered reasonable if the creditor performed a credit check or had other valid reasons for relying on your statements, such as a previous business relationship with you.

- You must have intended to deceive the creditor. This is hard to prove, so most courts look at the disparity between what's on the statement and the truth. For instance, if you wrote that you make $150,000 a year, but you only make $15,000, the court will conclude you intended to deceive. If, on the other hand, you establish that the error came from genuine carelessness, you may get the debt discharged.

2. Debts From Willful and Malicious Acts

Debts caused by your willful and malicious injury to another person or property are not dischargeable if the creditor successfully objects. The obvious question is what constitutes a willful and malicious act.

Law can be broken down into two major areas: criminal and civil. Generally, crimes in which you intentionally injure people or property are considered willful and malicious acts. An example is stabbing someone with a knife because you're angry. Your liability for the injury or damage caused the victim will probably be ruled nondischargeable.

An example of a crime that isn't willful and malicious is driving over the speed limit. Even if you hit another car and cause damage, your act can't be described as intentional. It is negligent for sure, maybe even reckless. But while you may have intended to speed, you did not intend to hit the other vehicle.

The area of civil law that covers injuries to another person or property is called tort law. Just as with criminal acts, there are two kinds of torts: intentional and negligent. Damages arising out of an intentional tort, such as libel or slander—making a false and damaging statement about a person to a third party—generally will not be discharged in bankruptcy. But damages from negligent, or even reckless, acts usually will be. (See *Kawaauhau v. Geiger*, 118 S.Ct. 974 (1998).)

Examples of acts that may be considered willful and malicious include:

- false imprisonment (unlawfully restraining someone)
- intentional infliction of emotional distress (deliberately causing extreme anxiety, fear or shock)
- libel or slander (making false and damaging statements about someone to a third person)

- deliberate infringement of a copyright, patent or trademark
- forcible entry and detainer (activities of a landlord to evict a tenant, such as removing a door or changing the locks)
- conversion of personal property (taking someone's property or cash), such as hiding assets from your spouse during a divorce proceeding or destroying collateral, and
- engaging in malicious prosecution or vexatious litigation (filing a lawsuit based on false allegations with the intent to injure the defendant financially and emotionally).

Secured creditors often see willfulness and malice when the collateral securing a loan has been destroyed. For example, you bought a car on credit and junked it rather than return it when you filed for bankruptcy. The creditor may claim that you willfully and maliciously destroyed the collateral, and that your debt for the balance due should not be discharged. If you can show that you junked the car because you thought you didn't owe any more money, you thought the car had no value or you desperately needed money for necessities, you may be able to discharge the debt because your actions were not necessarily intentionally malicious.

3. Debts From Embezzlement, Larceny or Breach of Fiduciary Duty

A debt incurred as a result of embezzlement, larceny or breach of fiduciary duty is nondischargeable if the creditor successfully objects to its discharge.

Embezzlement is taking property entrusted to you for another and using it for yourself. Examples of embezzlement are when a trustee misappropriates trust funds or a bank clerk takes money from the bank.

Larceny is another word for theft. If you owe a debt because you stole property or services, you can't discharge the debt if the victim goes to court and proves the larceny.

Breach of fiduciary duty is the failure to live up to a duty of trust you owe someone, based on a relationship where you're required to manage property or money for another, or where your relationship is a close and confidential one. In general, common fiduciary relationships are:

- agent and principal
- partnerships
- attorney and client
- bailor and bailee (a bailor is someone who stores property for someone else, the bailee)
- bank officer and customer
- broker and customer
- estate executor and beneficiary
- guardian and ward
- husband and wife, and
- landlord and tenant.

Many bankruptcy courts, however, limit the definition of fiduciary. Many require the relationship to have been formed by a technical or express trust (such as an estate executor and beneficiary), not just by the general laws of a state (such as a partnership).

4. Debts From a Divorce Decree or Marital Settlement Agreement

Any debt arising from a separation agreement or divorce, or in connection with a marital settlement agreement, divorce decree or other court order, can be considered dischargeable, with one exception: debts that are in the nature of alimony, maintenance or support are almost never dischargeable. (See Section B.4 in this chapter.) If your obligation is not alimony or child support, you can usually discharge it unless your ex-spouse or child challenges the discharge of the debt in bankruptcy court. Once the challenge is raised, the court will allow the debt to be discharged unless:

- you have the ability to pay the debt from income or property not reasonably necessary for your support and not reasonably necessary for you to continue, preserve and operate a business, or
- discharging the debt would result in a detriment to your former spouse or child that would out-weigh the benefit you would receive from the discharge.

The majority of courts have held that the burden of proving the debtor's ability/inability to pay or proving who would be harmed more by the discharge/nondischarge is on the debtor. (See, for example, *In re Hill*, 184 B.R. 750 (N.D. Ill. 1995).) A few courts, however, have held that the burden is on the non-filing ex-spouse.

Decisions interpreting this provision of the Bankruptcy Code include the following:

- A debtor could not prove that the benefit he would receive by the discharge of a property equalizing payment would outweigh the detriment to his ex-wife. The court therefore focused on his ability to pay and determined that it would be a hardship for him to pay it all (nearly $19,000) at once. The court ordered him to pay $10,000 of it at a rate of $200 per month. (*In re Comisky*, 183 B.R. 883 (N.D. Cal. 1995).)

- A debtor proved that she could not afford to pay the marital debts she agreed to pay in her divorce because most of her assets were tied up by her ex-husband—she'd get her share of the marital property if and when he decided to sell the property. The court further found that the benefit she'd receive by the discharge would outweigh the detriment to her ex-husband who would have to pay the debts because he held most of the marital property, was receiving child support payments from her and earned approximately $2,000 per month. (*In re Becker*, 185 B.R. 567 (W.D. Mo. 1995).)

- A court concluded that a debtor clearly could not afford to pay the debts he agreed to pay in his divorce, and that the benefit to him in discharging the debts was substantial—he'd receive a necessary fresh start. But the court also found that the detriment to his ex-wife in having to pay the debts was significant—that she might be forced to file for bankruptcy, too. The court concluded that this wasn't so bad, allowed the ex-husband to discharge the debts and suggested that a "discharge of the debts by both parties ... [was] the most sensible solution to the combined problems." (*In re Hill*, 184 B.R. 750 (N.D. Ill. 1995).)

- A debtor filed for bankruptcy and sought to discharge the debts he was assigned in his divorce on the ground that he could not pay because of a lack of income. After his divorce, he had voluntarily reduced his income from $48,000 per year to well under $10,000. He lived off a small amount he received helping out in a bar and grill where he was a shareholder and in helping his new wife in her dog grooming business. His ex-wife had paid over $22,000 satisfying some of the debts on which he had defaulted. The court wasted no time stating that he had failed to show a lack of ability to pay, and furthermore, that any benefit he'd receive through the discharge of his debts would be outweighed by the detriment to his ex-wife. (*In re Molino*, 225 B.R. 904 (6th Cir. 1998).)

Debts Your Creditors Claim Are Nondischargeable

Some of your creditors may be claiming that the debts you owe them cannot be wiped out in bankruptcy. In fact, computer leases—software and hardware—often contain clauses stating that if you're unable to complete the lease period, you can't eliminate the balance of the debt in bankruptcy.

Hogwash. The only debts you can't discharge in bankruptcy are the ones the Bankruptcy Code lists as nondischargeable—and we've described them in this chapter. Don't let your creditors intimidate you into thinking otherwise.

CHAPTER

9

Help Beyond the Book

Although this book covers routine bankruptcy procedures in some detail, it doesn't come close to covering everything. That would require a 1,000-page treatise, most of which would be irrelevant for nearly all readers. That said, here are some suggestions if you need more information or advice than this book provides.

The major places to go for follow-up help are:

- **Bankruptcy Petition Preparers:** When you're ready to file for bankruptcy, but need typing assistance in filling out the forms.
- **Lawyers:** When you want information, advice or legal representation.
- **Law Libraries:** When you want more information on an issue raised in the course of your bankruptcy.

Before we discuss each of these approaches in more detail, here's a general piece of advice: Maintain control of your case whenever possible. By getting this book and filing for Chapter 7 bankruptcy, you've taken responsibility for your own legal affairs. If you decide to get help from others, shop around until you find someone who respects your efforts as a self-helper and recognizes your right to participate in the case as a valuable partner.

A. Bankruptcy Petition Preparers

Even though you should be able to handle routine bankruptcy procedures yourself, you may want someone familiar with the bankruptcy courts in your area to:

- type your forms
- provide some basic information about local procedures and requirements, or
- help you prepare for negotiations with your creditors.

For this level of assistance—routine form preparation and basic, general information rather than specific advice on a course of action—consider employing a bankruptcy petition preparer (BPP). BPPs will type your bankruptcy papers for about $50 to $175. (Most bankruptcy courts have set such a limit.)

BPPs are very different from lawyers. They can't give legal advice or represent you in court—only lawyers are allowed to do those things. That means they cannot advise you to file or not file for bankruptcy, tell you what to include or not include on your forms, tell you which exemption schedule to use or recommend a particular course of action regarding a debt or piece of property. If you need help doing any of these things, you should see an attorney.

Congress created the BPP designation for the specific purpose of regulating non-lawyers who assist people filing for bankruptcy with completing their forms. (11 U.S.C. § 110(g)(1).) On its face, the law is meant to protect consumers. For instance, the law makes it difficult for a BPP to charge an unreasonable fee—that is, a fee not reasonably related to the amount of service the BPP was authorized to provide. The law also permits a bankruptcy court to fine a BPP up to $500 for:

- failing to put the BPP's name, address and Social Security number on a bankruptcy petition
- failing to give the customer a copy of the documents at the time the documents are signed
- using the word "legal" or any similar term in advertisements or advertising under a category that includes such terms, or
- accepting court filing fees from the person filing for bankruptcy—that is, you must pay the filing fee to the court yourself or give the BPP a cashier's check made out to the court.

The law also allows a trustee or creditor to get $1,000 from a BPP who:

- commits a fraudulent, unfair or deceptive act
- violates any of the technical rules listed above, or
- causes a case to be dismissed by failing to file the papers, acting negligently, violating the bankruptcy statutes or regulations, or intentionally disregarding the law or procedural rules.

In addition, the BPP must pay you any actual monetary loss, plus $2,000, or twice the amount you paid to the BPP, whichever is greater.

BPPs are springing up all over the country to help people who don't want or can't afford to hire a lawyer, but you're still more likely to find a BPP if you live on the West Coast. A recommendation from someone who has used a particular BPP is the best way to find a reputable one in your area.

BPPs often advertise in classified sections of local newspapers and in the Yellow Pages. You may have to look hard to find BPPs because the Bankruptcy Code bars them from using the term "legal" in their advertisements or from advertising under a category which contains the word "legal." And many BPPs have display ads in local throwaway papers like the Classified Flea Market or Giant Nickel.

If you decide to use a BPP, remember that you are representing yourself and are responsible for knowing your rights under the bankruptcy law. A lot of what you will need to know can be found in this book. However, you may need to go beyond the book and either hit the law library or hire a lawyer (Sections B and C below).

B. Bankruptcy Lawyers

If you need to prepare custom-made court papers, show up at a court hearing to argue your side of a dispute during your bankruptcy or negotiate with a creditor or the trustee, you may need to consult a bankruptcy lawyer. You can't use a BPP because BPPs cannot represent you in court. Nor can they legally give you guidance on how to handle matters yourself. Also, non-routine bankruptcy procedures often require a knowledge of federal court procedure and the ability to engage in legal analysis. An experienced lawyer should have expertise in these areas. A bankruptcy lawyer can also provide valuable assistance in negotiating with a creditor or trustee.

You may be able to hire an attorney to handle only a specific procedure while you handle the main part of the bankruptcy yourself. As a general rule, you should bring an attorney into the case whenever a dispute involves something of sufficient value to justify the attorney's fees. If a creditor objects to the discharge of a $500 debt, and it will cost you $400 to hire an attorney, you may be better off trying to handle the matter yourself, even though this increases the risk that the creditor will win. If, however, the dispute is worth $1,000 and the attorney will cost you $200, hiring the attorney makes sense.

1. How to Find a Bankruptcy Lawyer

Where there's a bankruptcy court, there are bankruptcy lawyers. They're listed in the Yellow Pages under attorneys and often advertise in newspapers. You

should use an experienced bankruptcy lawyer, not a general practitioner, to advise you or handle matters associated with bankruptcy.

There are several ways to find the best bankruptcy lawyer for your job:

- **Personal Referrals:** This is your best approach. If you know someone who was pleased with the services of a lawyer, call that lawyer first. If that lawyer doesn't handle bankruptcies or can't take on your case, she may recommend someone else who's experienced, competent and available.
- **Bankruptcy Petition Preparers:** If there's a BPP in your area, chances are she works closely with bankruptcy attorneys who are both competent and sympathetic to self-helpers.
- **Group Legal Plans:** Some unions, employers and consumer action organizations offer group plans to their members or employees, who can obtain comprehensive legal assistance free or for low rates. If you're a member of such a plan, and the plan covers bankruptcies, check with it first for a lawyer.
- **Prepaid Legal Insurance:** Prepaid legal insurance plans offer some services for a low monthly fee and charge more for additional or different work. That means that participating lawyers may use the plan as a way to get clients, who are attracted by the low-cost basic services, and then sell them more expensive services. If the lawyer recommends an expensive course of action, get a second opinion before you agree.

But if a plan offers extensive free advice, your initial membership fee may be worth the consultation you receive, even if you use it only once. You can always join a plan for a specific service and then not renew. For bankruptcy purposes, however, a plan won't be much help unless it offers the services of bankruptcy attorneys.

There's no guarantee that the lawyers available through these plans are of the best caliber; sometimes they aren't. As with any consumer transaction, check out the plan carefully before signing up. Ask about the plan's complaint system, whether you get to choose your lawyer and whether or not the lawyer will represent you in court.

- **Lawyer Referral Panels:** Most county bar associations will give you the names of some bankruptcy attorneys who practice in your area. But bar associations usually provide only minimal screening for the attorneys listed, which means those who participate may not be the most experienced or competent. You may find a skilled attorney willing to work for a reasonable fee this way, but take the time to check out the credentials and experience of the person to whom you're referred.

2. What to Look for in a Lawyer

No matter what approach you take to finding a lawyer, here are three suggestions on how to make sure you have the best possible working relationship.

First, fight the urge you may have to surrender your will and be intimidated by a lawyer. You should be the one who decides what you feel comfortable doing about your legal and financial affairs. Keep in mind that you're hiring the lawyer to perform a service for you; shop around if the price or personality isn't right.

Second, it's important that you be as comfortable as possible with any lawyer you hire. When making an appointment, ask to talk directly to the lawyer. If you can't, this may give you a hint as to how accessible he or she is. Of course, if you're told that a paralegal will be handling the routine aspects of your case under the supervision of a lawyer, you may be satisfied with that arrangement.

If you do talk directly to the lawyer, ask some specific questions. Do you get clear, concise answers? If not, try someone else.

Also, pay attention to how the lawyer responds to your considerable knowledge. If you've read this book, you're already better informed about the law than most clients. Many lawyers are threatened when the client knows too much—in some cases, anything.

Finally, once you find a lawyer you like, make an hour-long appointment to discuss your situation fully. Your goal at the initial conference is to find out what the lawyer recommends and how much it will cost. Go home and think about the lawyer's suggestions. If they don't make complete sense or you have other reservations, call someone else.

3. How Bankruptcy Attorneys Are Paid

Commonly, bankruptcy attorneys charge a flat fee for a routine case and then charge additional amounts for extra procedures if they're necessary. For instance, the flat fee may be $750, but it may cost $150 more to respond to a motion brought by a creditor and $250 more to file a motion to establish the fair market value of secured property.

Most bankruptcy attorneys allow you to pay in installments. But even so, many require that you pay the entire fee before the bankruptcy petition is filed. Some even require that you pay for post-petition services (such as defending a creditor's challenge to the dischargeability of a debt) before you file the petition. This is because many courts classify attorneys' fees incurred after the bankruptcy petition is filed as dischargeable debts. That means that if you refuse to pay, the attorney can't force collection. Some courts, however, have allowed attorneys to collect post-petition fees. (For example, *In re Hines*, 147 F.3d 1185 (9th Cir. 1998).) Attorneys practicing before those courts will often allow debtors to pay fees after the petition has been filed.

If an attorney requires that you pay for post-petition services before you file the petition, consider this: If the court orders the attorney to turn the fee over (because it is deemed an illegal preference—that is, favoring one creditor, the attorney, over others), that money will go into the pot to pay your other creditors. If you hadn't paid the fees up-front, you may have been able to convert those funds to exempt assets (see Ch. 2, Section C) or exempt part or all of it through a wild-card exemption.

C. Legal Research

 Get some additional research help if you need it.

Legal research can vary from the very simple to the hopelessly complex. In this section we are way over on the simple side. If you would like to learn more about legal research or find our suggestions come up a bit short in your particular case, we recommend that you obtain a copy of *Legal Research: How to Find & Understand the Law,* by Elias and Levinkind (Nolo). *Legal Research* provides a plain-English tutorial on the ins and outs of legal research in the law library and on the Internet.

1. Sources of Bankruptcy Law

Bankruptcy is governed by several different sources of law:

- federal bankruptcy laws (statutes) passed by Congress
- federal bankruptcy procedural rules issued by a federal judicial agency
- local rules issued by individual bankruptcy courts
- federal and bankruptcy court cases applying bankruptcy laws to specific disputes
- laws (statutes) passed by state legislatures that define property you can keep in bankruptcy, and
- state court cases interpreting state exemption statutes.

A few years ago you would have had to visit a law library to find these law sources. Now you can find most of these same resources on the Internet. However, if you are able to visit a decent-sized law library, your research will be the better for it. This is because the law library hardcopy resources permit you to more easily find and read relevant court interpretations of the underlying statutes and rules—which are crucial to

getting a clear picture of what the laws and rules really mean.

There is another important reason to visit the law library if possible. While you can find superficial discussions and overviews of various aspects of bankruptcy on the Internet, you'll find in-depth encyclopedias and treatises in the law library that delve into every aspect of bankruptcy. In other words, you can not only find the law itself in the law library but you'll also be able to learn what the experts have to say about all the picky little issues that have arisen over the years.

Below, we get you to the resources you'll most likely be using, whether you are doing your research on the Internet or in the law library.

How to Use Law Libraries

Law libraries open to the public are most often found in and around courthouses. Law schools also frequently admit the public during certain times. Assuming you are welcome as a member of the public, find a way to feel at home even if it seems that the library is run mostly to serve members of the legal community—judges, lawyers and paralegals. Almost without exception, law libraries come with law librarians. The law librarians will be helpful as long as you ask them the right questions. Quite simply, the law librarian will help you find specific library resources (for instance, where you can find the federal bankruptcy statutes or rules) but they normally won't teach you the ins and outs of legal research. Nor will they give an opinion about what a law means, how you should deal with the court or how your particular question should be answered. For instance if you want to find a state case interpreting a particular exemption, the law librarian will show you where your state code is located on the shelves and he or she may even point out the volumes that contain the exemptions. The librarian won't, however, help you interpret the exemption, or apply the exemption to your specific facts, or how to raise the exemption in your bankruptcy case. Nor is he or she likely to tell you what additional research steps you can or should take. When it comes to legal research in the law library, self-help is the order of the day.

2. Bankruptcy Background Materials: Overviews, Encyclopedias and Treatises

Before digging into the primary law sources (statutes, rules, cases, etc., that we discuss below), you may want to do some background reading to get a firm grasp of your issue or question.

a. The Internet

A number of Internet sites contain large collections of articles written by experts about various aspects of bankruptcy. A starting place is the debt and bank-ruptcy law center hosted by Nolo at www.nolo.com. To find the center, browse down the Nolo home page till you see the "Debt and Bankruptcy law" center at the left. Click on it. Our next favorite jumping-off site for this type of research is The Bankruptcy Lawfinder page for consumer resources at www.agin.com/lawfind/level1b.html. You can also use www.findlaw.com (first click in Legal Subjects and then on the bankruptcy link).

If you feel a tad challenged by the bankruptcy lingo you encounter in these resources, we recommend that you become acquainted with A Dictionary of Bank-ruptcy Terminology published by the law firm of Bernstein and Bernstein at www.bernsteinlaw.com/publications/bankdict.html.

b. The Law Library

Finding a good treatise or encyclopedia discussion of bankruptcy is where the law library shines.

i. *Collier on Bankruptcy*

It's a good idea to get an overview of your subject be-fore trying to find a precise answer to a precise ques-tion. The best way to do this is to find a general commentary on your subject by a bankruptcy expert. For example, if you want to find out whether a particu-lar debt is nondischargeable, you should start by read-ing a general discussion about the type of debt you're dealing with. Or, if you don't know whether you're en-titled to claim certain property as exempt, a good over-view of your state's exemptions would get you started on the right track.

The most complete source of this type of background information is a multi-volume treatise known as *Collier on Bankruptcy*, by Lawrence P. King, et al. (Matthew Bender). It's available in virtually all law libraries. *Collier* is both incredibly thorough and meticulously up-to-date; semiannual supplements, with all the latest developments, are located at the front of each volume. In addition to comments on every aspect of bankruptcy law, *Collier* contains the bankruptcy statutes, rules and exemption lists for every state.

Collier is organized according to the bankruptcy statutes. This means that the quickest way to find infor-mation in it is to know what statute you're looking for. If you don't know the governing statute, start with the *Collier* subject-matter index. Be warned, however, that the index can be difficult to use; it contains a lot of bankruptcy jargon you may be unfamiliar with.

ii. Other Background Resources

For general discussions of bankruptcy issues, there are several other good places to start. An excellent all-around resource is called *Consumer Bankruptcy Law*

One-Stop Research: Using the CCH *Bankruptcy Law Reporter*

Most law libraries carry a looseleaf publication known as the Commerce Clearing House (CCH) *Bankruptcy Law Reporter* (BLR). In this publication, you can find all three primary source materials relating to bankruptcy: statutes, rules and cases.

Here is a brief tutorial on using this extremely helpful resource. More complete instructions are at the beginning of BLR Volume 1.

Assume Pamela buys a car from John for $2,000. She pays for the car by check, which bounces two days later. Before John can collect the money, Pamela files for Chapter 7 bankruptcy, listing John as a creditor for $2,000. John asks the bankruptcy court to declare the debt nondischargeable on the ground that writing a bad check is fraud. Pamela wants to know whether or not John is right.

Pamela visits her local law library and finds the *Bankruptcy Law Reporter*. The instructions at the beginning of Volume 1 lead her to the "topical index" which is organized by subject matter. She looks up "debt," "bad check" and "fraud." Under "fraud" she finds an entry for "discharge of debts" and a paragraph reference number: 9228.

Pamela locates paragraph 9228 in Volume 2, which contains:

- the federal bankruptcy statute defining fraud
- an explanation of the statute
- summaries of court decisions interpreting the statute

- a table of contents covering the summaries.

Pamela reads the statute, which states that debts arising from fraud can survive bankruptcy. Then, in the table of contents to paragraph 9228, she locates a reference to cases dealing with bad checks and is referred to subsection 9228.27. There she finds a summary of a possibly relevant case, with a cross-reference to paragraph number 69,195, where the full text of the case is printed. She finds the case and reads it, but it isn't helpful.

Next, Pamela turns to the "cumulative index" in Volume 3 and looks for paragraph 9228 in the left margin. The cumulative index tells her if any newer cases have been decided on this issue. She finds several possibly relevant references, including one that says, "Dishonored check not a false representation without a false statement" and a cross-reference to paragraph number 72,876.

Pamela turns to paragraph 72,876 (located in Volume 3, section "New Developments") and finds two new bankruptcy court cases dealing with when a debt from writing a bad check can survive bankruptcy. She reads the cases and learns that writing a bad check isn't considered fraud without showing an intent to commit fraud. Had Pamela told John that the check was good, the bankruptcy court would probably consider it fraud, and the debt would survive bankruptcy.

and Practice. This volume, published by the National Consumer Law Center, is updated every year. It contains a complete discussion of Chapter 7 bankruptcy procedures, the official bankruptcy forms and a marvelous bibliography.

Another good treatise is a legal encyclopedia called *American Jurisprudence*, 2nd Series. Almost all law libraries carry it. The article on bankruptcy has an extensive table of contents, and the entire encyclopedia has an index. Between these two tools, you should be able to zero in on helpful material.

If you are looking for information on adversary proceedings (such as how to defend against a creditor's challenge to the dischargeability of a debt), turn to *Represent Yourself in Court*, by Paul Bergman and Sara J. Berman-Barrett (Nolo). It has an entire chapter on representing yourself in adversary proceedings in bankruptcy court.

Researching bankruptcy procedure. If you need information on court procedures or the local rules of a specific court, consult the *Collier Bankruptcy Practice Manual.*

3. Finding Federal Bankruptcy Statutes

Title 11 of the United States Code contains all the statutes that govern your bankruptcy.

a. The Internet

If you are using the Internet, you'll want to become familiar with a reference page in The Bankruptcy Lawfinder website, at www.agin.com/lawfind/level1a.html.

This page provides several different links to the federal bankruptcy laws, including a link to a site maintained by Cornell Law School at www4.law.cornell.edu/uscode/11. The Cornell version of the federal bankruptcy laws lets you browse the laws by subject matter and also offers a key word search. To help you in your browsing, here is a table setting out the various subject-matter sections of the U.S. Code that apply to bankruptcy:

Bankruptcy Code Sections (11 U.S.C.)

§ 109 Who may file for which type of bankruptcy
§ 110 Non-attorney bankruptcy petition preparers
§ 302 Who qualifies for filing joint cases
§ 341 Meeting of creditors
§ 342 Giving notice of meeting of creditors
§ 343 Examination of debtor at meeting of creditors
§ 347 Property the trustee doesn't want
§ 348 Converting from one type of bankruptcy to another
§ 349 Dismissing a case
§ 350 Closing and reopening a case
§ 362 The automatic stay
§ 366 Continuing or reconnecting utility service
§ 501 Filing of creditors' claims
§ 506 Allowed secured claims & lien avoidance
§ 507 Claims having priority
§ 522 Exemptions
§ 523 Nondischargeable debts
§ 524 Reaffirmation of debts
§ 525 Prohibited postbankruptcy discrimination
§ 541 Property of the estate
§ 547 Preferences
§ 548 Fraudulent transfers
§ 553 Setoffs
§ 554 Trustee's abandonment of property
§ 722 Avoiding lien that impairs exemption; redemption
§ 726 Distribution of the property of the estate
§ 727 Discharge

---

b. The Law Library

Virtually every law library has at least one complete set of the annotated United States Code. If you already have a citation to the statute you are seeking, you can use the citation to find the statute. However, if you have no citation—which is frequently the case—you can either use the index to Title 11 (the part of the Code that applies to bankruptcy) or you can use the table we set out just above that matches various issues that are likely to interest you with specific chapters or sections of Title 11.

Once you have found and read the statute, you can browse the one-paragraph summaries of written opinions issued by courts that have interpreted that particular statute. You will be looking to see whether a court has addressed your particular issue. If so, assuming you are in the law library, you will most likely be able to find and read the entire case for yourself. Reading what a judge has had to say about the statute regarding facts similar to yours is an invaluable guide to understanding how a judge is likely to handle the issue in your case.

4. Finding the Federal Rules of Bankruptcy Procedure

The Federal Rules of Bankruptcy Procedure govern what happens if an issue is contested in the bankruptcy court. Most cases sail through the court without any need for the bankruptcy judge's intervention. However, lawsuits are sometimes filed. If you are representing yourself in such a lawsuit, you'll want to become familiar with these rules.

a. The Internet

You can find the Rules by visiting The Bankruptcy Lawfinder page for statutes, rules and cases at www.high-tech-law.com/lawfind/levelA.html. Click on the link to the bankruptcy rules maintained by Cornell, which takes you to www2.law.cornell.edu/cgi-bin/foliocgi.exe/frb?.

b. The Law Library

The Law Library also contains the Federal Rules of Bankuptcy Procedure. These can be found in the larger collection of federal laws published either as United States Code Annotated or United State Code Service. As with the federal bankruptcy statutes, once you read a rule you can also browse summaries of court opinions that interpret the particular rule. And again, because you are in the law library, you can also usually find the full text of any case that you want to read.

5. Finding Local Court Rules

Every bankruptcy court operates under a set of local rules that govern how it does business and what is expected of the parties who use it. Throughout this book we have cautioned you to read the rules for your particular court so that your dealings with the court will go smoothly—and so you won't end up getting tossed out of court if you become involved in litigation, such as an action to determine the dischargeability of a debt or a creditor's motion to lift the automatic stay.

a. The Internet

In addition to making its local rules available in the court clerk's office, most courts now post their local rules on their own websites. To find the website for your court, take these steps:

Step 1: Go to www.uscourts.gov/links.html.

Step 2: Click the number on the map that is closest to where you live.

Step 3: Browse the list until you find your court and click on it.

Step 4: Click on the local rules link.

These court websites usually contain other helpful information as well, including case information, official and local bankruptcy forms, court guidelines (in addition to the local rules), information about the court and its judges and the court calendar.

b. The Law Library

Your best shot at finding the local rules in your library is to consult *Collier on Bankruptcy*, the best-known bankruptcy treatise (described in subsection 2 above). This publication contains the local rules for most (if not all) of the nation's bankruptcy courts.

6. Finding Federal Court Bankruptcy Cases

Court opinions are vital to understanding how a particular law might apply to your individual case. There are four levels of federal courts that issue bankruptcy-related opinions:

- The U.S. Supreme Court

- The U.S. Courts of Appeal
- The U.S. District Courts
- The bankruptcy court (a subdivision of the U.S. District Court).

Most bankruptcy-related opinions are, not surprisingly, issued by the bankruptcy courts. By comparison, very few bankruptcy opinions come out of the U.S. Supreme Court. The Circuit and District Courts are somewhere in the middle.

a. The Internet

Depending on the date the case was decided, U.S. Supreme Court decisions and U.S. Court of Appeal decisions are available for free on the Internet. For a reasonable fee of $6.95 a month you can also subscribe to VersusLaw (at www.versuslaw.com), which provides U.S. Court of Appeal cases for an earlier period than you can get for free. VersusLaw also publishes some U.S. District Court cases on its website. Opinions by the bankruptcy courts are not yet available over the Internet unless you subscribe to Lexis or Westlaw, both of which are extremely pricey.

U.S. Supreme Court. To find a Supreme Court case, go to www.findlaw.com/casecode/supreme.html and use one of the search options to locate a particular case. If you don't know the case name and you don't have a citation, enter some relevant words relating to your issue and see what you pull up. You can search cases all the way back to 1893.

U.S. Court of Appeals. To find a U.S Circuit Court of Appeals case back to roughly 1996:

Step 1: go to www.findlaw.com/casecode/index.html

Step 2: scroll down to the U.S Court of Appeals opinions and websites

Step 3: click on the link that contains your state's abbreviation

Step 4: use one of the search options to find your case.

If you are looking for a case decided prior to 1996, your best bet is to sign up for VersusLaw, a proprietary Internet legal research site, at www.versuslaw.com. For a modest monthly fee you can search for cases back to the 1950s (in most circuits).

U.S. District Court and Bankruptcy Court. As mentioned, as of this writing (May 2002), very few U.S. District Court or bankruptcy court cases are available

online unless you subscribe to Westlaw or Lexis. Internet legal research will fail you here. You will have to take a trip to a law library if you want to know what the judges are doing in the courts—where the legal rubber meets the judicial road.

b. The Law Library

U.S. Supreme Court cases are published in three different book series:

- Supreme Court Reports
- Supreme Court Reporter
- Supreme Court Lawyer's Edition.

Some law libraries carry all three of these publications; others have only one. The cases are the same but each series has different editorial enhancements.

U.S. Court of Appeals cases are published in the Federal Reporter (abbreviated simply as "F."). Most law libraries, large and small, carry this series.

Many U.S. District Court cases are published in the Federal Supplement (F.Supp), a series available in most law libraries. Written opinions of bankruptcy judges are published in the Bankruptcy Reporter (B.R.), available in most mid- to large-size libraries. To accurately understand how your bankruptcy court is likely to interpret the laws in your particular case, you will sooner or later need access to the Bankruptcy Reporter.

7. State Statutes

As we stress throughout the book, the secret to understanding what property you can keep frequently lies in the exemptions that your state allows you to claim against creditors in and out of bankruptcy. These exemptions are found in your state's statutes, the laws passed by your state's legislature.

a. The Internet

Every state has its statutes online, including its exemption statutes. This means that you can read your state's exemption statutes for yourself. To do this:

Step 1: Go to Appendix 1. At the top of your state's exemption table, you'll see a general reference to the collection of state laws for your state that contain the exemption statutes. For example, if you are in Georgia you are told to look in the Official Code of Georgia Annotated.

Step 2: Go to www.nolo.com.

Step 3: Scroll to Legal Research Center.

Step 4: Click on state laws.

Step 5: Click on your state.

Step 6: Locate the collection of statutes mentioned in Appendix 1.

Step 7: Use the exemption citation to the far right of your state's exemption table to search for the statute.

b. The Law Library

Your law library will almost certainly have your state's statutes in book form, usually referred to as your state's code, annotated statutes or "compiled laws." Use Appendix 1 in this book to find a reference to the exemption statute you want to pursue further, then use that reference to locate the exemption statute in the code. Once you find and read the exemption of interest, you can browse the summaries of court opinions interpreting the statute and, if you wish, read the cases in their entirety.

Alternatively, if your library has a copy of *Colliers on Bankruptcy* (see Section 5 above), you can find the exemptions for your state accompanied by annotations summarizing state court interpretations.

8. State Court Cases

State courts are sometimes called on to interpret exemption statutes. If a court has interpreted the statute in which you are interested, you'll definitely want to chase down the relevant case and read it for yourself.

a. The Internet

All states make their more recent cases available for free on the internet—usually back to about 1996. To find these cases for your state:

Step 1: Go to http://www.law.cornell.edu/ opinions.html#state.

Step 2: Click on your state.

Step 3: Locate the link to the court opinions for your state. This may be one link or there may be separate links for your state's supreme court and your state's courts of appeal (the lower trial courts seldom publish their opinions, so you probably won't be able to find them).

If you want to go back to an earlier case, consider subscribing to VersusLaw at www.versuslaw.com. It only costs $6.95 a month and makes available state court cases going back 50 years or more (to 1934 for California and some other states).

b. The Law Library

Your law library will almost certainly have a collection of books that contain opinions issued by your state's courts. If you have a citation, you can go right to the case. If you don't have a citation, you'll need to use a digest to find relevant bankruptcy cases. Finding cases by subject matter is a little too advanced for this brief summary. See *Legal Research: How to Find & Understand the Law,* by Elias and Levinkind (Nolo), for more help.

9. Other Helpful Resources

You can download any official bankruptcy form from www.uscourts.gov/bankform.

As part of the bankruptcy process, you are required to give a fair market value for all the property you list in Schedule A (real property) and Schedule B (personal property). These figures also are crucial in determining which of your property is exempt. You can find the fair market value for your car by using the *Kelley Blue Book* at www.kbb.com. You can find the fair market value for most other personal property items by browsing on e-bay at www.ebay.com. You can determine the fair market value for your home by checking the prices that other comparable homes have sold for in the recent past. Many states have this information online; you can find it at www.homeadvisor.msn.com. Or, check with a local broker for the most appropriate Internet address. ■

State and Federal Exemptions Tables

Using the Exemption Tables

Every state lets people who file for bankruptcy keep certain property, called exemptions. Ch. 2, *Your Property and Bankruptcy*, Section B.6, discusses exemptions in detail.

1. What This Appendix Contains

- lists of each state's exemptions
- list of the federal bankruptcy exemptions (available as a choice in 14 states and the District of Columbia)
- list of the federal non-bankruptcy exemptions (available as additional exemptions when the state exemptions are chosen), and
- glossary defining exemption terms.

Each list is divided into three columns. Column 1 lists the major exemption categories: homestead, insurance, miscellaneous, pensions, personal property, public benefits, tools of the trade, wages and wildcard. (These categories differ on the federal non-bankruptcy exemptions chart.)

Column 2 gives the specific property that falls into each large category with noted limitations.

For example, the federal bankruptcy exemptions allow married couples filing jointly to each claim a full set of exemptions. This is called "doubling." Many state exemption systems do not allow doubling or do not allow doubling for certain types of property, such as the homestead exemption (which exempts equity in your residence). In some states, the legislature has expressly allowed or prohibited doubling. In others, the courts have allowed or prohibited doubling. In still others, neither the courts nor the legislature has addressed the issue. If that is the case, doubling is probably allowed. In Column 2, we've noted whether a court or state legislature has expressly allowed or prohibited doubling. If the chart doesn't say, it is probably safe to double. However, keep in mind that this area of the law changes rapidly—legislation or court decisions regarding doubling issued after the publication date of this book will not be reflected in the chart.

Column 3 lists the applicable law, which must be included on Schedule C.

2. Choosing Between State and Federal Exemptions

Each state chart indicates whether the federal exemptions are available for that state. The list of federal exemptions follows Wyoming.

3. Using the Glossary

Many of the terms used in exemption statutes are unfamiliar and can be looked up in the glossary. Even if you think you understand the terms in the chart, at least skim the glossary; some terms have special legal meanings that differ from their everyday meanings.

4. Houses and Pensions

If you own a house, you should also read Ch. 6, *Your House.*

With pensions, some states exempt only the money building up in the pension fund, and a few exempt only payments actually being received. Most exempt both. If the pension listing doesn't indicate otherwise, it means the state exempts both.

5. Wages, Benefits and Other Payments

Many states exempt insurance proceeds, pension payments, alimony and child support payments, public benefits or wages. This means that payments you received before filing are exempt if you haven't mixed them with other money or, if you have mixed them, you can trace the exempt portion back to its source.

If, when you file for bankruptcy, you're entitled to receive an exempt payment but haven't yet received it, you can exempt the payment when it comes in by amending Schedules B (personal property you own or possess) and C (property you claim as exempt).

Alabama

Federal Bankruptcy Exemptions not available. All law references are to Alabama Code.

ASSET	EXEMPTION	LAW
homestead	Real property or mobile home to $5,000; property cannot exceed 160 acres (husband & wife may double)	6-10-2
	Must record homestead declaration before attempted sale of home	6-10-20
insurance	Annuity proceeds or avails to $250 per month	27-14-32
	Disability proceeds or avails to an average of $250 per month	27-14-31
	Fraternal benefit society benefits	27-34-27
	Life insurance proceeds or avails	6-10-8; 27-14-29
	Life insurance proceeds or avails if clause prohibits proceeds from being used to pay beneficiary's creditors	27-15-26
	Mutual aid association benefits	27-30-25
pensions	IRAs and other retirement accounts	19-3-1
	Judges (only payments being received)	12-18-10(a),(b)
	Law enforcement officers	36-21-77
	State employees	36-27-28
	Teachers	16-25-23
personal property	Books of debtor and family	6-10-6
	Burial place for self and family	6-10-5
	Church pew for self and family	6-10-5
	Clothing of debtor and family	6-10-6
	Family portraits or pictures	6-10-6
public benefits	Aid to blind, aged, disabled, and other public assistance	38-4-8
	Crime victims' compensation	15-23-15(e)
	Southeast Asian War POWs' benefits	31-7-2
	Unemployment compensation	25-4-140
	Workers' compensation	25-5-86(b)
tools of trade	Arms, uniforms, equipment that state military personnel are required to keep	31-2-78
wages	With respect to consumer loans, consumer credit sales, and consumer leases, 75% of weekly net earnings or 30 times the federal minimum hourly wage; all other cases, 75% of earned but unpaid wages; bankruptcy judge may authorize more for low-income debtors	5-19-15; 6-10-7
wildcard	$3,000 of any personal property, except wages (husband and wife may double)	6-10-6

Alaska

Alaska law states that only the items found in Alaska Statutes §§ 9.38.010, 9.38.015(a), 9.38.017, 9.38.020, 9.38.025 and 9.38.030 may be exempted in bankruptcy. In *In re McNutt*, 87 B.R. 84 (9th Cir. 1988), however, an Alaskan debtor used the federal bankruptcy exemptions. All law references are to Alaska Statutes.

Alaska exemption amounts are adjusted regularly by administrative order. Current amounts are found at 8 Alaska Admin. Code tit. 8, § 95.030.

ASSET	EXEMPTION	LAW
homestead	$64,800 (joint owners may each claim a portion, but total can't exceed $64,800)	09.38.010(a)
insurance	Disability benefits	09.38.015(b), 09.38.030(e)(1),(5)
	Fraternal benefit society benefits	21.84.240
	Life insurance or annuity contract[s], total aggregate cash surrender value to $12,000	09.38.025
	Life insurance proceeds payable to beneficiary	09.38.025(c)
	Medical, surgical or hospital benefits	09.38.015(a)(3)
miscellaneous	Alimony, to extent wages exempt	09.38.030(e)(2)
	Child support payments made by collection agency	09.38.015(b)
	Liquor licenses	09.38.015(a)(7)
	Permits for limited entry into Alaska Fisheries	09.38.015(a)(8)
	Property of business partnership	09.38.100(b)
pensions	Elected public officers (only benefits building up)	09.38.015(b)
	ERISA-qualified benefits deposited more than 120 days before filing bankruptcy	09.38.017
	Judicial employees (only benefits building up)	09.38.015(b)
	Public employees, (only benefits building up)	09.38.015(b); 39.35.505
	Roth & traditional IRAs, medical savings accounts	09.38.017(e)(3)
	Teachers (only benefits building up)	09.38.015(b)
	Other pensions, to extent wages exempt (only payments being received)	09.38.030(e)(5)
personal property	Books, musical instruments, clothing, family portraits, household goods & heirlooms to $3,600 total	09.38.020(a)
	Building materials	34.35.105
	Burial plot	09.38.015(a)(1)
	Cash or other liquid assets to $1,680	09.38.030(b)
	Deposit in apartment or condo owners association	09.38.010(e)
	Health aids needed	09.38.015(a)(2)
	Jewelry to $1,200	09.38.020(b)
	Motor vehicle to $3,600; vehicle's market value can't exceed $24,000	09.38.020(e)
	Personal injury recoveries, to extent wages exempt	09.38.030(e)(3)
	Pets to $1,200	09.38.020(d)
	Proceeds for lost, damaged or destroyed exempt property	09.38.060
	Tuition credits under an advance college tuition payment contract	09.38.015(a)(9)
	Wrongful death recoveries, to extent wages exempt	09.38.030(e)(3)
public benefits	Adult assistance to elderly, blind, disabled	47.25.550
	Alaska longevity bonus	09.38.015(a)(5)
	Crime victims' compensation	09.38.015(a)(4)
	Federally exempt public benefits paid or due	09.38.015(a)(6)
	General relief assistance	47.25.210
	20% of permanent fund dividends	43.23.065
	Unemployment compensation	09.38.015(b); 23.20.405
	Workers' compensation	23.30.160
tools of trade	Implements, books & tools of trade to $3,360	09.38.020(c)
wages	Weekly net earnings to $420; for sole wage earner in a household, $660; if you don't receive weekly, or semi-monthly pay, can claim $1,680 in cash or liquid assets paid any month; for sole wage earner in household, $2,640	9.38.030(a),(b), 9.38.050(b)
wildcard	None	

Arizona

Federal Bankruptcy Exemptions not available. All law references are to Arizona Revised Statutes unless otherwise noted.

Note: Doubling is permitted for noted exemptions by Arizona Revised Statutes § 33-1121.01.

ASSET	EXEMPTION	LAW
homestead	Real property, an apartment or mobile home you occupy to $100,000; sale proceeds exempt 18 months after sale or until new home purchased, whichever occurs first (husband & wife may not double)	33-1101(A)
	May record homestead declaration to clarify which one of multiple eligible parcels are being claimed as homestead.	33-1102
insurance	Fraternal benefit society benefits	20-877
	Group life insurance policy or proceeds	20-1132
	Health, accident or disability benefits	33-1126(A)(4)
	Life insurance cash value or proceeds to $25,000 total	33-1126(A)(6); 20-1131(D)
	Life insurance proceeds to $20,000 if beneficiary is spouse or child	33-1126(A)(1)
miscellaneous	Alimony, child support needed for support	33-1126(A)(3)
	Minor child's earnings, unless debt is for child	33-1126(A)(2)
Pensions *also see wages*	Board of regents members	15-1628(I)
	District employees	48-227
	ERISA-qualified benefits deposited over 120 days before filing	33-1126(C)
	IRAs	*In re Herrscher,* 121 B.R. 29 (D. Ariz. 1990)
	Firefighters	9-968
	Police officers	9-931
	Public safety personnel	38-850(C)
	Rangers	41-955
	State employees retirement and disability	38-792; 38-797.11
personal property *husband & wife may double all personal property*	2 beds & bedding; 1 living room chair per person; 1 dresser, table, lamp; kitchen table; dining room table & 4 chairs (1 more per person); living room carpet or rug; couch; 3 lamps; 3 coffee or end tables; pictures, paintings, personal drawings, family portraits; refrigerator, stove, washer, dryer, vacuum cleaner; TV, radio, stereo, alarm clock to $4,000 total	33-1123
	Bank deposit to $150 in one account	33-1126(A)(8)
	Bible; bicycle; sewing machine; typewriter; burial plot; rifle, pistol or shotgun to $500 total	33-1125
	Books to $250; clothing to $500; wedding & engagement rings to $1,000; watch to $100; pets, horses, milk cows & poultry to $500; musical instruments to $250	33-1125
	Food & fuel to last 6 months	33-1124
	Funeral deposits	32-1391.04
	Health aids	33-1125(9)
	Motor vehicle to $5,000 ($10,000, if disabled)	33-1125(8)
	Prepaid rent or security deposit to $1,000 or 1 1/2 times your rent, whichever is less, in lieu of homestead	33-1126(D)
	Proceeds for sold or damaged exempt property	33-1126(A)(5),(7)
public benefits	Unemployment compensation	23-783(A)
	Welfare benefits	46-208
	Workers' compensation	23-1068(B)
tools of trade *(husband & wife may double)*	Arms, uniforms & accoutrements profession or office requires by law	33-1130(3)
	Farm machinery, utensils, seed, instruments of husbandry, feed, grain & animals to $2,500 total	33-1130(2)
	Library & teaching aids of teacher	33-1127
	Tools, equipment, instruments & books to $2,500	33-1130(1)
wages	75% of earned but unpaid weekly net earnings or 30 times the federal minimum hourly wage; 50% of wages for support orders; bankruptcy judge may authorize more for low-income debtors	33-1131
wildcard	None	

Arkansas

Federal Bankruptcy Exemptions available. All law references are to Arkansas Code Annotated unless otherwise noted.

ASSET	EXEMPTION	LAW
homestead *choose option 1 or 2*	1. For married person or head of family: unlimited exemption on real or personal property used as residence to 1/4 acre in city, town, or village, or 80 acres elsewhere; if property is between 1/4 -1 acre in city, town or village, or 80-160 acres elsewhere, additional limit is $2,500; homestead may not exceed 1 acre in city, town or village, or 160 acres elsewhere (husband & wife may not double)	Constitution 9-3, 9-4, 9-5; 16-66-210, 16-66-218(b)(3), (4) *In re Stevens,* 829 F.2d 693 (8th Cir. 1987)
	2. Real or personal property used as residence to $800 if single; $1,250 if married	16-66-218(a)(1)
insurance	Annuity contract	23-79-134
	Disability benefits	23-79-133
	Fraternal benefit society benefits	23-74-403
	Group life insurance	23-79-132
	Life, health, accident or disability cash value or proceeds paid or due to $500, *In re Holt,* 97 B.R. 997 (W.D. Ark. 1988)	16-66-209; Constitution 9-1, 9-2
	Life insurance proceeds if clause prohibits proceeds from being used to pay beneficiary's creditors	23-79-131
	Life insurance proceeds or avails if beneficiary isn't the insured	23-79-131
	Mutual assessment life or disability benefits to $1,000	23-72-114
	Stipulated insurance premiums	23-71-112
miscellaneous	Property of business partnership (Will be repealed in 2005)	4-42-502
pensions	Disabled firefighters	24-11-814
	Disabled police officers	24-11-417
	Firefighters	24-10-616
	IRA deposits to $20,000 if deposited over 1 year before filing for bankruptcy	16-66-218(b)(16)
	Police officers	24-10-616
	School employees	24-7-715
	State police officers	24-6-205, 24-6-223
personal property	Burial plot to 5 acres, if choosing Federal homestead exemption (option 2)	16-66-207, 16-66-218(a)(1)
	Clothing	Constitution 9-1, 9-2
	Motor vehicle to $1,200	16-66-218(a)(2)
	Wedding rings	16-66-219
public benefits	Crime victims' compensation	16-90-716(e)
	Unemployment compensation	11-10-109
	Workers' compensation	11-9-110
tools of trade	Implements, books & tools of trade to $750	16-66-218(a)(4)
wages	Earned but unpaid wages due for 60 days; in no event under $25 per week	16-66-208, 16-66-218(b)(6)
wildcard	$500 of any personal property if married or head of family; $200 if not married	Constitution 9-1, 9-2; 16-66-218(b)(1),(2)

California—System 1

Federal Bankruptcy Exemptions not available. California has two systems; you must select one or the other. All law references are to California Code of Civil Procedure unless otherwise noted.

ASSET	EXEMPTION	LAW
homestead	Real or personal property you occupy including mobile home, boat, stock cooperative, community apartment, planned development or condo to $50,000 if single & not disabled; $75,000 for families if no other member has a homestead (if only one spouse files, may exempt one-half of amount if home held as community property and all of amount if home held as tenants in common); $125,000 if 65 or older, or physically or mentally disabled; $125,000 if 55 or older, single & earn under $15,000 or married & earn under $20,000 & creditors seek to force the sale of your home; sale proceeds received exempt for 6 months after (husband & wife may not double)	704.710, 704.720, 704.730 *In re McFall*, 112 B.R. 336 (9th Cir. B.A.P. 1990)
	May file homestead declaration	704.920
insurance	Disability or health benefits	704.130
	Fidelity bonds	Labor 404
	Fraternal unemployment benefits	704.120
	Homeowners' insurance proceeds for 6 months after received, to homestead exemption amount	704.720(b)
	Life insurance proceeds if clause prohibits proceeds from being used to pay beneficiary's creditors	Ins. 10132, Ins. 10170, Ins. 10171
	Matured life insurance benefits needed for support	704.100(c)
	Unmatured life insurance policy loan value to $8,000 (husband & wife may double)	704.100(b)
miscellaneous	Business or professional licenses	695.060
	Inmates' trust funds to $1,000 (husband and wife may not double)	704.090
	Property of business partnership	Corp. 16501-04
pensions	County employees	Gov't 31452
	County firefighters	Gov't 32210
	County peace officers	Gov't 31913
	Private retirement benefits, including IRAs & Keoghs	704.115
	Public employees	Gov't 21201
	Public retirement benefits	704.110
Personal property	Appliances, furnishings, clothing & food	704.020
	Bank deposits from Social Security Administration to $2,000 ($3,000 for husband and wife)	704.080
	Building materials to repair or improve home to $2,000 (husband and wife may not double)	704.030
	Burial plot	704.200
	Funds held in escrow	Fin. 17410
	Health aids	704.050
	Homeowners' Association Assessments	Civil 1366(c)
	Jewelry, heirlooms & art to $5,000 total (husband and wife may not double)	704.040
	Motor vehicles to $1,900, or $1,900 in auto insurance for loss or damages (husband and wife may not double)	704.010
	Personal injury & wrongful death causes of action	704.140(a), 704.150(a)
	Personal injury & wrongful death recoveries needed for support; if receiving installments, at least 75%	704.140(b),(c),(d), 704.150(b),(c)
public benefits	Aid to blind, aged, disabled, public assistance	704.170
	Financial aid to students	704.190
	Relocation benefits	704.180
	Unemployment benefits	704.120
	Union benefits due to labor dispute	704.120(b)(5)
	Workers' compensation	704.160
tools of trade	Tools, implements, materials, instruments, uniforms, books, furnishings & equipment to $5,000 total ($10,000 total if used by both spouses in same occupation)	704.060
	Commercial vehicle (Vehicle Code § 260) to $4,000 ($8,000 total if used by both spouses in same occupation)	704.060
wages	Minimum 75% of wages paid within 30 days prior to filing	704.070
	Public employees vacation credits; if receiving installments, at least 75%	704.113
wildcard	None	

California—System 2

Federal Bankruptcy Exemptions not available. All law references are to California Code of Civil Procedure unless otherwise noted.

Note: Married couples may not double any exemptions. (*In re Talmadge,* 832 F.2d 1120 (9th Cir. 1987); *In re Baldwin,* 70 B.R. 612 (9th Cir. B.A.P. 1987)

ASSET	EXEMPTION	LAW
homestead	Real or personal property, including co-op, used as residence to $17,425; unused portion of homestead may be applied to any property	703.140 (b)(1)
insurance	Disability benefits	703.140 (b)(10)(C)
	Life insurance proceeds needed for support of family	703.140 (b)(11)(C)
	Unmatured life insurance contract accrued avails to $9,300	703.140 (b)(8)
	Unmatured life insurance policy other than credit	703.140 (b)(7)
miscellaneous	Alimony, child support needed for support	703.140 (b)(10)(D)
pensions	ERISA-qualified benefits needed for support	703.140 (b)(10)(E)
personal property	Animals, crops, appliances, furnishings, household goods, books, musical instruments & clothing to $450 per item	703.140 (b)(3)
	Burial plot to $17,425, in lieu of homestead	703.140 (b)(1)
	Health aids	703.140 (b)(9)
	Jewelry to $1,150	703.140 (b)(4)
	Motor vehicle to $2,725	703.140 (b)(2)
	Personal injury recoveries to $17,425 (not to include pain & suffering; pecuniary loss)	703.140 (b)(11)(D),(E)
	Wrongful death recoveries needed for support	703.140 (b)(11)(B)
public benefits	Crime victims' compensation	703.140 (b)(11)(A)
	Public assistance	703.140 (b)(10)(A)
	Social Security	703.140 (b)(10)(A)
	Unemployment compensation	703.140 (b)(10)(A)
	Veterans' benefits	703.140 (b)(10)(B)
tools of trade	Implements, books & tools of trade to $1,750	703.140 (b)(6)
wages	None (use Federal non-bankruptcy wage exemption)	
wildcard	$925 of any property	703.140 (b)(5)
	Unused portion of homestead or burial exemption, of any property	703.140 (b)(5)

Colorado

Federal Bankruptcy Exemptions not available. All law references are to Colorado Revised Statutes.

ASSET	EXEMPTION	LAW
homestead	Real property, mobile home, manufactured home or house trailer you occupy to $45,000; sale proceeds exempt 1 year after received (husband & wife may double)	38-41-201, 38-41-201.6, 38-41-203, 38-41-207; *In re Pastrana*, 216 B.R. 948 (Colo., 1998)
	Spouse or child of deceased owner may claim homestead exemption	38-41-204
insurance	Disability benefits to $200 per month; if receive lump sum, entire amount exempt	10-16-212
	Fraternal benefit society benefits	10-14-403
	Group life insurance policy or proceeds	10-7-205
	Homeowners' insurance proceeds for 1 year after received, to homestead exemption amount	38-41-209
	Life insurance cash surrender value to $25,000, except contributions to policy within past 24 months	13-54-102(1)(l)
	Life insurance proceeds if clause prohibits proceeds from being used to pay beneficiary's creditors	10-7-106
miscellaneous	Child support	13-54-102.5
	Property of business partnership	7-60-125
pensions *see also wages*	ERISA-qualified benefits, including IRAs	13-54-102(1)(s)
	Firefighters & police officers	31-30.5-208; 31-31-203
	Public employees	24-51-212
	Teachers	22-64-120
	Veterans	13-54-102(1)(h), 13-54-104
personal property	1 burial plot per family member	13-54-102(1)(d)
	Clothing to $1,500	13-54-102(1)(a)
	Food & fuel to $600	13-54-102(1)(f)
	Health aids	13-54-102(1)(p)
	Household goods to $3,000	13-54-102(1)(e)
	Jewelry & articles of adornment to $1,000	13-54-102(1)(b)
	Motor vehicles or bicycles used for work to $3,000; to $6,000 if used by a debtor or by a dependent who is disabled or 65 or over	13-54-102(j)(I), (II)
	Personal injury recoveries	13-54-102(1)(n)
	Family pictures & books to $1,500	13-54-102(1)(c)
	Proceeds for damaged exempt property	13-54-102(1)(m)
	Security deposits	13-54-102(1)(r)
Public benefits	Aid to blind, aged, disabled, public assistance	26-2-131
	Crime victims' compensation	13-54-102(1)(q); 24-4.1-114
	Earned income tax credit	13-54-102(1)(o)
	Unemployment compensation	8-80-103
	Veterans' benefits for veteran, spouse or child if veteran served in war	13-54-102(1)(h)
	Workers' compensation	8-42-124
tools of trade	Livestock or other animals, machinery, tools, equipment & seed of person engaged in agriculture, to $25,000 total	13-54-102(1)(g)
	Professional's library to $3,000 (if not claimed under other tools of trade exemption)	13-54-102(1)(k)
	Stock in trade, supplies, fixtures, tools, machines, electronics, equipment, books & other business materials, to $10,000 total	13-54-102(1)(i)
wages	Minimum 75% of weekly net earnings or 30 times the federal minimum wage, whichever is greater, including pension and insurance payments	13-54-104
wildcard	None	

Connecticut

Federal Bankruptcy Exemptions available. All law references are to Connecticut General Statutes Annotated.

ASSET	EXEMPTION	LAW
homestead	Real property, including mobile or manufactured home, to $75,000 (husband & wife may double); applies only to claims arising after 1993.	52-352a(e); 52-352b(t)
insurance	Disability benefits paid by association for its members	52-352b(p)
	Fraternal benefit society benefits	38a-637
	Health or disability benefits	52-352b(e)
	Life insurance proceeds if clause prohibits proceeds from being used to pay beneficiary's creditors	38a-454
	Life insurance proceeds or avails	38a-453
	Unmatured life insurance policy loan value to $4,000	52-352b(s)
miscellaneous	Alimony, to extent wages exempt	52-352b(n)
	Child support	52-352b(h)
	Farm partnership animals and livestock feed reasonably required to run farm where at least 50% of partners are members of same family	52-352d
pensions	ERISA-qualified benefits, including IRAs and Keoghs, to extent wages exempt	52-321a 52-352b(m)
	Medical savings account	52-321a
	Municipal employees	7-446
	Probate judges & employees	45-29o
	State employees	5-171, 5-192w
	Teachers	10-183q
personal property	Appliances, food, clothing, furniture, bedding	52-352b(a)
	Burial plot	52-352b(c)
	Health aids needed	52-352b(f)
	Motor vehicle to $1,500	52-352b(j)
	Proceeds for damaged exempt property	52-352b(q)
	Residential utility & security deposits for 1 residence	52-352b(l)
	Spendthrift trust funds required for support of debtor & family	51-321(d)
	Transfers to a nonprofit debt adjuster	52-352b(u)
	Wedding & engagement rings	52-352b(k)
public benefits	Crime victims' compensation	52-352b(o); 54-213
	Public assistance	52-352b(d)
	Social Security	52-352b(g)
	Unemployment compensation	31-272(c); 2-352b(g)
	Veterans' benefits	52-352b(g)
	Vietnam veterans' death benefits	27-140i
	Wages from earnings incentive program	52-352b(d)
	Workers' compensation	52-352b(g)
	Arms, military equipment, uniforms, musical instruments of military personnel	52-352b(i)
tools of trade	Tools, books, instruments & farm animals needed	52-352b(b)
wages	Minimum 75% of earned but unpaid weekly disposable earnings, or 40 times the state or federal hourly minimum wage, whichever is greater	52-361a(f)
wildcard	$1,000 of any property	52-352b(r)

Delaware

Federal Bankruptcy Exemptions not available. All law references are to Delaware Code Annotated unless otherwise noted.

Note: A single person may exempt no more than $5,000 total in all exemptions; a husband & wife may exempt no more than $10,000 total (10-4914).

ASSET	EXEMPTION	LAW
homestead	None, however, property held as tenancy by the entirety may be exempt against debts owed by only one spouse	In re Hovatter, 25 B.R. 123 (D. Del. 1982)
insurance	Annuity contract proceeds to $350 per month	18-2728
	Fraternal benefit society benefits	18-6218
	Group life insurance policy or proceeds	18-2727
	Health or disability benefits	18-2726
	Life insurance proceeds if clause prohibits proceeds from being used to pay beneficiary's creditors	18-2729
	Life insurance proceeds or avails	18-2725
miscellaneous	Property of business partnership	6-1525
pensions	IRAs	In re Yuhas, 104 F.3d 612 (3rd Cir. 1997)
	Kent County employees	9-4316
	Police officers	11-8803
	State employees	29-5503
	Volunteer firefighters	16-6653
personal property	Bible, books & family pictures	10-4902(a)
	Burial plot	10-4902(a)
	Church pew or any seat in public place of worship	10-4902(a)
	Clothing, includes jewelry	10-4902(a)
	College investment plan account (limit for year before filing is $5,000 or average of past two years' contribution whichever is more)	10-4916
	Pianos and leased organs	10-4902(d)
	Sewing machines	10-4902(c)
public benefits	Aid to blind	31-2309
	Aid to aged, disabled, general assistance	31-513
	Unemployment compensation	19-3374
	Workers' compensation	19-2355
tools of trade	Tools, implements & fixtures to $75 in New Castle & Sussex Counties; to $50 in Kent County	10-4902(b)
wages	85% of earned but unpaid wages	10-4913
wildcard	$500 of any personal property, except tools of trade, if head of family	10-4903

District of Columbia

Federal Bankruptcy Exemptions available. All law references are to District of Columbia Code unless otherwise noted.

ASSET	EXEMPTION	LAW
homestead	Any property used as a residence or coop that debtor or debtor's dependent uses as a residence	15-501(a)(14)
	(Property held as tenancy by the entirety may be exempt against debts owed by only one spouse)	Estate of Wall, 440 F.2d 215 (D.C. Cir. 1971)
insurance	Disability benefits	15-501(a)(7)
	Fraternal benefit society benefits	31-5315
	Group life insurance policy or proceeds	31-4717
	Life insurance payments	15-501(a)(11)
	Life insurance proceeds if clause prohibits proceeds from being used to pay beneficiary's creditors	31-4719
	Life insurance proceeds or avails	31-4716
	Other insurance proceeds to $200 per month, maximum 2 months, for head of family; else $60 per month	15-503
	Unmatured life insurance contract other than credit life insurance	15-501(a)(5)
	alimony or child support	15-501(a)(7)
pensions also see wages	ERISA-qualified benefits, IRAs, Keoghs, etc. to maximum deductible contribution	15-501(b)(9)
	Any stock bonus, annuity, pension or profit sharing plan	15-501(a)(7)
	Judges	11-1570(d)
	Public school teachers	38-2001.17, 38-2021.17
personal property	Appliances, books, clothing, household furnishings and goods, musical instruments, pets to $425 per item or $8,625 total	15-501(a)(2)
	Cooperative association holdings to $50	29-928
	Food for 3 months	15-501(a)(12)
	Health aids	15-501(a)(6)
	Higher education tuition savings account	47-4510
	Residential condominium deposit	42-1904.09
	All family pictures; and all the family library, to $400	15-501(a)(8)
	Motor vehicle to $2,575	15-501(a)(1)
	Payment including pain & suffering for loss of debtor or person depended on	15-501(a)(11)
	Uninsured motorist benefits	31-2408.01(h)
	Wrongful death damages	15-501(a)(11)
public benefits	Aid to blind, aged, disabled, general assistance	4-215.01
	Crime victims' compensation	15-501(a)(11)
	Social Security	15-501(a)(7)
	Unemployment compensation	51-118
	Veterans' benefits	15-501(a)(7)
	Workers' compensation	32-1517
tools of trade	Library, furniture, tools of professional or artist to $300	15-501(a)(13)
	Tools of trade or business to $1,625;	15-501(a)(5),
	mechanic's tools to $200	15-503(b)
	Seal & documents of notary public	1-1206
wages	Minimum 75% of earned but unpaid wages, pension payments; bankruptcy judge may authorize more for low-income debtors	16-572
	Non-wage (including pension & retirement) earnings to $200/mo for head of family; else $60/mo for a maximum of two mos.	15-503
	Payment for loss of future earnings	15-501(e)(11)
wildcard	Up to $850 in any property, plus up to $ 8,075 of unused homestead exemption	15-501(a)(3)

Florida

Federal Bankruptcy Exemptions not available. All law references are to Florida Statutes Annotated unless otherwise noted.

ASSET	EXEMPTION	LAW
homestead	Real or personal property including mobile or modular home to unlimited value; cannot exceed half acre in municipality or 160 acres elsewhere; spouse or child of deceased owner may claim homestead exemption; (husband & wife may double)	222.01, 222.02, 222.03, 222.05;Constitution 10-4 *In re Colwell,* 196 F.3d (11th Cir. 1999)
	May file homestead declaration	222.01
	Property held as tenancy by the entirety may be exempt against debts owed by only one spouse	*Havoco of America, Ltd. v. Hill,* 197 F.3d 1135 (11th Cir Fla.,1999)
insurance	Annuity contract proceeds; does not include lottery winnings	222.14; *In re Pizzi,* 153 B.R. 357 (S.D. Fla. 1993)
	Death benefits payable to a specific beneficiary, not the deceased's estate	222.13
	Disability or illness benefits	222.18
	Fraternal benefit society benefits,	632.619
	Life insurance cash surrender value	222.14
miscellaneous	Alimony, child support needed for support	222.201
	Damages to employees for injuries in hazardous occupations	769.05
pensions *also see wages*	County officers, employees	122.15
	ERISA-qualified benefits	222.21(2)
	Firefighters	175.241
	Police officers	185.25
	State officers, employees	121.131
	Teachers	238.15
personal property	Any personal property to $1,000 (husband & wife may double)	Constitution 10-4 *In re Hawkins,* 51 B.R. 348 (S.D. Fla. 1985)
	Federal income tax refund or credit	222.25
	Health aids	222.25
	Motor vehicle to $1,000	222.25
	Pre-need funeral contract deposits	497.413(8)
	Pre-paid college education trust deposits	222.22(1)
	Pre-paid medical savings account deposits	222.22(2)
public benefits	Crime victims' compensation unless seeking to discharge debt for treatment of injury incurred during the crime	960.14
	Hazardous occupation injury recoveries	769.05
	Public assistance	222.201
	Social Security	222.201
	Unemployment compensation	222.201; 443.051(2),(3)
	Veterans' benefits	222.201; 744.626
	Workers' compensation	440.22
tools of trade	None	
wages	100% of wages for heads of family up to $500 per week either unpaid or paid and deposited into bank account for up to 6 months	222.11
	Federal government employees pension payments needed for support & received 3 months prior	222.21
wildcard	See personal property	

Georgia

Federal Bankruptcy Exemptions not available. All law references are to the Official Code of Georgia Annotated, not to the Georgia Code Annotated.

ASSET	EXEMPTION	LAW
homestead	Real or personal property, including co-op, used as residence to $10,000 (husband & wife may double); up to $5,000 of unused portion of homestead may be applied to any property	44-13-100(a)(1) 44-13-100(a)(6)
insurance	Annuity & endowment contract benefits	33-28-7
	Disability or health benefits to $250 per month	33-29-15
	Fraternal benefit society benefits	33-15-62
	Group insurance	33-30-10
	Proceeds and avails of life insurance	33-26-5; 33-25-11
	Life insurance proceeds if policy owned by someone you depended on, needed for support	44-13-100(a)(11)(C)
	Unmatured life insurance contract	44-13-100(a)(8)
	Unmatured life insurance dividends, interest, loan value or cash value to $2,000 if beneficiary is you or someone you depend on	44-13-100(a)(9)
miscellaneous	Alimony, child support needed for support	44-13-100(a)(2)(D)
pensions	Employees of non-profit corporations	44-13-100(a)(2.1)(B)
	ERISA-qualified benefits	18-4-22
	Public employees	44-13-100(a)(2.1)(A); 47-2-332
	Other pensions needed for support	18-4-22; 44-13-100(a)(2)(E), 44-13-100(a)(2.1)(C)
personal property	Animals, crops, clothing, appliances, books, furnishings, household goods, musical instruments to $300 per item, $5,000 total	44-13-100(a)(4)
	Burial plot, in lieu of homestead	44-13-100(a)(1)
	Health aids	44-13-100(a)(10)
	Jewelry to $500	44-13-100(a)(5)
	Lost future earnings needed for support	44-13-100(a)(11)(E)
	Motor vehicles to $3,500 (husband & wife may double)	44-13-100(a)(3)
	Personal injury recoveries to $10,000	44-13-100(a)(11)(C)
	Wrongful death recoveries needed for support	44-13-100(a)(11)(B)
public benefits	Aid to blind	49-4-58
	Aid to disabled	49-4-84
	Crime victims' compensation	44-13-100(a)(11)(A)
	Local public assistance	44-13-100(a)(2)(A)
	Old age assistance	49-4-35
	Social Security	44-13-100(a)(2)(A)
	Unemployment compensation	44-13-100(a)(2)(A)
	Veterans' benefits	44-13-100(a)(2)(B)
	Workers' compensation	34-9-84
tools of trade	Implements, books & tools of trade to $1,500	44-13-100(a)(7)
wages	Minimum 75% of earned but unpaid weekly disposable earnings, or 40 times the state or federal hourly minimum wage, whichever is greater for private & federal workers; bankruptcy judge may authorize more for low-income debtors	18-4-20, 18-4-21
wildcard	$600 of any property	44-13-100(a)(6)
	Unused portion of homestead exemption to $5,000	44-13-100(a)(6)

Hawaii

Federal Bankruptcy Exemptions available. All law references are to Hawaii Revised Statutes unless otherwise noted.

ASSET	EXEMPTION	LAW
homestead	Head of family or over 65 to $30,000; all others to $20,000; property cannot exceed 1 acre; sale proceeds exempt for 6 months after sale (husband & wife may not double)	651-91, 651-92, 651-96
	Property held as tenancy by the entirety may be exempt against debts owed by only one spouse	*Security Pacific Bank v. Chang,* 818 F.Supp. 1343 (D. Ha. 1993)
insurance	Annuity contract or endowment policy proceeds if beneficiary is insured's spouse, child or parent	431:10-232(b)
	Disability benefits	431:10-231
	Fraternal benefit society benefits	432:2-403
	Group life insurance policy or proceeds	431:10-233
	Life or health insurance policy for spouse or child	431:10-234
	Life insurance proceeds if clause prohibits proceeds from being used to pay beneficiary's creditors	431:10D-112
miscellaneous	Property of business partnership	425-125
pensions	ERISA-qualified benefits deposited over 3 years before filing bankruptcy	651-124
	Firefighters	88-169
	Police officers	88-169
	Public officers & employees	88-91; 653-3
personal property	Appliances & furnishings	651-121(1)
	Books	651-121(1)
	Burial plot to 250 sq. ft. plus tombstones, monuments & fencing	651-121(4)
	Clothing	651-121(1)
	Jewelry, watches & articles of adornment to $1,000	651-121(1)
	Motor vehicle to wholesale value of $2,575	651-121(2)
	Proceeds for sold or damaged exempt property; sale proceeds exempt for 6 months after sale	651-121(5)
public benefits	Public assistance paid by Dept. of Health Services for work done in home or workshop	346-33
	Unemployment compensation	383-163
	Unemployment work relief funds to $60 per month	653-4
	Workers' compensation	386-57
tools of trade	Tools, implements, books, instruments, uniforms, furnishings, fishing boat, nets, motor vehicle & other property needed for livelihood	651-121(3)
wages	Unpaid wages due for services of past 31 days	651-121(6)
	Prisoner's wages held by Dept. of Public Safety	353-22
wildcard	None	

Idaho

Federal Bankruptcy Exemptions not available. All law references are to Idaho Code.

ASSET	EXEMPTION	LAW
homestead	Real property or mobile home to $50,000; sale proceeds exempt for 6 months (husband and wife may not double)	55-1003, 55-1113
	Must record homestead exemption for property that is not yet occupied	55-1004
insurance	Annuity contract proceeds to $350 per month	41-1836
	Death or disability benefits	11-604(1)(a); 41-1834
	Fraternal benefit society benefits	41-3218
	Group life insurance benefits	41-1835
	Homeowners' insurance proceeds to amount of homestead exemption	55-1008
	Life insurance proceeds if clause prohibits proceeds from being used to pay beneficiary's creditors	41-1930
	Life insurance proceeds or avails for beneficiary other than the insured	11-604(d); 41-1833
	Medical, surgical or hospital care benefits	11-603(5)
	Unmatured life insurance contract, other than credit life insurance, owned by debtor	11-605(8)
	Unmatured life insurance contract interest or dividends to $5,000 owned by debtor or person debtor depends on	11-605(9)
miscellaneous	Alimony, child support	11-604(1)(b)
	Liquor licenses	23-514
	Property of business partnership	53-325
Pension *also see wages*	ERISA-qualified benefits	55-1011
	Firefighters	72-1422
	Government & private pensions, retirement plans, IRAs, Keoghs, etc.	11-604A
	Police officers	50-1517
	Public employees	59-1317
personal property	Appliances, furnishings, books, clothing, pets, musical instruments, 1 firearm, family portraits & sentimental heirlooms to $500 per item, $5,000 total	11-605(1)
	Building materials	45-514
	Burial plot	11-603(1)
	College savings program account	11-604A(4)(b)
	Crops cultivated on maximum of 50 acres, to $1,000; water rights to 160 inches	11-605(6)
	Health aids	11-603(2)
	Jewelry to $1,000	11-605(2)
	Motor vehicle to $3,000	11-605(3)
	Personal injury recoveries	11-604(1)(c)
	Proceeds for damaged exempt property for 3 months after proceeds received	11-606
	Wrongful death recoveries	11-604(1)(c)
public benefits	Aid to blind, aged, disabled	56-223
	Federal, state & local public assistance	11-603(4)
	General assistance	56-223
	Social Security	11-603(3)
	Unemployment compensation	11-603(6)
	Veterans' benefits	11-603(3)
	Workers' compensation	72-802
tools of trade	Arms, uniforms & accoutrements that peace officer, national guard or military personnel is required to keep	11-605(5)
	Implements, books & tools of trade to $1,500	11-605(3)
wages	Minimum 75% of earned but unpaid weekly disposable earnings, or 30 times the federal hourly minimum wage, whichever is greater, pension payments; bankruptcy judge may authorize more for low-income debtors	11-207
wildcard	$800 in any tangible personal property	11-605(10)

Illinois

Federal Bankruptcy Exemptions not available. All law references are to Illinois Annotated Statutes.

ASSET	EXEMPTION	LAW
homestead	Real or personal property including a farm, lot & buildings, condo, co-op or mobile home to $7,500 (husband and wife may double); sale proceeds exempt for 1 year	735-5/12-901, 735-5/12-906
	Spouse or child of deceased owner may claim homestead exemption	735-5/12-902
insurance	Fraternal benefit society benefits	215-5/299.1a
	Health or disability benefits	735-5/12-1001(g)(3)
	Homeowners proceeds if home destroyed, to $7,500	735-5/12-907
	Life insurance, annuity proceeds or cash value if beneficiary is insured's child, parent, spouse or other dependent	215-5/238; 735-5/12-1001(f)
	Life insurance proceeds to a spouse or dependent of debtor to extent needed for support	735-5/12-1001(f),(g)(3)
miscellaneous	Alimony, child support	735-5/12-1001(g)(4)
	Property of business partnership	805-205/25
pensions	Civil service employees	40-5/11-223
	County employees	40-5/9-228
	Disabled firefighters; widows & children of firefighters	40-5/22-230
	ERISA-qualified benefits	735-5/12-1006
	Firefighters	40-5/4-135, 40-5/6-213
	General assembly members	40-5/2-154
	House of correction employees	40-5/19-117
	Judges	40-5/18-161
	Municipal employees	40-5/7-217(a), 40-5/8-244
	Park employees	40-5/12-190
	Police officers	40-5/3-144.1, 40-5/5-218
	Public employees	735-5/12-1006
	Public library employees	40-5/19-218
	Sanitation district employees	40-5/13-805
	State employees	40-5/14-147
	State university employees	40-5/15-185
	Teachers	40-5/16-190, 40-5/17-151
personal property	Bible, family pictures, schoolbooks & clothing	735-5/12-1001(a)
	Health aids	735-5/12-1001(e)
	Motor vehicle to $1,200	735-5/12-1001(c)
	Personal injury recoveries to $7,500	735-5/12-1001(h)(4)
	Prepaid tuition trust fund	110-979/45 (g)
	Proceeds of sold exempt property	735-5/12-1001
	Wrongful death recoveries	735-5/12-1001(h)(2)
public benefits	Aid to aged, blind, disabled, public assistance	305-5/11-3
	Crime victims' compensation	735-5/12-1001(h)(1)
	Restitution payments on account of WWII relocation of Aleuts and Japanese Americans	735-5/12-1001(12)(h)(5)
	Social Security	735-5/12-1001(g)(1)
	Unemployment compensation	735-5/12-1001(g) (1),(3)
	Veterans' benefits	735-5/12-1001(g)(2)
	Workers' compensation	820-305/21
	Workers' occupational disease compensation	820-310/21
tools of trade	Implements, books & tools of trade to $750	735-5/12-1001(d)
wages	Minimum 85% of earned but unpaid weekly wages or 45 times the Federal minimum hourly wage; bankruptcy judge may authorize more for low-income debtors	740-170/4
wildcard	$2,000 of any personal property (does not include wages)	735-5/12-1001(b)

Indiana

Federal Bankruptcy Exemptions not available. All law references are to Indiana Statutes Annotated.

ASSET	EXEMPTION	LAW
homestead *also see wildcard*	Real or personal property used as residence to $7,500 (husband and wife may double); homestead plus personal property—except health aids—can't exceed $10,000	34-55-10-2(b)(1); 34-55-10-2(c)
	Property held as tenancy by the entirety may be exempt against debts incurred by only one spouse	34-55-10-2(b)(5)
insurance	Employer's life insurance policy on employee	27-1-12-17.1
	Fraternal benefit society benefits	27-11-6-3
	Group life insurance policy	27-1-12-29
	Life insurance policy, proceeds, cash value or avails if beneficiary is insured's spouse or dependent	27-1-12-14
	Life insurance proceeds if clause prohibits proceeds to be used to pay beneficiary's creditors	27-2-5-1
	Mutual life or accident proceeds	27-8-3-23
miscellaneous	Property of business partnership	23-4-1-25
pensions	Firefighters	36-8-7-22, 36-8-8-17
	Police officers	10-1-2-9; 36-8-8-17
	Public employees	5-10.3-8-9
	Public or private retirement benefits	34-55-10-2(b)(6)
	Sheriffs	36-8-10-19
	State teachers	21-6.1-5-17
personal property *see wild card*	Health aids	34-55-10-2(b)(4)
	Money in medical care savings account	34-55-10-2(b)(7)
	Spendthrift trusts	30-4-3-2
	$100 of any intangible personal property, except money owed to you	34-55-10-2(b)(3)
public benefits	Crime victims' compensation unless seeking to discharge the debts for which the victim was compensated	5-2-6.1-38
	Unemployment compensation	22-4-33-3
	Workers' compensation	22-3-2-17
tools of trade	National guard uniforms, arms & equipment	10-2-6-3
wages	Minimum 75% of earned but unpaid weekly disposable earnings, or 30 times the federal hourly minimum wage; bankruptcy judge may authorize more for low-income debtors	24-4.5-5-105
wildcard	$4,000 of any real estate or tangible personal property, but wildcard plus homestead cannot exceed $10,000	34-55-10-2(b)(2)

Iowa

Federal Bankruptcy Exemptions not available. All law references are to Iowa Code Annotated.

ASSET	EXEMPTION	LAW
homestead	Real property or an apartment to an unlimited value; property cannot exceed 1/2 acre in town or city, 40 acres elsewhere (husband & wife may not double)	499A.18; 561.2, 561.16
	May record homestead declaration	561.4
insurance	Accident, disability, health, illness or life proceeds or avails	627.6(6)
	Disability or illness benefit	627.6(8)(c)
	Employee group insurance policy or proceeds	509.12
	Life insurance proceeds paid to spouse, child or other dependent (limited to $10,000 if acquired within 2 years of filing for bankruptcy)	627.6(6)
	Upon death of insured, up to $15,000 total proceeds from all matured life, accident, health, or disability policies exempt from beneficiary's debts contracted before insured's death.	627.6(6)
	Life insurance proceeds if clause prohibits proceeds from being used to pay beneficiary's creditors	508.32
miscellaneous	Alimony, child support needed for support	627.6(8)(d)
	Liquor licenses	123.38
pensions *also see* wages	Disabled firefighters, police officers (only payments being received)	410.11
	Federal government pension	627.8
	Firefighters	411.13
	Peace officers	97A.12
	Police officers	411.13
	Public employees	97B.39
	Other pensions, annuities and contracts fully exempt; however, contributions made within 1 year prior to filing for bankruptcy not exempt to the extent they exceed normal and customary amounts	627.6(8)(e)
	Retirement plans, Keoghs, IRAs, Roth IRAs, ERISA-qualified benefits	627.6(8)(f)
Personal property	Appliances, furnishings & household goods to $2,000 total	627.6(5)
	Bibles, books, portraits, pictures & paintings to $1,000 total	627.6(3)
	Burial plot to 1 acre	627.6(4)
	Clothing and its storage containers to $1,000	627.6(1)
	Health aids	627.6(7)
	Motor vehicle, musical instruments & tax refund & accrued wages to $5,000 total, no more than $1,000 from tax refunds and accrued wages.	627.6(9)
	Residential security or utility deposit, or advance rent, to $500	627.6(14)
	Rifle or musket; shotgun	627.6(2)
	Wedding or engagement rings	627.6(1)
public benefits	Adopted child assistance	627.19
	Any public assistance benefit	627.6(8)(a)
	Social Security	627.6(8)(a)
	Unemployment compensation	627.6(8)(a)
	Veterans' benefits	627.6(8)(b)
	Workers' compensation	627.13
tools of trade	Farming equipment; includes livestock, feed to $10,000	627.6(11)
	Non-farming equipment to $10,000	627.6(10)
wages	Expected annual earnings — Amount NOT exempt per year	642.21
	$0 to 12,000 — $250	
	$12,000 to 16,000 — $400	
	$16,000 to 24,000 — $800	
	$24,000 to 35,000 — $1,000	
	$35,000 to 50,000 — $2,000	
	More than $50,000 — 10%	
	Not exempt from spousal or child support	
wildcard	$100 of any personal property, including cash	627.6(13)

Kansas

Federal Bankruptcy Exemptions not available. All law references are to Kansas Statutes Annotated unless otherwise noted.

ASSET	EXEMPTION	LAW
homestead	Real property or mobile home you occupy or intend to occupy to unlimited value; property cannot exceed 1 acre in town or city, 160 acres on farm	60-2301; Constitution 15-9
insurance	Disability and illness benefits	60-2313(a)(1)
	Fraternal life insurance benefits	60-2313(a)(8)
	Cash value of life insurance; not exempt if obtained within 1 year prior to bankruptcy with fraudulent intent.	60-2313(a)(7); 40-414(b)
	Life insurance proceeds	40-414(a)
miscellaneous	Alimony, maintenance and support	60-2312(b)
	Liquor licenses	41-326
pensions	Elected & appointed officials in cities with populations between 120,000 & 200,000	13-14a10
	ERISA-qualified benefits	60-2308(b)
	Federal government pension needed for support & paid within 3 months of filing for bankruptcy (only payments being received)	60-2308(a)
	Firefighters	12-5005(e); 14-10a10
	Judges	20-2618
	Police officers	12-5005(e); 13-14a10
	Public employees	74-4923, 74-49,105
	State highway patrol officers	74-4978g
	State school employees	72-5526
	Payment under a stock bonus, pension, profit-sharing, annuity, or similar plan or contract on account of illness, disability, death, age, or length of service, to the extent reasonably necessary for the support	60-2312(b)
personal property	Burial plot or crypt	60-2304(d)
	Clothing to last 1 year	60-2304(a)
	Food & fuel to last 1 year	60-2304(a)
	Funeral plan prepayments	16-310(d)
	Furnishings & household equipment	60-2304(a)
	Jewelry & articles of adornment to $1,000	60-2304(b)
	Motor vehicle to $20,000; if designed or equipped for disabled person, no limit	60-2304(c)
public benefits	Crime victims' compensation	74-7313(d)
	General assistance	39-717(c)
	Social Security	60-2312(b)
	Unemployment compensation	44-718(c)
	Veteran's benefits	60-2312(b)
	Workers' compensation	44-514
tools of trade	Books, documents, furniture, instruments, equipment, breeding stock, seed, grain & stock to $7,500 total	60-2304(e)
	National Guard uniforms, arms & equipment	48-245
wages	Minimum 75% of disposable weekly wages or 30 times the federal minimum hourly wage per week, whichever is greater; bankruptcy judge may authorize more for low-income debtors	60-2310
wildcard	None	

Kentucky

Federal Bankruptcy Exemptions not available. All law references are to Kentucky Revised Statutes.

ASSET	EXEMPTION	LAW
homestead	Real or personal property used as residence to $5,000; sale proceeds exempt	427.060, 427.090
insurance	Annuity contract proceeds to $350 per month	304.14-330
	Cooperative life or casualty insurance benefits	427.110(1)
	Fraternal benefit society benefits	427.110(2)
	Group life insurance proceeds	304.14-320
	Health or disability benefits	304.14-310
	Life insurance policy if beneficiary is a married woman	304.14-340
	Life insurance proceeds if clause prohibits proceeds from being used to pay beneficiary's creditors	304.14-350
	Life insurance proceeds or cash value if beneficiary is someone other than insured	304.14-300
miscellaneous	Alimony, child support needed for support	427.150(1)
	Property of business partnership	362.270
pensions	Firefighters	67A.620; 95.878
	Police officers	427.120, 427.125
	ERISA-qualified benefits, including IRAs, SEPs, and Keoghs deposited more than 120 days before filing	427.150
	State employees	61.690
	Teachers	161.700
	Urban county government employees	67A.350
personal property	Burial plot to $5,000, in lieu of homestead	427.060
	Clothing, jewelry, articles of adornment & furnishings to $3,000 total	427.010(1)
	Health aids	427.010(1)
	Lost earnings payments needed for support	427.150(2)(d)
	Medical expenses paid & reparation benefits received under motor vehicle reparation law	304.39-260
	Motor vehicle to $2,500	427.010(1)
	Personal injury recoveries to $7,500 (not to include pain & suffering or pecuniary loss)	427.150(2)(c)
	Prepaid tuition payment fund account	164A.707(3)
	Wrongful death recoveries for person you depended on, needed for support	427.150(2)(b)
public benefits	Aid to blind, aged, disabled, public assistance	205.220(c)
	Crime victims' compensation	427.150(2)(a)
	Unemployment compensation	341.470(4)
	Workers' compensation	342.180
tools of trade	Library, office equipment, instruments & furnishings of minister, attorney, physician, surgeon, chiropractor, veterinarian or dentist to $1,000	427.040
	Motor vehicle of auto mechanic, mechanical or electrical equipment servicer, minister, attorney, physician, surgeon, chiropractor, veterinarian or dentist to $2,500	427.030
	Tools, equipment, livestock & poultry of farmer to $3,000	427.010(1)
	Tools of non-farmer to $300	427.030
wages	Minimum 75% of disposable weekly earnings or 30 times the federal minimum hourly wage per week, whichever is greater; bankruptcy judge may authorize more for low-income debtors	427.010(2),(3)
wildcard	$1,000 of any property	427.160

Louisiana

Federal Bankruptcy Exemptions not available. All law references are to Louisiana Revised Statutes Annotated unless otherwise noted.

ASSET	EXEMPTION	LAW
homestead	Property you occupy to $25,000 (if debt is result of catastrophic or terminal illness or injury, limit is full value of property as of 1 year before filing); cannot exceed 5 acres in city or town, 200 acres elsewhere (husband & wife may not double)	20:1(A)(1),(2),(3)
	Spouse or child of deceased owner may claim homestead exemption; spouse given home in divorce gets homestead	20:1(B)
insurance	Annuity contract proceeds and avails	22:647
	Fraternal benefit society benefits	22:558
	Group insurance policies or proceeds	22:649
	Health, accident or disability proceeds or avails	22:646
	Life insurance proceeds or avails; if policy issued within 9 months of filing, exempt only to $35,000	22:647
miscellaneous	Property of minor child	13:3881(A)(3); Civil Code Art. 223
pensions	Assessors	11:1403
	Court clerks	11:1526
	District attorneys	11:1583
	ERISA-qualified benefits, including IRAs and Keoghs, if contributions made over 1 year before filing for bankruptcy	13:3881(D)(1); 20:33(1)
	Firefighters	11:2263
	Gift or bonus payments from employer to employee or heirs whenever paid	20:33(2)
	Judges	11:1378
	Louisiana University employees	11:952.3
	Municipal employees	11:1735
	Parochial employees	11:1905
	Police officers	11:3513
	School employees	11:1003
	Sheriffs	11:2182
	State employees	11:405
	Teachers	11:704
	Voting registrars	11:2033
personal property	Arms, military accoutrements; bedding; dishes, glassware, utensils, silverware (non-sterling); clothing, family portraits, musical instruments; bedroom, living room & dining room furniture; poultry, 1 cow, household pets; heating & cooling equipment, refrigerator, freezer, stove, washer & dryer, iron, sewing machine	13:3881(A)(4)
	Cemetery plot, monuments	8:313
	Engagement & wedding rings to $5,000	13:3881(A)(5)
	Spendthrift Trusts	9:2004
public benefits	Aid to blind, aged, disabled, public assistance	46:111
	Crime victims' compensation	46:1811
	Unemployment compensation	23:1693
	Workers' compensation	23:1205
tools of trade	Tools, instruments, books, pickup truck (maximum 3 tons) or non-luxury auto & utility trailer, needed to work	13:3881(A)(2)
wages	Minimum 75% of disposable weekly earnings or 30 times the federal minimum hourly wage per week, whichever is greater; bankruptcy judge may authorize more for low-income debtors	13:3881(A)(1)
wildcard	None	

Maine

Federal Bankruptcy Exemptions not available. All law references are to Maine Revised Statutes Annotated.

ASSET	EXEMPTION	LAW
homestead	Real or personal property (including cooperative) used as residence to $25,000; if debtor has minor dependents in residence, to $50,000; if debtor over age 60 or physically or mentally disabled, $60,000 (joint debtors in this category may double); proceeds of sale exempt for six months	14-4422(1)
insurance	Annuity proceeds to $450 per month	24-A-2431
	Disability or health proceeds, benefits or avails	14-4422(13)(A),(C); 24-A-2429
	Fraternal benefit society benefits	24-A-4118
	Group health or life policy or proceeds	24-A-2430
	Life, endowment, annuity or accident policy, proceeds or avails	14-4422(14)(C); 24-A-2428
	Life insurance policy, interest, loan value or accrued dividends for policy from person you depended on, to $4,000	14-4422(11)
	Unmatured life insurance policy, except credit insurance policy	14-4422(10)
miscellaneous	Alimony & child support needed for support	14-4422(13)(D)
	Property of business partnership	31-305
pensions	ERISA-qualified benefits	14-4422(13)(E)
	Judges	4-1203
	Legislators	3-703
	State employees	5-17054
personal property	Animals, crops, musical instruments, books, clothing, furnishings, household goods, appliances to $200 per item	14-4422(3)
	Balance due on repossessed goods; total amount financed can't exceed $2,000	9-A-5-103
	Burial plot in lieu of homestead exemption	14-4422(1)
	Cooking stove; furnaces & stoves for heat	14-4422(6)(A),(B)
	Food to last 6 months	14-4422(7)(A)
	Fuel not to exceed 10 cords of wood, 5 tons of coal or 1,000 gal. of heating oil	14-4422(6)(C)
	Health aids	14-4422(12)
	Jewelry to $750; no limit for one wedding & one engagement ring	14-4422(4)
	Lost earnings payments needed for support	14-4422(14)(E)
	Military clothes, arms & equipment	37-B-262
	Motor vehicle to $5,000	14-4422(2)
	Personal injury recoveries to $12,500	14-4422(14)(D)
	Seeds, fertilizers & feed to raise & harvest food for 1 season	14-4422(7)(B)
	Tools & equipment to raise & harvest food	14-4422(7)(C)
	Wrongful death recoveries needed for support	14-4422(14)(B)
public benefits	Crime victims' compensation	14-4422(14)(A)
	Public assistance	22-3766
	Social Security	14-4422(13)(A)
	Unemployment compensation	14-4422(13)(A),(C)
	Veterans' benefits	14-4422(13)(B)
	Workers' compensation	39-A-106
tools of trade	Commercial fishing boat, 5 ton limit	14-4422(9)
	Books, materials & stock to $5,000	14-4422(5)
	One of each farm implement (and its maintenance equipment needed to harvest and raise crops)	14-4422(8)
wages	None (use Federal non-bankruptcy wage exemption)	
wildcard	Unused portion of exemption in homestead to $6,000; or unused exemption in animals, crops, musical instruments, books, clothing, furnishings, household goods, appliances, tools of the trade & personal injury recoveries	14-4422(15)
	$400 of any property	14-4422(15)

Maryland

Federal Bankruptcy Exemptions not available. All law references are to Maryland Code of Courts & Judicial Proceedings unless otherwise noted.

ASSET	EXEMPTION	LAW
homestead	None, however, property held as tenancy, by the entirety is exempt against debts owed by only one spouse	*In re Birney,* 200 F.3d 225 (4th Cir. 1999)
insurance	Disability or health benefits, including court awards, arbitrations & settlements	11-504(b)(2)
	Fraternal benefit society benefits	Ins. 8-431; Estates & Trusts 8-115
	Life insurance or annuity contract proceeds or avails if beneficiary is insured's dependent, child or spouse	Ins. 16-111(a); Estates & Trusts 8-115
	Medical insurance benefits deducted from wages plus medical insurance payments to $145 per week or 75% of disposable wages.	Commercial Law 15-601.1(3)
miscellaneous	Property of business partnership	Corps. & Ass'ns. 9-502
pensions	ERISA-qualified benefits, except IRAs	11-504(h)(1)
	State employees	State Pers. & Pen. 21-502
personal property	Appliances, furnishings, household goods, books, pets & clothing to $500 total	11-504(b)(4)
	Burial plot	Code of 1957, 23-164
	Health aids	11-504(b)(3)
	Lost future earnings recoveries	11-504(b)(2)
public benefits	Crime victims' compensation	Crim. Proc. 11-816(b)
	General assistance	Code of 1957 88A-73
	Unemployment compensation	Labor & Employment 8-106
	Workers' compensation	Labor & Employment 9-732
tools of trade	Clothing, books, tools, instruments & appliances to $2,500;	11-504(b)(1)
wages	Earned but unpaid wages, the greater of 75% or $145 per week; in Kent, Caroline, & Queen Anne's of Worcester Counties, the greater of 75% or 30 times Federal minimum hourly wage	Commercial Law 15-601.1
wildcard	$5,500 of any property (may include up to $3,000 in cash); must claim exemption within 30 days of levy or attachment	11-504(b)(5),(f)

Massachusetts

Federal Bankruptcy Exemptions available. All law references are to Massachusetts General Laws Annotated.

ASSET	EXEMPTION	LAW
homestead	Property you occupy or intend to occupy (including mobile home) to $300,000; if over 65 or disabled, $300,000 (joint owners may not double)	188-1, 188-1A
	If statement of homestead is not in title to property, must record homestead declaration before filing bankruptcy	188-2
	Spouse or children of deceased owner may claim homestead exemption	188-4
	Property held as tenancy by the entirety may be exempt against non-necessity owed by only one spouse.	209-1
insurance	Disability benefits to $400 per week	175-110A
	Fraternal benefit society benefits	176-22
	Group annuity policy or proceeds	175-132C
	Group life insurance policy	175-135
	Life or endowment policy, proceeds or cash value	175-125
	Life insurance policy if beneficiary is married woman	175-126
	Life insurance or annuity contract proceeds if clause prohibits proceeds from being used to pay beneficiary's creditors	175-119A
	Medical malpractice self-insurance	175F-15
miscellaneous	Property of business partnership	108A-25
pensions	Credit union employees	171-84
also see wages	ERISA-qualified benefits, including IRAs	235-34A; 246-28
	Private retirement benefits	32-41
	Public employees	32-19
	Savings bank employees	168-41, 168-44
personal property	Bank deposits to $125	235-34
	Beds & bedding; heating unit; clothing	235-34
	Bibles & books to $200 total; sewing machine to $200	235-34
	Burial plots, tombs & church pew	235-34
	Cash for fuel, heat, water or light to $75 per month	235-34
	Cash to $200/month for rent, in lieu of homestead	235-34
	Cooperative association shares to $100	235-34
	2 cows, 12 sheep, 2 swine, 4 tons of hay	235-34
	Food or cash for food to $300	235-34
	Furniture to $3,000; motor vehicle to $700	235-34
	Moving expenses for eminent domain	79-6A
	Trust company, bank or credit union deposits to $500	246-28A
public benefits	Public assistance	235-34
	Aid to families with dependent children	118-10
	Unemployment compensation	151A-36
	Veterans' benefits	115-5
	Workers' compensation	152-47
tools of trade	Arms, accoutrements & uniforms required	235-34
	Fishing boats, tackle & nets to $500	235-34
	Materials you designed & procured to $500	235-34
	Tools, implements & fixtures to $500 total	235-34
wages	Earned but unpaid wages to $125 per week	246-28
wildcard	None	

Michigan

Federal Bankruptcy Exemptions available. All law references are to Michigan Compiled Laws Annotated unless otherwise noted.

ASSET	EXEMPTION	LAW
homestead	Real property including condo to $3,500; property cannot exceed 1 lot in town, village, city, or 40 acres elsewhere; spouse or children of deceased owner may claim homestead exemption	559.214; 600.6023(1)(h),(i) 600.6023(3)
	Property held as tenancy by the entirety may be exempt against debts owed by only one spouse	*In re Smith*, 246 B.R. 540 (Bkrtcy. E.D. Mich., 2000).
insurance	Disability, mutual life or health benefits	600.6023(1)(f)
	Fraternal benefit society benefits	500.8181
	Life, endowment or annuity proceeds if clause prohibits proceeds from being used to pay beneficiary's creditors	500.4054
miscellaneous	Property of business partnership	449.25
pensions	Firefighters, police officers	38.559(6); 38.1683
	ERISA-qualified benefits, except contributions within last 120 days	600.6023(1)(l)
	IRAs, except contributions within last 120 days	600.6023(1)(k)
	Judges	38.2308; 38.1683
	Legislators	38.1057; 38.1683
	Probate judges	38.2308; 38.1683
	Public school employees	38.1346; 38.1683
	State employees	38.40; 38.1683
personal property	Appliances, utensils, books, furniture & household goods to $1,000 total	600.6023(1)(b)
	Building & loan association shares to $1,000 par value, in lieu of homestead	600.6023(1)(g)
	Burial plots, cemeteries; church pew, slip, seat for entire family	600.6023(1)(c)
	Clothing; family pictures	600.6023(1)(a)
	2 cows, 100 hens, 5 roosters, 10 sheep, 5 swine & feed to last 6 months	600.6023(1)(d)
	Food & fuel to last family for 6 months	600.6023(1)(a)
public benefits	Crime victims' compensation	18.362
	Social welfare benefits	400.63
	Unemployment compensation	421.30
	Veterans' benefits for Korean War veterans	35.977
	Veterans' benefits for Vietnam veterans	35.1027
	Veterans' benefits for WWII veterans	35.926
	Workers' compensation	418.821
tools of trade	Arms & accoutrements required	600.6023(1)(a)
	Tools, implements, materials, stock, apparatus, team, motor vehicle, horse & harness to $1,000 total	600.6023(1)(e)
wages	head of household may keep 60% of earned but unpaid wages (no less than $15/week), plus $2/week per non-spouse dependent; if not head of household may keep 40% (no less than $10/week)	600.5311
wildcard	None	

Minnesota

Federal Bankruptcy Exemptions available. All law references are to Minnesota Statutes Annotated.

NOTE: Section 550.37(4)(a) requires certain exemptions to be adjusted for inflation on July 1 of even-numbered years; this table includes all changes made through July 1, 2000. Exemptions are published in the May 1 issue of the Minnesota State Register, www.comm.media.state.mn.us/bookstore/stateregister.asp, or Minnesota Dept. of Commerce at (651) 296-7977.

ASSET	EXEMPTION	LAW
homestead	Home and land on which it is situated to $200,000; if homestead is used for agricultural purposes, $500,000; cannot exceed 1/2 acre in city, 160 acres elsewhere (husband & wife may not double);	510.01, 510.02
	Manufactured home to an unlimited value	550.37 subd. 12
insurance	Accident or disability proceeds	550.39
	Fraternal benefit society benefits	64B.18
	Life insurance proceeds to $36,000, if beneficiary is spouse or child of insured, plus $9,000 per dependent	550.37 subd. 10
	Police, fire or beneficiary association benefits	550.37 subd. 11
	Unmatured life insurance contract dividends, interest or loan value to $7,200 if insured is debtor or person debtor depends on	550.37 subd. 23
miscellaneous	Earnings of minor child	550.37 subd. 15
	Property of business partnership	323.24
pensions	ERISA-qualified benefits or needed for support, up to $54,000 in present value	550.37 subd. 24
	IRAs needed for support, up to $54,000 in present value	550.37 subd. 24
	Public employees	353.15
	State employees	352.96 subd. 6
	State troopers	352B.071
personal property	Appliances, furniture, jewelry, radio, phonographs & TV to $8,100 total	550.37 subd. 4(b)
	Bible and books	550.37 subd. 2
	Burial plot; church pew or seat	550.37 subd. 3
	Clothing, one watch, food & utensils for family	550.37 subd. 4(a)
	Motor vehicle to $3,600 (up to $36,000 if vehicle has been modified for disability)	550.37 subd. 12(a)
	Personal injury recoveries	550.37 subd. 22
	Proceeds for damaged exempt property	550.37 subds. 9, 16
	Wrongful death recoveries	550.37 subd. 22
public benefits	Crime victims' compensation	611A.60
	Public benefits	550.37 subd. 14
	Unemployment compensation	268.192 subd. 2
	Veterans' benefits	550.38
	Workers' compensation	176.175
tools of trade *total (except teaching materials) can't exceed $13,000*	Farm machines, implements, livestock, produce & crops	550.37 subd. 5
	Teaching materials of college, university, public school or public institution teacher	550.37 subd. 8
	Tools, machines, instruments, stock in trade, furniture & library to $9,000 total	550.37 subd. 6
wages	Wages, paid within 6 mos. of returning to work, after receiving welfare or after incarceration; includes earnings deposited in a financial institution in the last 60 days	550.37 subd. 14
	Minimum 75% of weekly disposable earnings or 40 times federal minimum hourly wage, whichever is greater	571.922
	Wages deposited into bank accounts for 20 days after depositing	550.37 subd. 13
wildcard	None	

NOTE: Some courts have held "unlimited" exemptions unconstitutional under the Minnesota Constitution, which allows debtors to exempt only a "reasonable amount" of property. See *In re Tveten*, 402 N.W. 2d 551 (Minn. 1987) and *In re Medill*, 119 B.R. 685, (D. Minn. 1990).

Mississippi

Federal Bankruptcy Exemptions not available. All law references are to Mississippi Code.

ASSET	EXEMPTION	LAW
homestead	Property you own & occupy to $75,000; if over 60 and married or widowed may claim a former residence; property cannot exceed 160 acres; sale proceeds exempt.	85-3-1(b)(i), 85-3-21, 85-3-23
	Mobile home does not qualify as homestead unless you own land on which it is located.	*In re Cobbins*, 234 B.R. 882 (S.D. Miss. 1999)
	May file homestead declaration	85-3-27, 85-3-31
insurance	Disability benefits	85-3-1(b)(ii)
	Fraternal benefit society benefits	83-29-39
	Homeowners' insurance proceeds to $75,000	85-3-23
	Life insurance proceeds if clause prohibits proceeds from being used to pay beneficiary's creditors	83-7-5
miscellaneous	Property of business partnership	79-12-49
pensions	ERISA-qualified benefits, IRAs, Keoghs deposited over 1 yr. before filing bankruptcy	85-3-1(b)(iii), (f)
	Firefighters (includes death benefits)	21-29-257, 45-2-1
	Highway patrol officers	25-13-31
	Law enforcement officers' death benefits	45-2-1
	Private retirement benefits to extent tax-deferred	71-1-43
	Police officers (includes death benefits)	21-29-257, 45-2-1
	Public employees retirement & disability benefits	25-11-129
	State employees	25-14-5
	Teachers	25-11-201(1)(d)
	Volunteer firefighters death benefits	45-2-1
personal property	Tangible personal property to $10,000: any item worth less than $200, furniture, dishes, kitchenware, household goods, appliances, 1 radio & 1 TV, 1 gun, 1 lawnmover, clothing, wedding rings, motor vehicles, tools of the trade, books, crops, health aids, domestic animals (does not include works of art, antiques, jewelry or electronic entertainment equipment)	85-3-1(a)
	Personal injury judgments to $10,000	85-3-17
	Sale or insurance proceeds for exempt property	85-3-1(b)(i)
public benefits	Assistance to aged	43-9-19
	Assistance to blind	43-3-71
	Assistance to disabled	43-29-15
	Crime victims' compensation	99-41-23
	Social Security	25-11-129
	Unemployment compensation	71-5-539
	Workers' compensation	71-3-43
tools of trade	See personal property	
wages	Earned but unpaid wages owed for 30 days; after 30 days, minimum 75% of earned but unpaid weekly disposable earnings, or 30 times the federal hourly minimum wage, whichever is greater (bankruptcy judge may authorize more for low-income debtors)	85-3-4
wildcard	See personal property	

Missouri

Federal Bankruptcy Exemptions not available. All law references are to Annotated Missouri Statutes unless otherwise noted.

ASSET	EXEMPTION	LAW
homestead	Real property to $8,000 or mobile home to $1,000 (joint owners may not double)	513.430(6), 513.475 *In re Smith*, 254 B.R. 751 (W.D. Mo. 2000)
	Property held as tenancy by the entirety may be exempt against debts owed by only one spouse	*In re Eads*, 271 B.R. 371 (Bkrtcy.W.D.Mo. 2002).
insurance	Assessment or insurance premium proceeds	377.090
	Disability or illness benefits	513.430(10)(c)
	Fraternal benefit society benefits to $5,000, bought over 6 months before filing	513.430(8)
	Life insurance dividends, loan value or interest to $5,000, bought over 6 months before filing	513.430(8)
	Life insurance proceeds if policy owned by a woman & insures her husband	376.530
	Life insurance proceeds if policy owned by unmarried woman & insures her father or brother	376.550
	Stipulated insurance premiums	377.330
	Unmatured life insurance policy	513.430(7)
miscellaneous	Alimony, child support to $500 per month	513.430(10)(d)
	Property of business partnership	358.250
pensions	Employees of cities with 100,000 or more people	71.207
	ERISA-qualified benefits needed for support (only payments being received)	513.430(10)(e)
	Firefighters	87.090, 87.365, 87.485
	Highway & transportation employees	104.250
	Police department employees	86.190, 86.353, 86.493, 86.780
	Public officers & employees	70.695, 70.755
	State employees	104.540
	Teachers	169.090
personal property	Appliances, household goods, furnishings, clothing, books, crops, animals & musical instruments to $1,000 total	513.430(1)
	Burial grounds to 1 acre or $100	214.190
	Health aids	513.430(9)
	Jewelry to $500	513.430(2)
	Motor vehicle to $1,000	513.430(5)
	Personal injury causes of action	*In re Mitchell*, 73 B.R. 93 (E.D. Mo. 1987)
	Wrongful death recoveries for person you depended on	513.430(11)
public benefits	Public assistance	513.430(10)(a)
	Social Security	513.430(10)(a)
	Unemployment compensation	288.380(10)(l); 513.430(10)(c)
	Veterans' benefits	513.430(10)b)
	Workers' compensation	287.260
tools of trade	Implements, books & tools of trade to $2,000	513.430(4)
wages	Minimum 75% of weekly earnings (90% of weekly earnings for head of family) , or 30 times the federal minimum hourly wage, whichever is more; bankruptcy judge may authorize more for low-income debtors	525.030
	Wages of servant or common laborer to $90	513.470
wildcard	$1,250 of any property if head of family, else $400; head of family may claim additional $250 per child.	513.430(3), 513.440

Montana

Federal Bankruptcy Exemptions not available. All law references are to Montana Code Annotated.

ASSET	EXEMPTION	LAW
homestead	Real property or mobile home you occupy to $60,000; sale, condemnation or insurance proceeds exempt 18 months	70-32-104, 70-32-201, 70-32-213
	Must record homestead declaration before filing for bankruptcy	70-32-105
insurance	Annuity contract proceeds to $350 per month	33-15-514
	Disability or illness proceeds, avails or benefits	25-13-608(1)(d); 33-15-513
	Fraternal benefit society benefits	33-7-522
	Group life insurance policy or proceeds	33-15-512
	Hail insurance benefits	80-2-245
	Life insurance proceeds if clause prohibits proceeds from being used to pay beneficiary's creditors	33-20-120
	Medical, surgical or hospital care benefits	25-13-608(1)(f)
	Unmatured life insurance contracts to $4,000	25-13-609(4)
miscellaneous	Alimony, child support	25-13-608(1)(g)
pensions	ERISA-qualified benefits deposited over 1 year before filing bankruptcy in excess of 15% of debtor's yearly income	31-2-106
	Firefighters	19-18-612(1)
	IRA contributions & earnings made before judgment filed	25-13-608(1)(e)
	Police officers	19-19-504(1)
	Public employees	19-2-1004
	Teachers	19-20-706(2)
	University system employees	19-21-212
personal property	Appliances, household furnishings, goods, animals with feed, crops, musical instruments, books, firearms, sporting goods, clothing & jewelry to $600 per item, $4,500 total	25-13-609(1)
	Burial plot	25-13-608(1)(h)
	Cooperative association shares to $500 value	35-15-404
	Health aids	25-13-608(1)(a)
	Motor vehicle to $2,500	25-13-609(2)
	Proceeds from sale or for damage or loss of exempt property for 6 mos. after received	25-13-610
public benefits	Aid to aged, disabled	53-2-607
	Crime victims' compensation	53-9-129
	Local public assistance	25-13-608(1)(b)
	Silicosis benefits	39-73-110
	Social Security	25-13-608(1)(b)
	Subsidized adoption payments	53-2-607
	Unemployment compensation	31-2-106(2); 39-51-3105
	Veterans' benefits	25-13-608(1)(c)
	Vocational rehabilitation to the blind	53-2-607
	Workers' compensation	39-71-743
tools of trade	Implements, books & tools of trade to $3,000	25-13-609(3)
	Uniforms, arms, accoutrements needed to carry out government functions	25-13-613(b)
wages	Minimum 75% of earned but unpaid weekly disposable earnings, or 30 times the federal hourly minimum wage, whichever is greater; bankruptcy judge may authorize more for low-income debtors	25-13-614
wildcard	None	

Nebraska

Federal Bankruptcy Exemptions not available. All law references are to Revised Statutes of Nebraska.

ASSET	EXEMPTION	LAW
homestead	$12,500 for married debtor or head of household; cannot exceed 2 lots in city or village, 160 acres elsewhere; sale proceeds exempt 6 months after sale (husband & wife may not double)	40-101, 40-111, 40-113
	May record homestead declaration	40-105
insurance	Fraternal benefit society benefits to $10,000 loan value unless beneficiary convicted of a crime related to benefits	44-1089
	Life insurance or annuity contract proceeds to $10,000 loan value	44-371
miscellaneous	Property of business partnership	67-325
pensions *also see* *wages*	County employees	23-2322
	ERISA-qualified benefits needed for support	25-1563.01
	Military disability benefits	25-1559
	School employees	79-948
	State employees	84-1324
personal property	Burial plot	12-517
	Clothing	25-1556(2)
	Crypts, lots, tombs, niches, vaults	12-605
	Furniture, household goods & appliances, household electronics, personal computers, books & musical instruments to $1,500	25-1556(3)
	Health aids	25-1556(5)
	Perpetual care funds	12-511
	Personal injury recoveries	25-1563.02
	Personal possessions	25-1556
public benefits	Aid to disabled, blind, aged, public assistance	68-1013
	Unemployment compensation	48-647
	Workers' compensation	48-149
tools of trade	Equipment or tools including a vehicle used in/or for commuting to principal place of business to $2,400 (husband & wife may double)	25-1556(4); *In re Keller,* 50 B.R. 23 (D. Neb. 1985)
wages	Minimum 85% of earned but unpaid weekly disposable earnings or pension payments for head of family; minimum 75% of earned but unpaid weekly disposable earnings, or 30 times the federal hourly minimum wage, whichever is greater for all others; bankruptcy judge may authorize more for low-income debtors	25-1558
wildcard	$2,500 of any personal property, except wages, in lieu of homestead	25-1552

Nevada

Federal Bankruptcy Exemptions not available. All law references are to Nevada Revised Statutes Annotated.

ASSET	EXEMPTION	LAW
homestead	Real property or mobile home to $125,000 (husband & wife may not double)	115.010, 21.090(1)(m)
	Must record homestead declaration before filing for bankruptcy	115.020
insurance	Annuity contract proceeds to $350 per month	687B.290
	Fraternal benefit society benefits	695A.220
	Group life or health policy or proceeds	687B.280
	Health proceeds or avails	687B.270
	Life insurance policy or proceeds if annual premiums not over $1,000 (husband & wife may double)	21.090(1)(k) *In re Bower,* 234 B.R. 109 (Nev. 1999)
	Life insurance proceeds if you're not the insured	687B.260
miscellaneous	Alimony and child support	21.090(1)(r)
	Property of business partnership	87.250
pensions	ERISA-qualified benefits or IRAs to $500,000	21.090(1)(q)
	Public employees	286.670
personal property	Appliances, household goods, furniture, home & yard equipment to $3,000 total	21.090(1)(b)
	Books to $1,500	21.090(1)(a)
	Burial plot purchase money held in trust	689.700
	Funeral service contract money held in trust	689.700
	Health aids	21.090(1)(p)
	Keepsakes & pictures	21.090(1)(a)
	Metal-bearing ores, geological specimens, art curiosities or paleontological remains; must be arranged, classified, catalogued & numbered in reference books	21.100
	Mortgage impound accounts	645B.180
	Motor vehicle to $4,500; no limit on vehicle equipped for disabled person	21.090(1)(f),(o)
	One gun	21.090(1)(i)
public benefits	Aid to blind, aged, disabled, public assistance	422.291
	Industrial insurance (workers' compensation)	616C.205
	Unemployment compensation	612.710
	Vocational rehabilitation benefits	615.270
tools of trade	Arms, uniforms & accoutrements you're required to keep	21.090(1)(j)
	Cabin or dwelling of miner or prospector; mining claim, cars, implements & appliances to $4,500 total (for working claim only)	21.090(1)(e)
	Farm trucks, stock, tools, equipment & seed to $4,500	21.090(1)(c)
	Library, equipment, supplies, tools & materials to $4,500	21.090(1)(d)
wages	Minimum 75% of disposable weekly earnings or 30 times the federal minimum hourly wage per week, whichever is more; bankruptcy judge may authorize more for low-income debtors	21.090(1)(g)
wildcard	None	

New Hampshire

Federal Bankruptcy Exemptions available. All law references are to New Hampshire Revised Statutes Annotated.

ASSET	EXEMPTION	LAW
homestead	Real property or manufactured housing (and the land it's on if you own it) to $30,000	480:1
insurance	Firefighters' aid insurance	402:69
	Fraternal benefit society benefits	418:24
	Homeowners' insurance proceeds to $5,000	512:21(VIII)
miscellaneous	Child support	161-C-11
	Jury, witness fees	512:21(VI)
	Property of business partnership	304-A:25
	Wages of minor child	512:21(III)
pensions	Federally created pension (only benefits building up)	512:21(IV)
	Firefighters	102:23
	Police officers	103:18
	Public employees	100-A:26
personal property	Beds, bedding & cooking utensils	511:2(II)
	Bibles & books to $800	511:2(VIII)
	Burial plot, lot	511:2(XIV)
	Church pew	511:2(XV)
	Clothing	511:2(I)
	Cooking & heating stoves, refrigerator	511:2(IV)
	1 cow, 6 sheep & their fleece, 4 tons of hay	511:2(XI), (XII)
	Domestic fowl to $300	511:2(XIII)
	Food & fuel to $400	511:2(VI)
	Furniture to $3,500	511:2(III)
	1 hog or pig or its meat (if slaughtered)	511:2(X)
	Jewelry to $500	511:2(XVII)
	Motor vehicle to $4,000	511:2(XVI)
	Proceeds for lost or destroyed exempt property	512:21(VIII)
	Sewing machine	511:2(V)
public benefits	Aid to blind, aged, disabled, public assistance	167:25
	Unemployment compensation	282-A:159
	Workers' compensation	281-A:52
tools of trade	Tools of your occupation to $5,000	511:2(IX)
	Uniforms, arms & equipment of military member	511:2(VII)
	Yoke of oxen or horse needed for farming or teaming	511:2(XII)
wages	50 times the federal minimum hourly wage per week	512:21(II)
	Earned but unpaid wages of spouse	512:21(III)
wildcard	$1,000 of any property	511:2(XVIII)
	Unused portion of bibles & books, food & fuel, furniture, jewelry, motor vehicle and tools of trade exemptions to $7,000	511:2(XVIII)

New Jersey

Federal Bankruptcy Exemptions available. All law references are to New Jersey Statutes Annotated.

ASSET	EXEMPTION	LAW
homestead	None, but survivorship interest of a spouse in property held as tenancy by the entirety is exempt from creditors of a single spouse.	*Freda v. Commercial Trust Co. of New Jersey*, 570 A.2d 409 (N.J.,1990).
insurance	Annuity contract proceeds to $500 per month	17B:24-7
	Disability or death benefits for military member	38A:4-8
	Disability, death, medical or hospital benefits for civil defense workers	App. A:9-57.6
	Group life or health policy or proceeds	17B:24-9
	Health or disability benefits	17:18-12, 17B:24-8
	Life insurance proceeds if clause prohibits proceeds from being used to pay beneficiary's creditors	17B:24-10
	Life insurance proceeds or avails if you're not the insured	17B:24-6b
pensions	Alcohol beverage control officers	43:8A-20
	City boards of health employees	43:18-12
	Civil defense workers	App. A:9-57.6
	County employees	43:10-57, 43:10-105
	ERISA-qualified benefits for city employees	43:13-9
	Firefighters, police officers, traffic officers	43:16-7, 43:16A-17
	IRAs	*In re Yuhas*, 104 F.3d 612 (3rd Cir. 1997)
	Judges	43:6A-41
	Municipal employees	43:13-44
	Prison employees	43:7-13
	Public employees	43:15A-53
	School district employees	18A:66-116
	State police	53:5A-45
	Street & water department employees	43:19-17
	Teachers	18A:66-51
	Trust containing personal property created pursuant to federal tax law, including 401(k) plans and higher education (529) savings plans.	25:2-1
personal property	Personal property & possessions of any kind, stock or interest in corporations to $1,000 total	2A:17-19
	Burial plots	8A:5-10
	Clothing	2A:17-19
	Furniture & household goods to $1,000	2A:26-4
public benefits	Crime victims' compensation	52:4B-30
	Old age, permanent disability assistance	44:7-35
	Unemployment compensation	43:21-53
	Workers' compensation	34:15-29
tools of trade	None	
wages	90% of earned but unpaid wages if annual income under $7,500; if annual income over $7,500, judge decides amount that is exempt	2A:17-56
	Wages or allowances received by military personnel	38A:4-8
wildcard	None	

New Mexico

Federal Bankruptcy Exemptions available. All law references are to New Mexico Statutes Annotated.

ASSET	EXEMPTION	LAW
homestead	$30,000 (joint owners may double)	42-10-9
insurance	Benevolent association benefits to $5,000	42-10-4
	Fraternal benefit society benefits	59A-44-18
	Life, accident, health or annuity benefits, withdrawal or cash value, if beneficiary is a New Mexico resident	42-10-3
	Life insurance proceeds	42-10-5
miscellaneous	Ownership interest in unincorporated association	53-10-2
	Property of business partnership	54-1A-501
pensions	Pension or retirement benefits	42-10-1, 42-10-2
	Public school employees	22-11-42A
personal property	Books & furniture	42-10-1, 42-10-2
	Building materials	48-2-15
	Clothing	42-10-1, 42-10-2
	Cooperative association shares, minimum amount needed to be member	53-4-28
	Health aids	42-10-1, 42-10-2
	Jewelry to $2,500	42-10-1, 42-10-2
	Materials, tools & machinery to dig, drill, complete, operate or repair oil line, gas well or pipeline	70-4-12
	Motor vehicle to $4,000	42-10-1, 42-10-2
public benefits	Crime victims' compensation (will be repealed in 2006)	31-22-15
	General assistance	27-2-21
	Occupational disease disablement benefits	52-3-37
	Unemployment compensation	51-1-37
	Workers' compensation	52-1-52
tools of trade	$1,500	42-10-1, 42-10-2
wages	Minimum 75% of disposable earnings or 40 times the federal hourly minimum wage, whichever is more; bankruptcy judge may authorize more for low-income debtors	35-12-7
wildcard	$500 of any personal property	42-10-1
	$2,000 of any real or personal property, in lieu of homestead	42-10-10

New York

Federal Bankruptcy Exemptions not available. Law references to Consolidated Laws of New York, Civil Practice Law & Rules, are abbreviated C.P.L.R.

ASSET	EXEMPTION	LAW
homestead	Real property including co-op, condo or mobile home, to $10,000 (husband & wife may double)	C.P.L.R. 5206(a); In re Pearl, 723 F.2d 193 (2nd Cir. 1983)
insurance	Annuity contract benefits due the debtor, if debtor paid for the contract; $5,000 limit if purchased within 6 mos. prior to filing & not tax-deferred	Ins. 3212(d); Debt. & Cred. 283(1)
	Disability or illness benefits to $400/month	Ins. 3212(c)
	Life insurance proceeds left at death with the insurance company, if clause prohibits proceeds from being used to pay beneficiary's creditors	Est. Powers & Trusts 7-1.5(a)(2)
	Life insurance proceeds and avails if the beneficiary is not the debtor, or if debtor's spouse has taken out policy	Ins. 3212(b)
miscellaneous	Alimony, child support	C.P.L.R. 5205 (d)(3); Debt. & Cred. 282(2)(d)
	Property of business partnership	Partnership 51
pensions	ERISA-qualified benefits, IRAs, & Keoghs & income needed for support	C.P.L.R. 5205(c); Debt. & Cred. 282(2)(e)
	Public retirement benefits	Ins. 4607
	State employees	Ret. & Soc. Sec. 10
	Teachers	Educ. 524
	Village police officers	Unconsolidated 5711-o
	Volunteer ambulance workers' benefits	Vol. Amb. Wkr. Ben. 23
	Volunteer firefighters' benefits	Vol. Firefighter Ben. 23
personal property	Bible, schoolbooks, other books to $50; pictures; clothing; church pew or seat; sewing machine, refrigerator, TV, radio; furniture, cooking utensils & tableware, dishes; food to last 60 days; stoves with fuel to last 60 days; domestic animal with food to last 60 days, to $450; wedding ring; watch to $35; exemptions may not exceed $5,000 total (including tools of trade & limited annuity)	C.P.L.R. 5205(a)(1)-(6); Debt. & Cred. 283(1)
	Burial plot, without structure to 1/4 acre	C.P.L.R. 5206(f)
	Cash (including savings bonds, tax refunds, bank & credit union deposits) to $2,500, or to $5,000 after exemptions for personal property taken, whichever amount is less (for debtors who do not claim homestead)	Debt. & Cred. 283(2)
	College tuition savings program trust fund	C.P.L.R. 5205(j)
	Health aids, including service animals with food	C.P.L.R. 5205(h)
	Lost future earnings recoveries needed for support	Debt. & Cred. 282(3)(iv)
	Motor vehicle to $2,400 (husband & wife may double)	Debt. & Cred. 282(1) In re Miller, 167 B.R. 782 (S.D. N.Y. 1994)
	Personal injury recoveries up to 1 year after receiving	Debt. & Cred. 282(3)(iii)
	Recovery for injury to exempt property up to 1 year after receiving	C.P.L.R. 5205(b)
	Savings & Loan Savings to $600	Banking 407
	Security deposit to landlord, utility company	C.P.L.R. 5205(g)
	Spendthrift trust fund principal, 90% of income if not created by debtor	C.P.L.R. 5205(c), (d)
	Wrongful death recoveries for person you depended on	Debt. & Cred. 282(3)(ii)
public benefits	Aid to blind, aged, disabled	Debt. & Cred. 282(2)(c)
	Crime victims' compensation	Debt. & Cred. 282(3)(i)
	Home relief, local public assistance	Debt. & Cred. 282(2)(a)
	Public assistance	Soc. Serv. 137
	Social Security	Debt. & Cred. 282(2)(a)
	Unemployment compensation	Debt. & Cred. 282(2)(a)
	Veterans' benefits	Debt. & Cred. 282(2)(b)
	Workers' compensation	Debt. & Cred. 282(2)(c); Work. Comp. 33, 218
tools of trade	Farm machinery, team & food for 60 days; professional furniture, books & instruments to $600 total	C.P.L.R. 5205(a), (b)
	Uniforms, medal, emblem, equipment, horse, arms & sword of member of military	C.P.L.R. 5205(e)
wages	90% of earned but unpaid wages received within 60 days before & anytime after filing	C.P.L.R. 5205(d)
	90% of earnings from dairy farmer's sales to milk dealers	C.P.L.R. 5205(f)
	100% of pay of non-commissioned officer, private or musician in U.S. or N.Y. state armed forces	C.P.L.R. 5205(e)
wildcard	None	

North Carolina

Federal Bankruptcy Exemptions not available. All law references are to General Statutes of North Carolina unless otherwise noted.

ASSET	EXEMPTION	LAW
homestead	Real or personal property, including co-op, used as residence to $10,000; up to $3,500 of unused portion of homestead may be applied to any property (husband and wife may double)	1C-1601(a)(1),(2)
	Property held as tenancy by the entirety may be exempt against debts owed by only one spouse	In re Chandler, 148 B.R. 13 (E.D. N.C., 1992)
insurance	Employee group life policy or proceeds	58-58-165
	Life insurance on spouse or children	1C-1601(a)(6); Const. Art. X § 5
	Fraternal benefit society benefits	58-24-85
miscellaneous	Property of business partnership	59-55
	Support received by a surviving spouse for 1 year, up to $10,000	30-15
pensions	Firefighters & rescue squad workers	58-86-90
	IRAs	1C-1601(a)(9)
	Law enforcement officers	143-166.30(g)
	Legislators	120-4.29
	Municipal, city & county employees	128-31
	Teachers & state employees	135-9, 135-95
personal property	Animals, crops, musical instruments, books, clothing, appliances, household goods & furnishings to $3,500 total; may add $750 per dependent, up to $3,000 total additional (all property must have been purchased at least 90 days before filing)	1C-1601(a)(4),(d)
	Burial plot to $10,000, in lieu of homestead	1C-1601(a)(1)
	Health aids	1C-1601(a)(7)
	Motor vehicle to $1,500	1C-1601(a)(3)
	Personal injury and wrongful death recoveries for person you depended on	1C-1601(a)(8)
public benefits	Aid to blind	111-18
	Crime victims' compensation	15B-17
	Special adult assistance	108A-36
	Unemployment compensation	96-17
	Workers' compensation	97-21
tools of trade	Implements, books & tools of trade to $750	1C-1601(a)(5)
wages	Earned but unpaid wages received 60 days before filing for bankruptcy, needed for support	1-362
wildcard	$3,500 less any amount claimed for homestead or burial exemption, of any property	1C-1601(a)(2)
	$500 of any personal property	Constitution Art. X §1

North Dakota

Federal Bankruptcy Exemptions not available. All law references are to North Dakota Century Code.

ASSET	EXEMPTION	LAW
homestead	Real property, house trailer or mobile home to $80,000 (husband & wife may not double)	28-22-02(10); 47-18-01
insurance	Fraternal benefit society benefits	26.1-15.1-18, 26.1-33-40
	Life insurance proceeds payable to deceased's estate, not to a specific beneficiary	26.1-33-40
	Life insurance surrender value to $100,000 per policy, if beneficiary is insured's dependent & policy was owned over 1 year before filing for bankruptcy; limit does not apply if more needed for support	28-22-03.1(3)
miscellaneous	Child support payments	14-09-09.31
pensions	Disabled veterans' benefits, except military retirement pay	28-22-03.1(4)(d)
	ERISA-qualified benefits, IRAs & Keoghs to $100,000 per plan; limit does not apply if more needed for support; total (with life insurance surrender value exemption cannot exceed $200,000)	28-22-03.1(3)
	Public employees	28-22-19(1)
personal property	1. All debtors may exempt:	
	Bible, schoolbooks; other books to $100	28-22-02(4)
	Burial plots, church pew	28-22-02(2),(3)
	Cash to $7,500, in lieu of homestead	28-22-03.1(1)
	Clothing & family pictures	28-22-02(1),(5)
	Crops or grain raised by debtor on 1 tract 160 acres	28-22-02(8)
	Food & fuel to last 1 year	28-22-02(6)
	Insurance proceeds for exempt property	28-22-02(9)
	Motor vehicle to $1,200	28-22-03.1(2)
	Personal injury recoveries to $7,500	28-22-03.1(4)(b)
	Wrongful death recoveries to $7,500	28-22-03.1(4)(a)
	2. Head of household not claiming crops or grain may claim $5,000 of any personal property or:	28-22-03
	Books & musical instruments to $1,500	28-22-04(1)
	Household & kitchen furniture, beds & bedding, to $1,000	28-22-04(2)
	Library & tools of professional, tools of mechanic & stock in trade, to $1,000	28-22-04(4)
	Livestock & farm implements to $4,500	28-22-04(3)
	3. Non-head of household not claiming crops or grain, may claim $2,500 of any personal property	28-22-05
public benefits	Crime victims' compensation	28-22-19(2)
	Public assistance	28-22-19(3)
	Social Security	28-22-03.1(4)(c)
	Unemployment compensation	52-06-30
	Workers' compensation	65-05-29
tools of trade	See personal property, option 2	
wages	Minimum 75% of disposable weekly earnings or 40 times the federal minimum wage, whichever is more; bankruptcy judge may authorize more for low-income debtors	32-09.1-03
wildcard	See personal property, options 2 or 3	

Ohio

Federal Bankruptcy Exemptions not available. All law references are to Ohio Revised Code unless otherwise noted.

ASSET	EXEMPTION	LAW
homestead	Real or personal property used as residence to $5,000	2329.66(A)(1)(b)
	Property held as tenancy by the entirety may be exempt against debts owed by only one spouse	In re Pernus, 143 B.R. 856 (N.D. Ohio, 1992)
insurance	Benevolent society benefits to $5,000	2329.63, 2329.66(A)(6)(a)
	Disability benefits to $600 per month	2329.66(A)(6)(e); 3923.19
	Fraternal benefit society benefits	2329.66(A)(6)(d); 3921.18
	Group life insurance policy or proceeds	2329.66(A)(6)(c); 3917.05
	Life, endowment or annuity contract avails for your spouse, child or dependent	2329.66(A)(6)(b); 3911.10
	Life insurance proceeds for a spouse	3911.12
	Life insurance proceeds if clause prohibits proceeds from being used to pay beneficiary's creditors	3911.14
miscellaneous	Alimony, child support needed for support	2329.66(A)(11)
	Property of business partnership	1775.24; 2329.66(A)(14)
Pensions	ERISA-qualified benefits needed for support	2329.66(A)(10)(b)
	Firefighters, police officers	742.47
	Public safety officers death benefit	2329.66(A)(10)(a)
	IRAs & Keoghs needed for support	2329.66(A)(10)(c)
	Public employees	145.56
	Public school employees	3309.66
	State highway patrol employees	5505.22
	Volunteer firefighters' dependents	146.13
Personal property	Animals, crops, books, musical instruments, appliances, household goods, furnishings, firearms, hunting & fishing equipment to $200 per item; jewelry to $400 for 1 item, $200 for all others; $1,500 total ($2,000 if no homestead exemption claimed) (husband & wife may double)	2329.66(A)(4)(b),(c),(d) In re Szydlowski, 186 B.R. 907 (N.D. Ohio 1995)
	Beds, bedding, clothing to $200 per item	2329.66(A)(3)
	Burial plot	517.09, 2329.66(A)(8)
	Cash, money due within 90 days, tax refund, bank, security & utility deposits to $400 total (husband & wife may double)	2329.66(A)(4)(a) In re Szydlowski, 186 B.R. 907 (N.D. Ohio 1995)
	Cooking unit & refrigerator to $300 each	2329.66(A)(3)
	Health aids	2329.66(A)(7)
	Lost future earnings needed for support, received during 12 months before filing	2329.66(A)(12)(d)
	Motor vehicle to $1,000	2329.66(A)(2)(b)
	Personal injury recoveries to $5,000, received during 12 months before filing	2329.66(A)(12)(c)
	Tuition credit or payment	2329.66(A)(16)
	Wrongful death recoveries for person debtor depended on, needed for support, received during 12 months before filing	2329.66(A)(12)(b)
public benefits	Crime victim's compensation, received during 12 months before filing	2329.66(A)(12)(a); 2743.66(D)
	Disability assistance payments	2329.66(A)(9)(f);
	Public assistance	2329.66(A)(9)(d); 5107.12
	Unemployment compensation	2329.66(A)(9)(c); 4141.32
	Vocational rehabilitation benefits	2329.66(A)(9)(a); 3304.19
	Workers' compensation	2329.66(A)(9)(b); 4123.67
tools of trade	Implements, books & tools of trade to $750	2329.66(A)(5)
wages	Minimum 75% of disposable weekly earnings or 40 times the federal hourly minimum wage, whichever is higher; bankruptcy judge may authorize more for low-income debtors	2329.66(A)(13)
wildcard	$400 of any property	2329.66(A)(17)

Oklahoma

Federal Bankruptcy Exemptions not available. All law references are to Oklahoma Statutes Annotated.

ASSET	EXEMPTION	LAW
homestead	Real property or manufactured home to unlimited value; property cannot exceed 1 acre in city, town or village, or 160 acres elsewhere; $5,000 limit if more than 25% of total sq. ft. area used for business purposes; okay to rent homestead as long as no other residence is acquired	31-1(A)(1), 31-1(A)(2), 31-2
insurance	Annuity benefits & cash value	36-3631.1
	Assessment or mutual benefits	36-2410
	Fraternal benefit society benefits	36-2718.1
	Funeral benefits prepaid & placed in trust	36-6125
	Group life policy or proceeds	36-3632
	Life, health, accident & mutual benefit insurance proceeds & cash value, if clause prohibits proceeds from being used to pay beneficiary's creditors	36-3631.1
	Limited stock insurance benefits	36-2510
miscellaneous	Alimony, child support	31-1(A)(19)
	Property of business partnership	54-1-504
pensions	County employees	19-959
	Disabled veterans	31-7
	ERISA-qualified benefits, IRAs & Keoghs	31-1(A)(20),(23),(24)
	Firefighters	11-49-126
	Judges	20-1111
	Law enforcement employees	47-2-303.3
	Police officers	11-50-124
	Public employees	74-923
	Tax exempt benefits	60-328
	Teachers	70-17-109
personal property	Books, portraits & pictures	31-1(A)-7
	Burial plots	31-1(A)(4); 8-7
	Clothing to $4,000	31-1(A)(8)
	Federal earned income tax credit	31-1(A)(25)
	Food & seed for growing to last 1 year	31-1(A)(17)
	1 gun	31-1(A)(14)
	Health aids	31-1(A)(9)
	Household & kitchen furniture	31-1(A)(3)
	Livestock for personal or family use: 5 dairy cows & calves under 6 months; 100 chickens; 20 sheep; 10 hogs; 2 horses, bridles & saddles; forage & feed to last 1 year	31-1(A)(10),(11),(12), (15),(16),(17)
	Motor vehicle to $3,000	31-1(A)(13)
	Personal injury & wrongful death recoveries to $50,000	31-1(A)(21)
	Prepaid funeral benefits	36-6125(H)
	War bond payroll savings account	51-42
public benefits	Crime victims' compensation	21-142.13
	Public assistance	56-173
	Social Security	56-173
	Unemployment compensation	40-2-303
	Workers' compensation	85-48
tools of trade	Implements needed to farm homestead, tools, books & apparatus to $5,000 total	31-1(A)(5),(6), 31-1(C)
wages	75% of wages earned in 90 days before filing bankruptcy; bankruptcy judge may allow more if you show hardship	12-1171.1; 31-1(A)(18); 31-1.1
wildcard	None	

Oregon

Federal Bankruptcy Exemptions not available. All law references are to Oregon Revised Statutes.

ASSET	EXEMPTION	LAW
homestead	Real property you occupy or intend to occupy to $25,000 ($33,000 for joint owners); mobile home on property you own or houseboat to $23,000 ($30,000 for joint owners); mobile home not on your land to $20,000 ($27,000 for joint owners); property cannot exceed 1 block in town or city or 160 acres elsewhere; sale proceeds exempt 1 year from sale, if you intend to purchase another home	23.164, 23.240, 23.250
	Tenancy by entirety not exempt, but subject to rights of non-debtor spouse	*In re Pletz*, 225 B.R. 206 (D. Or., 1997)
	Real property of a soldier or sailor during time of war	408.440
insurance	Annuity contract benefits to $500 per month	743.049
	Fraternal benefit society benefits	748.207
	Group life policy or proceeds not payable to insured	743.047
	Health or disability proceeds or avails	743.050
	Life insurance proceeds or cash value if you are not the insured	743.046
miscellaneous	Alimony, child support needed for support	23.160(1)(i)
	Liquor licenses	471.292 (1)
	Property of business partnership	68.420
pensions	ERISA-qualified benefits, including IRAs and SEPs	23.170
	Public officers, employees	237.980; 238.445; 23.166 (2)
personal property	Bank deposits to $7,500; cash for sold exempt property	23.166
	Books, pictures & musical instruments to $600 total (husband & wife may double)	23.160(1)(a)
	Burial plot	65.870
	Clothing, jewelry & other personal items to $1,800 total (husband & wife may double)	23.160(1)(b)
	Domestic animals, poultry & pets to $1,000 plus food to last 60 days	23.160(1)(e)
	Federal earned income tax credit	23.160(1)(n)
	Food & fuel to last 60 days if debtor is house-holder	23.160(1)(f)
	Furniture, household items, utensils, radios & TVs to $3,000 total	23.160(1)(f)
	Health aids	23.160(1)(h)
	Higher education tuition savings account to $7,500	348.863; 23.166(1)
	Lost earnings payments for debtor or someone debtor depended on, to extent needed (husband & wife may double)	23.160(1)(L),(3)
	Motor vehicle to $1,700 (husband & wife may double)	23.160(1)(d),(3)
	Personal injury recoveries to $10,000 (husband & wife may double)	23.160(1)(k),(3)
	Pistol; rifle or shotgun (owned by person over 16) to $1,000	23.200
public benefits	Aid to blind	412.115
	Aid to disabled	412.610
	Civil defense & disaster relief	401.405
	Crime victims' compensation (husband & wife each claim)	23.160(1)(j)(A),(3); 147.325
	General assistance	411.760
	Injured inmates' benefits	655.530
	Medical assistance	414.095
	Old-age assistance	413.130
	Unemployment compensation	657.855
	Veterans' benefits	407.125
	Vocational rehabilitation	344.580
	Workers' compensation	656.234
tools of trade	Tools, library, team with food to last 60 days, to $3,000 (husband & wife may double)	23.160(1)(c),(3)
wages	75% of disposable wages or $170 per week, whichever is greater; bankruptcy judge may authorize more for low-income debtors	23.186
	Wages withheld in state employee's bond savings accounts	292.070
wildcard	$400 of any personal property not already covered by existing exemption	23.160(1)(o)

Pennsylvania

Federal Bankruptcy Exemptions available. All law references are to Pennsylvania Consolidated Statutes Annotated.

ASSET	EXEMPTION	LAW
homestead	None, however, property held as tenancy by the entirety may be exempt against debts owed by only one spouse	*In re Martin*, 259 B.R. 119 (M.D. Pa. 2001)
insurance	Accident or disability benefits	42-8124(c)(7)
	Fraternal benefit society benefits	42-8124(c)(1),(8)
	Group life policy or proceeds	42-8124(c)(5)
	Insurance policy or annuity contract payments, where insured is the beneficiary, cash value or proceeds to $100 per month	42-8124(c)(3)
	Life insurance annuity policy cash value or proceeds if beneficiary is insured's dependent, child or spouse	42-8124(c)(6)
	Life insurance and annuity proceeds if clause prohibits proceeds from being used to pay beneficiary's creditors	42-8214(c)(4)
	No-fault automobile insurance proceeds	42-8124(c)(9)
miscellaneous	Property of business partnership	15-8342
pensions	City employees	53-13445, 53-23572, 53-39383; 42-8124(b)(1)(iv)
	County employees	16-4716
	Municipal employees	53-881.115; 42-8124(b)(1)(vi)
	Police officers	53-764, 53-776, 53-23666; 42-8124(b)(1)(iii)
	Private retirement benefits to extent tax-deferred, if clause prohibits proceeds from being used to pay beneficiary's creditors; exemption limited to deposits of $15,000 per year made at least 1 year before filing (limit does not apply to rollovers from other exempt funds or accounts)	42-8124(b)(1)(vii), (viii),(ix)
	Public school employees	24-8533; 42-8124(b)(1)(i)
	State employees	71-5953; 42-8124(b)(1)(ii)
personal property	Bibles & schoolbooks	42-8124(a)(2)
	Clothing	42-8124(a)(1)
	Military uniforms & accoutrements	42-8124(a)(4); 51-4103
	Sewing machines	42-8124(a)(3)
public benefits	Crime victims' compensation	18-11.708
	Korean conflict veterans' benefits	51-20098
	Unemployment compensation	42-8124(a)(10); 43-863
	Veterans' benefits	51-20012, 20048, 20098; 20127
	Workers' compensation	42-8124(c)(2)
tools of trade	Seamstress' sewing machine	42-8124(a)(3)
wages	Earned but unpaid wages	42-8127
wildcard	$300 of any property, including cash, real property, securities or proceeds from sale of exempt property	42-8123

Rhode Island

Federal Bankruptcy Exemptions available. All law references are to General Laws of Rhode Island.

ASSET	EXEMPTION	LAW
homestead	$150,000 in land & buildings you occupy or intend to occupy as a principal residence (husband & wife may not double)	9-26-4.1
insurance	Accident or sickness proceeds, avails or benefits	27-18-24
	Fraternal benefit society benefits	27-25-18
	Life insurance proceeds if clause prohibits proceeds from being used to pay beneficiary's creditors	27-4-12
	Temporary disability insurance	28-41-32
miscellaneous	Earnings of a minor child	9-26-4(9)
	Property of business partnership	7-12-36
pensions	ERISA-qualified benefits	9-26-4(12)
	Firefighters	9-26-5
	IRAs	9-26-4(11)
	Police officers	9-26-5
	Private employees	28-17-4
	State & municipal employees	36-10-34
personal property	Beds, bedding, furniture, household goods & supplies, to $8,600 total (husband & wife may not double)	9-26-4(3) *In re Petrozella*, 247 B.R. 591 (R.I. 2000)
	Bibles & books to $300	9-26-4(4)
	Burial plot	9-26-4(5)
	Clothing	9-26-4(1)
	Consumer cooperative association holdings to $50	7-8-25
	Debt secured by promissory note or bill of exchange	9-26-4(7)
	Jewelry to $1,000	9-26-4 (14)
	Motor vehicles to $10,000	9-26-4 (13)
	Prepaid tuition program or tuition savings account	9-26-4 (15)
public benefits	Aid to blind, aged, disabled, general assistance	40-6-14
	State disability benefits	28-41-32
	Unemployment compensation	28-44-58
	Veterans' disability or survivors' death benefits	30-7-9
	Workers' compensation	28-33-27
tools of trade	Library of practicing professional	9-26-4(2)
	Working tools to $1,200	9-26-4(2)
wages	Earned but unpaid wages to $50	9-26-4(8)(iii)
	Earned but unpaid wages due military member on active duty	30-7-9
	Earned but unpaid wages due seaman	9-26-4(6)
	Wages of any person who had been receiving public assistance are exempt for 1 year after going off of relief	9-26-4(8)(ii)
	Wages of spouse & minor children	9-26-4(9)
	Wages paid by charitable organization or fund providing relief to the poor	9-26-4(8)(i)
wildcard	None	

South Carolina

Federal Bankruptcy Exemptions not available. All law references are to Code of Laws of South Carolina.

ASSET	EXEMPTION	LAW
homestead	Real property, including co-op, to $5,000 (joint owners may double)	15-41-30(1)
insurance	Accident & disability benefits	38-63-40(D)
	Benefits accruing under life insurance policy after death of insured, where proceeds left with insurance company pursuant to agreement; benefits not exempt from action to recover necessaries if parties so agree	38-63-50
	Disability or illness benefits	15-41-30(10)(C)
	Fraternal benefit society benefits	38-38-330
	Group life insurance proceeds; cash value to $50,000	38-63-40(C), 38-65-90
	Life insurance avails from policy for person you depended on to $4,000	15-41-30(8)
	Life insurance proceeds from policy for person you depended on, needed for support	15-41-30(11)(C)
	Proceeds & cash surrender value of life insurance payable to beneficiary other than insured's estate and for the express benefit of insured's spouse, children or dependents (must be purchased 2 years before filing)	38-63-40(A)
	Proceeds of life insurance or annuity contract	38-63-40(B)
	Unmatured life insurance contract, except credit insurance policy	15-41-30(7)
miscellaneous	Alimony, child support	15-41-30(10)(D)
	Property of business partnership	33-41-720
pensions	ERISA-qualified benefits; your share of the pension plan fund	15-41-30(10)(E),(13)
	Firefighters	9-13-230
	General assembly members	9-9-180
	IRAs	15-41-30(12)
	Judges, solicitors	9-8-190
	Police officers	9-11-270
	Public employees	9-1-1680
personal property	Animals, crops, appliances, books, clothing, household goods, furnishings, musical instruments to $2,500 total	15-41-30(3)
	Burial plot to $5,000, in lieu of homestead (joint owners may double)	15-41-30(1)
	Cash & other liquid assets to $1,000, in lieu of burial or homestead exemption	15-41-30(5)
	College investment program trust fund	59-2-140
	Health aids	15-41-30(9)
	Jewelry to $500	15-41-30(4)
	Motor vehicle to $1,200	15-41-30(2)
	Personal injury & wrongful death recoveries for person you depended on for support	15-41-30(11)(B)
public benefits	Crime victims' compensation	15-41-30(11)(A); 16-3-1300
	General relief, aid to aged, blind, disabled	43-5-190
	Local public assistance	15-41-30(10)(A)
	Social Security	15-41-30(10)(A)
	Unemployment compensation	15-41-30(10)(A)
	Veterans' benefits	15-41-30(10)(B)
	Workers' compensation	42-9-360
tools of trade	Implements, books & tools of trade to $750	15-41-30(6)
wages	None (use Federal non-bankruptcy wage exemption)	
wildcard	None	

South Dakota

Federal Bankruptcy Exemptions not available. All law references are to South Dakota Codified Laws.

ASSET	EXEMPTION	LAW
homestead	Real property to unlimited value or mobile home (larger than 240 sq. ft. at its base and registered in state at least 6 months before filing) to unlimited value; property cannot exceed 1 acre in town or 160 acres elsewhere; sale proceeds to $30,000 (no limit if over age 70 or widow or widower who hasn't remarried) exempt for 1 year after sale (husband & wife may not double)	43-31-1, 43-31-2, 43-31-3, 43-31-4
	(Gold or silver mine, mill or smelter not exempt, 43-31-5.)	
	Spouse or child of deceased owner may claim homestead exemption	43-31-13
	May file homestead declaration	43-31-6
insurance	Annuity contract proceeds to $250 per month	58-12-6, 58-12-8
	Endowment, life insurance, policy proceeds to $20,000; if policy issued by mutual aid or benevolent society, cash value to $20,000	58-12-4
	Fraternal benefit society benefits	58-37A-18
	Health benefits to $20,000	58-12-4
	Life insurance proceeds, if clause prohibits proceeds from being used to pay beneficiary's creditors	58-15-70
	Life insurance proceeds to $10,000, if beneficiary is surviving spouse or child	43-45-6
pensions	City employees	9-16-47
	ERISA-qualified benefits, limited to income & distribution on $250,000	43-45-16
	Public employees	3-12-115
personal property	Bible, schoolbooks; other books to $200	43-45-2(4)
	Burial plots, church pew	43-45-2(2),(3)
	Clothing	43-45-2(5)
	Family pictures	43-45-2(1)
	Food & fuel to last 1 year	43-45-2(6)
public benefits	Crime victim's compensation	23A-28B-24
	Public assistance	28-7A-18
	Unemployment compensation	61-6-28
	Workers' compensation	62-4-42
tools of trade	None	
wages	Earned wages owed 60 days before filing bankruptcy, needed for support of family	15-20-12
	Wages of prisoners in work programs	24-8-10
wildcard	Head of family may claim $6,000 or non-head of family may claim $4,000 of any personal property	43-45-4

Tennessee

Federal Bankruptcy Exemptions not available. All law references are to Tennessee Code Annotated unless otherwise noted.

ASSET	EXEMPTION	LAW
homestead	$5,000; $7,500 for joint owners	26-2-301
	Life estate	26-2-302
	2-15 year lease	26-2-303
	Spouse or child of deceased owner may claim homestead exemption	26-2-301
	Property held as tenancy by the entirety may be exempt against debts owed by only one spouse	*In re Arango,* 136 B.R. 740 aff'd, 992 F.2d 611 (6th Cir. 1993)
insurance	Accident, health or disability benefits for resident & citizen of Tennessee	26-2-110
	Disability or illness benefits	26-2-111(1)(C)
	Fraternal benefit society benefits	56-25-1403
	Homeowners' insurance proceeds to $5,000	26-2-304
miscellaneous	Alimony, child support owed for 30 days before filing for bankruptcy	26-2-111(1)(E)
	Property of business partnership	61-1-124
pensions	ERISA-qualified benefits, IRAs & Roth IRAs	26-2-111(1)(D)
	Public employees	8-36-111
	State & local government employees	26-2-105
	Teachers	49-5-909
personal property	Bible, schoolbooks, family pictures & portraits	26-2-104
	Burial plot to 1 acre	26-2-305, 46-2-102
	Clothing & storage containers	26-2-104
	Health aids	26-2-111(5)
	Lost future earnings payments for you or person you depended on	26-2-111(3)
	Personal injury recoveries to $7,500; wrongful death recoveries to $10,000 ($15,000 total for personal injury, wrongful death & crime victims' compensation)	26-2-111(2)(B),(C)
public benefits	Aid to blind	71-4-117
	Aid to disabled	71-4-1112
	Crime victims' compensation to $5,000 (see personal property)	26-2-111(2)(A), 29-13-111
	Local public assistance	26-2-111(1)(A)
	Old-age assistance	71-2-216
	Social Security	26-2-111(1)(A)
	Unemployment compensation	26-2-111(1)(A)
	Veterans' benefits	26-2-111(1)(B)
	Workers' compensation	50-6-223
tools of trade	Implements, books & tools of trade to $1,900	26-2-111(4)
wages	Minimum 75% of disposable weekly earnings or 30 times the federal minimum hourly wage, whichever is more, plus $2.50 per week per child; bankruptcy judge may authorize more for low-income debtors	26-2-106,107
wildcard	$4,000 of any personal property including deposits on account with any bank or financial institution	26-2-103

Texas

Federal Bankruptcy Exemptions available. All law references are to Texas Revised Civil Statutes Annotated unless otherwise noted.

ASSET	EXEMPTION	LAW
homestead	Unlimited; property cannot exceed 10 acres in town, village, city or 100 acres (200 for families) elsewhere; sale proceeds exempt for 6 months after sale (renting okay if another home not acquired, Prop. 41.003)	Prop. 41.001, 41.002; Const. Art. 16 § 50, 51
	Must file homestead declaration, or court will file it for you and charge you for doing so.	Prop. 41.005(f), 41.021 to 41.023
insurance	Church benefit plan benefits	1407a (6)
	Fraternal benefit society benefits	Ins. 10.28
	Life, health, accident or annuity benefits, monies, policy proceeds & cash values due or paid to beneficiary or insured	Ins. 21.22
	Texas employee uniform group insurance	Ins. 3.50-2(10)(a)
	Texas public school employees group insurance	Ins. 3.50-4(11)(a)
	Texas state college or university employee benefits	Ins. 3.50-3(9)(a)
miscellaneous	Alimony and child support	Prop. 42.001(b)(3)
	Property of business partnership	6132b-5.01
pensions	County & district employees	Gov't. 811.006
	ERISA-qualified government or church benefits, including Keoghs and IRAs	Prop. 42.0021
	Firefighters	6243e(5); 6243a-1(8.03); 6243b(15); 6243e(5); 6243e.1(1.04)
	Judges	Gov't. 831.004
	Law enforcement officers', firefighters', emergency medical personnel survivors	Gov't. 615.005
	Municipal employees & elected officials, state employees	6243h(22), Gov't. 811.005
	Police officers	6243d-1(17), 6243j(20); 6243a-1(8.03); 6243b(15); 6243d-1(17)
	Retirement benefits to extent tax-deferred	Prop. 42.0021
	Teachers	Gov't. 821.005
personal property	Athletic and sporting equipment, including bicycles	Prop. 42.002(a)(8)
to $60,000 total for family,	Clothing & food	Prop. 42.002(a)(2),(5)
$30,000	2 firearms	Prop. 42.002(a)(7)
for single adult	Higher education savings plan trust account	Educ. 54.709(e)
	Home furnishings including family heirlooms	Prop. 42.002(a)(1)
(see also tools of trade)	Jewelry (limited to 25% of total exemption)	Prop. 42.002(a)(6)
	1 two-, three- or four-wheeled motor vehicle per family member or per single adult who holds a driver's license; or, if not licensed, who relies on someone else to operate vehicle	Prop. 42.002(a)(9)
	Pets & domestic animals plus their food: 2 horses, mules or donkeys & tack; 12 head of cattle; 60 head of other livestock; 120 fowl	Prop. 42.002(a)(10),(11)
	Burial plots (exempt from total)	Prop. 41.001
	Health aids (exempt from total)	Prop. 42.001(b)(2)
public benefits	Crime victims' compensation	Crim. Proc. 56.49
	Medical assistance	Hum. Res. 32.036
	Public assistance	Hum. Res. 31.040
	Unemployment compensation	Labor 207.075
	Workers' compensation	Labor 408.201
tools of trade	Farming or ranching vehicles & implements	Prop. 42.002(a)(3)
included in aggregate dollar limits for personal property	Tools, equipment (includes boat & motor vehicles used in trade) & books	Prop. 42.002(a)(4)
wages	Earned but unpaid wages	Prop. 42.001(b)(1)
	Unpaid commissions not to exceed 25% of total personal property exemptions	Prop. 42.001(d)
wildcard	None	

Utah

Federal Bankruptcy Exemptions not available. All law references are to Utah Code.

ASSET	EXEMPTION	LAW
homestead	Real property, mobile home or water rights to $20,000 if primary residence; $5,000 if not primary residence (joint owners may double)	78-23-3(1),(2),(4)
	Must file homestead declaration before attempted sale of home	78-23-4
	Sale proceeds exempt for 1 year	78-23-3(5)(b)
insurance	Disability, illness, medical or hospital benefits	78-23-5(1)(a)(iii)
	Fraternal benefit society benefits	31A-9-603
	Life insurance policy cash surrender value to $5,000	78-23-7
	Life insurance proceeds if beneficiary is insured's spouse or dependent, as needed for support	78-23-6(2)
	Medical, surgical and hospital benefits	78-23-5(1)(a)(iv)
miscellaneous	Alimony needed for support	78-23-5(1)(a)(vi), 78-23-6(1)
	Child support	78-23-5(1)(f), (k)
	Property of business partnership	48-1-22
pensions	ERISA-qualified benefits, IRAs, Keoghs (benefits that have accrued & contributions that have been made at least 1 year prior to filing)	78-23-5(1)(a)(x)
	Public employees	49-1-609
	Other pensions & annuities needed for support	78-23-6(3)
Personal property	Animals, books & musical instruments to $500	78-23-8(1)(c)
	Artwork depicting, or done by, a family member	78-23-5(1)(a)(viii)
	Bed, bedding, carpets	78-23-5(1)(a)(vii)
	Burial plot	78-23-5(1)(a)(i)
	Clothing (cannot claim furs or jewelry)	78-23-5(1)(a)(vii)
	Dining & kitchen tables & chairs to $500	78-23-8(1)(b)
	Food to last 12 months	78-23-5(1)(a)(vii)
	Health aids	78-23-5(1)(a)(ii)
	Heirlooms to $500	78-23-8(1)(d)
	Motor vehicle	78-23-8(3)
	Personal injury, wrongful death recoveries for you or person you depended on	78-23-5(1)(a)(ix)
	Proceeds for sold, lost or damaged exempt property	78-23-9
	Refrigerator, freezer, microwave, stove, sewing machine, washer & dryer	78-23-5(1)(a)(vii)
	Sofas, chairs & related furnishings to $500	78-23-8(1)(a)
public benefits	Crime victims' compensation	63-25a-421(4)
	General assistance	35A-3-112
	Occupational disease disability benefits	34A-3-107
	Unemployment compensation	35A-4-103(4)(b)
	Veterans' benefits	78-23-5(1)(a)(v)
	Workers' compensation	34A-2-422
tools of trade	Implements, books & tools of trade to $3,500	78-23-8(2)
	Military property of National Guard member	39-1-47
wages	Minimum 75% of disposable weekly earnings or 30 times the federal hourly minimum wage, whichever is more; bankruptcy judge may authorize more for low-income debtors	70C-7-103
wildcard	None	

Vermont

Federal Bankruptcy Exemptions available. All law references are to Vermont Statutes Annotated unless otherwise noted.

ASSET	EXEMPTION	LAW
homestead	Real property or mobile home to $75,000; may also claim rents, issues, profits & out-buildings (husband and wife may double)	27-101
	Spouse of deceased owner may claim homestead exemption	27-105
	Property held as tenancy by the entirety may be exempt against debts owed by only one spouse	In re McQueen, 21 B.R. 736 (D. Ver. 1982)
insurance	Annuity contract benefits to $350 per month	8-3709
	Disability benefits that supplement life insurance or annuity contract	8-3707
	Disability or illness benefits needed for support	12-2740(19)(C)
	Fraternal benefit society benefits	8-4478
	Group life or health benefits	8-3708
	Health benefits to $200 per month	8-4086
	Life insurance proceeds if beneficiary is not the insured	8-3706
	Life insurance proceeds for person you depended on	12-2740(19)(H)
	Life insurance proceeds if clause prohibits proceeds from being used to pay beneficiary's creditors	8-3705
	Unmatured life insurance contract other than credit	12-2740(18)
miscellaneous	Alimony, child support	12-2740(19)(D)
pensions	Municipal employees	24-5066
	Self-directed accounts (IRAs, Keoghs); contributions must be made 1 year before filing	12-2740(16)
	State employees	3-476
	Teachers	16-1946
	Other pensions	12-2740(19)(J)
personal property	Appliances, furnishings, goods, clothing, books, crops, animals, musical instruments to $2,500 total	12-2740(5)
	Bank deposits to $700	12-2740(15)
	Cow, 2 goats, 10 sheep, 10 chickens & feed to last 1 winter; 3 swarms of bees plus honey; 5 tons coal or 500 gal. heating oil, 10 cords of firewood; 500 gal. bottled gas; growing crops to $5,000; yoke of oxen or steers, plow & ox yoke; 2 horses with harnesses, halters & chains	12-2740(6),(9)-(14)
	Health aids	12-2740(17)
	Jewelry to $500; wedding ring unlimited	12-2740(3),(4)
	Motor vehicles to $2,500	12-2740(1)
	Personal injury, lost future earnings, wrongful death recoveries for you or person you depended on	12-2740(19)(F),(G),(I)
	Stove, heating unit, refrigerator, freezer, water heater & sewing machines	12-2740(8)
public benefits	Aid to blind, aged, disabled, general assistance	33-124
	Crime victims' compensation needed for support	12-2740(19)(E)
	Social Security needed for support	12-2740(19)(A)
	Unemployment compensation	21-1367
	Veterans' benefits needed for support	12-2740(19)(B)
	Workers' compensation	21-681
tools of trade	Books & tools of trade to $5,000	12-2740(2)
wages	Minimum 75% of weekly disposable earnings or 30 times the federal minimum hourly wage, whichever is greater; bankruptcy judge may authorize more for low-income debtors	12-3170
	Entire wages, if you received welfare during 2 months before filing	12-3170
wildcard	Unused exemptions for motor vehicle, tools of trade, jewelry, household furniture, appliances, clothing & crops to $7,000	12-2740(7)
	$400 of any property	12-2740(7)

Virginia

Federal Bankruptcy Exemptions not available. All law references are to Code of Virginia unless otherwise noted.

ASSET	EXEMPTION	LAW
homestead	$5,000 plus $500 per dependent; rents & profits; sale proceeds exempt to $5,000 (husband & wife may double, unused portion of homestead may be applied to any personal property)	Cheeseman v. Nachman, 656 F.2d 60 (4th Cir. 1981); 34-4, 34-18, 34-20
	May include mobile home	In re Goad, 161 B.R. 161 (W.D. Va. 1993)
	Must file homestead declaration before filing for bankruptcy	34-6
	Property held as tenancy by the entirety may be exempt against debts owed by only one spouse	In re Harris, 155 B.R. 948 (E.D. Va. 1993)
	Surviving spouse may claim $10,000; if no surviving spouse, minor children may claim exemption	64.1-151.3
insurance	Accident or sickness benefits	38.2-3406
	Burial society benefits	38.2-4021
	Cooperative life insurance benefits	38.2-3811
	Fraternal benefit society benefits	38.2-4118
	Group life or accident insurance for government officials	51.1-510
	Group life insurance policy or proceeds	38.2-3339
	Industrial sick benefits	38.2-3549
	Life insurance proceeds	38.2-3122
miscellaneous	Property of business partnership	50-73.108
pensions also see wages	City, town & county employees	51.1-802
	ERISA-qualified benefits to $17,500	34-34
	Judges	51.1-300
	State employees	51.1-124.4(A)
	State police officers	51.1-200
personal property	Bible	34-26(1)
	Burial plot	34-26(3)
	Clothing to $1,000	34-26(4)
	Family portraits & heirlooms to $5,000 total	34-26(2)
	Health aids	34-26(6)
	Household furnishings to $5,000	34-26(4a)
	Motor vehicle to $2,000	34-26(8)
	Personal injury causes of action & recoveries	34-28.1
	Pets	34-26(5)
	Wedding and engagement rings	34-26(1a)
public benefits	Aid to blind, aged, disabled, general relief	63.1-88
	Crime victims' compensation unless seeking to discharge debt for treatment of injury incurred during crime	19.2-368.12
	Unemployment compensation	60.2-600
	Workers' compensation	65.2-531
tools of trade	For farmer, pair of horses or mules with gear; one wagon or cart, one tractor to $3,000; 2 plows & wedges; one drag, harvest cradle, pitchfork, rake; fertilizer to $1,000	34-27
	Tools, books and instruments of trade, including motor vehicles, to $10,000, needed in your occupation or education	34-26(7)
	Uniforms, arms, equipment of military member	44-96
wages	Minimum 75% of weekly disposable earnings or 30 times the federal minimum hourly wage, whichever is greater; bankruptcy judge may authorize more for low-income debtors	34-29
wildcard	Unused portion of homestead or personal property exemption	34-13
	$2,000 of any property for disabled veterans	34-4.1

Washington

Federal Bankruptcy Exemptions available. All law references are to Revised Code of Washington Annotated.

ASSET	EXEMPTION	LAW
homestead	Real property or mobile home to $40,000; unimproved property intended for residence to $15,000 (husband and wife may not double)	6.13.010, 6.13.030
	Must record homestead declaration before sale of home if property unimproved or home unoccupied	6.15.040
insurance	Annuity contract proceeds to $250 per month	48.18.430
	Disability proceeds, avails or benefits	48.36A.180
	Group life insurance policy or proceeds	48.18.420
	Life insurance proceeds or avails if beneficiary is not the insured	48.18.410
miscellaneous	Property of business partnership	25.05.215
pensions	City employees	41.28.200, 41.44.240
	ERISA-qualified benefits, IRAs & Keoghs	6.15.020
	Judges	2.10.180, 2.12.090
	Law enforcement officials & firefighters	41.26.053
	Police officers	41.20.180
	Public & state employees	41.40.052
	State patrol officers	43.43.310
	Teachers	41.32.052
	Volunteer firefighters	41.24.240
personal property	Appliances, furniture, household goods, home & yard equipment to $2,700 total for individual ($5,400 for community)	6.15.010(3)(a)
	Books to $1,500	6.15.010(2)
	Burial plots sold by nonprofit cemetery association	68.20.120
	Clothing, no more than $1,000 in furs, jewelry, ornaments	6.15.010(1)
	Food & fuel for comfortable maintenance	6.15.010(3)(a)
	Fire insurance proceeds for lost, stolen or destroyed exempt property	6.15.030
	Keepsakes & family pictures	6.15.010(2)
	Health aids prescribed	6.15.010(3)(e)
	Motor vehicle to $2,500 total for individual (two vehicles to $5,000 for community)	6.15.010(3)(c)
	Personal injury recoveries to $16,150	6.15.010(3)(f)
public benefits	Child welfare	74.13.070
	Crime victims' compensation	7.68.070
	General assistance	74.04.280
	Industrial insurance (workers' compensation)	51.32.040
	Old-age assistance	74.08.210
	Unemployment compensation	50.40.020
tools of trade	Commercial fishing license	75.28.011
	Farmer's trucks, stock, tools, seed, equipment & supplies to $5,000 total	6.15.010(4)(a)
	Library, office furniture, office equipment & supplies of physician, surgeon, attorney, clergy or other professional to $5,000 total	6.15.010(4)(b)
	Tools & materials used in any other trade to $5,000	6.15.010(4)(c)
wages	Minimum 75% of weekly disposable earnings or 30 times the federal minimum hourly wage, whichever is greater; bankruptcy judge may authorize more for low-income debtors	6.27.150
wildcard	$2,000 of any personal property (no more than $200 in cash, bank deposits, bonds, stocks & securities)	6.15.010(3)(b)

West Virginia

Federal Bankruptcy Exemptions not available. All law references are to West Virginia Code.

ASSET	EXEMPTION	LAW
homestead	Real or personal property used as residence to $25,000; unused portion of homestead may be applied to any property (husband & wife may double)	38-10-4(a)
insurance	Fraternal benefit society benefits	33-23-21
	Group life insurance policy or proceeds	33-6-28
	Health or disability benefits	38-10-4(j)(3)
	Life insurance payments from policy for person you depended on, needed for support	38-10-4(k)(3)
	Unmatured life insurance contract, except credit insurance policy	38-10-4(g)
	Unmatured life insurance contract's accrued dividend, interest or loan value to $8,000, if debtor owns contract & insured is either debtor or a person on whom debtor is dependent	38-10-4(h)
miscellaneous	Alimony, child support needed for support	38-10-4(j)(4)
	Property of business partnership	47-8A-25
pensions	ERISA-qualified benefits, IRAs needed for support	38-10-4(j)(5)
	Public employees	5-10-46
	Teachers	18-7A-30
personal property	Animals, crops, clothing, appliances, books, household goods, furnishings, musical instruments to $400 per item, $8,000 total	38-10-4(c)
	Burial plot to $15,000, in lieu of homestead	38-10-4(a)
	Health aids	38-10-4(i)
	Jewelry to $1,000	38-10-4(d)
	Lost earnings payments needed for support	38-10-4(k)(5)
	Motor vehicle to $2,400	38-10-4(b)
	Personal injury recoveries to $15,000	38-10-4(k)(4)
	Prepaid higher education tuition trust fund and savings plan payments	38-10-4(k)(6)
	Wrongful death recoveries for person you depended on, needed for support	38-10-4(k)(2)
public benefits	Aid to blind, aged, disabled, general assistance	9-5-1
	Crime victims' compensation	38-10-4(k)(1)
	Social Security	38-10-4(j)(1)
	Unemployment compensation	38-10-4(j)(1)
	Veterans' benefits	38-10-4(j)(2)
	Workers' compensation	23-4-18
tools of trade	Implements, books & tools of trade to $1,500	38-10-4(f)
wages	Minimum 30 times the federal minimum hourly wage per week; bankruptcy judge may authorize more for low-income debtors	38-5A-3
wildcard	$800 plus unused portion of homestead or burial exemption, of any property	38-10-4(e)

Wisconsin

Federal Bankruptcy Exemptions available. All law references are to Wisconsin Statutes Annotated.

ASSET	EXEMPTION	LAW
homestead	Property you occupy or intend to occupy to $40,000; sale proceeds exempt for 2 years if you intend to purchase another home (husband & wife's exemption may not exceed $40,000)	815.20
insurance	Federal disability insurance	815.18(3)(ds)
	Fraternal benefit society benefits	614.96
	Life insurance proceeds held in trust by insurer, if clause prohibits proceeds from being used to pay beneficiary's creditors	632.42
	Life insurance proceeds for someone debtor depended on, needed for support	815.18(3)(i)(a)
	Unmatured life insurance contract (except credit insurance contract) if debtor owns contract & insured is debtor or dependents, or someone debtor is dependent on	815.18(3)(f)
	Unmatured life insurance contract's accrued dividends, interest or loan value to $4,000 total, if debtor owns contract & insured is debtor or dependents, or someone debtor is dependent on	815.18(3)(f)
miscellaneous	Alimony, child support needed for support	815.18(3)(c)
	Property of business partnership	178.21(3)(c)
pensions	Certain municipal employees	62.63(4)
	Firefighters, police officers who worked in city with population over 100,000	815.18(3)(ef)
	Military pensions	815.18(3)(n)
	Private or public retirement benefits	815.18(3)(j)
	Public employees	40.08(1)
personal property	Burial plot, tombstone, coffin (husband & wife may double)	815.18(3)(a)
	College savings account or tuition trust fund	14.64(7), 14.63(8)
	Deposit accounts to $1,000	815.18(3)(k)
	Fire & casualty proceeds for destroyed exempt property for 2 years from receiving	815.18(3)(e)
	Household goods and furnishings, clothing, keepsakes, jewelry, appliances, books, musical instruments, firearms, sporting goods, animals and other tangible personal property to $5,000 total (husband & wife may double)	815.18(3)(d)
	Lost future earnings recoveries, needed for support	815.18(3)(i)(d)
	Motor vehicles to $1,200 (husband & wife may double; unused portion of $5,000 personal property exemption may be added)	815.18(3)(g)
	Personal injury recoveries to $25,000	815.18(3)(i)(c)
	Tenant's lease or stock interest in housing co-op, to homestead amount	182.004(6)
	Wages used to purchase savings bonds	20.921(1)(e)
	Wrongful death recoveries, needed for support	815.18(3)(i)(b)
public benefits	Crime victims' compensation	949.07
	Social services payments	49.96
	Unemployment compensation	108.13
	Veterans' benefits	45.35(8)(b)
	Workers' compensation	102.27
tools of trade	Equipment, inventory, farm products, books and tools of trade to $7,500 total	815.18(3)(b)
wages	75% of weekly net income or 30 times the greater of the federal or state minimum hourly wage; bankruptcy judge may authorize more for low-income debtors	815.18(3)(h)
wildcard	None	

Wyoming

Federal Bankruptcy Exemptions not available. All law references are to Wyoming Statutes Annotated unless otherwise noted.

ASSET	EXEMPTION	LAW
homestead	Real property you occupy to $10,000 or house trailer you occupy to $6,000 (joint owners may double)	1-20-101,102,104
	Spouse or child of deceased owner may claim homestead exemption	1-20-103
	Property held as tenancy by the entirety may be exempt against debts owed by only one spouse	In re Anselmi, 52 B.R. 479 (D. Wy. 1985)
insurance	Annuity contract proceeds to $350 per month	26-15-132
	Disability benefits if clause prohibits proceeds from being used to pay beneficiary's creditors	26-15-130
	Fraternal benefit society benefits	26-29-218
	Group life or disability policy or proceeds, cash surrender & loan values, premiums waived and dividends	26-15-131
	Individual life insurance policy proceeds, cash surrender & loan values, premiums waived and dividends	26-15-129
	Life insurance proceeds held by insurer, if clause prohibits proceeds from being used to pay beneficiary's creditors	26-15-133
miscellaneous	Liquor licenses & malt beverage permits	12-4-604
pensions	Criminal investigators, highway officers	9-3-620
	Firefighters' death benefits	15-5-209
	Game & fish wardens	9-3-620
	Police officers	15-5-313(c)
	Private or public retirement funds & accounts	1-20-110
	Public employees	9-3-426
personal property	Bedding, furniture, household articles & food to $2,000 per person in the home	1-20-106(a)(iii)
	Bible, schoolbooks & pictures	1-20-106(a)(i)
	Burial plot	1-20-106(a)(ii)
	Clothing & wedding rings to $1,000	1-20-105
	Motor vehicle to $2,400	1-20-106(a)(iv)
	Prepaid funeral contracts	26-32-102
public benefits	Crime victims' compensation	1-40-113
	General assistance	42-2-113(b)
	Unemployment compensation	27-3-319
	Workers' compensation	27-14-702
tools of trade	Library & implements of professional to $2,000 or tools, motor vehicle, implements, team & stock in trade to $2,000	1-20-106(b)
wages	Earnings of National Guard members	19-9-401
	Minimum 75% of disposable weekly earnings or 30 times the federal hourly minimum wage, whichever is more.	1-15-511
	Wages of inmates on work release	7-16-308
wildcard	None	

Federal Bankruptcy Exemptions

Married couples may double all exemptions. All references are to 11 U.S.C. § 522. These exemptions were last adjusted in 2001. Every three years ending on April 1, these amounts will be adjusted to reflect changes in the Consumer Price Index. Debtors in the following states may select the Federal Bankruptcy Exemptions:

Arkansas	Massachusetts	New Jersey	Texas
Connecticut	Michigan	New Mexico	Vermont
District of Columbia	Minnesota	Pennsylvania	Washington
Hawaii	New Hampshire	Rhode Island	Wisconsin

ASSET	EXEMPTION	SUBSECTION
homestead	Real property, including co-op or mobile home, to $17,425; unused portion of homestead to $8,075 may be applied to any property	(d)(1)
insurance	Disability, illness or unemployment benefits	(d)(10)(C)
	Life insurance payments for person you depended on, needed for support	(d)(11)(C)
	Life insurance policy with loan value, in accrued dividends or interest, to $9,300	(d)(8)
	Unmatured life insurance contract, except credit insurance policy	(d)(7)
miscellaneous	Alimony, child support needed for support	(d)(10)(D)
pensions	ERISA-qualified benefits needed for support; may include IRAs	(d)(10)(E); *Carmichael v. Osherow*, 100 F.3d 375 (5th Cir. 1996)
personal property	Animals, crops, clothing, appliances, books, furnishings, household goods, musical instruments to $450 per item, $9,300 total	(d)(3)
	Health aids	(d)(9)
	Jewelry to $1,150	(d)(4)
	Lost earnings payments	(d)(11)(E)
	Motor vehicle to $2,775	(d)(2)
	Personal injury recoveries to $17,425 (not to include pain & suffering or pecuniary loss)	(d)(11)(D)
	Wrongful death recoveries for person you depended on	(d)(11)(B)
public benefits	Crime victims' compensation	(d)(11)(A)
	Public assistance	(d)(10)(A)
	Social Security	(d)(10)(A)
	Unemployment compensation	(d)(10)(A)
	Veterans' benefits	(d)(10)(A)
tools of trade	Implements, books & tools of trade to $1,750	(d)(6)
wages	None	
wildcard	$925 of any property	(d)(5)
	$8,725 less any amount of homestead exemption claimed, of any property	(d)(5)

Federal Non-Bankruptcy Exemptions

These exemptions are available only if you select your state exemptions. You may use them for any exemptions in addition to those allowed by your state, but they cannot be claimed if you file using federal bankruptcy exemptions. All law references are to the United States Code.

ASSET	EXEMPTION	LAW
retirement	Civil service employees	5 § 8346
	Foreign Service employees	22 § 4060
	Military Medal of Honor roll pensions	38 § 1562(c)
	Military service employees	10 § 1440
	Railroad workers	45 § 231m
	Social Security	42 § 407
	Veterans' benefits	38 § 5301
survivor's benefits	Judges, U.S. court & judicial center directors, administrative assistants to U.S. Supreme Court Chief Justice	28 § 376
	Lighthouse workers	33 § 775
	Military service	10 § 1450
death & disability benefits	Government employees	5 § 8130
	Longshoremen & harbor workers	33 § 916
	War risk hazard death or injury compensation	42 § 1717
miscellaneous	Indian lands or homestead sales or lease proceeds	25 § 410
	Klamath Indians tribe benefits for Indians residing in Oregon	25 § 543, 545
	Military deposits in savings accounts while on permanent duty outside U.S.	10 § 1035
	Military group life insurance	38 § 1970(g)
	Railroad workers' unemployment insurance	45 § 352(e)
	Seamen's clothing	46 § 11110
	Seamen's wages (while on a voyage) pursuant to a written contract	46 § 11109
	Minimum 75% of disposable weekly earnings or 30 times the federal minimum hourly wage, whichever is more; bankruptcy judge may authorize more for low-income debtors	15 § 1673

Exemption Glossary

This glossary defines some of the terms that appear in the Appendix 1: *State and Federal Exemption Tables.*

Animals

The "animal" exemption varies among states. In many places, pets or livestock and poultry are specifically exempt. If your state simply allows you to exempt "animals," you may include livestock, poultry or pets. Some states exempt only domestic animals, which are usually considered to be all animals but pets.

Annuity

Insurance that pays out during the life of the insured, unlike life insurance, which pays out at the insured's death. A person who purchases an annuity contract and reaches a specified age, such as 65, gets back monthly payments until death. Thus, an annuity is really a type of retirement plan.

Appliance

Any household apparatus or machine, usually operated by electricity, gas or propane. Examples include refrigerators, stoves, washing machines, dishwashers, vacuum cleaners, air conditioners and toasters.

Arms & accoutrements

Arms are weapons (e.g., pistols, rifles, swords); accoutrements are the furnishings of a soldier's outfit, such as a belt or pack, but not clothes or weapons. A soldier's clothing is his uniform.

Articles of adornment

See Jewelry.

Assessment benefits

See Stipulated insurance.

Avails

Any amount available to the owner of an insurance policy other than the actual proceeds of the policy. Avails include dividend payments, interest, cash or surrender value (the money you'd get if you sold your policy back to the insurance company) and loan value (the amount of cash you can borrow against the policy).

Benefit or benevolent society benefits

See Fraternal benefit society benefits.

Building materials

Items such as lumber, brick, stone, iron, paint and varnish used to build or improve a structure.

Burial plot

Cemetery plot.

Clothing

The everyday clothes needed by you and your family for work, school, household use and protection from the elements. In many states luxury items and furs are not exempt.

Condo

Condominium, a form of housing in which multiple units are constructed on a commonly owned piece of land, but each unit is individually owned. The common areas (lobby, hallways, stairways, etc.) are jointly owned by the unit owners and managed by an owners' association.

Co-op

Cooperative housing. Cooperative housing involves a group of people forming a corporation to own a residential building; stockholders are entitled to live in certain dwelling units.

Cooperative insurance

Compulsory employment benefits provided by a state or federal government, such as Old Age, Survivors, Disability and Health Insurance, to assure a minimum standard of living for lower and middle income people. Also called social insurance.

Credit insurance

Insurance taken to cover a borrower for an outstanding loan. If the borrower dies or becomes disabled before paying off the loan, the policy will pay off the balance due.

Crops

All products of the soil or earth that are grown and raised annually and gathered in a single season. Thus, oranges (on the tree or harvested) are crops; an orange tree isn't.

Disability benefits

Payments made under a disability insurance plan (or a retirement plan) when the insured (or employee) is unable to work (or retires early) because of disability, accident or sickness.

Domestic animals

See Animals.

Doubling

The ability of married couples to double the amount of an exemption for certain property when filing for bankruptcy together. The federal bankruptcy exemptions allow doubling. State laws vary — some permit and some prohibit doubling. Check Appendix 1, *State and Federal Exemption Tables*, for the doubling rules in your state.

Endowment insurance

Provides that an insured who lives the specified endowment period receives the face value (the amount paid at death). If the insured dies sooner, the beneficiary named in the policy receives the proceeds.

ERISA-qualified benefits

ERISA (Employee Retirement Income Security Act), a federal law governing pensions, provides benefits to employers and rights to employees. Pensions must meet certain requirements to qualify for ERISA coverage. Many private pensions, including Keoghs and IRAs, qualify.

Farm tools

Tools used by a person whose primary occupation is farming. Some states limit farm tools of the trade to items which can be held in the hand: hoes, axes, pitchforks, shovels, scythes and the like. In other states, farm tools also include plows, harnesses, mowers, reapers, etc. To determine which definition applies in your state, read your state statute, noted in your state exemption chart.

Fraternal benefit society benefits

Benefits, often group life insurance, paid for by fraternal societies, such as the Elks, Masons, Knights of Columbus or the Knights of Maccabees, to their members. Also called benefit society, benevolent society or mutual aid association benefits.

Furnishings

Furniture, fixtures in your home, such as a heating unit, furnace or built-in lighting, and other items with which a home is furnished (e.g., carpets and drapes).

Goods & chattels

Same as Personal property.

Group life or group health insurance

A single policy under which individuals in a group (for example, employees) and their dependents are covered.

Head of family or head of household

A person who supports and maintains, in one household, one or more people who are closely related to him by blood, marriage or adoption.

Health aids

Items needed to maintain their owner's health, such as a wheelchair, crutches, prosthesis and hearing aid. Many states require that health aids be prescribed by a physician.

Health benefits

Benefits paid under health insurance plans, such as Blue Cross/Blue Shield, to cover the costs of health care.

Heirloom

An item with special monetary or sentimental value passed from generation to generation.

Homestead

An exemption that protects up to a specified value (or specified number of acres) in a home from being taken to satisfy creditors. *See* Ch. 6, *Your House.*

Homestead declaration

A form filed with the county recorder's office to put on record your right to a homestead exemption.

Household good

An item of permanent nature (as opposed to items consumed, like food or cosmetics) used in or about the house. It includes linens, dinnerware, utensils, pots and pans and small electronic equipment like radios.

Householder or housekeeper

A person who supports and maintains a household, with or without other people.

Implement

An instrument, tool or utensil used by a person to accomplish her job.

In lieu of homestead (or burial) exemption

This means that the given exemption is available only if you don't claim the homestead (or burial) exemption.

Intangible personal property

See Intangible property.

Intangible property

Property that has no physical existence such as stocks, bonds, notes, franchises, goodwill, trade secrets, patents, copyrights and trademarks. Some intangible items may be represented by a certificate, but it represents the value of the property and isn't the property itself.

Jewelry

Items created for personal adornment; usually includes watches. Also called articles of adornment.

Life estate

The right to live in, but not own, a specific home until your death.

Life insurance

Provides for the payment of money to an individual (called the beneficiary) in the event of the death of another (called the insured). If the insured is alive, the policy is unmatured; when the insured dies, the policy matures.

Life insurance avails

See Avails.

Liquid assets

Cash or an item easily convertible into cash, such as a money market account, stocks, U.S. Treasury bill or bank deposit.

Lost earnings payments or recoveries

See Lost future earnings.

Lost future earnings

The portion of a lawsuit judgment intended to pay an injured person the equivalent of the future earnings lost because of the injury. Also called lost earnings payments or recoveries.

Matured life insurance benefits

Benefits currently payable because of the death of the insured.

Motor vehicle

A self-propelled vehicle suitable for use on a street or road. It includes a car, truck, motorcycle, van and moped. *See also* Tools of the trade.

Musical instrument

An instrument having the capacity, in and of itself, when properly operated, to produce a musical sound. Pianos, guitars, drums, drum machines, synthesizers and harmonicas are musical instruments.

Mutual aid association benefits
See Fraternal benefit society benefits.

Mutual assessment or mutual life
See Stipulated insurance.

Necessities
Articles needed to sustain life, such as food, clothing, medical care and shelter.

Pain and suffering damages
The portion of a court judgment intended to compensate for past, present and future mental and physical pain, suffering, impairment of ability to work, anxiety about the injury, and mental distress caused by an injury.

Pension
A fund into which payments are made to provide an employee income after retirement.

Personal injury cause of action
The right to seek compensation for physical and mental suffering, including injury to body, reputation or both.
EXAMPLE: Joyce is hit by a car while crossing the street. Her right to sue the driver (and anyone else who might be responsible) for her injuries is a personal injury cause of action.

Personal injury recovery
The amount that comes from a lawsuit or insurance settlement to compensate someone for physical and mental suffering, including physical injury, injury to reputation or both. Bankruptcy exemptions usually do not apply to compensation for pain or suffering or punitive damages.

Personal property
All property not classified as real property (land, and structures permanently attached to the land). Examples: money, stocks, furniture, cars, bank accounts, pensions, jewelry, oil paintings and patents.

Pets
See Animals.

Proceeds for damaged exempt property
The money collected through insurance, arbitration, mediation, settlement or a lawsuit to pay for exempt property that's no longer exemptible because it has been damaged or destroyed.
EXAMPLE: Hiro, who lives in Hawaii, planned to exempt the equity in his family's home under Hawaii's exemption ($30,000). Right before filing, however, a fire destroyed his house. Rather than claim his home's equity, Hiro now will claim as exempt $30,000 of the insurance proceeds he'll be paid from his insurance company.

Property of business partnership
A partnership's business property having the following characteristics:
- Each partner has a right to possess the property for partnership purposes, but has no right to possess it for any other purpose without consent of the partners.
- At a partner's death, his share of the partnership property passes to the surviving partners.
- The property isn't subject to state non-partnership property laws such as dower, curtesy, spouse's share or inheritance.

Sickness benefits
See Disability benefits.

Stipulated insurance
An insurance policy that allows the insurance company to assess an amount on the insured, above the standard premium payments, if the company experiences losses worse than had been calculated into the standard premium. Also called assessment, mutual assessment or mutual life insurance.

Surrender value
See Avails.

Tangible personal property
See Tangible property and Personal property.

Tangible property

Property that may be felt or touched. Examples: money, furniture, cars, jewelry, artwork and houses. Compare Intangible property.

Tenancy by the entirety

A property ownership form available only to married couples in certain states. Each spouse may possess and enjoy the property, and when one spouse dies, his share goes automatically to the survivor. Most states that exempt tenancy by the entirety property allow the exemption only against debts incurred by one spouse. If a spouse tries to discharge jointly incurred marital debts, the tenancy by the entirety property loses its exempt status.

To ___ acres

The designation "to ___ acres" (for example, "to 160 acres") is a limitation on the size of a homestead that may be exempted.

Tools of the trade

Items needed to perform a line of work that you are currently doing and relying on for support. For a mechanic, plumber or carpenter, tools of trade are the implements used to repair, build and install. For a doctor, tools of trade are the items found in the doctor's office and bag. For a clergyperson, tools of trade often consist of no more than books. Traditionally, tools of the trade were limited to items that could be held in the hand. Most states, however, now embrace a broader definition and a debtor may be able to fit many items under a tool of trade exemption. The following list shows examples of what a creative debtor may exempt. This list isn't meant to be a specific guideline, as each state's law differs. At the same time, this list isn't exhaustive; use your imagination.

- Art camera, scanner (artist)
- Car, truck or van that is used for more than just commuting (sales manager, insurance adjuster, physician, firewood salesperson, traveling salesperson, real estate salesperson, mechanic)
- Cream separator, dairy cows, animal feed (farmer)
- Drills, saws (carpenter)
- Electric motor & lathe (mechanic)
- Guitar, acoustic amplifier, coronet, violin & bow, organ, speaker cabinet (musician)
- Hair dye, shampoo, cash register, furniture, dryer, fan, curler, magazine rack (barber, beauty parlor operator)
- Oven & mixer (baker)
- Personal computer & printer (insurance salesperson, lawyer, accountant)
- Photographic lens (photographer)
- Power chain saw (firewood salesperson)
- Sewing machine (tailor)
- Truck (logger, tire retreader, truck driver, farmer, electrician).

Unmatured life insurance

A policy whose benefits aren't yet payable because the insured is still alive.

Weekly net earnings

The earnings left after mandatory deductions such as income tax, mandatory union dues and Social Security contributions have been subtracted from an employee's gross income.

Wildcard exemption

An exemption that you may apply toward the property of your choice. Some states limit the exemption to personal property; others include any property, real or personal. In nearly all states, you can apply the exemption to nonexempt property (such as expensive jewelry or clothes) or use it to increase the amount for an already partially exempt item. For example, if your state has no specific motor vehicle exemption but does have a wildcard exemption, you can use the wildcard exemption to exempt the car. If your state has a specific motor vehicle exemption, but the amount is limited, you can use the wildcard exemption to increase the exempt amount.

Wrongful death cause of action

The right to seek compensation for having to live without a deceased person. Usually only the spouse and children of the deceased have a wrongful death cause of action.

EXAMPLE: Joyce is killed by a speeding car while crossing the street. Her husband and children's right to sue the driver (and anyone else who might be responsible) for her death is a wrongful death cause of action.

Wrongful death recoveries

The portion of a lawsuit judgment intended to compensate a plaintiff for having to live without a deceased person. The compensation's intended to cover the earnings and the emotional comfort and support the deceased would have provided. ■

APPENDIX

3

Addresses of Bankruptcy Courts

Alabama

Northern District of Alabama
Eastern Division
103 Federal Court House
12th and Noble Streets
Anniston, AL 36202
256-741-1500 (voice)
www.alnb.uscourts.gov

Northern District of Alabama
Birmingham Division
1800 5th Avenue North, Room 120
Birmingham, AL 35203-2111
205-714-4000
www.alnb.uscourts.gov

Northern District of Alabama
Northern Division
P.O. Box 2748
Decatur, AL 35602
256-353-2817 (voice)
www.alnb.uscourts.gov

Northern District of Alabama
Western Division
1118 Greensboro Avenue
P.O. Box 3226
Tuscaloosa, AL 35401
205-752-0426 (voice)
205-752-6468 (fax)
www.alnb.uscourts.gov

Southern District of Alabama
201 St. Louis Street
Mobile, AL 36602
334-441-5391 (voice)
334-441-5612 (fax)
www.alsb.uscourts.gov

Middle District of Alabama
Montgomery Division
One Court Square, Room 127
Montgomery, AL 36102
334-206-6300 (voice)
334-206-6374 (fax)
www.almb.uscourts.gov

Alaska

District of Alaska
Historical Courthouse
605 West Fourth Avenue, Room 138
Anchorage, AK 99501-2296
907-271-2655 (voice)
907-271-2645 (fax)
www.akb.uscourts.gov

District of Alaska
U.S. Courthouse
101 12th Avenue, Room 370
Fairbanks, AK
907-456-0349
www.akb.uscourts.gov

District of Alaska
U.S. District Court
709 W. 9th Avenue, Room 979
Juneau, AK 99802
907-586-7458
www.akb.uscourts.gov
(This court forwards bankruptcy
filings to Anchorage for processing.)

District of Alaska
648 Mission Street, Room 507
Ketchikan, AK 99901
907-247-7576
www.akb.uscourts.gov

District of Alaska
U.S. District Court
Front Street
P.O. Box 130
Nome, AK 99762
907-443-5216 (voice)
www.akb.uscourts.gov

Arizona

District of Arizona
Phoenix Division
2929 North Central Avenue
Ninth Floor
P.O. Box 34151
Phoenix, AZ 85067-4151
602-640-5800 (voice)
602-640-5846 (fax)
www.azb.uscourts.gov

District of Arizona
Tucson Division
110 South Church Street
Room 8-112
Tucson, AZ 85702
520-620-7500 (voice)
520-620-7457 (fax)
www.azb.uscourts.gov

District of Arizona
Yuma Division
325 W. 19th St., Suite D
Yuma, AZ 85364
520-783-2288
www.azb.uscourts.gov

Arkansas

Western and Eastern Districts
300 West 2nd Street
P.O. Box 3777
Little Rock, AR 72201
501-918-5500
www.arb.uscourts.gov

California

Eastern District of California
Fresno Division
1130 O Street, Suite 2656
Fresno, CA 93721
559-498-7217 (voice)
www.caeb.uscourts.gov

Central District of California
Los Angeles Division
Federal Building
300 N. Los Angeles Street
Los Angeles, CA 90012
213-894-3118 (voice)
213-894-0225 (fax)
www.cacb.uscourts.gov

Eastern District of California
Modesto Division
1130 Twelfth Street, Room C
Modesto, CA 95352
209-521-5160 (voice)
www.caeb.uscourts.gov

Northern District of California
Oakland Division
P.O. Box 2070
Oakland, CA 94604-2070
510-879-3600 (voice)
www.canb.uscourts.gov

Eastern District of California
Sacramento Division
501 I Street, Suite 3-200
Sacramento, CA 95814
916-930-4400 (voice)
916-498-5469 (fax)
www.caeb.uscourts.gov

Central District of California
San Bernardino Division
3420 12th Street
Riverside, CA 92501-3819
909-774-1000 (voice)
www.cacb.uscourts.gov

Southern District of California
325 West "F" Street
San Diego, CA 92101-6998
619-557-5620 (voice)
619-557-2646 (fax)
www.casb.uscourts.gov

Central District of California
San Fernando Division
21041 Burbank Boulevard
Woodland Hills, CA 91367
818-587-2900 (voice)
www.cacb.uscourts.gov

Northern District of California
San Francisco Division
P.O. Box 7341
235 Pine Street, 19th Floor
San Francisco, CA 94120-7341
415-268-2300 (voice)
www.canb.uscourts.gov

Northern District of California
San Jose Division
280 South First Street, Room 3035
San Jose, CA 95113-3099
408-535-5118 (voice)
www.canb.uscourts.gov

Central District of California
Santa Ana Division
U.S. Courthouse
411 West Fourth Street
Santa Ana, CA 92701
714-338-5300 (voice)
www.cacb.uscourts.gov

Central District of California
Santa Barbara Division
1415 State Street
Santa Barbara, CA 93101
805-884-4800 (voice)
www.cacb.uscourts.gov

Northern District of California
Santa Rosa Division
99 South E Street
Santa Rosa, CA 95404
707-525-8539 (voice)
www.canb.uscourts.gov

Colorado

District of Colorado
U.S. Customs House
721 – 19th Street
Denver, CO 80202-2508
303-844-4045 (voice)
888-213-4715 (toll free)
www.cob.uscourts.gov/bindex.htm

Connecticut

District of Connecticut
915 Lafayette Boulevard
Bridgeport, CT 06604
203-579-5808 (voice)
www.ctb.uscourts.gov

District of Connecticut
Hartford Division
450 Main Street
Hartford, CT 06103
860-240-3675 (voice)
www.ctb.uscourts.gov

District of Connecticut
157 Church Street
New Haven, CT 06510
203-773-2009 (voice)

Delaware

District of Delaware
824 Market Street, Fifth Floor
Wilmington, DE 19801
302-252-2900 (voice)
www.deb.uscourts.gov/general.htm

District of Columbia

District of Columbia
D.C. Division
333 Constitution Avenue, NW
Washington, DC 20001
202-273-0042 (voice)
www.dcb.uscourts.gov

Florida

Middle District
2110 First Street
Fort Myers, FL 33901
www.flmb.uscourts.gov
(Cases filed and maintained in
Tampa court.)

Middle District of Florida
Jacksonville Division
311 West Monroe Street, Room 206
Jacksonville, FL 32202
904-232-2852 (voice)
www.flmb.uscourts.gov

Southern District of Florida
Miami Division
51 Southwest First Avenue, Rm 1517
Miami, FL 33130
305-536-5216 (voice)

Middle District of Florida
Orlando Division
135 West Central Boulevard, Rm 960
Orlando, FL 32801
407-648-6365 (voice)
www.flmb.uscourts.gov

Northern District of Florida
227 North Bronough Street
Suite 3120
Tallahassee, FL 32301-1378
850-942-8933 (voice)

Middle District of Florida
801 N. Florida Avenue
Tampa, FL 33602
813-301-5134 (voice)
www.flmb.uscourts.gov

Southern District of Florida
West Palm Beach Division
701 Clematis Street, Room 202
West Palm Beach, FL 33401
561-665-6774 (voice)

Georgia

Northern District of Georgia
75 Spring Street Southwest, Room 1340
Atlanta, GA 30303
404-215-1000 (voice)
404-730-2216 (fax)
www.ganb.uscourts.gov

Southern District of Georgia
Augusta Division
500 Ford St.
Augusta, GA 30901
706-724-2421 (voice)

Middle District of Georgia
P.O. Box 1957
433 Cherry Street
Macon, GA 31202
912-752-3506 (voice)
912-752-8157 (fax)
www.gamb.uscourts.gov

Northern District of Georgia
Newnan Division
18 Greenville Street
Newnan, GA 30264
770-251-5583 (voice)
www.ganb.uscourts.gov

Northern District of Georgia
Rome Division
600 E. First Street
Rome, GA 30161-3187
706-291-5639 (voice)
www.ganb.uscourts.gov

Southern District of Georgia
125 Bull Street
Savannah, GA 31401
912-650-4100 (voice)
www.gasb.uscourts.gov

Hawaii

1132 Bishop Street, Suite 250-L
Honolulu, HI 96813
808-522-8100 (voice)
808-522-8120 (fax)
www.hib.uscourts.gov

Idaho

District of Idaho
550 West Fort Street
MSC 042
Boise, ID 83724
208-334-1074 (voice)
208-334-1361 (fax)
www.id.uscourts.gov

Northern Division
205 North 4th Street, Room 202
Coeur d'Alene, ID 83814
208-664-4925 (voice)
208-765-0270 (fax)
www.id.uscourts.gov

Northern Division
220 E. 5th Street, Room 304
Moscow, ID 83843
208-882-7612 (voice)
208-883-1576 (fax)
www.id.uscourts.gov

Eastern Division
801 E. Sherman St.
Pocatello, ID 83201
208-478-4123 (voice)
208-478-4106 (fax)
www.id.uscourts.gov

Illinois

Northern District of Illinois
Eastern Division
219 South Dearborn Street
Chicago, IL 60604
312-435-5694 (voice)
312-408-7750 (fax)
www.ilnb.uscourts.gov

Central District of Illinois
Danville Division
201 N. Vermillion Street
Danville, IL 61832
217-431-4820 (voice)
217-431-2694 (fax)
www.ilcb.uscourts.gov

Southern District of Illinois
750 Missouri Avenue, 1st Floor
East St. Louis, IL 62201
618-482-9400 (voice)
www.ilsb.uscourts.gov

Central District of Illinois
Peoria Division
100 Northeast Monroe Street
1st Floor, Room 131
Peoria, IL 61602
309-671-7035 (voice)
309-671-7076 (fax)
www.ilcb.uscourts.gov

Northern District of Illinois
Western Division
211 South Court Street, Room 110
Rockford, IL 61101
815-987-4350 (voice)
815-987-4205 (fax)
www.ilnb.uscourts.gov

Central District of Illinois
600 East Monroe Street, Room 226
Springfield, IL 62701
217-492-4551 (voice)
www.ilcb.uscourts.gov

Indiana

Southern District of Indiana
Evansville Division
352 Federal Building
101 NW MLK Boulevard
Evansville, IN 47708
812-465-6440 (voice)
812-465-6453 (fax)
www.insb.uscourts.gov

Northern District of Indiana
Fort Wayne Division
1300 South Harrison Street
Fort Wayne, IN 46802
Mailing Address
P.O. Box 2547
Fort Wayne, IN 46801-2547
260-420-5100 (voice)
260-422-1668 (fax)
www.innb.uscourts.gov

Northern District of Indiana
Gary Division
610 Connecticut Street
Gary, IN 46402-2595
219-881-3335 (voice)
219-881-3307 (fax)
www.innb.uscourts.gov

Northern District of Indiana
South Bend Division
401 South Michigan Street
South Bend, IN 46601
Mailing Address
P.O. Box 7003
South Bend, IN 46634-7003
574-968-2100 (voice)
574-968-2205 (fax)
www.innb.uscourts.gov

Southern District of Indiana
Indianapolis Division
116 U.S. Courthouse
46 East Ohio Street
Indianapolis, IN 46204
317-229-3800 (voice)
317-229-3801 (fax)
www.insb.uscourts.gov

Southern District of Indiana
New Albany Division
110 U.S. Courthouse
121 West Spring Street
New Albany, IN 47150
812-948-5254 (voice)
812-948-5262 (fax)
www.insb.uscourts.gov

Iowa

Northern District of Iowa
P.O. Box 74890
425 Second Street, Southeast
Cedar Rapids, IA 52407
319-286-2200 (voice)
319-286-2280 (fax)
www.ianb.uscourts.gov/index.asp

Southern District of Iowa
P.O. Box 9264
Des Moines, IA 50306
515-284-6230 (voice)
515-284-6418 (fax)
www.iasb.uscourts.gov/asp/home/
default.asp

Northern District of Iowa
Sioux City Division
Federal Building
320 Sixth Street, Room 117
Sioux City, IA 51101
Mailing Address
P.O. Box 3857
Sioux City, IA 51102-3857
712-233-3939 (voice)
712-233-3942 (fax)
www.ianb.uscourts.gov/index.asp

Kansas

District of Kansas
Kansas City Division
161 U.S. Courthouse
500 State Avenue
Kansas City, KS 66101
913-551-6732 (voice)
www.ksb.uscourts.gov

District of Kansas
Topeka Division
240 U.S. Courthouse
444 Southeast Quincy Street
Topeka, KS 66683
785-295-2750 (voice)
www.ksb.uscourts.gov

District of Kansas
Wichita Division
167 U.S. Courthouse
401 North Market Street
Wichita, KS 67202
316-269-6486 (voice)
316-269-6181 (fax)

Kentucky

Eastern District of Kentucky
100 East Vine Street, Suite 200
Lexington, KY 40507
Mailing Address
Box 1111
Lexington, KY 40588-1111
859-233-2608 (voice)
www.kyeb.uscourts.gov

Western District of Kentucky
601 W. Broadway, Suite 546
Snyder Courthouse
Louisville, KY 40202
502-627-5700 (voice)
502-627-5710 (fax)
www.kywb.uscourts.gov/fpweb/
louisville.htm

Louisiana

Western District of Louisiana
Alexandria Division
300 Jackson Street, Suite 116
Alexandria, LA 71301
318-445-1890 (voice)
www.lawb.uscourts.gov

Middle District of Louisiana
707 Florida Street, Suite 119
Baton Rouge, LA 70801
225-389-0211 (voice)
225-389-3501 (fax)
www.lamb.uscourts.gov

Eastern District of Louisiana
501 Magazine Street, Room 601
New Orleans, LA 70130
504-589-7878 (voice)
504-589-2076 (fax)
www.laeb.uscourts.gov

Western District of Louisiana
Lafayette-Opelousas Division
231 South Union Street, 2nd Floor
Opelousas, LA 70570
337-948-3451 (voice)
www.lawb.uscourts.gov

Western District of Louisiana
300 Fannin Street, Suite 2201
Shreveport, LA 71101
318-676-4267 (voice)
www.lawb.uscourts.gov

Maine

District of Maine
P.O. Box 1109
300 U.S. Courthouse
202 Harlow Street, 3rd Floor
Bangor, ME 04401-1109
207-945-0348 (voice)
207-945-0304 (fax)
www.meb.uscourts.gov

District of Maine
537 Congress Street, Second Floor
Portland, ME 04101-0048
Mailing Address
P.O. Box 17575
Portland, ME 04112-8575
207-780-3482 (voice)
207-780-3679 (fax)
www.meb.uscourts.gov

Maryland

District of Maryland
Baltimore Division
U.S. Courthouse
101 West Lombard Street, Suite 8308
Baltimore, MD 21201
410-962-2688 (voice)
410-942-9319 (fax)
www.mdb.uscourts.gov

District of Maryland
6500 Cherry Wood Lane
Room 300
Greenbelt, MD 20770
301-344-8018 (voice)
301-344-0415 (fax)
www.mdb.uscourts.gov

Massachusetts

District of Massachusetts
Eastern Division
1101 Thomas P. O'Neill
Federal Building
10 Causeway Street
Boston, MA 02222
617-565-8950 (voice)
617-565-6650 (fax)
www.mab.uscourts.gov

District of Massachusetts
Barnstable Town Hall
376 Main Street
Hyannis, MA 02601-3917
617-565-6073 (voice)
www.mab.uscourts.gov
(Pleadings must be filed in the
Boston court.)

District of Massachusetts
Federal Building and Courthouse
1550 Main Street
Springfield, MA 01103
508-770-8936 (voice)
www.mab.uscourts.gov
(Pleadings must be filed in the
Worcester court.)

District of Massachusetts
Western Division
Harold Donahue Federal Building
595 Main Street, Second Floor
Worcester, MA 01608-2076
508-770-8900 (voice)
508-793-0189 (fax)
www.mab.uscourts.gov

Michigan

Eastern District of Michigan
Bay City Division
111 First Street
Bay City, MI 48707
989-894-8840 (voice)
www.mieb.uscourts.gov/index1.html

Eastern District of Michigan
1060 Federal Building
211 West Fort Street
Detroit, MI 48226
313-234-0065 (voice)
313-234-5399 (fax)
www.mieb.uscourts.gov/index1.html

Eastern District of Michigan
Flint Division
226 West Second Street
Flint, MI 48502
810-235-4126 (voice)
www.mieb.uscourts.gov/index1.html

Western District of Michigan
Southern Division
Ford Federal Building
110 Michigan Street Northwest, Rm 299
Grand Rapids, MI 49501
Mailing Address
P.O. Box 3310
Grand Rapids, MI 49501
616-456-2693 (voice)
www.miwb.uscourts.gov

Western District of Michigan
Marquette Division
202 West Washington Street
3rd Floor
Marquette, MI 49855
Mailing Address
P.O. Box 909
Marquette, MI 49855
906-226-2117 (voice)
www.miw.uscourts.gov

Minnesota

District of Minnesota
Duluth Division
416 U.S. Courthouse
515 West First Street
Duluth, MN 55802
218-529-3600 (voice)
www.mnb.uscourts.gov

District of Minnesota
Fergus Falls Office
204 U.S. Courthouse
118 South Mill Street
Fergus Falls, MN 56537
218-739-4671 (voice)
www.mnb.uscourts.gov

District of Minnesota
301 U.S. Courthouse
300 South Fourth Street
Minneapolis, MN 55415
612-664-5200 (voice)
612-664-5303 (fax)
612-664-5301 (TTY)
www.mnb.uscourts.gov

District of Minnesota
St. Paul Division
200 U.S. Courthouse
316 North Robert Street
St. Paul, MN 55101
651-848-1000 (voice)
www.mnb.uscourts.gov

Mississippi

Northern District of Mississippi
P.O. Drawer 867
205 Federal Building
301 W. Commerce Building
Aberdeen, MS 39730-0867
662-369-2596 (voice)
www.msnb.uscourts.gov

Southern District of Mississippi
725 Lashington Loop, Suite 117
Biloxi, MS 39530
601-432-5542 (voice)

Southern District of Mississippi
100 E. Capital Street
Jackson, MS 39201
Mailing Address
P.O. Drawer 2448
Jackson, MS 39225
601-965-5301 (voice)

Missouri

Western District of Missouri
400 E. 9th Street, Room 1800
Kansas City, MO 64106
816-512-1800 (voice)

Eastern District of Missouri
Thomas F. Eagleton U.S. Courthouse
111 South 10th St., Fourth Floor
St. Louis, MO 63102
314-244-4500 (voice)
314-244-4990 (fax)
www.moeb.uscourts.gov

Montana

District of Montana
400 North Main Street
Butte, MT 59701
406-782-9878 (voice)
406-782-0537 (fax)
www.mtb.uscourts.gov

Nebraska

District of Nebraska
111 South 18th Plaza, Suite 1125
Omaha, NE 68102
402-661-7444 (voice)
402-661-7441 (fax)
www.neb.uscourts.gov

District of Nebraska
460 Federal Building
100 Centennial Mall North
Lincoln, NE 68508
402-437-5100 (voice)
402-437-5454 (fax)

Nevada

District of Nevada
300 Las Vegas Boulevard South
Room 2130
Las Vegas, NV 89101
702-388-6257 (voice)
www.nvb.uscourts.gov

District of Nevada
300 Booth Street, Room 1109
Reno, NV 89509
702-784-5559 (voice)
www.nvb.uscourts.gov

New Hampshire

District of New Hampshire
275 Chestnut Street, Room 404
Manchester, NH 03101
603-222-2600 (voice)
603-666-7408 (fax)
www.nhb.uscourts.gov

New Jersey

District of New Jersey
Camden Division
401 Market Street, Second Floor
Camden, NJ 08102-1104
856-757-5485 (voice)
www.njb.uscourts.gov

District of New Jersey
Newark Division
50 Walnut Street
Newark, NJ 07102
973-645-4764 (voice)
www.njb.uscourts.gov

District of New Jersey
Trenton Division
U.S. Courthouse
402 East State Street
Trenton, NJ 08608
609-989-2129 (voice)
609-989-0580 (fax)
www.njb.uscourts.gov

New Mexico

District of New Mexico
421 Gold Avenue Southwest, Rm 316
Albuquerque, NM 87102
Mailing Address
P.O. Box 546
Albuquerque, NM 87103
505-348-2500 (voice)
505-348-6521 (fax)
www.nmcourt.fed.us/bkdocs

New York

Northern District of New York
445 Broadway, Suite 330
James T. Foley Courthouse
Albany, NY 12207
518-257-1661 (voice)
www.nynb.uscourts.gov

Eastern District of New York
U.S. Courthouse
225 Cadman Plaza East
Brooklyn, NY 11201
718-330-2188 (voice)
718-330-2833 (fax)

Western District of New York
Olympic Towers
300 Pearl Street, Suite 250
Buffalo, NY 14202-2501
716-551-4130 (voice)
www.nywb.uscourts.gov

Southern District of New York
Alexander Hamilton Custom House
One Bowling Green
New York, NY 10004-1408
212-668-2870 (voice)
www.nysb.uscourts.gov

Western District of New York
Rochester Division
1220 U.S. Courthouse
100 State Street
Rochester, NY 14614
716-263-3148 (voice)

Northern District of New York
Utica Division
Alexander Pirnie U.S. Court House
10 Broad Street, Room 230
Utica, NY 13502
315-793-8101 (voice)
www.nynb.uscourts.gov

Southern District of New York
White Plains Division
300 Quarropas Street
White Plains, NY 10601-4150
914-390-4100 (voice)
www.nysb.uscourts.gov

North Carolina

Western District of North Carolina
Jonas Federal Building
401 West Trade Street, Room 111
Charlotte, NC 28202
Mailing Address
P.O. Box 34189
Charlotte, NC 28234-4189
704-350-7500 (voice)
704-344-6403 (fax)
www.ncwb.uscourts.gov

Middle District of North Carolina
101 S. Edgeworth Street,
Greensboro, NC 27401
Mailing Address
P.O. Box 26100
Greensboro, NC 27420-6100
336-333-5647 (voice)
www.ncmb.uscourts.gov

Eastern District of North Carolina
P.O. Box 2807
1760 Parkwood Boulevard
Wilson, NC 27894-2807
252-237-0248 (voice)
www.nceb.uscourts.gov

North Dakota

District of North Dakota
655 First Avenue North, Suite 210
Fargo, ND 58102-4932
701-297-7100 (voice)
701-297-7105 (fax)
www.ndb.uscourts.gov

Ohio

Northern District of Ohio
Akron Division
455 U.S. Courthouse
Two South Main Street
Akron, OH 44308
330-375-5840 (voice)
www.ohnb.uscourts.gov

Northern District of Ohio
Canton Division
107 Frank T. Bow Federal Building
201 Cleveland Avenue Southwest
Canton, OH 44702-1929
330-489-4426 (voice)
www.ohnb.uscourts.gov

Southern District of Ohio
Western Division
Atrium Two, Room 800
221 East Fourth Street
Cincinnati, OH 45202
513-684-2572 (voice)
www.ohsb.uscourts.gov

Northern District of Ohio
Key Tower, Room 3001
127 Public Square
Cleveland, OH 44114-1309
216-522-4373 (voice)
www.ohnb.uscourts.gov

Southern District of Ohio
Eastern Division
170 N. High Street
Columbus, OH 43215
614-469-6638 (voice)

Southern District of Ohio
Western Division
120 W. Third Street
Dayton, OH 45402
937-225-2516 (voice)
937-225-2954 (voice)

Northern District of Ohio
Toledo Division
411 U.S. Courthouse
1716 Spielbusch Avenue
Toledo, OH 43624
419-259-6440 (voice)
www.ohnb.uscourts.gov

Northern District of Ohio
Youngstown Division
Federal Building
125 Market Street
Youngstown, OH 44501
330-746-7027 (voice)
www.ohnb.uscourts.gov

Oklahoma

Western District of Oklahoma
Old Post Office Building
Seventh Floor
215 Dean A. McGee Avenue
Oklahoma City, OK 73102
405-231-5642 (voice)

Eastern District of Oklahoma
P.O. Box 1347
111 West 4th Street
Okmulgee, OK 74446
918-758-0127 (voice)
918-756-9248 (fax)
www.okeb.uscourts.gov

Northern District of Oklahoma
224 S. Boulder, Room 122
Tulsa, OK 74103-4217
918-581-7181 (voice)
www.oknb.uscourts.gov

Oregon

District of Oregon
1001 Southwest Fifth Avenue
Room 700
Portland, OR 97204
503-326-2231 (voice)
www.orb.uscourts.gov

Pennsylvania

Western District of Pennsylvania
Erie Division
717 State Street, Suite 501
Erie, PA 16501
814-453-7580 (voice)
814-453-3795 (fax)
www.pawb.uscourts.gov

Middle District of Pennsylvania
Harrisburg Division
P.O. Box 908
320 Federal Bldg.
228 Walnut Street
Harrisburg, PA 17101-0908
717-901-2800 (voice)
717-901-2822 (fax)
www.pamb.uscourts.gov

Eastern District of Pennsylvania
900 Market Street, Suite 400
Philadelphia, PA 19107
215-408-2800 (voice)
www.paeb.uscourts.gov

Western District of Pennsylvania
5414 U.S. Tower
600 Grant Street
Pittsburgh, PA 15219
412-644-2700 (voice)
412-644-6512 (fax)
www.pawb.uscourts.gov

Eastern District of Pennsylvania
Reading Division
The Madison Building, Suite 300
400 Washington Street
Reading, PA 19601-3915
610-320-5255 (voice)
www.paeb.uscourts.gov

Middle District of Pennsylvania
Wilkes-Barre Division
Federal Building
197 South Main Street, Suite 161
Wilkes-Barre, PA 18701
570-826-6450 (voice)
www.pamb.uscourts.gov

Rhode Island

District of Rhode Island
380 Westminster Street, 6th Floor
Providence, RI 02903
401-528-4477 (voice)
401-528-4089 (fax)
www.rib.uscourts.gov

South Carolina

District of South Carolina
P.O. Box 1448
1100 Laurel Street
Columbia, SC 29202
803-765-5436 (voice)
www.scb.uscourts.gov

South Dakota

District of South Dakota
Central Division
Federal Building
225 South Pierre Street, Room 210
Pierre, SD 57501
605-224-6013 (voice)
605-224-9808 (fax)
www.sdb.uscourts.gov

District of South Dakota
Western Division
515 9th Street, Room 318
Rapid City, SD 57701
605-343-6335 (voice)
605-343-4367 (fax)
www.sdb.uscourts.gov

District of South Dakota
Southern Division
U.S. Courthouse
400 South Phillips Avenue
Room 104
P.O. Box 5060
Sioux Falls, SD 57117-5060
605-330-4541 (voice)
605-330-4548 (fax)
www.sdb.uscourts.gov

Tennessee

Eastern District of Tennessee
Southern Division
Historic U.S. Courthouse 361
31 East 11th Street
Chattanooga, TN 37402-2722
423-752-5163 (voice)
www.tneb.uscourts.gov

Western District of Tennessee
Eastern Division
111 South Highland, Room 107
Jackson, TN 38301
901-421-9300 (voice)
www.tnwb.uscourts.gov

Eastern District of Tennessee
Knoxville Division
U.S. Courthouse
800 Market Street, Suite 330
Knoxville, TN 37902
865-545-4279 (voice)
www.tneb.uscourts.gov

Western District of Tennessee
Western Division
200 Jefferson Avenue, Suite 413
Memphis, TN 38103
901-328-3500 (voice)
www.tnwb.uscourts.gov

Middle District of Tennessee
701 Broadway
P.O. Box 24890
Nashville, TN 37203
615-736-5584 (voice)
615-736-2305 (fax)
www.tnmb.uscourts.gov

Texas

Western District of Texas
Austin Division
903 San Jacinto Boulevard, Suite 322
Austin, TX 78701
512-916-5248
512-916-5278 (fax)
www.txwb.uscourts.gov

Southern District of Texas
Corpus Christi Division
1133 N. Shoreline Blvd.
Corpus Christi, TX 78401
361-888-3483 (voice)
www.txsb.uscourts.gov

Northern District of Texas
U.S. Courthouse, 12th Floor
1100 Commerce Street
Dallas, TX 75242
214-753-2000 (voice)
214-767-3588 (fax)
www.txnb.uscourts.gov

Northern District of Texas
Fort Worth Division
501 West 10th Street, Room 147
Fort Worth, TX 76102
817-333-6000 (voice)
www.txnb.uscourts.gov

Southern District of Texas
P.O. Box 61010
Federal Building
515 Rusk Avenue
Houston, TX 77208-1010
713-250-5500 (voice)
713-250-5550 (fax)
www.txsb.uscourts.gov

Northern District of Texas
306 Federal Building
1205 Texas Avenue
Lubbock, TX 79401
806-472-5000 (voice)
www.txnb.uscourts.gov

Western District of Texas
Post Office Building Alamo Plaza
615 East Houston Street
P.O. Box 1439
San Antonio, TX 78295-1439
210-472-6720, ext. 228 (voice)
210-472-5196 (fax)
www.txwb.uscourts.gov

Eastern District of Texas
200 East Ferguson Street, Room 200
Tyler, TX 75702
903-590-1212 (voice)
www.txeb.uscourts.gov

Utah

District of Utah
U.S. Courthouse
350 South Main Street, Suite 301
Salt Lake City, UT 84101
801-524-6687 (voice)
801-524-4409 (fax)
www.utb.uscourts.gov

Vermont

District of Vermont
Opera House, Second Floor
67 Merchants Row
P.O. Box 6648
Rutland, VT 05702-6648
802-776-2000 (voice)
802-776-2020 (fax)
www.vtb.uscourts.gov

Virginia

Eastern District of Virginia
Alexandria Division
200 South Washington Street
P.O. Box 19247
Alexandria, VA 22320-0247
703-258-1200 (voice)
www.vaeb.uscourts.gov

Western District of Virginia
Harrisonburg Division
223 Federal Building
116 North Main Street
Harrisonburg, VA 22801
540-434-8327 (voice)
www.vawb.uscourts.gov

Western District of Virginia
Lynchburg Division
P.O. Box 6400
1100 Main Street, Room 226
Lynchburg, VA 24504
804-845-0317 (voice)
804-845-1801 (fax)
www.vawb.uscourts.gov

Eastern District of Virginia
Newport News Division
101 25th Street
P.O. Box 1938
Newport News, VA 23607
757-222-7500 (voice)
www.vaeb.uscourts.gov

Eastern District of Virginia
Norfolk Division
600 Granby Street, 4th Floor
Norfolk, VA 23510
757-222-7500 (voice)
www.vaeb.uscourts.gov

Eastern District of Virginia
Richmond Division
1100 East Main Street
Room 301
Richmond, VA 23219
804-916-2400 (voice)
www.vaeb.uscourts.gov

Western District of Virginia
Roanoke Division
210 Church Avenue, Southwest
Room 200
Roanoke, VA 24011
540-857-2391 (voice)
540-857-2873 (fax)
www.vawb.uscourts.gov

Washington

Western District of Washington
Park Place Building
1200 Sixth Avenue, Room 315
Seattle, WA 98101
206-553-7545 (voice)
206-553-0187 (fax)
www.wawb.uscourts.gov

Eastern District of Washington
P.O. Box 2164
904 West Riverside Avenue, Suite 304
Spokane, WA 92210-2164
509-353-2404 (voice)
509-353-2448 (fax)
www.waeb.uscourts.gov

Western District of Washington
Tacoma Division
1717 Pacific Avenue, Room 2100
Tacoma, WA 98402-3233
253-593-6310 (voice)
www.wawb.uscourts.gov

West Virginia

Southern District of West Virginia
P.O. Box 3924
Charleston, WV 25339
304-347-3000 (voice)
www.wvsd.uscourts.gov/bankruptcy/
    index.htm

Northern District of West Virginia
U.S. Post Office and Courthouse Bldg.
Twelfth and Chapline Streets, Rm 300
P.O. Box 70
Wheeling, WV 26003
304-233-1655 (voice)
304-233-0185 (fax)
www.wvnb.uscourts.gov

Wisconsin

Western District of Wisconsin
Eau Claire Division
500 South Barstow Street
P.O. Box 5009
Eau Claire, WI 54702
715-839-2980 (voice)
715-839-2996 (fax)
www.wiw.uscourts.gov/bankruptcy

Western District of Wisconsin
P.O. Box 548
120 North Henry Street
Room 340
Madison, WI 53703
608-264-5178 (voice)
608-264-5105 (fax)

Eastern District of Wisconsin
Milwaukee Division
126 U.S. Courthouse
517 East Wisconsin Avenue
Suite 126
Milwaukee, WI 53202
414-297-3291(voice)
www.wieb.uscourts.gov

Wyoming

District of Wyoming
111 South Wolcott Street
Casper, WY 82601
307-261-5444 (voice)
www.wyb.uscourts.gov

District of Wyoming
P.O. Box 1107
2120 Capitol Avenue
Cheyenne, WY 82001-1107
307-772-2191 (voice)
307-772-2298 (fax)
www.wyb.uscourts.gov

Tear-Out Forms

 Do not complete these forms until you have read the appropriate chapters in this book.

Personal Property Checklist

1. Cash on hand
- [ ] In your home
- [ ] In your wallet
- [ ] Under your mattress
- [ ] Stashed in your secret place

2. Checking/savings account, certificate of deposit, other bank accounts
- [ ] Checking accounts
- [ ] Savings accounts
- [ ] Brokerage accounts (with stockbroker)
- [ ] Certificates of deposit (CDs)
- [ ] Credit union account
- [ ] Escrow account
- [ ] Money market account
- [ ] Money in a safe deposit box
- [ ] Savings and loan account

3. Security deposits held by utility companies, landlord
- [ ] Electric
- [ ] Gas
- [ ] Heating oil
- [ ] Security deposit on a rental unit
- [ ] Prepaid rent
- [ ] Rented furniture or equipment
- [ ] Telephone

4. Household goods, furniture, including audio, video, and computer equipment
- [ ] Antiques
- [ ] Appliances
- [ ] Carpentry tools
- [ ] China and crystal
- [ ] Clocks
- [ ] Dishes
- [ ] Food (total value)
- [ ] Furniture
- [ ] Gardening tools
- [ ] Home computer (for personal use)
- [ ] Iron and ironing board
- [ ] Lamps
- [ ] Lawn mower or tractor
- [ ] Microwave oven
- [ ] Patio or outdoor furniture
- [ ] Radios
- [ ] Rugs
- [ ] Sewing machine
- [ ] Silverware and utensils
- [ ] Small appliances
- [ ] Snow blower
- [ ] Stereo system
- [ ] Telephone and answering machines
- [ ] Televisions
- [ ] Vacuum cleaner
- [ ] Video equipment (VCR, camcorder)

5. Books, pictures, art objects, records, compact discs, collectibles
- [ ] Art prints
- [ ] Bibles
- [ ] Books
- [ ] Coins
- [ ] Collectibles (such as political buttons, baseball cards)
- [ ] Family portraits
- [ ] Figurines
- [ ] Original art works
- [ ] Photographs
- [ ] Records, CDs, audiotapes
- [ ] Stamps
- [ ] Video tapes

6. Clothing

7. Furs and jewelry
- [ ] Furs
- [ ] Engagement and wedding rings
- [ ] Gems
- [ ] Precious metals
- [ ] Watches

8. Sports, photographic, hobby equipment, firearms
- [ ] Board games
- [ ] Bicycle
- [ ] Camera equipment
- [ ] Electronic musical equipment
- [ ] Exercise machine
- [ ] Fishing gear
- [ ] Guns (rifles, pistols, shotguns, muskets)
- [ ] Model or remote cars or planes
- [ ] Musical instruments
- [ ] Scuba diving equipment
- [ ] Ski equipment
- [ ] Other sports equipment
- [ ] Other weapons (swords and knives)

9. Interest in insurance policies—specify refund or cancellation value
- [ ] Credit insurance
- [ ] Disability insurance
- [ ] Health insurance
- [ ] Homeowner's or renter's insurance
- [ ] Term life insurance
- [ ] Whole life insurance

10. Annuities

11. Interests in pension or profit sharing plans
- [ ] IRA
- [ ] Keogh
- [ ] Pension or retirement plan
- [ ] 401(k) plan

12. Stock and interests in incorporated/unincorporated business

13. Interests in partnerships/joint ventures
- [ ] Limited partnership interest
- [ ] General partnership interest

14. Bonds
- [ ] Corporate bonds
- [ ] Municipal bonds
- [ ] Promissory notes
- [ ] U.S. Savings bonds

15. Accounts receivable
- [ ] Accounts receivable from business
- [ ] Commissions already earned

16. Alimony/family support to which you are entitled
- ☐ Alimony (spousal support, maintenance) due under court order
- ☐ Child support payments due under court order
- ☐ Payments due under divorce property settlement

17. Other liquidated debts owed to you, including tax refunds
- ☐ Disability benefits due
- ☐ Disability insurance due
- ☐ Judgments obtained against third parties you haven't yet collected
- ☐ Sick pay earned
- ☐ Social Security benefits due
- ☐ Tax refund due under returns already filed
- ☐ Vacation pay earned
- ☐ Wages due
- ☐ Workers' compensation due

18. Equitable or future interests or life estates
- ☐ Right to receive, at some future time cash, stock or other personal property placed in an irrevocable trust
- ☐ Current payments of interest or principal from a trust
- ☐ General power of appointment over personal property

19. Interests in estate of decedent or life insurance plan or trust
- ☐ Beneficiary of a living trust, if the trustor has died
- ☐ Expected proceeds from a life insurance policy where the insured has died
- ☐ Inheritance from an existing estate in probate (the owner has died and the court is overseeing the distribution of the property) even if the final amount is not yet known

- ☐ Inheritance under a will that is contingent upon one or more events occurring, but only if the owner has died

20. Other contigent/unliquidated claims, including tax refunds, counterclaims
- ☐ Claims against a corporation, government entity or individual
- ☐ Potential tax refund but return not yet filed

21. Patents, copyrights, other intellectual property
- ☐ Copyrights
- ☐ Patents
- ☐ Trade secrets
- ☐ Trademarks
- ☐ Trade names

22. Licenses, franchises
- ☐ Building permits
- ☐ Cooperative association holdings
- ☐ Exclusive licenses
- ☐ Liquor licenses
- ☐ Nonexclusive licenses
- ☐ Patent licenses
- ☐ Professional licenses

23. Automobiles, trucks, trailers, and accessories.
- ☐ Car
- ☐ Mini bike or motor scooter
- ☐ Mobile or motor home if on wheels
- ☐ Motorcycle
- ☐ Recreational vehicle (RV)
- ☐ Trailer
- ☐ Truck
- ☐ Van

24. Boats, motors, and accessories
- ☐ Boat (canoe, kayak, rowboat, shell, sailboat, pontoon, yacht, etc.)
- ☐ Boat radar, radio or telephone
- ☐ Outboard motor

25. Aircraft and accessories
- ☐ Aircraft
- ☐ Aircraft radar, radio and other accessories

26. Office equipment, supplies
- ☐ Artwork in your office
- ☐ Computers, software, modems, printers
- ☐ Copier
- ☐ Fax machine
- ☐ Furniture
- ☐ Rugs
- ☐ Supplies
- ☐ Telephones
- ☐ Typewriters

27. Machinery, fixtures, etc., for business
- ☐ Military uniforms and accoutrements
- ☐ Tools of your trade

28. Inventory

29. Animals
- ☐ Birds
- ☐ Cats
- ☐ Dogs
- ☐ Fish and aquarium equipment
- ☐ Horses
- ☐ Other pets
- ☐ Livestock and poultry

30. Crops—growing or harvested

31. Farming equipment and implements

32. Farm supplies, chemicals, feed

33. Other personal property of any kind not listed
- ☐ Church pew
- ☐ Health aids (for example, wheelchair, crutches)
- ☐ Hot tub or portable spa
- ☐ Season tickets
- ☐ Other items not listed elsewhere

Worksheet: What Property Can You Keep in Chapter 7 Bankruptcy?

Part A: Real Estate

1. Address and description of property:_____

_____

_____

2. Market value of property $ _____

Mortgages, home equity loans and liens:

Creditors name and address   Amount

_____   _____

_____   _____

_____   _____

3. Total liens and mortgages   _____

4. Total ownership equity (line 2 – line 3)   _____

5. Exemptions   _____

6. Equity less exemptions (line 4 – line 5) $ _____

Part B: Personal Property

1 Property	2 Market Value	3 Exemption	4 Statute No.
1. Cash on hand			
_____	_____	_____	_____
_____	_____	_____	_____
_____	_____	_____	_____
_____	_____	_____	_____
2. Checking/savings account, certificate of deposit, other bank accounts			
_____	_____	_____	_____
_____	_____	_____	_____
_____	_____	_____	_____
_____	_____	_____	_____
_____	_____	_____	_____
_____	_____	_____	_____
_____	_____	_____	_____
3. Security deposits held by utility companies, landlord			
_____	_____	_____	_____
_____	_____	_____	_____
_____	_____	_____	_____

4. Household goods, furniture, including audio, video, and computer equipment

5. Books, pictures, art objects, records, compact discs, collectibles

6. Clothing

	1 Property	2 Market Value	3 Exemption	4 Statute No.

7. Furs and jewelry

_____ _____ _____ _____
_____ _____ _____ _____
_____ _____ _____ _____
_____ _____ _____ _____
_____ _____ _____ _____
_____ _____ _____ _____

8. Sports, photographic, hobby equipment, firearms

_____ _____ _____ _____
_____ _____ _____ _____
_____ _____ _____ _____
_____ _____ _____ _____

9. Interest in insurance policies—specify refund or cancellation value

_____ _____ _____ _____
_____ _____ _____ _____
_____ _____ _____ _____

10. Annuities

_____ _____ _____ _____
_____ _____ _____ _____
_____ _____ _____ _____

11. Interests in pension or profit sharing plans

_____ _____ _____ _____
_____ _____ _____ _____
_____ _____ _____ _____

12. Stock and interests in incorporated/unincorporated business

_____ _____ _____ _____
_____ _____ _____ _____
_____ _____ _____ _____
_____ _____ _____ _____
_____ _____ _____ _____
_____ _____ _____ _____
_____ _____ _____ _____
_____ _____ _____ _____
_____ _____ _____ _____

13. Interests in partnerships/joint ventures

14. Bonds

15. Accounts receivable

16. Alimony/family support to which you are entitled

17. Other liquidated debts owed to you, including tax refunds

18. Equitable or future interests or life estates

19. Interests in estate of decedent or life insurance plan or trust

20. Other contigent/unliquidated claims, including tax refunds, counterclaims

21. Patents, copyrights, other intellectual property

22. Licenses, franchises

23. Automobiles, trucks, trailers, and accessories.

24. Boats, motors, and accessories

25. Aircraft and accessories

26. Office equipment, supplies

27. Machinery, fixtures, etc., for business

NOLO
www.nolo.com

Worksheet:
What Property Can You Keep in Chapter 7 Bankruptcy?

Page 5 of 6

28. Inventory

29. Animals

30. Crops—growing or harvested

31. Farming equipment and implements

32. Farm supplies, chemicals, feed

33. Other personal property of any kind not listed

COURT CLERK
United States Bankruptcy Court

TO THE COURT CLERK:

Please send me the following information:

1. Copies of all local forms required by this court for an individual (not corporation) filing a Chapter 7 bankruptcy and for making amendments.

2. The number of copies or sets required for filing.

3. The order in which forms should be submitted.

4. Complete instructions on this court's emergency filing procedures and deadlines.

I would also appreciate answers to three questions:

1. Do you require a separate creditor mailing list (matrix)? If so, do you have specific requirements for its format?

2. Is the filing fee still $155? Is the administrative fee still $45? If either have changed, please advise.

3. Should I two-hole punch my papers or is that done by the court?

I've enclosed a self-addressed envelope for your reply. Thank you.

Sincerely,

FORM B1	United States Bankruptcy Court _____District of_____	Voluntary Petition

Name of Debtor (if individual, enter Last, First, Middle):	Name of Joint Debtor (Spouse) (Last, First, Middle):
All Other Names used by the Debtor in the last 6 years (include married, maiden, and trade names):	All Other Names used by the Joint Debtor in the last 6 years (include married, maiden, and trade names):
Soc. Sec./Tax I.D. No. (if more than one, state all):	Soc. Sec./Tax I.D. No. (if more than one, state all):
Street Address of Debtor (No. & Street, City, State & Zip Code):	Street Address of Joint Debtor (No. & Street, City, State & Zip Code):
County of Residence or of the Principal Place of Business:	County of Residence or of the Principal Place of Business:
Mailing Address of Debtor (if different from street address):	Mailing Address of Joint Debtor (if different from street address):

Location of Principal Assets of Business Debtor
(if different from street address above):

Information Regarding the Debtor (Check the Applicable Boxes)

Venue (Check any applicable box)

☐ Debtor has been domiciled or has had a residence, principal place of business, or principal assets in this District for 180 days immediately
   preceding the date of this petition or for a longer part of such 180 days than in any other District.

☐ There is a bankruptcy case concerning debtor's affiliate, general partner, or partnership pending in this District.

Type of Debtor (Check all boxes that apply)

☐ Individual(s)	☐ Railroad
☐ Corporation	☐ Stockbroker
☐ Partnership	☐ Commodity Broker
☐ Other_____	

**Chapter or Section of Bankruptcy Code Under Which
the Petition is Filed** (Check one box)

☐ Chapter 7   ☐ Chapter 11   ☐ Chapter 13
☐ Chapter 9   ☐ Chapter 12
☐ Sec. 304 - Case ancillary to foreign proceeding

Nature of Debts (Check one box)

☐ Consumer/Non-Business   ☐ Business

Filing Fee (Check one box)

☐ Full Filing Fee attached
☐ Filing Fee to be paid in installments (Applicable to individuals only)
  Must attach signed application for the court's consideration
  certifying that the debtor is unable to pay fee except in installments.
  Rule 1006(b). See Official Form No. 3.

Chapter 11 Small Business (Check all boxes that apply)

☐ Debtor is a small business as defined in 11 U.S.C. § 101
☐ Debtor is and elects to be considered a small business under
  11 U.S.C. § 1121(e) (Optional)

Statistical/Administrative Information (Estimates only)

☐ Debtor estimates that funds will be available for distribution to unsecured creditors.

☐ Debtor estimates that, after any exempt property is excluded and administrative expenses paid, there will
  be no funds available for distribution to unsecured creditors.

THIS SPACE IS FOR COURT USE ONLY

Estimated Number of Creditors	1-15	16-49	50-99	100-199	200-999	1000-over
	☐	☐	☐	☐	☐	☐

Estimated Assets

$0 to $50,000	$50,001 to $100,000	$100,001 to $500,000	$500,001 to $1 million	$1,000,001 to $10 million	$10,000,001 to $50 million	$50,000,001 to $100 million	More than $100 million
☐	☐	☐	☐	☐	☐	☐	☐

Estimated Debts

$0 to $50,000	$50,001 to $100,000	$100,001 to $500,000	$500,001 to $1 million	$1,000,001 to $10 million	$10,000,001 to $50 million	$50,000,001 to $100 million	More than $100 million
☐	☐	☐	☐	☐	☐	☐	☐

Voluntary Petition *(This page must be completed and filed in every case)*	Name of Debtor(s):

Prior Bankruptcy Case Filed Within Last 6 Years (If more than one, attach additional sheet)

Location Where Filed:	Case Number:	Date Filed:

Pending Bankruptcy Case Filed by any Spouse, Partner or Affiliate of this Debtor (If more than one, attach additional sheet)

Name of Debtor:	Case Number:	Date Filed:
District:	Relationship:	Judge:

Signatures

Signature(s) of Debtor(s) (Individual/Joint)

I declare under penalty of perjury that the information provided in this petition is true and correct.
[If petitioner is an individual whose debts are primarily consumer debts and has chosen to file under chapter 7] I am aware that I may proceed under chapter 7, 11, 12 or 13 of title 11, United States Code, understand the relief available under each such chapter, and choose to proceed under chapter 7.
I request relief in accordance with the chapter of title 11, United States Code, specified in this petition.

X _____
Signature of Debtor

X _____
Signature of Joint Debtor

_____
Telephone Number (If not represented by attorney)

_____
Date

Signature of Attorney

X _____
Signature of Attorney for Debtor(s)

_____
Printed Name of Attorney for Debtor(s)

_____
Firm Name

_____
Address

_____
Telephone Number

_____
Date

Signature of Debtor (Corporation/Partnership)

I declare under penalty of perjury that the information provided in this petition is true and correct, and that I have been authorized to file this petition on behalf of the debtor.

The debtor requests relief in accordance with the chapter of title 11, United States Code, specified in this petition.

X _____
Signature of Authorized Individual

_____
Printed Name of Authorized Individual

_____
Title of Authorized Individual

_____
Date

Exhibit A

(To be completed if debtor is required to file periodic reports (e.g., forms 10K and 10Q) with the Securities and Exchange Commission pursuant to Section 13 or 15(d) of the Securities Exchange Act of 1934 and is requesting relief under chapter 11)

☐ Exhibit A is attached and made a part of this petition.

Exhibit B

(To be completed if debtor is an individual whose debts are primarily consumer debts)

I, the attorney for the petitioner named in the foregoing petition, declare that I have informed the petitioner that [he or she] may proceed under chapter 7, 11, 12, or 13 of title 11, United States Code, and have explained the relief available under each such chapter.

X _____
Signature of Attorney for Debtor(s)   Date

Exhibit C

Does the debtor own or have possession of any property that poses or is alleged to pose a threat of imminent and identifiable harm to public health or safety?

☐ Yes, and Exhibit C is attached and made a part of this petition.
☐ No

Signature of Non-Attorney Petition Preparer

I certify that I am a bankruptcy petition preparer as defined in 11 U.S.C. § 110, that I prepared this document for compensation, and that I have provided the debtor with a copy of this document.

_____
Printed Name of Bankruptcy Petition Preparer

_____
Social Security Number

_____
Address

Names and Social Security numbers of all other individuals who prepared or assisted in preparing this document:

If more than one person prepared this document, attach additional sheets conforming to the appropriate official form for each person.

X _____
Signature of Bankruptcy Petition Preparer

_____
Date

A bankruptcy petition preparer's failure to comply with the provisions of title 11 and the Federal Rules of Bankruptcy Procedure may result in fines or imprisonment or both 11 U.S.C. §110; 18 U.S.C. §156.

Form B1, Exhibit C
(9/01)

United States Bankruptcy Court
District of _____

In re _____   Case No._____
                                    _____
                                    Debtor(s)   Chapter _____

Exhibit "C" to Voluntary Petition

1. Identify and briefly describe all real or personal property owned by or in possession of the debtor that, to the best of the debtor's knowledge, poses or is alleged to pose a threat of imminent and identifiable harm to the public health or safety (attach additional sheets if necessary):

_____

_____

_____

_____

_____

_____

_____

_____

_____

2. With respect to each parcel of real property or item of personal property identified in question 1, describe the nature and location of the dangerous condition, whether environmental or otherwise, that poses or is alleged to pose a threat of imminent and identifiable harm to the public health or safety (attach additional sheets if necessary):

_____

_____

_____

_____

_____

_____

_____

_____

_____

_____

_____

_____

_____

Form B6A
(6/90)

In re _____, Case No._____
             Debtor   (If known)

SCHEDULE A—REAL PROPERTY

Except as directed below, list all real property in which the debtor has any legal, equitable, or future interest, including all property owned as a co-tenant, community property, or in which the debtor has a life estate. Include any property in which the debtor holds rights and powers exercisable for the debtor's own benefit. If the debtor is married, state whether husband, wife, or both own the property by placing an "H," "W," "J," or "C" in the column labeled "Husband, Wife, Joint, or Community." If the debtor holds no interest in real property, write "None" under "Description and Location of Property."

Do not include interests in executory contracts and unexpired leases on this schedule. List them in Schedule G—Executory Contracts and Unexpired Leases.

If an entity claims to have a lien or hold a secured interest in any property, state the amount of the secured claim. See Schedule D. If no entity claims to hold a secured interest in the property, write "None" in the column labeled "Amount of Secured Claim."

If the debtor is an individual or if a joint petition is filed, state the amount of any exception claimed in the property only in Schedule C—Property Claimed as Exempt.

DESCRIPTION AND LOCATION OF PROPERTY	NATURE OF DEBTOR'S INTEREST IN PROPERTY	HUSBAND, WIFE, JOINT, OR COMMUNITY	CURRENT MARKET VALUE OF DEBTOR'S INTEREST IN PROPERTY WITHOUT DEDUCTING ANY SECURED CLAIM OR EXEMPTION	AMOUNT OF SECURED CLAIM

Total ➡ $ _____

(Report also on Summary of Schedules.)

In re _____,   Case No._____
_____Debtor_____   _____(If known)_____

SCHEDULE B—PERSONAL PROPERTY

Except as directed below, list all personal property of the debtor of whatever kind. If the debtor has no property in one or more of the categories, place an "X" in the appropriate position in the column labeled "None." If additional space is needed in any category, attach a separate sheet properly identified with the case name, case number, and the number of the category. If the debtor is married, state whether husband, wife, or both own the property by placing an "H," "W," "J," or "C" in the column labeled "Husband, Wife, Joint, or Community." If the debtor is an individual or a joint petition is filed, state the amount of any exemptions claimed only in Schedule C—Property Claimed as Exempt.

Do not include interests in executory contracts and unexpired leases on this schedule. List them in Schedule G—Executory Contracts and Unexpired Leases.

If the property is being held for the debtor by someone else, state that person's name and address under "Description and Location of Property."

TYPE OF PROPERTY	NONE	DESCRIPTION AND LOCATION OF PROPERTY	HUSBAND, WIFE, JOINT, OR COMMUNITY	CURRENT MARKET VALUE OF DEBTOR'S INTEREST IN PROPERTY, WITHOUT DEDUCTING ANY SECURED CLAIM OR EXEMPTION
1. Cash on hand.				
2. Checking, savings or other financial accounts, certificates of deposit, or shares in banks, savings and loan, thrift, building and loan, and homestead associations, or credit unions, brokerage houses, or cooperatives.				
3. Security deposits with public utilities, telephone companies, landlords, and others.				
4. Household goods and furnishings, including audio, video, and computer equipment.				

In re _____,   Case No._____
Debtor   (If known)

SCHEDULE B—PERSONAL PROPERTY
(Continuation Sheet)

TYPE OF PROPERTY	NONE	DESCRIPTION AND LOCATION OF PROPERTY	HUSBAND, WIFE, JOINT, OR COMMUNITY	CURRENT MARKET VALUE OF DEBTOR'S INTEREST IN PROPERTY, WITHOUT DEDUCTING ANY SECURED CLAIM OR EXEMPTION
5. Books, pictures and other art objects, antiques, stamp, coin, record, tape, compact disc, and other collections or collectibles.				
6. Wearing apparel.				
7. Furs and jewelry.				
8. Firearms and sports, photo-graphic, and other hobby equipment.				
9. Interests in insurance policies. Name insurance company of each policy and itemize surrender or refund value of each.				
10. Annuities. Itemize and name each issuer.				
11. Interests in IRA, ERISA, Keogh, or other pension or profit sharing plans. Itemize.				
12. Stock and interests in incor-porated and unincorporated businesses. Itemize.				
13. Interests in partnerships or joint ventures. Itemize.				

In re _____,   Case No._____
                          Debtor   (If known)

SCHEDULE B—PERSONAL PROPERTY
(Continuation Sheet)

TYPE OF PROPERTY	NONE	DESCRIPTION AND LOCATION OF PROPERTY	HUSBAND, WIFE, JOINT, OR COMMUNITY	CURRENT MARKET VALUE OF DEBTOR'S INTEREST IN PROPERTY, WITHOUT DEDUCTING ANY SECURED CLAIM OR EXEMPTION
14. Government and corporate bonds and other negotiable and non-negotiable instruments.				
15. Accounts receivable.				
16. Alimony, maintenance, support, and property settlements to which the debtor is or may be entitled. Give particulars.				
17. Other liquidated debts owing debtor including tax refunds. Give particulars.				
18. Equitable or future interest, life estates, and rights or powers exercisable for the benefit of the debtor other than those listed in Schedule of Real Property.				
19. Contingent and noncontingent interests in estate of a decedent, death benefit plan, life insurance policy, or trust.				
20. Other contingent and unliquidated claims of every nature, including tax refunds, counterclaims of the debtor, and rights to setoff claims. Give estimated value of each.				
21. Patents, copyrights, and other intellectual property. Give particulars.				
22. Licenses, franchises, and other general intangibles. Give particulars.				

In re _____ ,   Case No._____
                      Debtor   (If known)

SCHEDULE B—PERSONAL PROPERTY
(Continuation Sheet)

TYPE OF PROPERTY	NONE	DESCRIPTION AND LOCATION OF PROPERTY	HUSBAND, WIFE, JOINT, OR COMMUNITY	CURRENT MARKET VALUE OF DEBTOR'S INTEREST IN PROPERTY, WITHOUT DEDUCTING ANY SECURED CLAIM OR EXEMPTION
23. Automobiles, trucks, trailers, and other vehicles and accessories.				
24. Boats, motors, and accessories.				
25. Aircraft and accessories.				
26. Office equipment, furnishings, and supplies.				
27. Machinery, fixtures, equipment, and supplies used in business.				
28. Inventory.				
29. Animals.				
30. Crops—growing or harvested. Give particulars.				
31. Farming equipment and implements.				
32. Farm supplies, chemicals, and feed.				
33. Other personal property of any kind not already listed, such as season tickets. Itemize.				
			Total ➡	$

_____ continuation sheets attached

(Include amounts from any continuation sheets attached. Report total also on Summary of Schedules.)

Form B6C
(6/90)

In re _____,   Case No._____
                              Debtor   (If known)

SCHEDULE C—PROPERTY CLAIMED AS EXEMPT

Debtor elects the exemptions to which debtor is entitled under:

(Check one box)

☐ 11 U.S.C. § 522(b)(1):   Exemptions provided in 11 U.S.C. § 522(d). **Note: These exemptions are available only in certain states.**

☐ 11 U.S.C. § 522(b)(2):   Exemptions available under applicable nonbankruptcy federal laws, state or local law where the debtor's domicile has been located for the 180 days immediately preceding the filing of the petition, or for a longer portion of the 180-day period than in any other place, and the debtor's interest as a tenant by the entirety or joint tenant to the extent the interest is exempt from process under applicable nonbankruptcy law.

DESCRIPTION OF PROPERTY	SPECIFY LAW PROVIDING EACH EXEMPTION	VALUE OF CLAIMED EXEMPTION	CURRENT MARKET VALUE OF PROPERTY WITHOUT DEDUCTING EXEMPTIONS

Form B6D
(6/90)

In re _____ ,   Case No._____
                Debtor   (If known)

SCHEDULE D—CREDITORS HOLDING SECURED CLAIMS

State the name, mailing address, including zip code, and account number, if any, of all entities holding claims secured by property of the debtor as of the date of filing of the petition. List creditors holding all types of secured interest such as judgment liens, garnishments, statutory liens, mortgages, deeds of trust, and other security interests. List creditors in alphabetical order to the extent practicable. If all secured creditors will not fit on this page, use the continuation sheet provided.

If any entity other than a spouse in a joint case may be jointly liable on a claim, place an "X" in the column labeled "Codebtor," include the entity on the appropriate schedule of creditors, and complete Schedule H—Codebtors. If a joint petition is filed, state whether husband, wife, both of them, or the marital community may be liable on each claim by placing an "H," "W," "J," or "C" in the column labeled "Husband, Wife, Joint, or Community."

If the claim is contingent, place an "X" in the column labeled "Contingent." If the claim is unliquidated, place an "X" in the column labeled "Unliquidated." If the claim is disputed, place an "X" in the column labeled "Disputed." (You may need to place an "X" in more than one of these three columns.)

Report the total of all claims listed on this schedule in the box labeled "Total" on the last sheet of the completed schedule. Report this total also on the Summary of Schedules.

☐   Check this box if debtor has no creditors holding secured claims to report on this Schedule D.

CREDITOR'S NAME AND MAILING ADDRESS INCLUDING ZIP CODE	CODEBTOR	HUSBAND, WIFE, JOINT, OR COMMUNITY	DATE CLAIM WAS INCURRED, NATURE OF LIEN, AND DESCRIPTION AND MARKET VALUE OF PROPERTY SUBJECT TO LIEN	CONTINGENT	UNLIQUIDATED	DISPUTED	AMOUNT OF CLAIM WITHOUT DEDUCTING VALUE OF COLLATERAL	UNSECURED PORTION, IF ANY
ACCOUNT NO.								
			VALUE $					
ACCOUNT NO.								
			VALUE $					
ACCOUNT NO.								
			VALUE $					
ACCOUNT NO.								
			VALUE $					

_____ continuation sheets attached

                                             Subtotal ➡ $
                                   (Total of this page)

                                             Total ➡ $
                                  (Use only on last page)

(Report total also on Summary of Schedules)

In re _____,   Case No._____

                   Debtor   (If known)

SCHEDULE D—CREDITORS HOLDING SECURED CLAIMS
(Continuation Sheet)

CREDITOR'S NAME AND MAILING ADDRESS INCLUDING ZIP CODE	CODEBTOR	HUSBAND, WIFE, JOINT, OR COMMUNITY	DATE CLAIM WAS INCURRED, NATURE OF LIEN, AND DESCRIPTION AND MARKET VALUE OF PROPERTY SUBJECT TO LIEN	CONTINGENT	UNLIQUIDATED	DISPUTED	AMOUNT OF CLAIM WITHOUT DEDUCTING VALUE OF COLLATERAL	UNSECURED PORTION, IF ANY
ACCOUNT NO.								
			VALUE $					
ACCOUNT NO.								
			VALUE $					
ACCOUNT NO.								
			VALUE $					
ACCOUNT NO.								
			VALUE $					
ACCOUNT NO.								
			VALUE $					
ACCOUNT NO.								
			VALUE $					

Subtotal ➡ $
(Total of this page)

Total ➡ $
(Use only on last page)

Sheet no. _____ of _____ continuation sheets attached to
Schedule of Creditors Holding Secured Claims

(Report total also on Summary of Schedules)

In re _____,   Case No._____
              Debtor   (If known)

SCHEDULE E—CREDITORS HOLDING UNSECURED PRIORITY CLAIMS

A complete list of claims entitled to priority, listed separately by type of priority, is to be set forth on the sheets provided. Only holders of unsecured claims entitled to priority should be listed in this schedule. In the boxes provided on the attached sheets, state the name and mailing address, including zip code, and account number, if any, of all entities holding priority claims against the debtor or the property of the debtor, as of the date of the filing of the petition.

If any entity other than a spouse in a joint case may be jointly liable on a claim, place an "X" in the column labeled "Codebtor," include the entity on the appropriate schedule of creditors, and complete Schedule H—Codebtors. If a joint petition is filed, state whether husband, wife, both of them, or the marital community may be liable on each claim by placing an "H," "W," "J," or "C" in the column labeled "Husband, Wife, Joint, or Community."

If the claim is contingent, place an "X" in the column labeled "Contingent." If the claim is unliquidated, place an "X" in the column labeled "Unliquidated." If the claim is disputed, place an "X" in the column labeled "Disputed." (You may need to place an "X" in more than one of these three columns.)

Report the total of all claims listed on each sheet in the box labeled "Subtotal" on each sheet. Report the total of all claims listed on this Schedule E in the box labeled "Total" on the last sheet of the completed schedule. Repeat this total also on the Summary of Schedules.

☐ **Check this box if debtor has no creditors holding unsecured priority claims to report on this Schedule E.**

TYPES OF PRIORITY CLAIMS (Check the appropriate box(es) below if claims in that category are listed on the attached sheets)

☐ **Extensions of credit in an involuntary case**

Claims arising in the ordinary course of the debtor's business or financial affairs after the commencement of the case but before the earlier of the appointment of a trustee or the order for relief. 11 U.S.C. § 507(a)(2).

☐ **Wages, salaries, and commissions**

Wages, salaries, and commissions, including vacation, severance, and sick leave pay owing to employees and commissions owing to qualifying independent sales representatives up to $4,650* per person, earned within 90 days immediately preceding the filing of the original petition, or the cessation of business, whichever occurred first, to the extent provided in 11 U.S.C. § 507(a)(3).

☐ **Contributions to employee benefit plans**

Money owed to employee benefit plans for services rendered within 180 days immediately preceding the filing of the original petition, or the cessation of business, whichever occurred first, to the extent provided in 11 U.S.C. § 507(a)(4).

☐ **Certain farmers and fishermen**

Claims of certain farmers and fishermen, up to a maximum of $4,650* per farmer or fisherman, against the debtor, as provided in 11 U.S.C. § 507(a)(5).

☐ **Deposits by individuals**

Claims of individuals up to a maximum of $2,100* for deposits for the purchase, lease, or rental of property or services for personal, family, or household use, that were not delivered or provided. 11 U.S.C. § 507(a)(6).

☐ **Alimony, Maintenance, or Support**

Claims of a spouse, former spouse, or child of the debtor for alimony, maintenance, or support, to the extent provided in 11 U.S.C. § 507(a)(7).

☐ **Taxes and Certain Other Debts Owed to Governmental Units**

Taxes, customs, duties, and penalties owing to federal, state, and local governmental units as set forth in 11 U.S.C. § 507(a)(8).

☐ **Commitments to Maintain the Capital of an Insured Depository Institution**

Claims based on commitments to the FDIC, RTC, Director of the Office of Thrift Supervision, Comptroller of the Currency, or Board of Governors of the Federal Reserve system, or their predecessors or successors, to maintain the capital of an insured depository institution. 11 U.S.C. § 507 (a)(9).

* Amounts are subject to adjustment on April 1, 2004, and every three years thereafter with respect to cases commenced on or after the date of adjustment.

_____ continuation sheets attached

B6E
(Rev. 4/98)

In re _____,   Case No._____
                        Debtor   (If known)

SCHEDULE E—CREDITORS HOLDING UNSECURED PRIORITY CLAIMS
(Continuation Sheet)

_____

TYPE OF PRIORITY

CREDITOR'S NAME AND MAILING ADDRESS INCLUDING ZIP CODE	CODEBTOR	HUSBAND, WIFE, JOINT, OR COMMUNITY	DATE CLAIM WAS INCURRED AND CONSIDERATION FOR CLAIM	CONTINGENT	UNLIQUIDATED	DISPUTED	TOTAL AMOUNT OF CLAIM	AMOUNT ENTITLED TO PRIORITY
ACCOUNT NO.								
ACCOUNT NO.								
ACCOUNT NO.								
ACCOUNT NO.								
ACCOUNT NO.								

Subtotal ➡ $ _____
(Total of this page)

Total ➡ $ _____
(Use only on last page)

Sheet no. _____ of _____ sheets attached to
Schedule of Creditors Holding Unsecured Priority Claims

(Report total also on Summary of Schedules)

Form B6F (Official Form 6F)
(9/97)

In re _____,   Case No._____
                        Debtor   (If known)

SCHEDULE F—CREDITORS HOLDING UNSECURED NONPRIORITY CLAIMS

State the name, mailing address, including zip code, and account number, if any, of all entities holding unsecured claims without priority against the debtor or the property of the debtor as of the date of filing of the petition. Do not include claims listed in Schedules D and E. If all creditors will not fit on this page, use the continuation sheet provided.

If any entity other than a spouse in a joint case may be jointly liable on a claim, place an "X" in the column labeled "Codebtor," include the entity on the appropriate schedule of creditors, and complete Schedule H—Codebtors. If a joint petition is filed, state whether husband, wife, both of them, or the marital community may be liable on each claim by placing an "H," "W," "J," or "C" in the column labeled "Husband, Wife, Joint, or Community."

If the claim is contingent, place an "X" in the column labeled "Contingent." If the claim is unliquidated, place an "X" in the column labeled "Unliquidated." If the claim is disputed, place an "X" in the column labeled "Disputed." (You may need to place an "X" in more than one of these three columns.)

Report the total of all claims listed on this schedule in the box labeled "Total" on the last sheet of the completed schedule. Report this total also on the Summary of Schedules.

☐ Check this box if debtor has no creditors holding unsecured nonpriority claims to report on this Schedule F.

CREDITOR'S NAME AND MAILING ADDRESS INCLUDING ZIP CODE	CODEBTOR	HUSBAND, WIFE, JOINT, OR COMMUNITY	DATE CLAIM WAS INCURRED AND CONSIDERATION FOR CLAIM. IF CLAIM IS SUBJECT TO SETOFF, SO STATE	CONTINGENT	UNLIQUIDATED	DISPUTED	AMOUNT OF CLAIM
ACCOUNT NO.							
ACCOUNT NO.							
ACCOUNT NO.							
ACCOUNT NO.							

_____ continuation sheets attached

Subtotal ➡ $ _____
(Total of this page)

Total ➡ $ _____
(Use only on last page)

(Report total also on Summary of Schedules)

Form B6F—Cont.
(10/89)

In re _____,   Case No._____
                          Debtor   (If known)

SCHEDULE F—CREDITORS HOLDING UNSECURED NONPRIORITY CLAIMS
(Continuation Sheet)

CREDITOR'S NAME AND MAILING ADDRESS INCLUDING ZIP CODE	CODEBTOR	HUSBAND, WIFE, JOINT, OR COMMUNITY	DATE CLAIM WAS INCURRED AND CONSIDERATION FOR CLAIM. IF CLAIM IS SUBJECT TO SETOFF, SO STATE	CONTINGENT	UNLIQUIDATED	DISPUTED	AMOUNT OF CLAIM
ACCOUNT NO.							
ACCOUNT NO.							
ACCOUNT NO.							
ACCOUNT NO.							
ACCOUNT NO.							
			Subtotal ➤ (Total of this page)				$
			Total ➤ (Use only on last page)				$

Sheet no. _____ of _____ continuation sheets attached to
Schedule of Creditors Holding Unsecured Nonpriorty Claims

(Report total also on Summary of Schedules)

Form B6G
(10/89)

In re _____, Case No._____
                        Debtor   (If known)

SCHEDULE G—EXECUTORY CONTRACTS AND UNEXPIRED LEASES

Describe all executory contracts of any nature and all unexpired leases of real personal property. Include any timeshare interests.

State nature of debtor's interest in contract, i.e., "Purchaser," "Agent," etc. State whether debtor is the lessor or lessee of a lease.

Provide the names and complete mailing addresses of all other parties to each lease or contract described.

NOTE: A party listed on this schedule will not receive notice of the filing of this case unless the party is also scheduled in the appropriate schedule of creditors.

☐ Check this box if debtor has no executory contracts or unexpired leases.

NAME AND MAILING ADDRESS, INCLUDING ZIP CODE, OF OTHER PARTIES TO LEASE OR CONTRACT	DESCRIPTION OF CONTRACT OR LEASE AND NATURE OF DEBTOR'S INTEREST. STATE WHETHER LEASE IS FOR NONRESIDENTIAL REAL PROPERTY. STATE CONTRACT NUMBER OF ANY GOVERNMENT CONTRACT

Form B6H
(6/90)

In re _____,   Case No._____
                     Debtor   (If known)

SCHEDULE H—CODEBTORS

Provide the information requested concerning any person or entity, other than a spouse in a joint case, that is also liable on any debts listed by debtor in the schedules of creditors. Include all guarantors and co-signers. In community property states, a married debtor not filing a joint case should report the name and address of the nondebtor spouse on this schedule. Include all names used by the nondebtor spouse during the six years immediately preceding the commencement of this case.

☐ Check this box if debtor has no codebtors.

NAME AND ADDRESS OF CODEBTOR	NAME AND ADDRESS OF CREDITOR

Form B6I
(6/90)

In re _____,   Case No._____
                        Debtor   (If known)

SCHEDULE I—CURRENT INCOME OF INDIVIDUAL DEBTOR(S)

The column labled "Spouse" must be completed in all cases filed by joint debtors and by a married debtor in a Chapter 12 or 13 case whether or not a joint petition is filed, unless the spouses are separated and a joint petition is not filed.

DEBTOR'S MARITAL STATUS:	DEPENDENTS OF DEBTOR AND SPOUSE		
	NAMES	AGE	RELATIONSHIP

Employment:	DEBTOR	SPOUSE
Occupation		
Name of Employer		
How long employed		
Address of Employer		

INCOME: (Estimate of average monthly income)	DEBTOR	SPOUSE
Current monthly gross wages, salary, and commissions (pro rate if not paid monthly)	$ _____	$ _____
Estimated monthly overtime	$ _____	$ _____
SUBTOTAL	$ _____	$ _____
LESS PAYROLL DEDUCTIONS		
a. Payroll taxes and Social Security	$ _____	$ _____
b. Insurance	$ _____	$ _____
c. Union dues	$ _____	$ _____
d. Other (Specify: _____)	$ _____	$ _____
SUBTOTAL OF PAYROLL DEDUCTIONS	$ _____	$ _____
TOTAL NET MONTHLY TAKE HOME PAY	$ _____	$ _____
Regular income from operation of business or profession or farm (attach detailed statement)	$ _____	$ _____
Income from real property	$ _____	$ _____
Interest and dividends	$ _____	$ _____
Alimony, maintenance or support payments payable to the debtor for the debtor's use or that of dependents listed above	$ _____	$ _____
Social Security or other government assistance (Specify:_____)	$ _____	$ _____
Pension or retirement income	$ _____	$ _____
Other monthly income (Specify:_____)	$ _____	$ _____
_____	$ _____	$ _____
TOTAL MONTHLY INCOME	$ _____	$ _____

TOTAL COMBINED MONTHLY INCOME $ _____   (Report also on Summary of Schedules)

Describe any increase or decrease of more than 10% in any of the above categories anticipated to occur within the year following the filing of this document:

Form B6J
(6/90)

In re _____,   Case No._____

Debtor   (If known)

SCHEDULE J—CURRENT EXPENDITURES OF INDIVIDUAL DEBTOR(S)

Complete this schedule by estimating the average monthly expenses of the debtor and the debtor's family. Pro rate any payments made bi-weekly, quarterly, semi-annually, or annually to show monthly rate.

☐ Check this box if a joint petition is filed and debtor's spouse maintains a separate household. Complete a separate schedule of expenditures labeled "Spouse."

Rent or home mortgage payment (include lot rented for mobile home)	$ _____
Are real estate taxes included? Yes _____ No _____	
Is property insurance included? Yes _____ No _____	
Utilities: Electricity and heating fuel	$ _____
Water and sewer	$ _____
Telephone	$ _____
Other _____	$ _____
Home maintenance (repairs and upkeep)	$ _____
Food	$ _____
Clothing	$ _____
Laundry and dry cleaning	$ _____
Medical and dental expenses	$ _____
Transportation (not including car payments)	$ _____
Recreation, clubs and entertainment, newspapers, magazines, etc.	$ _____
Charitable contributions	$ _____
Insurance (not deducted from wages or included in home mortgage payments)	
Homeowner's or renter's	$ _____
Life	$ _____
Health	$ _____
Auto	$ _____
Other _____	$ _____
Taxes (not deducted from wages or included in home mortgage payments)	
(Specify: _____)	$ _____
Installment payments: (In Chapter 12 and 13 cases, do not list payments to be included in the plan)	
Auto	$ _____
Other _____	$ _____
Other _____	$ _____
Alimony, maintenance, and support paid to others	$ _____
Payments for support of additional dependents not living at your home	$ _____
Regular expenses from operation of business, profession, or farm (attach detailed statement)	$ _____
Other _____	$ _____
TOTAL MONTHLY EXPENSES (Report also on Summary of Schedules)	$ _____

[FOR CHAPTER 12 AND CHAPTER 13 DEBTORS ONLY]
Provide the information requested below, including whether plan payments are to be made bi-weekly, monthly, annually, or at some other regular interval.

A. Total projected monthly income	$ _____
B. Total projected monthly expenses	$ _____
C. Excess income (A minus B)	$ _____
D. Total amount to be paid into plan each_____	$ _____
(interval)	

United States Bankruptcy Court

_____ District of _____

In re _____,   Case No._____

            Debtor   (If known)

SUMMARY OF SCHEDULES

Indicate as to each schedule whether that schedule is attached and state the number of pages in each. Report the totals from Schedules A, B, D, E, F, I and J in the boxes provided. Add the amounts from Schedules A and B to determine the total amount of the debtor's assets. Add the amounts from Schedules D, E and F to determine the total amount of the debtor's liabilities.

NAME OF SCHEDULE		ATTACHED (YES/NO)	NUMBER OF SHEETS	AMOUNTS SCHEDULED		
				ASSETS	LIABILITIES	OTHER
A	Real Property			$		
B	Personal Property			$		
C	Property Claimed as Exempt					
D	Creditors Holding Secured Claims				$	
E	Creditors Holding Unsecured Priority Claims				$	
F	Creditors Holding Unsecured Nonpriority Claims				$	
G	Executory Contracts and Unexpired Leases					
H	Codebtors					
I	Current Income of Individual Debtor(s)					$
J	Current Expenditures of Individual Debtor(s)					$
Total Number of Sheets of All Schedules ➡						
Total Assets ➡				$		
Total Liabilities ➡					$	

Form B6—Cont.
(12/94)

In re _____, Case No._____
           Debtor   (If known)

DECLARATION CONCERNING DEBTOR'S SCHEDULES

DECLARATION UNDER PENALTY OF PERJURY BY INDIVIDUAL DEBTOR

I declare under penalty of perjury that I have read the foregoing summary and schedules consisting of _____
sheets, and that they are true and correct to the best of my knowledge, information, and belief.   (Total shown on summary page plus 1)

Date_____   Signature _____
                                                                        Debtor

Date_____   Signature _____
                                                               (Joint Debtor, if any)

[If joint case, both spouses must sign.]

_____

CERTIFICATION AND SIGNATURE OF NON-ATTORNEY BANKRUPTCY PETITION PREPARER (See 11 U.S.C. § 110)

I certify that I am a bankruptcy petition preparer as defined in 11 U.S.C. § 110, that I prepared this document for compensation, and that I have
provided the debtor with a copy of this document.

_____   _____
Printed or Typed Name of Bankruptcy Petition Preparer   Social Security No.

_____

Address

Names and Social Security numbers of all other individuals who prepared or assisted in preparing this document:

If more than one person prepared this document, attach additional signed sheets conforming to the appropriate Official Form for each person.

X_____   _____
Signature of Bankruptcy Petition Preparer   Date

*A bankruptcy petition preparer's failure to comply with the provisions of Title 11 and the Federal Rules of Bankruptcy Procedure may result in fine or imprisonment or both.
11 U.S.C. § 110; 18 U.S.C. § 156.*

_____

DECLARATION UNDER PENALTY OF PERJURY ON BEHALF OF CORPORATION OR PARTNERSHIP

I, the _____ [the president or other officer or an authorized agent of the corporation or a
member or an authorized agent of the partnership] of the _____ [corporation or partnership] named
as debtor in this case, declare under penalty of perjury that I have read the foregoing summary and schedules, consisting of
_____ sheets, and that they are true and correct to the best of my knowledge, information, and belief.
(Total shown on summary page plus 1)

Date_____   Signature _____

_____
[Print or type name of individual signing on behalf of debtor]

[An individual signing on behalf of a partnership or corporation must indicate position or relationship to debtor.]

_____

Penalty for making a false statement or concealing property: Fine of up to $500,000, imprisonment for up to 5 years, or both. 18 U.S.C. §§ 152 and 3571.

FORM 7. STATEMENT OF FINANCIAL AFFAIRS

UNITED STATES BANKRUPTCY COURT

_____ **DISTRICT OF** _____

In re: _____,   Case No. _____
              (Name)   (if known)
                        Debtor

STATEMENT OF FINANCIAL AFFAIRS

This statement is to be completed by every debtor. Spouses filing a joint petition may file a single statement on which the information for both spouses is combined. If the case is filed under chapter 12 or chapter 13, a married debtor must furnish information for both spouses whether or not a joint petition is filed, unless the spouses are separated and a joint petition is not filed. An individual debtor engaged in business as a sole proprietor, partner, family farmer, or self-employed professional, should provide the information requested on this statement concerning all such activities as well as the individual's personal affairs.

Questions 1 - 18 are to be completed by all debtors. Debtors that are or have been in business, as defined below, also must complete Questions 19 - 25. **If the answer to an applicable question is "None," mark the box labeled "None."** If additional space is needed for the answer to any question, use and attach a separate sheet properly identified with the case name, case number (if known), and the number of the question.

DEFINITIONS

"In business." A debtor is "in business" for the purpose of this form if the debtor is a corporation or partnership. An individual debtor is "in business" for the purpose of this form if the debtor is or has been, within the six years immediately preceding the filing of this bankruptcy case, any of the following: an officer, director, managing executive, or owner of 5 percent or more of the voting or equity securities of a corporation; a partner, other than a limited partner, of a partnership; a sole proprietor or self-employed.

"Insider." The term "insider" includes but is not limited to: relatives of the debtor; general partners of the debtor and their relatives; corporations of which the debtor is an officer, director, or person in control; officers, directors, and any owner of 5 percent or more of the voting or equity securities of a corporate debtor and their relatives; affiliates of the debtor and insiders of such affiliates; any managing agent of the debtor. 11 U.S.C. § 101.

_____

1. Income from employment or operation of business

None
☐
State the gross amount of income the debtor has received from employment, trade, or profession, or from operation of the debtor's business from the beginning of this calendar year to the date this case was commenced. State also the gross amounts received during the **two years** immediately preceding this calendar year. (A debtor that maintains, or has maintained, financial records on the basis of a fiscal rather than a calendar year may report fiscal year income. Identify the beginning and ending dates of the debtor's fiscal year.) If a joint petition is filed, state income for each spouse separately. (Married debtors filing under chapter 12 or chapter 13 must state income of both spouses whether or not a joint petition is filed, unless the spouses are separated and a joint petition is not filed.)

AMOUNT   SOURCE (if more than one)

2. Income other than from employment or operation of business

None

☐

State the amount of income received by the debtor other than from employment, trade, profession, or operation of the debtor's business during the **two years** immediately preceding the commencement of this case. Give particulars. If a joint petition is filed, state income for each spouse separately. (Married debtors filing under chapter 12 or chapter 13 must state income for each spouse whether or not a joint petition is filed, unless the spouses are separated and a joint petition is not filed.)

AMOUNT   SOURCE

---

3. Payments to creditors

None

☐

a. List all payments on loans, installment purchases of goods or services, and other debts, aggregating more than $600 to any creditor, made within **90 days** immediately preceding the commencement of this case. (Married debtors filing under chapter 12 or chapter 13 must include payments by either or both spouses whether or not a joint petition is filed, unless the spouses are separated and a joint petition is not filed.)

NAME AND ADDRESS OF CREDITOR	DATES OF PAYMENTS	AMOUNT PAID	AMOUNT STILL OWING

None

☐

b. List all payments made within **one year** immediately preceding the commencement of this case to or for the benefit of creditors who are or were insiders. (Married debtors filing under chapter 12 or chapter 13 must include payments by either or both spouses whether or not a joint petition is filed, unless the spouses are separated and a joint petition is not filed.)

NAME AND ADDRESS OF CREDITOR AND RELATIONSHIP TO DEBTOR	DATE OF PAYMENT	AMOUNT PAID	AMOUNT STILL OWING

---

4. Suits and administrative proceedings, executions, garnishments and attachments

None

☐

a. List all suits and administrative proceedings to which the debtor is or was a party within **one year** immediately preceding the filing of this bankruptcy case. (Married debtors filing under chapter 12 or chapter 13 must include information concerning either or both spouses whether or not a joint petition is filed, unless the spouses are separated and a joint petition is not filed.)

CAPTION OF SUIT AND CASE NUMBER	NATURE OF PROCEEDING	COURT OR AGENCY AND LOCATION	STATUS OR DISPOSITION

3

None ☐   b.   Describe all property that has been attached, garnished or seized under any legal or equitable process within **one year** immediately preceding the commencement of this case. (Married debtors filing under chapter 12 or chapter 13 must include information concerning property of either or both spouses whether or not a joint petition is filed, unless the spouses are separated and a joint petition is not filed.)

NAME AND ADDRESS OF PERSON FOR WHOSE BENEFIT PROPERTY WAS SEIZED	DATE OF SEIZURE	DESCRIPTION AND VALUE OF PROPERTY

---

5.   Repossessions, foreclosures and returns

None ☐   List all property that has been repossessed by a creditor, sold at a foreclosure sale, transferred through a deed in lieu of foreclosure or returned to the seller, within **one year** immediately preceding the commencement of this case. (Married debtors filing under chapter 12 or chapter 13 must include information concerning property of either or both spouses whether or not a joint petition is filed, unless the spouses are separated and a joint petition is not filed.)

NAME AND ADDRESS OF CREDITOR OR SELLER	DATE OF REPOSSESSION, FORECLOSURE SALE, TRANSFER OR RETURN	DESCRIPTION AND VALUE OF PROPERTY

---

6.   Assignments and receiverships

None ☐   a.   Describe any assignment of property for the benefit of creditors made within **120 days** immediately preceding the commencement of this case. (Married debtors filing under chapter 12 or chapter 13 must include any assignment by either or both spouses whether or not a joint petition is filed, unless the spouses are separated and a joint petition is not filed.)

NAME AND ADDRESS OF ASSIGNEE	DATE OF ASSIGNMENT	TERMS OF ASSIGNMENT OR SETTLEMENT

None ☐   b.   List all property which has been in the hands of a custodian, receiver, or court-appointed official within **one year** immediately preceding the commencement of this case. (Married debtors filing under chapter 12 or chapter 13 must include information concerning property of either or both spouses whether or not a joint petition is filed, unless the spouses are separated and a joint petition is not filed.)

NAME AND ADDRESS OF CUSTODIAN	NAME AND LOCATION OF COURT CASE TITLE & NUMBER	DATE OF ORDER	DESCRIPTION AND VALUE OF PROPERTY

7. Gifts

None ☐ List all gifts or charitable contributions made within **one year** immediately preceding the commencement of this case except ordinary and usual gifts to family members aggregating less than $200 in value per individual family member and charitable contributions aggregating less than $100 per recipient. (Married debtors filing under chapter 12 or chapter 13 must include gifts or contributions by either or both spouses whether or not a joint petition is filed, unless the spouses are separated and a joint petition is not filed.)

NAME AND ADDRESS OF PERSON OR ORGANIZATION	RELATIONSHIP TO DEBTOR, IF ANY	DATE OF GIFT	DESCRIPTION AND VALUE OF GIFT

---

8. Losses

None ☐ List all losses from fire, theft, other casualty or gambling within **one year** immediately preceding the commencement of this case **or since the commencement of this case**. (Married debtors filing under chapter 12 or chapter 13 must include losses by either or both spouses whether or not a joint petition is filed, unless the spouses are separated and a joint petition is not filed.)

DESCRIPTION AND VALUE OF PROPERTY	DESCRIPTION OF CIRCUMSTANCES AND, IF LOSS WAS COVERED IN WHOLE OR IN PART BY INSURANCE, GIVE PARTICULARS	DATE OF LOSS

---

9. Payments related to debt counseling or bankruptcy

None ☐ List all payments made or property transferred by or on behalf of the debtor to any persons, including attorneys, for consultation concerning debt consolidation, relief under the bankruptcy law or preparation of a petition in bankruptcy within **one year** immediately preceding the commencement of this case.

NAME AND ADDRESS OF PAYEE	DATE OF PAYMENT, NAME OF PAYOR IF OTHER THAN DEBTOR	AMOUNT OF MONEY OR DESCRIPTION AND VALUE OF PROPERTY

---

10. Other transfers

None ☐ List all other property, other than property transferred in the ordinary course of the business or financial affairs of the debtor, transferred either absolutely or as security within **one year** immediately preceding the commencement of this case. (Married debtors filing under chapter 12 or chapter 13 must include transfers by either or both spouses whether or not a joint petition is filed, unless the spouses are separated and a joint petition is not filed.)

NAME AND ADDRESS OF TRANSFEREE, RELATIONSHIP TO DEBTOR	DATE	DESCRIBE PROPERTY TRANSFERRED AND VALUE RECEIVED

11. Closed financial accounts

None
☐

List all financial accounts and instruments held in the name of the debtor or for the benefit of the debtor which were closed, sold, or otherwise transferred within **one year** immediately preceding the commencement of this case. Include checking, savings, or other financial accounts, certificates of deposit, or other instruments; shares and share accounts held in banks, credit unions, pension funds, cooperatives, associations, brokerage houses and other financial institutions. (Married debtors filing under chapter 12 or chapter 13 must include information concerning accounts or instruments held by or for either or both spouses whether or not a joint petition is filed, unless the spouses are separated and a joint petition is not filed.)

NAME AND ADDRESS OF INSTITUTION	TYPE AND NUMBER OF ACCOUNT AND AMOUNT OF FINAL BALANCE	AMOUNT AND DATE OF SALE OR CLOSING

12. Safe deposit boxes

None
☐

List each safe deposit or other box or depository in which the debtor has or had securities, cash, or other valuables within **one year** immediately preceding the commencement of this case. (Married debtors filing under chapter 12 or chapter 13 must include boxes or depositories of either or both spouses whether or not a joint petition is filed, unless the spouses are separated and a joint petition is not filed.)

NAME AND ADDRESS OF BANK OR OTHER DEPOSITORY	NAMES AND ADDRESSES OF THOSE WITH ACCESS TO BOX OR DEPOSITORY	DESCRIPTION OF CONTENTS	DATE OF TRANSFER OR SURRENDER, IF ANY

13. Setoffs

None
☐

List all setoffs made by any creditor, including a bank, against a debt or deposit of the debtor within **90 days** preceding the commencement of this case. (Married debtors filing under chapter 12 or chapter 13 must include information concerning either or both spouses whether or not a joint petition is filed, unless the spouses are separated and a joint petition is not filed.)

NAME AND ADDRESS OF CREDITOR	DATE OF SETOFF	AMOUNT OF SETOFF

14. Property held for another person

None

List all property owned by another person that the debtor holds or controls.

NAME AND ADDRESS OF OWNER	DESCRIPTION AND VALUE OF PROPERTY	LOCATION OF PROPERTY

15. Prior address of debtor

None ☐ If the debtor has moved within the **two years** immediately preceding the commencement of this case, list all premises which the debtor occupied during that period and vacated prior to the commencement of this case. If a joint petition is filed, report also any separate address of either spouse.

ADDRESS   NAME USED   DATES OF OCCUPANCY

---

16. Spouses and Former Spouses

None ☐ If the debtor resides or resided in a community property state, commonwealth, or territory (including Alaska, Arizona, California, Idaho, Louisiana, Nevada, New Mexico, Puerto Rico, Texas, Washington, or Wisconsin) within the **six-year period** immediately preceding the commencement of the case, identify the name of the debtor's spouse and of any former spouse who resides or resided with the debtor in the community property state.

NAME

---

17. Environmental Information.

For the purpose of this question, the following definitions apply:

"Environmental Law" means any federal, state, or local statute or regulation regulating pollution, contamination, releases of hazardous or toxic substances, wastes or material into the air, land, soil, surface water, groundwater, or other medium, including, but not limited to, statutes or regulations regulating the cleanup of these substances, wastes, or material.

"Site" means any location, facility, or property as defined under any Environmental Law, whether or not presently or formerly owned or operated by the debtor, including, but not limited to, disposal sites.

"Hazardous Material" means anything defined as a hazardous waste, hazardous substance, toxic substance, hazardous material, pollutant, or contaminant or similar term under an Environmental Law

---

None ☐ a. List the name and address of every site for which the debtor has received notice in writing by a governmental unit that it may be liable or potentially liable under or in violation of an Environmental Law. Indicate the governmental unit, the date of the notice, and, if known, the Environmental Law:

SITE NAME   NAME AND ADDRESS   DATE OF   ENVIRONMENTAL
AND ADDRESS   OF GOVERNMENTAL UNIT   NOTICE   LAW

None ☐ b. List the name and address of every site for which the debtor provided notice to a governmental unit of a release of Hazardous Material. Indicate the governmental unit to which the notice was sent and the date of the notice.

SITE NAME   NAME AND ADDRESS   DATE OF   ENVIRONMENTAL
AND ADDRESS   OF GOVERNMENTAL UNIT   NOTICE   LAW

None ☐   c.   List all judicial or administrative proceedings, including settlements or orders, under any Environmental Law with respect to which the debtor is or was a party. Indicate the name and address of the governmental unit that is or was a party to the proceeding, and the docket number.

NAME AND ADDRESS OF GOVERNMENTAL UNIT	DOCKET NUMBER	STATUS OR DISPOSITION

---

18 . Nature, location and name of business

None ☐   a.   If the debtor is an individual, list the names, addresses, taxpayer identification numbers, nature of the businesses, and beginning and ending dates of all businesses in which the debtor was an officer, director, partner, or managing executive of a corporation, partnership, sole proprietorship, or was a self-employed professional within the **six years** immediately preceding the commencement of this case, or in which the debtor owned 5 percent or more of the voting or equity securities within the **six years** immediately preceding the commencement of this case.

       If the debtor is a partnership, list the names, addresses, taxpayer identification numbers, nature of the businesses, and beginning and ending dates of all businesses in which the debtor was a partner or owned 5 percent or more of the voting or equity securities, within the **six years** immediately preceding the commencement of this case.

       If the debtor is a corporation, list the names, addresses, taxpayer identification numbers, nature of the businesses, and beginning and ending dates of all businesses in which the debtor was a partner or owned 5 percent or more of the voting or equity securities within the **six years** immediately preceding the commencement of this case.

NAME	TAXPAYER I.D. NUMBER	ADDRESS	NATURE OF BUSINESS	BEGINNING AND ENDING DATES

None ☐   b.   Identify any business listed in response to subdivision a., above, that is "single asset real estate" as defined in 11 U.S.C. § 101.

NAME	ADDRESS

     The following questions are to be completed by every debtor that is a corporation or partnership and by any individual debtor who is or has been, within the **six years** immediately preceding the commencement of this case, any of the following: an officer, director, managing executive, or owner of more than 5 percent of the voting or equity securities of a corporation; a partner, other than a limited partner, of a partnership; a sole proprietor or otherwise self-employed.

     *(An individual or joint debtor should complete this portion of the statement **only** if the debtor is or has been in business, as defined above, within the six years immediately preceding the commencement of this case. A debtor who has not been in business within those six years should go directly to the signature page.)*

8

19. Books, records and financial statements

None ☐

a. List all bookkeepers and accountants who within the **two years** immediately preceding the filing of this bankruptcy case kept or supervised the keeping of books of account and records of the debtor.

NAME AND ADDRESS   DATES SERVICES RENDERED

None ☐

b. List all firms or individuals who within the **two years** immediately preceding the filing of this bankruptcy case have audited the books of account and records, or prepared a financial statement of the debtor.

NAME   ADDRESS   DATES SERVICES RENDERED

None ☐

c. List all firms or individuals who at the time of the commencement of this case were in possession of the books of account and records of the debtor. If any of the books of account and records are not available, explain.

NAME   ADDRESS

None ☐

d. List all financial institutions, creditors and other parties, including mercantile and trade agencies, to whom a financial statement was issued within the **two years** immediately preceding the commencement of this case by the debtor.

NAME AND ADDRESS   DATE ISSUED

20. Inventories

None ☐

a. List the dates of the last two inventories taken of your property, the name of the person who supervised the taking of each inventory, and the dollar amount and basis of each inventory.

DATE OF INVENTORY   INVENTORY SUPERVISOR   DOLLAR AMOUNT OF INVENTORY
                                                     (Specify cost, market or other basis)

None ☐

b. List the name and address of the person having possession of the records of each of the two inventories reported in a., above.

DATE OF INVENTORY   NAME AND ADDRESSES OF CUSTODIAN
                                     OF INVENTORY RECORDS

21 . Current Partners, Officers, Directors and Shareholders

None ☐

a. If the debtor is a partnership, list the nature and percentage of partnership interest of each member of the partnership.

NAME AND ADDRESS	NATURE OF INTEREST	PERCENTAGE OF INTEREST

None ☐

b. If the debtor is a corporation, list all officers and directors of the corporation, and each stockholder who directly or indirectly owns, controls, or holds 5 percent or more of the voting or equity securities of the corporation.

NAME AND ADDRESS	TITLE	NATURE AND PERCENTAGE OF STOCK OWNERSHIP

22 . Former partners, officers, directors and shareholders

None ☐

a. If the debtor is a partnership, list each member who withdrew from the partnership within **one year** immediately preceding the commencement of this case.

NAME	ADDRESS	DATE OF WITHDRAWAL

None ☐

b. If the debtor is a corporation, list all officers, or directors whose relationship with the corporation terminated within **one year** immediately preceding the commencement of this case.

NAME AND ADDRESS	TITLE	DATE OF TERMINATION

23 . Withdrawals from a partnership or distributions by a corporation

None ☐

If the debtor is a partnership or corporation, list all withdrawals or distributions credited or given to an insider, including compensation in any form, bonuses, loans, stock redemptions, options exercised and any other perquisite during **one year** immediately preceding the commencement of this case.

NAME & ADDRESS OF RECIPIENT, RELATIONSHIP TO DEBTOR	DATE AND PURPOSE OF WITHDRAWAL	AMOUNT OF MONEY OR DESCRIPTION AND VALUE OF PROPERTY

24. Tax Consolidation Group.

None

☐

If the debtor is a corporation, list the name and federal taxpayer identification number of the parent corporation of any consolidated group for tax purposes of which the debtor has been a member at any time within the **six-year period** immediately preceding the commencement of the case.

NAME OF PARENT CORPORATION   TAXPAYER IDENTIFICATION NUMBER

25. Pension Funds.

None

☐

If the debtor is not an individual, list the name and federal taxpayer identification number of any pension fund to which the debtor, as an employer, has been responsible for contributing at any time within the **six-year period** immediately preceding the commencement of the case.

NAME OF PENSION FUND   TAXPAYER IDENTIFICATION NUMBER

* * * * *

[If completed by an individual or individual and spouse]

I declare under penalty of perjury that I have read the answers contained in the foregoing statement of financial affairs and any attachments thereto and that they are true and correct.

Date _____   Signature _____
                                  of Debtor

Date _____   Signature _____
                                  of Joint Debtor
                                  (if any)

_____

[If completed on behalf of a partnership or corporation]

I, declare under penalty of perjury that I have read the answers contained in the foregoing statement of financial affairs and any attachments thereto and that they are true and correct to the best of my knowledge, information and belief.

Date _____   Signature _____

                                  _____
                                  Print Name and Title

[An individual signing on behalf of a partnership or corporation must indicate position or relationship to debtor.]

_____ continuation sheets attached

Penalty for making a false statement: Fine of up to $500,000 or imprisonment for up to 5 years, or both. 18 U.S.C. § 152 and 3571

CERTIFICATION AND SIGNATURE OF NON-ATTORNEY BANKRUPTCY PETITION PREPARER (See 11 U.S.C. § 110)

I certify that I am a bankruptcy petition preparer as defined in 11 U.S.C. § 110, that I prepared this document for compensation, and that I have provided the debtor with a copy of this document.

_____   _____
Printed or Typed Name of Bankruptcy Petition Preparer   Social Security No.

_____

_____
Address

Names and Social Security numbers of all other individuals who prepared or assisted in preparing this document:

If more than one person prepared this document, attach additional signed sheets conforming to the appropriate Official Form for each person.

X _____   _____
Signature of Bankruptcy Petition Preparer   Date

A bankruptcy petition preparer's failure to comply with the provisions of title 11 and the Federal Rules of Bankruptcy Procedure may result in fines or imprisonment or both. 18 U.S.C. § 156.

Form 8. INDIVIDUAL DEBTOR'S STATEMENT OF INTENTION

UNITED STATES BANKRUPTCY COURT
_____ **DISTRICT OF** _____

In re _____,
          Debtor

Case No. _____

Chapter _____

CHAPTER 7 INDIVIDUAL DEBTOR'S STATEMENT OF INTENTION

1. I have filed a schedule of assets and liabilities which includes consumer debts secured by property of the estate.

2. I intend to do the following with respect to the property of the estate which secures those consumer debts:

    a. *Property to Be Surrendered.*

Description of Property   **Creditor's name**

    b. *Property to Be Retained*   *[Check any applicable statement.]*

Description of Property	Creditor's Name	Property is claimed as exempt	Property will be redeemed pursuant to 11 U.S.C. § 722	Debt will be reaffirmed pursuant to 11 U.S.C. § 524(c)

Date: _____

_____
Signature of Debtor

CERTIFICATION OF NON-ATTORNEY BANKRUPTCY PETITION PREPARER (See 11 U.S.C. § 110)

I certify that I am a bankruptcy petition preparer as defined in 11 U.S.C. § 110, that I prepared this document for compensation, and that I have provided the debtor with a copy of this document.

_____   _____
Printed or Typed Name of Bankruptcy Petition Preparer   Social Security No.

_____

_____
Address

Names and Social Security Numbers of all other individuals who prepared or assisted in preparing this document.

If more than one person prepared this document, attach additional signed sheets conforming to the appropriate Official Form for each person.

X_____   _____
Signature of Bankruptcy Petition Preparer   Date

A bankruptcy petition preparer's failure to comply with the provisions of title 11 and the Federal Rules of Bankruptcy Procedure may result in fines or imprisonment or both. 11 U.S.C. § 110; 18 U.S.C. § 156.

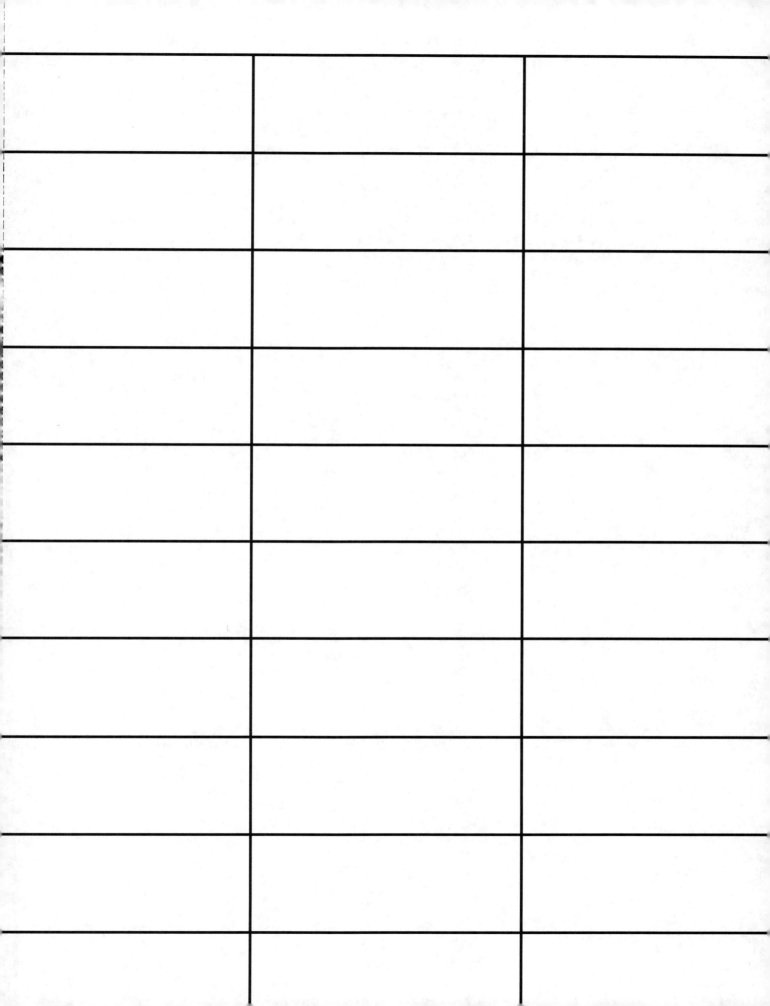

Form 3. APPLICATION AND ORDER TO PAY FILING FEE IN INSTALLMENTS
UNITED STATES BANKRUPTCY COURT
_____ DISTRICT OF _____

In re _____ ,
          Debtor

Case No. _____

Chapter _____

APPLICATION TO PAY FILING FEE IN INSTALLMENTS

1.   In accordance with Fed. R. Bankr. P. 1006, I apply for permission to pay the Filing Fee amounting to $_____ in installments.

2.   I certify that I am unable to pay the Filing Fee except in installments.

3.   I further certify that I have not paid any money or transferred any property to an attorney for services in connection with this case and that I will neither make any payment nor transfer any property for services in connection with this case until the filing fee is paid in full.

4.   I propose the following terms for the payment of the Filing Fee.*

        $ _____   Check one ☐   With the filing of the petition, or
                                         ☐   On or before _____

        $ _____   on or before _____

        $ _____   on or before _____

        $ _____   on or before _____

*   The number of installments proposed shall not exceed four (4), and the final installment shall be payable not later than 120 days after filing the petition. For cause shown, the court may extend the time of any installment, provided the last installment is paid not later than 180 days after filing the petition. Fed. R. Bankr. P. 1006(b)(2).

5.   I understand that if I fail to pay any installment when due my bankruptcy case may be dismissed and I may not receive a discharge of my debts.

_____
Signature of Attorney   Date

_____
Name of Attorney

_____
Signature of Debtor   Date
(In a joint case, both spouses must sign.)

_____
Signature of Joint Debtor (if any)   Date

CERTIFICATION AND SIGNATURE OF NON-ATTORNEY BANKRUPTCY PETITION (See 11 U.S.C. § 110)

  I certify that I am a bankruptcy petition preparer as defined in 11 U.S.C. § 110, that I prepared this document for compensation, and that I have provided the debtor with a copy of this document. I also certify that I will not accept money or any other property from the debtor before the filing fee is paid in full.

_____
Printed or Typed Name of Bankruptcy Petition Preparer

_____
Social Security No.

_____

_____
Address

Names and Social Security numbers of all other individuals who prepared or assisted in preparing this document:

If more than one person prepared this document, attach additional signed sheets conforming to the appropriate Official Form for each person.

x_____
Signature of Bankruptcy Petition Preparer

_____
Date

A bankruptcy petition preparer's failure to comply with the provisions of title 11 and the Federal Rules of Bankruptcy Procedure may result in fines or imprisonment or both. 11 U.S.C. § 110; 18 U.S.C. § 156.

**Form B3 continued
(9/97)**

UNITED STATES BANKRUPTCY COURT
_____ DISTRICT OF _____

In re _____,   Case No. _____
                    Debtor

                                                          Chapter _____

ORDER APPROVING PAYMENT OF FILING FEE IN INSTALLMENTS

       IT IS ORDERED that the debtor(s) may pay the filing fee in installments on the terms proposed in the foregoing application.

       IT IS FURTHER ORDERED that until the filing fee is paid in full the debtor shall not pay any money for services in connection with this case, and the debtor shall not relinquish any property as payment for services in connection with this case.

       BY THE COURT

Date: _____   _____
                                United States Bankruptcy Judge

To whom it may concern:

On _____, I filed a voluntary petition under Chapter 7 of the U.S. Bankruptcy Code. The case number is _____. Under 11 U.S.C. § 362(a), you may not:

- take any action against me or my property to collect any debt.
- enforce any lien on my real or personal property.
- repossess any property in my possession.
- discontinue any service or benefit currently being provided to me.
- take any action to evict me from where I live.

A violation of these prohibitions may be considered contempt of court and punished accordingly.

Very truly yours,

Form 20A. Notice of Motion or Objection

UNITED STATES BANKRUPTCY COURT

_____ DISTRICT OF _____

In re _____ ,   Case No. _____

                (Name)   (If known)

                     Debtor

                                                      Chapter _____

NOTICE OF [MOTION TO] [OBJECTION TO]

_____ has filed papers with the court to [relief sought in motion or objection].

<u>Your rights may be affected.</u> You should read these papers carefully and discuss them with your attorney, if you have one in this bankruptcy case. (If you do not have an attorney, you may wish to consult one.)

If you do not want the court to [relief sought in motion or objection], or if you want the court to consider your views on the [motion] [objection], then on or before <u>(date),</u> you or your attorney must:

File with the court a written request for a hearing [*or, if the court requires a written response,* an answer, explaining your position] at:

[address of the bankruptcy clerk's office]

If you mail your [request] [response] to the court for filing, you must mail it early enough so the court will **receive** it on or before the date stated above.

You must also mail a copy to:

[movant's attorney's name and address]

[names and addresses of others to be served]

[Attend the hearing scheduled to be held on (date) , (year) , at ___ a.m./p.m. in Courtroom _____, United States Bankruptcy Court, [address].]

[Other steps required to oppose a motion or objection under local rule or court order.]

If you or your attorney do not take these steps, the court may decide that you do not oppose the relief sought in the motion or objection and may enter an order granting that relief.

Date: _____   Signature: _____

                                          Name:_____

                                          Address: _____

Your Name, Address & Phone Number:

In Pro Per

UNITED STATES BANKRUPTCY COURT

_____ DISTRICT OF _____

In re   )
)   Case No. _____
)   Chapter _____
)   AMENDMENT COVER SHEET
)
                              Debtor(s))
_____

Presented herewith are the original and one copy of the following:

☐ Voluntary Petition (Note: Spouse may not be added or deleted subsequent to initial filing.)

☐ Schedule A—Real Property

☐ Schedule B—Personal Property

☐ Schedule C—Property Claimed as Exempt

☐ Schedule D—Creditors Holding Secured Claims

☐ Schedule E—Creditors Holding Unsecured Priority Claims

☐ Schedule F—Creditors Holding Unsecured Nonpriority Claims

☐ Schedule G—Executory Contracts and Unexpired Leases

☐ Schedule H—Codebtors

☐ Schedule I—Current Income of Individual Debtor(s)

☐ Schedule J—Current Expenditures of Individual Debtor(s)

☐ Summary of Schedules

☐ Statement of Financial Affairs

☐ I have enclosed a $20 fee because I am adding new creditors or changing addresses after the original
     Meeting of Creditors Notice has been sent.

_____   _____
Signature of Debtor   Signature of Debtor's Spouse

I (we) _____ and
_____, the debtor(s)
in this case, declare under penalty of perjury that the information set forth in the amendment attached hereto
consisting of _____ pages is true and correct to the best of my (our) information and belief.

Dated: _____, 20_____

_____   _____
Signature of Debtor   Signature of Debtor's Spouse

Your Name, Address & Phone Number: _____

In Pro Per

UNITED STATES BANKRUPTCY COURT

_____ DISTRICT OF _____

In re

)

)   Case No. _____

)   Chapter _____

)   NOTICE OF CHANGE OF ADDRESS

                   Debtor(s)   )

Social Security Number (H): _____

Social Security Number (W): _____

MY (OUR) FORMER MAILING ADDRESS AND PHONE NUMBER WAS:

Name: _____

Street: _____

City: _____

State/Zip: _____

Phone: (_____) _____

PLEASE BE ADVISED THAT AS OF_____, 20_____, MY (OUR) NEW MAILING ADDRESS AND PHONE NUMBER IS:

Name: _____

Street: _____

City: _____

State/Zip: _____

Phone: (_____) _____

_____
Signature of Debtor

_____
Signature of Debtor's Spouse

Your Name, Address & Phone Number:

In Pro Per

UNITED STATES BANKRUPTCY COURT

_____ DISTRICT OF _____

In re

Case No. _____

Chapter _____

SUPPLEMENTAL SCHEDULE FOR

PROPERTY ACQUIRED AFTER

Debtor(s)   )   BANKRUPTCY DISCHARGE

TO:_____, Trustee.

This is to inform you that I (we) have received the following item of property since my (our) discharge but within the 180-day period after filing my (our) Bankruptcy Petition under Bankruptcy Rule 1007 (h):

This property was obtained through an inheritance, marital settlement agreement or divorce decree, death benefits or life insurance proceeds, or other (specify):

☐   I (we) claim this property exempt under the following law:

I (we) _____ and

_____, the debtor(s)

in this case, declare under penalty of perjury that the foregoing is true and correct.

Dated: _____, 20_____   _____

Signature of Debtor

_____

Signature of Debtor's Spouse

Daily Expenses

Date:

Item	Cost

Date:

Item	Cost

Date:

Item	Cost

Date:

Item	Cost

1
2
3
4
5
6
7
8
9
10
11
12
13
14
15
16
17
18
19
20
21
22
23
24
25
26
27
28

Your Name, Address & Phone Number:

In Pro Per

UNITED STATES BANKRUPTCY COURT FOR THE
_____ DISTRICT OF _____

In re   )
)   Case No. _____
)
)
                        Debtor(s)   )
_____

PROOF OF SERVICE BY MAIL

I, _____, declare that:

I am over the age of 18 years and not a party to the within bankruptcy. I reside in or am employed in the

County of _____. My residence/business address is

_____.

On _____, I served the within _____

_____ by placing a true and correct copy of it in a sealed envelope with first-

class postage fully prepaid, in the United States mail at _____

_____, addressed as follows:

I declare under penalty of perjury that the foregoing is true and correct. Executed on

_____, 20_____ at _____

_____.

_____
Signature

Index

CATALOG

...more from Nolo

	PRICE	CODE

BUSINESS

	PRICE	CODE
Avoid Employee Lawsuits	$24.95	AVEL
The CA Nonprofit Corporation Kit (Binder w/CD-ROM)	$59.95	CNP
Consultant & Independent Contractor Agreements (Book w/CD-ROM)	$29.95	CICA
The Corporate Minutes Book (Book w/CD-ROM)	$69.99	CORMI
The Employer's Legal Handbook	$39.99	EMPL
Everyday Employment Law	$29.99	ELBA
Drive a Modest Car & 16 Other Keys to Small Business Success	$24.99	DRIV
Firing Without Fear	$29.95	FEAR
Form Your Own Limited Liability Company (Book w/CD-ROM)	$44.99	LIAB
Hiring Independent Contractors: The Employer's Legal Guide (Book w/CD-ROM)	$34.95	HICI
How to Create a Buy-Sell Agreement & Control the Destiny of your Small Business (Book w/Disk-PC)	$49.95	BSAG
How to Create a Noncompete Agreement	$44.95	NOCMP
How to Form a California Professional Corporation (Book w/CD-ROM)	$59.99	PROF
How to Form a Nonprofit Corporation (Book w/CD-ROM)—National Edition	$44.99	NNP
How to Form a Nonprofit Corporation in California (Book w/CD-ROM)	$44.99	NON
How to Form Your Own California Corporation (Binder w/CD-ROM)	$59.99	CACI
How to Form Your Own California Corporation (Book w/CD-ROM)	$34.99	CCOR
How to Get Your Business on the Web	$29.99	WEBS
How to Write a Business Plan	$29.99	SBS
The Independent Paralegal's Handbook	$29.95	PARA
Leasing Space for Your Small Business	$34.95	LESP
Legal Guide for Starting & Running a Small Business	$34.99	RUNS
Legal Forms for Starting & Running a Small Business (Book w/CD-ROM)	$29.95	RUNS2
Marketing Without Advertising	$22.00	MWAD
Music Law (Book w/CD-ROM)	$34.99	ML
Nolo's Guide to Social Security Disability	$29.99	QSS
Nolo's Quick LLC	$24.95	LLCQ
Nondisclosure Agreements	$39.95	NAG
The Small Business Start-up Kit (Book w/CD-ROM)	$29.99	SMBU
The Small Business Start-up Kit for California (Book w/CD-ROM)	$34.99	OPEN
The Partnership Book: How to Write a Partnership Agreement (Book w/CD-ROM)	$39.99	PART
Sexual Harassment on the Job	$24.95	HARS
Starting & Running a Successful Newsletter or Magazine	$29.99	MAG
Tax Savvy for Small Business	$34.99	SAVVY
Working for Yourself: Law & Taxes for the Self-Employed	$39.99	WAGE
Your Limited Liability Company: An Operating Manual (Book w/CD-ROM)	$49.99	LOP
Your Rights in the Workplace	$29.99	YRW

CONSUMER

	PRICE	CODE
Fed Up with the Legal System: What's Wrong & How to Fix It	$9.95	LEG
How to Win Your Personal Injury Claim	$29.99	PICL
Nolo's Encyclopedia of Everyday Law	$29.99	EVL
Nolo's Pocket Guide to California Law	$24.95	CLAW
Trouble-Free Travel...And What to Do When Things Go Wrong	$14.95	TRAV

ESTATE PLANNING & PROBATE

	PRICE	CODE
8 Ways to Avoid Probate	$19.95	PRO8

Prices subject to change.

	PRICE	CODE
9 Ways to Avoid Estate Taxes	$29.95	ESTX
Estate Planning Basics	$21.99	ESPN
How to Probate an Estate in California	$49.99	PAE
Make Your Own Living Trust (Book w/CD-ROM)	$39.99	LITR
Nolo's Law Form Kit: Wills	$24.95	KWL
Nolo's Simple Will Book (Book w/CD-ROM)	$34.99	SWIL
Plan Your Estate	$44.99	NEST
Quick & Legal Will Book	$15.99	QUIC

FAMILY MATTERS

	PRICE	CODE
Child Custody: Building Parenting Agreements That Work	$29.95	CUST
The Complete IEP Guide	$24.99	IEP
Divorce & Money: How to Make the Best Financial Decisions During Divorce	$34.99	DIMO
Do Your Own Divorce in Oregon	$29.95	ODIV
Get a Life: You Don't Need a Million to Retire Well	$24.99	LIFE
The Guardianship Book for California	$39.99	GB
How to Adopt Your Stepchild in California (Book w/CD-ROM)	$34.95	ADOP
A Legal Guide for Lesbian and Gay Couples	$29.99	LG
Living Together: A Legal Guide (Book w/CD-ROM)	$34.99	LTK
Using Divorce Mediation: Save Your Money & Your Sanity	$29.95	UDMD

GOING TO COURT

	PRICE	CODE
Beat Your Ticket: Go To Court and Win! (National Edition)	$19.99	BEYT
The Criminal Law Handbook: Know Your Rights, Survive the System	$34.99	KYR
Everybody's Guide to Small Claims Court (National Edition)	$24.95	NSCC
Everybody's Guide to Small Claims Court in California	$26.99	CSCC
Fight Your Ticket ... and Win! (California Edition)	$29.99	FYT
How to Change Your Name in California	$34.95	NAME
How to Collect When You Win a Lawsuit (California Edition)	$29.99	JUDG
How to Mediate Your Dispute	$18.95	MEDI
How to Seal Your Juvenile & Criminal Records (California Edition)	$34.95	CRIM
Nolo's Deposition Handbook	$29.99	DEP
Represent Yourself in Court: How to Prepare & Try a Winning Case	$34.99	RYC

HOMEOWNERS, LANDLORDS & TENANTS

	PRICE	CODE
California Tenants' Rights	$27.99	CTEN
Deeds for California Real Estate	$24.99	DEED
Dog Law	$21.95	DOG
Every Landlord's Legal Guide (National Edition, Book w/CD-ROM)	$44.99	ELLI
Every Tenant's Legal Guide	$26.95	EVTEN
For Sale by Owner in California	$29.99	FSBO
How to Buy a House in California	$34.99	BHCA
The California Landlord's Law Book: Rights & Responsibilities (Book w/CD-ROM)	$44.99	LBRT
The California Landlord's Law Book: Evictions (Book w/CD-ROM)	$44.99	LBEV
Leases & Rental Agreements	$29.99	LEAR
Neighbor Law: Fences, Trees, Boundaries & Noise	$26.99	NEI
The New York Landlord's Law Book (Book w/CD-ROM)	$39.95	NYLL
Renters' Rights (National Edition)	$24.99	RENT
Stop Foreclosure Now in California	$29.95	CLOS

HUMOR

	PRICE	CODE
29 Reasons Not to Go to Law School	$12.95	29R
Poetic Justice	$9.95	PJ

IMMIGRATION

	PRICE	CODE
Fiancé & Marriage Visas	$44.95	IMAR
How to Get a Green Card	$29.95	GRN
Student & Tourist Visas	$29.99	ISTU
U.S. Immigration Made Easy	$44.99	IMEZ

	PRICE	CODE

MONEY MATTERS

101 Law Forms for Personal Use (Book w/CD-ROM)	$29.99	SPOT
Bankruptcy: Is It the Right Solution to Your Debt Problems?	$19.99	BRS
Chapter 13 Bankruptcy: Repay Your Debts	$34.99	CH13
Creating Your Own Retirement Plan	$29.99	YROP
Credit Repair (Quick & Legal Series, Book w/CD-ROM)	$24.99	CREP
How to File for Chapter 7 Bankruptcy	$34.99	HFB
IRAs, 401(k)s & Other Retirement Plans: Taking Your Money Out	$29.99	RET
Money Troubles: Legal Strategies to Cope With Your Debts	$29.99	MT
Nolo's Law Form Kit: Personal Bankruptcy	$24.99	KBNK
Stand Up to the IRS	$24.99	SIRS
Surviving an IRS Tax Audit	$24.95	SAUD
Take Control of Your Student Loan Debt	$26.95	SLOAN

PATENTS AND COPYRIGHTS

The Copyright Handbook: How to Protect and Use Written Works (Book w/CD-ROM)	$39.99	COHA
Copyright Your Software	$34.95	CYS
Domain Names	$26.95	DOM
Getting Permission: How to License and Clear Copyrighted Materials Online and Off (Book w/CD-ROM)	$34.99	RIPER
How to Make Patent Drawings Yourself	$29.99	DRAW
The Inventor's Notebook	$24.99	INOT
Nolo's Patents for Beginners	$29.99	QPAT
License Your Invention (Book w/CD-ROM)	$39.99	LICE
Patent, Copyright & Trademark	$39.99	PCTM
Patent It Yourself	$49.99	PAT
Patent Searching Made Easy	$29.95	PATSE
The Public Domain	$34.95	PUBL
Web and Software Development: A Legal Guide (Book w/CD-ROM)	$44.95	SFT
Trademark: Legal Care for Your Business and Product Name	$39.95	TRD

RESEARCH & REFERENCE

Legal Research: How to Find & Understand the Law	$34.99	LRES

SENIORS

Choose the Right Long-Term Care: Home Care, Assisted Living & Nursing Homes	$21.99	ELD
The Conservatorship Book for California	$44.99	CNSV
Social Security, Medicare & Goverment Pensions	$29.99	SOA

SOFTWARE
Call or check our website at www.nolo.com
for special discounts on Software!

LeaseWriter CD—Windows	$129.95	LWD1
LLC Maker—Windows	$89.95	LLP1
PatentPro Plus—Windows	$399.99	PAPL
Personal RecordKeeper 5.0 CD—Windows	$59.95	RKD5
Quicken Lawyer 2003 Business Deluxe—Windows	$79.95	SBQB3
Quicken Lawyer 2003 Personal—Windows	$79.95	WQP3

Special Upgrade Offer
Save 35% on the latest edition of your Nolo book

Because laws and legal procedures change often, we update our books regularly. To help keep you up-to-date, we are extending this special upgrade offer. Cut out and mail the title portion of the cover of your old Nolo book and we'll give you **35% off** the retail price of the NEW EDITION of that book when you purchase directly from Nolo. This offer is to individuals only.

Prices and offer subject to change without notice.

Order Form

Name

Address

City

State, Zip

Daytime Phone

E-mail

Our "No-Hassle" Guarantee

Return anything you buy directly from Nolo for any reason and we'll cheerfully refund your purchase price. No ifs, ands or buts.

☐ Check here if you do not wish to receive mailings from other companies

Item Code	Quantity	Item	Unit Price	Total Price

Method of payment

☐ Check ☐ VISA ☐ MasterCard
☐ Discover Card ☐ American Express

Subtotal	
Add your local sales tax (California only)	
Shipping: RUSH $9, Basic $5 (See below)	
"I bought 3, ship it to me FREE!" (Ground shipping only)	
TOTAL	

Account Number

Expiration Date

Signature

Shipping and Handling

Rush Delivery—Only $9

We'll ship any order to any street address in the U.S. by UPS 2nd Day Air* for only $9!

* Order by noon Pacific Time and get your order in 2 business days. Orders placed after noon Pacific Time will arrive in 3 business days. P.O. boxes and S.F. Bay Area use basic shipping. Alaska and Hawaii use 2nd Day Air or Priority Mail.

Basic Shipping—$5

Use for P.O. Boxes, Northern California and Ground Service.

Allow 1-2 weeks for delivery. U.S. addresses only.

For faster service, use your credit card and our toll-free numbers

**Call our customer service group
Monday thru Friday 7am to 7pm PST**

Phone   1-800-728-3555
Fax   1-800-645-0895
Mail   Nolo
              950 Parker St.
              Berkeley, CA 94710

**Order 24 hours a day @
www.nolo.com**

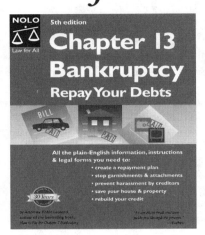

Remember:

Little publishers have big ears.
We really listen to you.

Take 2 Minutes & Give Us Your 2 cents

Your comments make a big difference in the development and revision of Nolo books and software. Please take a few minutes and register your Nolo product—and your comments—with us. Not only will your input make a difference, you'll receive special offers available only to registered owners of Nolo products on our newest books and software. Register now by:

PHONE
1-800-728-3555

FAX
1-800-645-0895

EMAIL
cs@nolo.com

or **MAIL** us
this registration card

fold here

- -

NOLO

Registration Card

NAME _____ DATE _____

ADDRESS _____

_____

CITY _____ STATE _____ ZIP _____

PHONE _____ E-MAIL _____

WHERE DID YOU HEAR ABOUT THIS PRODUCT? _____

WHERE DID YOU PURCHASE THIS PRODUCT? _____

DID YOU CONSULT A LAWYER? (PLEASE CIRCLE ONE)   YES   NO   NOT APPLICABLE

DID YOU FIND THIS BOOK HELPFUL?   (VERY)   5   4   3   2   1   (NOT AT ALL)

COMMENTS _____

_____

_____

WAS IT EASY TO USE?   (VERY EASY)   5   4   3   2   1   (VERY DIFFICULT)

We occasionally make our mailing list available to carefully selected companies whose products may be of interest to you.

❑ If you do not wish to receive mailings from these companies, please check this box.

❑ You can quote me in future Nolo promotional materials.
Daytime phone number _____.

HFB10.0

Nolo in the NEWS

"Nolo helps lay people perform legal tasks without the aid—or fees—of lawyers."

—USA TODAY

Nolo books are ..."written in plain language, free of legal mumbo jumbo, and spiced with witty personal observations."

—ASSOCIATED PRESS

"...Nolo publications...guide people simply through the how, when, where and why of law."

—WASHINGTON POST

"Increasingly, people who are not lawyers are performing tasks usually regarded as legal work... And consumers, using books like Nolo's, do routine legal work themselves."

—NEW YORK TIMES

"...All of [Nolo's] books are easy-to-understand, are updated regularly, provide pull-out forms...and are often quite moving in their sense of compassion for the struggles of the lay reader."

—SAN FRANCISCO CHRONICLE

- - - - - - - - - - - - - - - fold here - - - - - - - - - - - - - - - - - -

Place
stamp here

Nolo
950 Parker Street
Berkeley, CA 94710-9867

Attn: HFB10.0